THE STUDENTS, YES

AN ODYSSEY THROUGH STUDENT SOCIAL LIFE AT AMERICAN COLLEGES

DREW OTT

DESOLATE PUBLISHING

CONTENTS

LEGAL DISCLAIMER

Every story in this book is true. The only details that have been changed are names and identifying details to protect privacy. After these details have been changed, if any characters resemble any real persons, living or dead, it is entirely coincidental.

The dialogue throughout the book is accurate. I took notes in real-time, and when the conversation moved too fast for notes, I used an audio recorder with subject's consent.

All subjects agreed to participate in this book and gave me full permission to tell their stories, except for a few instances when I went undercover (Bob Jones and Tennessee). Each of my hosts has had the opportunity to read their chapter and suggest changes when it affects their privacy and anonymity. I have agreed to every change suggested.

These stories are about individuals, not about their schools. The students in this book are not representatives of their universities. I say this as a legal disclaimer, as well as a sincere expression of truth. You should not use this book to make any judgments about universities.

This book contains adult content and is not meant to be read by individuals under 18 years of age unless they have parental consent.

Dedicated to my K-12 classmates

INTRODUCTION

People everywhere seem to have a never-ending desire to know how their society's youth are living their lives. Perhaps this is because young people are inherently interesting—they're optimistic, overconfident, and reckless; they're sincere and curious; they're often brilliant because their minds are not yet set in their ways, but still naive and immature because they have not yet experienced enough of life to know how it all works. These characteristics make young people interesting, but it's not what makes them so fascinating. What fascinates us most about young people is that they represent the newest embodiment of living culture. Culture exists both out in the world—as media, education, language, etc.—and embodied in the minds of individuals—as thoughts, behaviors, and values. A permanent mystery of social life is the question of what the new generation of young people will absorb from the culture as it exists out in the world before they convert it into culture that lives in their minds and in turn acts upon the world. Society rushes forward, and nobody is holding the reins. In a free society, young people's values are not handed down from above by tradition or authority, but are instead formed from below by free, spontaneous choice; the adults can only sit back and hope that the youth choose well. To observe the social lives of young people is to see culture as it is actually being transmitted and absorbed right now. Their lives reveal the forces that are most vital in society and allow us to witness the stream of life and the flow of culture as it lives across time.

A young person leaves the comfort of childhood and encounters a new set of challenges that she will face for the rest of her life. If she longs to love and to be loved, she must go looking for it in a world of binge drinking and casual sex. If she longs for work that provides her a sense of meaning and significance, she must go looking for it in a world of fierce competition and financial necessity. If she longs for a sense of community and belonging, she must go looking for it in a world of strangers who may or may not like what she has to offer. In the United Sates, college—higher education and all that it entails—is our best attempt to guide young people through this nearly impossible process.

Parents never really know what's going on in the minds of their children. Parents send their children to college and imagine that they are having a good time, that they are being safely and pleasantly guided into a happy adulthood. For most college students, nothing could be further from the truth. Consider the unique psychosocial challenges of the college years:

A college student is in a near-constant state of identity confusion or identity crisis. Over the course of his childhood, he has developed his personality as an automatic reaction to his family, teachers, and peers, but as a college student, he realizes that he may now form his personality as a conscious choice. He is free to act however he wants, be whoever he wants, and believe whatever he wants. But how to act? Who to be? What to believe? He tries to answer these questions, but he is plagued by doubts and insecurities. He tries on different social masks, hesitates, falters, and then tries again. The task of identity formation is possibly the most important task in all of life, and every college student—consciously or unconsciously—recognizes its grave importance.

A college student has a desperate need to form intimate relationships—both platonic and romantic. Throughout childhood, her friendships have formed naturally and easily, but now she must start from scratch and see if she can relate to peers who grew up in different places and cultures. She dreams of finding a group of friends who understand her, a place where she belongs, and she must put concerted effort into finding these people, though she has no assurance that they will ever materialize. This is also a time when a young person attempts clumsily to learn the rules of the courtship process—a process that today has mostly descended into chaos and become a game with no rules. She finds a glimmer of hope that her romantic longings may be satisfied when she meets a classmate who seems interested in her, but often she is only led on, rejected, or ignored. If she succeeds in forming intimate relationships, she may experience her life as intensely pleasurable. If she fails, she may sink into despair.

A college student is in a profound transitional state of life—childhood into adulthood—and transitional states often bring existential questions into sharp focus. College students often ruminate and obsess over thoughts of meaninglessness, isolation, and death. Most grown-ups give up ever trying to answer the question, "What is the meaning of life?" but for many young people, no question is more important, and the search for a satisfactory answer can have life-or-death consequences.

In the classroom, a college student is theoretically learning about the truths of existence at the very highest level of understanding. There is no way to initiate a young person into adulthood while shielding him from the brutality of existence. The truth devastates, and higher education is where young people go to learn the truth. While life may at times be beautiful and complex and interesting, life is undoubtedly also horrific and barbaric and cruel. And so, theoretically, college is a time when wise elders tear down the guiding myths of childhood and force the student to confront the unvarnished, unpleasant truths of adulthood.

While the college years are some of the most high-stakes and difficult times in a person's life, all of these challenges take place in an atmosphere of intense fun and celebration. Parents call to check on their children. "Hey sweetie, are you having a good time at college?" "Yes, Mom and Dad, I'm having a blast."

This book is an odyssey through youth culture as it manifests itself at some of the nation's most interesting colleges. Specifically, this book contains the stories of 23 college students who were brave (or stupid) enough to allow an unknown writer to follow them everywhere they went for a week each in order to document a very sensitive time in their lives. At first glance, this is a story about sex, alcohol, and the college experience, but upon closer inspection, it is a story about the minds of young people and the future of life and culture in America.

———

While growing up, I always assumed I would go to college. When I was eight years old, the daughter in a family from our church was accepted into Stanford, and all the adults fawned over her. I wanted the adults to fawn over me as well, so I told my parents that I would also go to Stanford. They were proud of me just for the idea—"Wow, our son is going to Stanford!" Starting in kindergarten, our education system was designed to prepare us for college. They did a good job— by high school graduation, 97% of my graduating class was going to college, and our school was ranked nationally for college preparedness. We never questioned whether or not we would go to college, we just wondered where we would go.

Sometime during high school, I decided not to go to college. I was in my bedroom when I had an epiphany that it was possible to not go to college at all. To my surprise, the thought flooded me with euphoria. It gave me a sense of directing my own life, it satisfied a rebellious instinct, it took away the stress of applying for college, and it meant that I no longer had to compete with my peers for the highest grade point average. I also liked the idea of being self-made and self-taught. I quickly told my parents my plan.

"Drew, classy people *just go* to college," my mom said. "You can't not go."

I was so stubborn that my mom's response turned my half-formed idea into a fully formed decision: I was no longer going to college. For a couple of years, this decision gave me a great feeling of freedom and autonomy. I was living alone and working as a wedding videographer. I didn't know what I was going to do with my life yet, but I felt that there were an infinite number of possibilities before me. For a couple of years, I believed I had made a good decision.

But as time passed, the exciting life that I had dreamed of for myself became much less exciting. Until then, I had never experienced loneliness. Now my friends were across the country at their colleges, and I was mostly alone in my hometown. Living alone, I could sometimes go a week without talking to anyone. Meanwhile, other people my age were experiencing what were supposed to be the best times of their lives.

I also learned that it was far more painful to lose my family's approval than I had imagined. My great grandmother was the matriarch of a large extended family of college graduates, and we took pride in the fact that she had gone to college as a woman in the 1920s. Whenever she spoke, the whole room would respectfully quiet down to listen. The last time I saw her before she passed away, she asked me, "Andrew, where are you going to college?" The room full of my relatives went quiet.

When I told her that I wasn't going to college, a terrible look of disappointment came over her face and then spread to everyone in the room, then she slowly turned away from me and said nothing more.

In her old age, she was losing her short-term memory, so five minutes later she asked me again, "Andrew, where are you going to college?"

The room quieted down again. I gave her the same answer, which was followed by the same look of terrible disappointment and turning away.

When she asked the question a third time, my mom interrupted and said, "He's going to the University of Texas!" then looked at me for support.

I played along, though with great discomfort. This time a satisfied smile came to my great grandmother's face. She looked at me warmly and said, "That's wonderful."

Before long, I learned that girls were not interested in dating a guy who didn't go to college. When I decided not to go, I'd had a girlfriend of many years, and I naively thought we would be together forever. When she left for college and our relationship didn't survive the distance, I was newly single and saddled with what I repeatedly learned was a massive deal breaker. Girls would ask me, "What's your major?" and I'd have to tell them that I didn't even go to college. Rather than coming across as cool or self-reliant, I was often seen as beneath them and ineligible for anything romantic. Despite her not-so-tactful way of saying it, my mom's phrase that "classy people just go to college" contained more wisdom than I had realized.

Sometime during this period, I started to wonder if I had made a mistake.

As an adolescent, however, I still had a great deal of youthful confidence and arrogance. People loved to debate me about the value of college, and I would always entertain them. The most interesting and compelling argument I kept hearing, and often from trusted adults, was that the most important part of college was not the degree, the education, or the networking opportunities. The most important part of college was the college experience, the mystical totality of four years spent living as a student among students. I heard this argument so frequently that I began to wonder what exactly it meant, and if I was missing out on something important.

When I graduated high school, I went on a couple road trips to visit friends at their colleges, and I caught brief glimpses into their social worlds. I saw the lives of anarchist college students in California, musical theatre students in Ohio, and fraternity members in Oklahoma. Student life was drastically different from college to college. It made me wonder how the college experience could be something that everybody needs, while also being so different from school to school. What was it about the college experience that turned children into adults? Why was college our society's rite of passage?

One lonely night in my apartment, I began to daydream about visiting more colleges. I thought it would be fun to go on a road trip to a bunch of different colleges around the country to see what it was like to be a student at each one. Next I realized that this would make an entertaining book that I'd like to read, and then I thought that maybe I could be the person to write it. If I said I was writing a book, I could probably find students who would host me. This thought also flooded me with euphoria.

Here was the plan: I would travel around from college to college and live with one student for a week at each school. I'd sleep on their couch, sit next to them during class, watch them study, and go with them to parties. Each week I'd write a slice-of-life biography of what it's like to be a student at that school. But would anybody agree to let me write about them?

I began emailing around the country, looking for friends of friends of friends who would host me. To my surprise, lots of students were willing to be the subject of a chapter. Nobody asked if I had an agent (no), a publisher (no), or if I had ever written anything before (no). They just said yes. Since I had never written anything before, I'm not sure that I ever fully believed that I'd be able to turn my experiences into a book. In some sense, I felt I might just be lying about writing a book as an excuse to hang out with college students, but I believed in my lie so intensely and for so long that it came true.

So here you go. This book is the product of the strangest year of my life, the best year of my life, and perhaps the worst year of my life. I spent the year living with both men and women, at state schools, private schools, Ivy League schools, at fraternities and sororities, with athletes and art students, and at party schools and religious schools. I began with the noble intention to write straight journalism entirely about the students I was visiting. However, less than a week into the trip, the pressure to fit in, to be liked, and to have a good time completely eroded my original intention. I quickly started partying with my hosts and participating in their lives. I didn't intend to write about myself, but I realized that my story was interesting, too—the story of an outsider taking a tour through all that he was missing out on, trying in vain to somehow belong.

The schools I visited are organized chronologically in the same order that I visited them. I started in Texas and spent ten weeks in the southern United States, then went to the Northeast, and then went west. The book is divided into three parts. Part one is somewhat heavy with Greek life—there are two fraternities, two sororities, a baseball team that tries to start their own fraternity, and a week on the beach for college spring break. (Part one is also the sleaziest part of the book, by far.) The book undergoes a change in tone when I begin writing about visiting the prestigious colleges of the Northeast, starting with New York University, and then another change of tone when I head west, starting with Brigham-Young University. You might say that the book matures as it goes along, so I hope you'll stick with me through the early rough spots.

The world has changed dramatically since I began this project. This book contains stories that no traditional publisher would dare to publish in today's political climate. Today we live in a world where one wrong word, one small error in speech—even if well-intentioned —can cause a person to lose their reputation, their livelihood, and their dream of a happy future. This book surely contains not just one, but dozens or hundreds of wrong words. I began this project as a 19-year-old with a high school education, and today I am not much smarter. My original intention was to write fun and crazy stories about the college experience; however, along the way I encountered many situations that touched upon contentious social and political issues. I have no credentials or qualifications that allow me to properly discuss these issues. What I have tried to do instead is to give it to you straight, to give you the unfiltered truth exactly as I experienced it. I have done my very best, and I hope you will forgive my inevitable ignorance and moral shortcomings. I am learning new things every day, but I must publish this book before I've learned all that I need to know.

As I finish writing, I'm a 25-year-old who no longer approves of my behaviors from when I was 20. If I had to choose the most shameful year of my life to write about and share with the public, it would be this year. When I started this project, I didn't understand the implications of detailed self-disclosure; now I understand, and I have the deepest of regrets. But I have to finish what I started, and I'm grateful that I now know never to do something like this again.

Today I think that college is wonderful and that everyone who can afford it should go. If I had children, I would want them to go to college. As for me, I think that if I could live ten lives, I would go to college in nine of them. But for this one life, I'm still glad I didn't go. I learned that there is value in the story of an outsider, and I hope you find some value in it too.

PART I

1

UNIVERSITY OF TEXAS

Before I left for the long road trip to colleges around the country, I wanted to practice writing notes based on real life. I bought a book called *Writing Ethnographic Fieldnotes*, read two-thirds of it, and then started to sincerely think of myself as a self-taught ethnographer. I was clearly a moron, but my delusion of grandeur gave me awesome confidence. To practice writing fieldnotes, I would occasionally hang out with one of my friends from high school who went to The University of Texas and take notes in my phone. I did this for a few months before I left on my real trip. The following story comes from one of those nights.

It was the end of summer, one week before the start of the fall semester. My friend Danny had moved into his dorm room for his sophomore year on the earliest possible day. Since few other students had moved in yet, campus was mostly empty and there was little to do. We wanted to get drunk, but it was after midnight and we couldn't buy alcohol anymore. Danny messaged a few people who he thought might be on campus and asked what they were up to. An incoming freshman named Kyle responded. It was his first night ever at college, and he was hanging out with two other incoming freshmen. "Do you have any alcohol?" Danny asked. They had a bottle of whiskey and invited us over.

When we met them outside, two of them were already drunk, and they were giddy like it was the first time they'd ever had alcohol. One of the freshmen pissed on the side of the dorm building, Jester, then vomited in the grass. This was our cue to move inside. When we reached their dorm room, we learned that their bottle of whiskey was actually a plastic water bottle of whiskey, half empty. Then the two freshmen who had been so giddy outside became sleepy instead. The guy who had vomited fell asleep immediately on the tile floor in the middle of the room, and then Kyle, the guy who invited us over, lay down on his twin bed to go to sleep.

"You guys have to hear Peter's plan," Kyle said with sleepy eyes. "Peter, you have to tell them your plan."

Peter was the third freshman. We hadn't paid any attention to him until then. He hadn't said anything so far, and he didn't seem like he'd been drinking. Peter looked at Danny and me in a serious, concentrated way, and perhaps with a bit of pride. Whatever his plan was, he seemed to think that it would impress us.

"Get Peter to tell you about his plan," Kyle said again as his eyes were closing. "You guys need to hear Peter's plan." Then Kyle fell asleep too. It was his first night at college, the thing his entire life had been directed toward for as long as he could remember, and now he had arrived. He fell asleep with a little smile on his face.

Danny and I uncapped the water bottle of whiskey and each took a gross sip that killed our enthusiasm to drink any more. The night was a huge failure and an embarrassment. Danny and I were 19 years old. A 19-year-old is only slightly older than an 18-year-old in actuality, but he wants to believe that the small age difference contains a lifetime's worth of experiences—that he has accumulated so much wisdom during that single year that no 18-year-old could possibly know all that he knows. And here we were, 19 years old, but somehow without our own alcohol and forced to depend on guys who were only 18. I could tell that we both regretted coming here, but it felt impolite to leave so soon, even if our host had fallen asleep. With nothing else to do, Danny indulged the third freshman.

"What's this plan?" Danny asked Peter.

Peter took a moment to respond, really savoring his opportunity to finally speak.

"It's a very long plan," Peter said. "Do you have time for it?"

"I guess we do. What is it?"

"It's foolproof. Try to think of one thing that's wrong with it."

"Just tell us."

"I've had this plan for a long time. I've thought out every possibility, and trust me, there's nothing about it that wouldn't work."

"We get it," I said. "What's the plan?"

Peter glanced back and forth between Danny and me, took a long pause, then finally began:

"I had this internship over the summer, and I had a spot in an office that overlooked a lake. I sat in that office for eight hours a day, looking at this lake and the people kayaking and boating on the lake. And after weeks of staring out at this lake, I had a realization. I wasn't going to spend the rest of my life sitting in an office. I wasn't going to work a 9-to-5 just so I can make enough money for a big house where I can wait each day before I have to go back to work."

We weren't impressed.

"Is that the plan?" asked Danny.

"No." Peter's voice turned serious and conspiratorial. "It's nowhere close."

"What the fuck?"

"Just wait," said Peter. "So I realized that everybody in society is miserable. I realized that everybody hates their jobs and their lives. I realized that all of the normal world was just a big piece of shit. I decided I didn't want any of that."

"So what the fuck is the plan?"

"Just wait. Wait. So I was thinking about money, about alternate plans. I realized that nobody at their job really gives a shit about it. You just show up to work, and you do the bare minimum. Nobody cares at all to do anything they're told to do. Nobody gives a shit. And I also learned a very key piece of information."

"What?"

"Banks. There is a law that says that all banks are federally insured. If a bank loses its money for any reason, the federal government will just replenish its stock."

"You want to rob a bank?" I asked.

"No. No. Wait. Listen. A bank manager doesn't give a shit. He doesn't give a shit. He's an unhappy guy working 50 hours a week at his shitty job to support his shitty life. He doesn't give a shit."

"Dude, fucking hurry up," said Danny.

Every time Peter would say, "he doesn't give a shit," he'd put huge emphasis on the word *shit* as he pointed his finger dramatically. I could tell that Peter's slow and deliberate way of speaking was already irritating Danny.

"So banks are federally insured," Peter continued. "Banks are federally insured. If a bank loses money, it doesn't matter to the manager. He doesn't give a shit."

At this point, Danny and I were joining in with Peter every time he said, "he doesn't give a shit." Peter's intonation was so repetitive and predictable that Danny and I would say it in unison with him and imitate the hand gesture, then laugh together. Peter wasn't amused.

"I swear to fucking God, Peter, you need to hurry the fuck up with explaining this plan," said Danny. "Stop repeating the same shit."

"If I ask a bank manager to give me all of the money at the bank, he will do it," said Peter. "He doesn't give a shit. He hates his fucking job. He won't care."

"That's the stupidest shit I've ever heard."

"Try to find a flaw in it."

"Ok. What if he says no?"

"Why would he? He doesn't give a shit."

"Yes, he fucking does," said Danny. "It's actually the opposite. He might not give a shit about anything else in life, but this is his one responsibility, to not lose all of the money he is in charge of. If there's anything he does give a shit about, it's not letting you have all the money."

"I haven't finished explaining," said Peter. "So, I'm going to be there in the middle of the night. The manager might not even be there. I'm going to tell him I'm a film student and I want to make a movie in the bank. I'll say I want to shoot at night. He doesn't give a shit. He'll probably just give me the keys to the building so I can shoot. I'll get permits from school and everything. At most, there would only be one security guard. If I have a gun, he's just going to open the safes. He's instructed to. Banks are federally insured." Peter was full of intensity and conviction, otherwise we never would have bothered with taking him seriously.

"Dude, there is absolutely no chance a bank manager is going to let you shoot a movie in the middle of the night at his bank, unsupervised," I said. "There is absolutely no chance."

"I've made movies before, ok?" said Peter. "You don't understand. The bank manager doesn't give a shit. Neither does the security guard. They are federally insured."

"You're going to bring a gun. Are you going to shoot him if he contests you?"

"I don't want to harm anybody. He's not going to contest me. He doesn't give a shit."

"Ok now, here's where you're wrong," said Danny. "A security guard absolutely cares. He's been waiting for years to shoot a dude. Let's say he does hate his job. Still, he's been walking around with a gun for years and never gets to use it. You're his free excuse to use it."

"He wouldn't shoot me if I already had a gun pointed at him."

"What if there are multiple security guards?" I asked.

"I'd go like this." Peter made a pistol with his hand and pointed it back and forth between Danny and me like in some ridiculous gangster movie.

Danny and I burst out laughing. Since Peter thought he could beat two security guards in a standoff, we decided to test the limits of his claim by adding more and more hypothetical security guards. Peter was still convinced that he could win in a standoff against five security guards, all with guns pointed at him, just by waving his gun from guard to guard. We could never get him to admit how ridiculous this was, so we just moved on.

"Ok, so after that, how do you get away?" asked Danny. "What's the escape plan?

"I have this all figured out too," said Peter. "It's nine hours to Mexico. I'll make it out with the money, and after I'm out of the bank, they'll call the cops, probably. Well, I'll already be on my way. They won't be able to catch me, because I'll have a head start."

"Dude, that's not how it works," I said. "They call ahead and make a road block." (This is one of the stupidest things I've ever said. No, the police would not be able to call ahead and make a road block.)

"No they don't. They won't even know what kind of car I'm in. I'm going to park in a lot away from the bank to avoid the security cameras."

In the middle of all this, the guy who was asleep on the floor stood up, walked over to the sink, vomited again, and then went back to sleep without ever opening his eyes. Our conversation wasn't interrupted.

"First, you're not even going to get inside the bank," Danny said, "and the security guard isn't going to be able to open the safe for you. But even if that all goes down, the security guard is going to push the silent alarm, and all the cops are going to show. It's a bank."

"No," said Peter. "I'm going to keep the gun pointed at him until I'm out with the money. The cops won't be able to get there in time. I'll just be another car on the interstate."

"How much money is even kept at a bank in cash? Isn't that shit all electronic these days?"

"No. The kind of bank I'm going to rob can keep $80,000 cash on them. All of it is federally insured, so nobody working there gives a shit."

"What's the minimum amount of cash they can have?"

"At least $40,000."

"You're going to risk going to prison for bank robbery for $40,000?"

"That's the minimum amount. And yes, that's all I need to get started somewhere in another country."

"And then you can't re-enter the USA ever again? What about your friends and your family?"

"Nobody gives a shit about me. I've been rejected by everybody. The only person who really cares about me is my mom."

"You've been rejected by everybody?" asked Danny. "What are you talking about?"

"You have no idea what I've been through," said Peter.

"You have no idea what I've been through either. What are you talking about? I know the neighborhood you grew up in. You're a spoiled asshole."

Peter's eyes filled with rage. "You don't know poverty! You don't know destitution! You don't know starvation!"

"When the fuck did you experience that? Destitution? What the fuck are you talking about?"

Peter stood up and yelled. "No! You don't know!"

(In hindsight, I'm not sure why we didn't believe Peter's references to his abusive childhood, but we simply didn't—we thought he was full of shit.)

If this were another group of guys, a fight might have broken out. But I wasn't worried. In our suburban upbringing, physical violence didn't really exist. The closest thing to a punch in the face that any of us ever received was a really precise insult. Even so, the conversation had shifted from being fun and playful to being entirely adversarial. Somehow all of our egos had gotten mixed up in Peter's plan. Peter wasn't going to back down until we admitted that his plan was good, and we weren't going to back down until Peter admitted that his plan was terrible.

"Listen, Peter. You need to chill the fuck out," said Danny. "You don't know what you're talking about."

"What do you do with $40,000 in Mexico anyway?" I asked. "How is that so much better than here?"

"I'm not going to Mexico," said Peter. "I'm going to Chile."

"To Chile? What's in Chile?"

"They don't have shitty indoor jobs they all hate. There are all sorts of things you can do in Chile."

"Forty-thousand dollars isn't going to last you a lifetime," Danny said. "You'll still have to work."

"I'd rather farm beans in Chile. I would love to do that. I'd buy a plot of land and farm beans my whole life."

"Why don't you just go to Chile and do that then? Why don't you move down to Chile right now and start farming beans?"

"I need money to buy a plot of land."

"Dude, $40,000 isn't an impossible amount of money to earn legally," I said. "Your parents are paying that much for your school right now."

"I already told you, my parents don't give a shit about me."

"Yes, they do," said Danny. "It doesn't matter what you think. If they're paying for your college, they at least give some slight shit about you, and that's more than it is for a lot of kids."

"Listen," said Peter. "I told you before, you don't know what you're talking about. You don't know destitution. You don't know poverty. You don't know rejection."

"We don't know what you've been through, and you don't know what we've been through," I said. "Stop talking about what you think we know. Look, your ideas about not wanting to work a 9-to-5, I understand. I agree with a lot of what you have to say, it makes sense. Rejecting society, moving away, sure. I can sympathize. But you don't need to rob a bank. You are absolutely going to prison if you try to go through with this. You're going to end up killing a security guard and not even getting into the vault."

"I said I wouldn't shoot a security guard," said Peter. "Nobody gets hurt."

"What if he started shooting at you?" asked Danny. "What if you had to duck and then he kept firing?"

"The most I would do is shoot him in the leg."

"Ok. So he's on the ground, and he's still shooting at you. You can either die right there, or you shoot him. What do you do?"

"In that case, I would have to kill him."

Danny and I nodded with satisfaction: Peter's plan was crumbling apart.

"Ok. What about the five-security-guard scenario," I said. "You just killed their best friend, and four more run in. They're all shooting at you, trying to kill you. Do you fire?"

"That would never happen," said Peter.

"Would you fire?"

"Yes, I would have to."

"So you're saying that there's a scenario where for a small chance at $40,000, you'd kill five security guards and then leave the country, never to return again, so you can buy land in Chile to farm for beans?"

"That wouldn't happen. I've worked out all the details where that doesn't happen. Prove me wrong. Tell me where the idea doesn't work."

"We told you a hundred reasons that your idea is shitty," said Danny. "We told you all along."

"And I gave you answers," said Peter.

"No, dude, you're wrong about those. Your entire argument hangs on the fact that nobody gives a shit. People give shits. I give a shit about things. Drew, do you give a shit?"

"I give a shit," I said.

"You think a bank manager gives a shit?" Peter asked. "He works 50 hours a week for a shitty paycheck just so he can keep doing it."

"Yeah, he cares," said Danny. "He became a bank manager for a reason. He does give a shit. You trying to rob him would be the most excitement he's ever had. He and the security guards would love to kill you. It'd be incredibly fulfilling for them."

"And let's say everything goes according to plan," I said. "You make it to Chile, and their government doesn't arrest you, and nobody cares, and you buy your plot of land, and your beans grow.

You said your mom still cares about you. She still loves you and will want to see you. What happens when you've been there for 20 years and you want to see her again before she dies? Do you just leave her and never see her again, telling her you'd rather risk your life and risk killing someone to rob a bank instead of just getting a job for a couple years and saving money so you can leave the country legally? What's she going to think happened to you?"

"Yeah, what about your mom?" asked Danny. "Don't you love your mom more than that?"

It was quiet for a moment.

"Well," said Peter. "That's the one part I haven't figured out yet."

Danny and I realized that we had won, so we left shortly after that. The whiskey was still on the dresser as full as when we'd arrived. We laughed at Peter's terrible plan the whole way home, then after that night, we didn't talk about it much more. It was one weird night among many.

A year later, I ran into the freshman who had invited us over that night—one of the guys who was asleep during the conversation. He was a sophomore now. I asked him what Peter was up to, expecting to hear that he was still at UT studying engineering or something, but to my surprise, Peter had dropped out of school and moved to Chile. He was actually in Chile at that very moment. "Wow," I thought, "good for him." I was a little bit proud, actually, thinking that maybe we had convinced him not to rob the bank but to instead move to Chile legally so that he could still come home to visit his mom.

But a few weeks later, it occurred to me that maybe Peter did rob a bank. How would anyone know if he did or didn't? The news doesn't really publicize successful bank robberies, because that would encourage more people to become criminals. It's highly unlikely that he robbed a bank, but there was some tiny chance that he did.

Today when I ponder the possibility of Peter robbing a bank, I find that I enjoy imagining he really did it. The hypothetical Peter who robbed a bank and moved to Chile, the hypothetical Peter who looked into his future and saw a lifetime of meaningless work and then thought better of it, has become a strange hero of mine. Today I take an odd delight in imagining Peter as a sort of Andy Dufresne at the end of *The Shawshank Redemption*, sanding a little boat on an empty beach as the camera floats high up over the Pacific Ocean. So today, whenever I run into somebody who knows Peter, I never ask where he is, because I don't want to know.

2

BAYLOR UNIVERSITY

I began my trip with incredible excitement, a ridiculous nervous energy. Somewhere in this excitement was the naive belief that all change would be good, that all obstacles would lead to growth. I was headed to Waco, Texas to meet my first host. I did not believe in my own project, but this guy did, and that made it real.

Kevin studied evolutionary biology and worked as an assistant researcher on an experiment designed to better understand the mate selection behaviors of social tropical fish. Within ten minutes of meeting, we ·were seated next to a fish tank in his apartment as he sketched for me a diagram of fish DNA on a yellow legal pad. The tank buzzed and bubbled while inside one male and one female fish hovered on opposite sides. The buzzing and bubbling filled in the silences between Kevin's sentences, which were slow and deliberate so that I could follow along. To mate, he explained, a male fish will wait for a female to produce eggs. Then he will quiver and shake his tail, which attracts her to nibble on his tail. The male's tail is where the fish sperm are stored, so when the female nibbles his tail, she gets the fish sperm in her mouth. As she's nibbling his tail, the eggs she has produced eject out of her, and then she swims to pick up the eggs in her mouth, which causes the eggs to mix with the fish sperm and become fertilized. Once the eggs are fertilized, she has to hold them in her mouth for a four-week incubation period.

"What makes the female want to bite the male's tail?" I asked.

"It's like you wanna stick your P in a V," Kevin said. "It just happens."

Kevin's fish tank was on the table next to the couch where I would be sleeping. For the remainder of the week, I would observe the fish courtship as I went to bed, then I would let the tank's steady hum put me to sleep after I closed my eyes.

The fish tank we were looking at wasn't where Kevin did his actual research. On the evening of my arrival, I joined Kevin on a trip to his laboratory where his real experiment was taking place. The lab was in a small warehouse to which Kevin had his own set of keys. Inside were a dozen rows of PVC shelves, each holding tanks of murky water with fish in them. The air in the lab was thick with warm humidity that moistened the walls like in a steam room. As soon as we arrived, Kevin began his work, which involved collecting and counting all the eggs that had dropped in the bottoms of the tanks, then logging the data into spreadsheets.

The goal of Kevin's experiment was to determine the genetic factors that could predict a female's mate choice. To do this, Kevin's team took fish tanks and divided each tank into three sections using plastic grids. A male fish would be placed in each of the outside sections, and a female fish would be placed in the center section. The plastic grid dividing the three fish was sized such that the smaller females could swim through the grid, but the larger males could not. This meant that once the female had produced eggs and was ready to mate, she could choose which male she wanted to mate with by crossing into his section of the tank. (As you'll recall, this is like the climax of the first *Air Bud* movie where the dog had to choose between the boy protagonist and his former abusive owner.) After doing hundreds of trials over many months, Kevin's team hoped to be able to predict any given female's mate choice based on the DNA of the males.

My first three days with Kevin were oddly formal. We went to his classes, spent a lot of time in his lab, and mostly talked about academics (Kevin was studying Nietzsche's *On the Genealogy of Morality* in his philosophy class, and he was excited about it). Kevin was a junior, making him one year older than me. He was somewhat introverted. He had friends, but on weekdays he would spend most of his time alone in his lab or studying in his bedroom. Although we weren't having a great deal of fun yet, I was taking pleasure in being on campus surrounded by college students. The college atmosphere at Baylor had a certain magic and vitality. I was sitting in on classes, meeting people my own age, and somehow it all felt terribly important. Then on my fourth day with Kevin, after he had finished his classes and lab work, we bought a six-pack of beer and drank it together, sitting side by side on his porch. I wasn't sure at first if I should drink with Kevin. Was my role as a writer to stay sober and observe my hosts from afar, or should I participate with them? I decided to participate in this case, figuring that a few beers wouldn't be a problem. During this conversation, Kevin began to speak openly for the first time, as if during the previous three days he had been suppressing everything he had wanted to say.

He told me the story of one of his roommates. Kevin lived with three other guys in an off-campus apartment. One of the roommates, Andrew, was a dick, according to Kevin. He's mean to people, messy, doesn't take out the trash, doesn't lock the door, keeps the freezer full of fish he never eats, and uses Kevin's dishes without washing them. A few years earlier, Andrew met a girl at Baylor and they started dating. After some time, her family became unable to afford the cost of Baylor, so she was going to have to drop out of school and move back home. But Andrew's parents are very wealthy, so they offered to pay the girlfriend's tuition to keep her at Baylor, and she accepted their offer, which allowed her to continue to date Andrew. This story could have been viewed as a story about love, but Kevin didn't describe their relationship in terms of love; instead, he described it in terms of an economic transaction. "I guess she'll have to keep sucking his dick to keep that tuition," Kevin said. He said that Andrew was chemically addicted to his girlfriend, and that the chemical addiction would wear off in a few years.

"I've heard them fucking in there," Kevin said, "and she usually makes noise; sometimes he does. But she sounds like she's in pain, not like she's enjoying it, which makes me think he doesn't really spend any time on foreplay to get the juices flowing—he just sticks it right in and it's more of a power thing." According to Kevin, Andrew had no need to satisfy his girlfriend sexually because he had her financially trapped. Similarly, Kevin believed that Andrew was making a poor decision to invest his time and money into this particular girl, because she was likely to break up with him as soon as she graduated—after she had used up all the money and no longer needed him. Kevin's theory was that all relationships operate by similar principles. He told me this theory and others as if he were a wise elder teaching a naive pupil.

One of Kevin's more controversial theories was that men and women in relationships were almost always willing to cheat on one another. One night he told me that the only way to guarantee that your girlfriend wouldn't cheat on you is to give her powerful orgasms by using a dominant sexual technique. Later in the week, he even pulled out his laptop and showed me a porn clip of the specific technique he was talking about. (This was a bit more than I needed to see, but I went along with it.) Kevin didn't necessarily want this to be true, he just believed it to be true.

In the 1950s, Baylor began a tradition called Dr Pepper Hour. The tradition is effectively a marketing event for the soda company, which is headquartered in Waco, but nevertheless it became embedded in the culture of the school. Once a week, Baylor hosts an event where students can receive free Dr Pepper ice cream floats. When the tradition began, Baylor had a men's-only dorm and a women's-only dorm. Dr Pepper Hour was held in the ballroom of the Student Union building, so it mostly served as an excuse for the sexes to intermingle. Dr Pepper Hour was supposed to be an old-fashioned sort of event where young men and women could socialize, meet each other, and potentially begin dating. Most of the dorms at Baylor have since become co-ed, but the tradition of Dr Pepper Hour persists.

Kevin and I stopped by Dr Pepper Hour the following day. The ballroom appeared mostly as it must have 60 years ago—no furniture, just open polished floors for standing, and ice cream floats served from huge brass bowls at the far end of the room with a line of students stretched to the opposite door—except now, shortly after receiving their ice cream, the students would leave the ballroom to head somewhere else.

"Well, this is it," Kevin said with a hint of cynicism as we waited in line. He had built up the event to sound like something that was a little bit romantic or at least fun and social, but today the tradition seemed to be mostly about the ice cream.

That evening we went to a burger and beer place with a group of accounting majors, friends of Kevin's roommate Darren. One of the guys in the group had just graduated from Baylor and was apparently working 80 hours a week at a Big Four accounting firm. He wore a large work phone unfashionably on his waist, and he excused himself multiple times over dinner to take calls. Since he had received the best job that any of the accountants could hope for, his new lifestyle was both the envy and the fear of his younger accountant friends. The talk of the evening was the big party the following night, which would be the first big party of the new semester. The party's host, who was sitting with us, said that he wanted it to be the gold standard of parties. Kevin and I were the only people in the three booths of accounting students who weren't dressed in semi-formal attire. The accountants, who were mostly juniors, had all attended a recruitment fair that day. "Only two and a half years of college and it's already almost over," someone said. Tomorrow's party, at least, was something for them to look forward to.

Kevin and I continued drinking at his apartment, just the two of us, and as the night wore on, Kevin seemingly lost the ability to monitor his speech. Of all the students I wrote about, Kevin was the most loose-lipped while drunk. To make matters worse, on this night we unintentionally occupied the physical choreography of Freudian talk therapy—Kevin lying down on a couch facing the ceiling as I sat upright behind him taking notes. As he talked to me, he alternated between sipping whiskey, texting some girl he hadn't yet mentioned, and, for some reason, sharpening a pocket knife.

"It's easy to get caught up in the romance of college and forget your duties," he told me. "I've tried the dating thing. It takes too much time. Even if it's just a hookup thing, it takes at least an hour, you know?"

"Right," I said.

"And of course the girl wants more, even if she says she doesn't. Most girls at Baylor are looking for husbands. They're trying to find a guy with some success and go off with him. Girls love it when you act like you don't give a fuck until they find out you really don't give a fuck."

"What about you?"

"I wish there was a girl I could give a fuck about. Girls in college are like little girls. At 16, girls are more mature than guys, but then guys go out and get in trouble and mature. So girls are just idiots in college and spread their legs for anyone. This past year, all I've had to do is sit them down and talk about my research. I'll sit them by the fish and turn the lights off. That's all I need. Girls are so dumb."

It occurred to me that Kevin used the same seduction technique on me when we first met, but I didn't mention it.

"What about the girl you're texting right now?" I asked.

"Ah, we're actually starting to form a bit of a relationship. Some mutual respect is forming."

"How so?"

"I think you can form sexual attachment to anyone you fuck on the regular, which is different from that attachment when you have an actual crush. Sometimes you forget you don't like them. You can't trust how you feel about it. I don't know, love seems like it might be a reason why people get together, but not why they stay together."

"What makes them stay together?"

"It depends on the people. You can really grow into affection for somebody by having lots of sex with them. Over time you get accustomed to the softness of her back or the smell of her hair. You get used to them and the bond forms, but it goes away the same way. I think most relationships can't stay past six years. As it comes to an end, it's funny how you can be having sex and it's not that exciting anymore. But you don't believe it. It's amazing how you can just not believe some things. We choose to love people as much as we choose to hate people."

"How do you choose who to love?"

"I don't know," Kevin said, holding his pocket knife still for a moment. "But at some point you're going to meet that girl, and you're going to realize every other girl was just practice until that girl. Just pray you don't meet that girl too early. How unlucky."

"Have you had that?" I asked.

He sighed. "Who the fuck knows? I know I thought I had that."

Kevin told me the story of his last girlfriend. He loved her, but they had an extremely hostile breakup when they went to separate colleges. She now has a new boyfriend and studies Women and Gender Studies. I wondered if their opposing academic pursuits— her gender studies and his evolutionary biology—were somehow formed in contrast to one another.

"Sometimes girls just inspire that in guys," Kevin continued, referring to feelings of love. "And I'm sure whoever she's fucking right now is feeling the same way. But at least she's only with one guy. It sounds kinda primal, but I'd prefer one person fool around with my property rather than 12 guys playing with my toys."

I thought Kevin was joking. I was bad at playing the therapist, because when he said this, I let out a loud snort of laughter. He wasn't joking, though, and he didn't even smile.

Later in the night, Kevin received a phone call from a Baylor student who had graduated and now lived in California. She was presently drunk and was trying to convince Kevin not to hook up with other girls. This was a different girl from the one Kevin had been texting earlier. Kevin didn't seem to mind that I was still in the room taking notes. I could only hear Kevin's side of the conversation.

"You shouldn't obsess over me," he said.

"...Listen, I have no fuck buddy. I'm busy, I have a job, I can't whore around..."

"...My job is to get an education..."

"...How can you not think I'm an asshole? All I say are asshole things, and you hear them, and I don't know..."

"...I assure you, I'm not talking to anyone..."

"...That would feel amazing..."

I raised a brow and wondered if I should leave the room.

"...You're just teasing me because there's nothing I can do..." Kevin continued.

"...No, I'm not coming to San Francisco..."

"...You're asking my GPA because you want to know my potential value..."

"...No, I'm not labeling you as a typical Baylor girl..."

"...I'm not going to say it..."

"...3.68..."

"...Do my grades make you horny?..."

"...I like that my grades make you horny..."

"...Come May and we're both single and you want the shit fucked out of you, you know where I am..."

When Kevin hung up the phone, he turned to face me—the first time he'd seen me in his visual field in about an hour—and laughed. "Thinking about my research is a lot easier than thinking about girls," he said.

Later that night, when Kevin thought I was asleep, he snuck out the front door of the apartment and didn't return until the morning. The first girl, the one he had been texting, lived down the hall.

When Kevin wasn't drunk, he was often contemplative and philosophical. The following day, he brought me on a tour of campus, which included a visit to a museum dedicated to the works of poets Robert and Elizabeth Browning. Kevin hadn't been since he was a freshman, but he said he remembered it as being quite beautiful. The museum had a calming effect on both of us, and we began to talk much less. After circling the inside a few times, we found ourselves standing before Elizabeth's most famous poem, "How Do I Love

Thee?" which was etched in gold on a polished granite wall. In the poem, Browning lists the small, subtle aspects of love that add up to form her full love.

I didn't think Kevin would like the poem, considering that his worldview of biological motives and economic calculation didn't have any room for abstract, true love. But something about the poem caught his eye, and we stood transfixed before it for a long while without speaking. Other visitors to the museum would shuffle past us, stopping to look briefly at the poem before moving on, but we stayed put. I never learned what Kevin was thinking about during that time; I didn't think it was right to ask.

The philosophically minded adolescent frequently acts in accordance with whatever he has most recently read or studied. One day he reads a convincing essay on the existence of love and then finds himself writing love letters and composing poetry; the next day he reads an equally convincing essay claiming that love isn't real and then finds himself cringing with shame over what he believed just one day prior. As such, someone in the throes of a philosophically minded adolescence may seem mercurial and enigmatic to the people around him as he tests out new philosophies of life. In Kevin's case, his education was leading him toward a worldview of pure biological determinism, an amoral world where humans were only trying to combine DNA with the best possible mates and were willing to do anything necessary in order to do so. Although Kevin seemed to believe this, he also seemed to be wrestling against it. Beneath his dispassionate exterior, he seemed to be sensitive and hurting.

It was the final full day of my stay at Baylor, which happened to coincide with the first big party of the semester—the party thrown by the accountants who were longing to set the gold standard for parties. As we left the final class of the day, Kevin whistled, "Working for the Weekend," the song that goes, "Everybody's working for the weekend. Everybody wants a new romance."

"What do you think is the point of partying?" I asked. It was a dumb question, but I wanted to hear how Kevin would answer.

"I think it's an opportunity for people who have been pent up and involved with themselves all week to be themselves to the community," Kevin said. "Or be a fool and have nobody notice."

"Makes sense."

"It's a Friday night, and they feel they can nurse some of their vices. College students probably have a higher sex drive. You're just around each other all the time, and it's pretty well known that college girls are the biggest sluts. Afterward they restrict themselves more."

Kevin thought to himself for a minute, then offered a closing remark: "At the end of the day, dude, it's only the last dick that matters."

I again let out a snort of laughter at something that Kevin hadn't meant as a joke. He had just shared, in a rather crude way, a sentiment that is actually somewhat romantic: a woman may be with many men in her life, but it's the man who she ends up with—the last dick—who really counts. I took the remark to mean that Kevin still hoped he could someday end up with his ex-girlfriend.

Some of the accounting students—maybe 12 of them—came to Kevin and Darren's apartment to start drinking before the party. As we stood around the kitchen mixing drinks, one of the girls in the group, April, was standing very close to Kevin, smiling up at him, and laughing at all of his jokes.

"You make funny faces," April said to Kevin. There was a group conversation underway, but April and Kevin had started to talk between themselves.

Kevin sipped his whiskey. "I always make funny faces," he said.

Their conversation became quieter and more private, and during a few separate moments, April touched and held onto Kevin's arm for a little longer than what could be considered merely friendly. I was told later that April wasn't single; she had a boyfriend, and he was one of the other guys in the room with us. But he wasn't watching April and Kevin's flirting—he had gotten drunk early in the night and was sitting half-asleep on the couch. I made sure to keep my eye on Kevin and April to see what would develop.

(If you feel bad for the boyfriend, think again. While sitting half-asleep on the couch, he kept repeating, "Gay sex is icky... gay sex is icky..." for some unknown reason. That's all I ever heard him say.)

A little later, the accountants began plotting something that I didn't expect.

"We should get Drew laid," one of the girls said.

"Oh shit, let's do it. Yeah, we're gonna get you laid, dude," said one of the guys.

Everyone in the room agreed with this plan, and then they looked to me for my reaction. As soon as this happened, I felt a pleasant mixture of excitement and fear.

The reason for my excitement was simple and obvious: I was a 20-year-old dude and there was nothing at all extraordinary about me. Of course I wanted a roomful of strangers to try to help me have sex.

The reason for my fear was more complicated.

When I began this project, I was completely convinced that my book would be a work of anthropology. As far as I knew, anthropologists weren't supposed to try to sleep with anyone while on the job. But why had I chosen to write something anthropological? I had no publisher, no editor, no authority figure guiding my project in any way. Theoretically I was free to write whatever I wanted. I think I wanted to write something purely anthropological for two reasons.

First, I could not under any circumstance admit to myself that I made a mistake by choosing not to go to college. If I tried to have too much fun, if I let loose and tried to participate as an equal, as a peer, it would mean that college had something that I wanted, something that I was missing. I could not admit this to myself. By writing something anthropological, I could tell myself that I was only trying to research college students, not hang out with them. And yet, I was now doing exactly that. I had concocted a massive plan that would throw me right into the action of college life, but I still wanted to believe that I didn't want or need to be a part of it.

The second reason was perhaps the stronger of the two. I had been reasonably confident with girls when I was in high school, but in the two intervening years my self-esteem had plummeted and I had started to feel more like a Charlie Kaufman protagonist. Every time I met someone new, the inevitable question of where I went to college would arise. I didn't personally think it should matter that I didn't go to college, but it seemed to matter a whole lot to everybody else. You would think that with time I would have become better at answering the question, "Where do you go to college?", but instead my answers became worse with time. I had been rejected so many times at that exact moment in conversation that the question of where I went to college had become a huge insecurity for me. I had no identity, no way to explain who I was. The only thing a young man has to offer a woman is his enthusiasm, but after he's had his spirits crushed enough times he can't even offer her that. By writing something anthropological, it meant that I didn't have to participate at parties. I didn't have to face rejection. I could just stand in the corner and watch.

There is a psychological tool called the Johari Window that says that everyone has four selves: the public self, which is the part of you that everyone sees; the private self, the part of you that only you see; the unknown self, the part of you that nobody can see; and the blind self, the part of you that everyone but you can see. If everyone knows that Tommy is an asshole, but Tommy has no idea, then the part of him that is an asshole would be his blind self.

My blind self was the part of me that didn't want to stand in the corner and simply watch. I did want to participate. I did want to have a good time. To my hosts, this was completely obvious, but for me, this fact about myself was hidden beneath many layers of repression and denial.

And there was new hope for me as well, because I would be testing out a new identity. I was no longer "Drew, the guy who didn't go to college." I was now "Drew, the guy who's writing a book." If someone asked me where I went to college, I could say, "I don't go to college, but I am writing a book *about* college." Would that stupid trick work, or would women accurately detect that I was a phony? I was not sure.

So here it was, already, one week into the trip. "Let's get Drew laid." The accountants were all looking at me for my response. I blushed and then told them that I'd do my best.

Kevin wanted to buy some weed before the party, so we left with the fourth roommate, TJ, toward a house where a group of weed-dealing Baylor football players lived. (I am not breaking any news here. Some former Baylor football players have already told the press that they used to deal weed while at college. As far as I know, we might have bought weed from one of those guys.) We walked up the stairs of the apartment and waited in the bedroom of one of the players. He came in a few minutes later with a shoebox where he kept his weed and bong. He held up his bong.

"Say, how would I clean this piece?" the football player asked Kevin.

"Isopropyl alcohol and salt," said Kevin.

"If I just put it in the dishwasher, will that break it?"

"I wouldn't," said Kevin. He pointed to the bong. "Hey, mind if I load this?"

"Yeah, do your thing."

Kevin brought the bong to the bathroom to rinse it out. From behind the door, he whistled, "Working for the Weekend" again. The football player asked, "Is that Kevin whistlin'? Ain't nobody else be whistlin' classical shit like that."

I nodded, not having the guts to tell him that it was a popular song from the '80s.

Once Kevin cleaned out the bong, the three of them smoked (weed makes me paranoid, so I declined). As we left, Kevin assured us that he was ok to drive.

"I'm not as belligerent as I seem," he said. "I would usually just chill on a night like this, but I want to go see April."

"What's the deal with that?" I asked. "She seemed into you."

"She looks at me with these eyes! I don't know what she's doing!"

"Would you do it?" asked TJ.

"I'm pretty fond of her," said Kevin. "I don't think Darren likes to hear that, because he's close with her boyfriend. But I think he knows."

"So yes or no?" asked TJ.

"I'm not sure yet," said Kevin.

Kevin was faced with a moral quandary: if April was willing to cheat on her boyfriend with Kevin, how much of this wrongdoing was Kevin's responsibility?

A light rain began to fall. We ran from Kevin's parked car toward the party and into the house, where students' faces glowed red in the light cast by strings of red party bulbs, the only source of illumination. About 50 students, many of them the accountants from the other night, were spread around the large apartment. Rap music blared loud enough that we could barely hear anyone talking. The entryway to the apartment was in shadow, so nobody turned to look as we first arrived, but as Kevin entered into the pool of red light, the accountants one by one saw him and yelled to him or gave him high fives, although Kevin didn't stop long enough to talk to any of them, and instead he continued to the far side of the room where he found April standing alone. She hugged him, and he hugged her. Neither of them let go for a long while—it was strange. I turned around, expecting to see TJ behind me also watching Kevin and April's intimate hug, but he had gone off somewhere else. I looked around the room to see if April's boyfriend was nearby, but I didn't see him. Eventually Kevin and April dropped their arms to let go of the hug, but their bodies stayed close. April looked up at Kevin, not by tilting her head back, but by lifting her eyes up. Those must have been the eyes that Kevin mentioned.

Kevin looked back at April, except his eyes didn't seem to share her intention. Instead, Kevin's eyes tightened with apology and remorse, his shoulders slumped with heaviness, and his head lowered a few notches as he released the air that had inflated his chest. Kevin leaned in and whispered something into her ear. I couldn't hear his words over the music, but it seemed like Kevin made the difficult choice and told April that he wasn't willing to hook up with her. April gave him a disappointed look, and then they slowly moved away from each other. The two of them didn't talk again for the rest of the night. A few beers later, Kevin appeared back to full health.

Kevin and April weren't the only two students wrestling with a moral dilemma. Darren, Kevin's accountant roommate, was dating a girl named Katherine. The two of them had first been close friends before becoming romantically involved. Since then, Katherine had spent plenty of time alone with Darren in his bedroom, so Kevin assumed that they had had sex. But this was not the case. In the middle of the party, Katherine ran over to Kevin.

"Kevin! I need to talk to you!" she said.

"Talk!" Kevin yelled back.

"Darren hasn't had sex with me!"

"Are you serious?"

Kevin and Katherine stood face to face, yelling over the music. I stood perpendicular to them, blatantly eavesdropping. (Everyone was used to it by then.) Next, Darren—the guy they were talking about—came and stood next to me with his back to Kevin and Katherine, listening to them over his shoulder, while Kevin and Katherine somehow remained oblivious to him. This ridiculous arrangement was only possible because of the dim lighting and the alcohol.

"Yes, I'm serious!" Katherine yelled.

"You haven't fucked? Why not?" Kevin asked.

"He says he's Catholic! He's not supposed to have sex, but I don't understand how he can not want to!"

"He's insane!"

Darren took a sip of his drink, then braced himself as he listened to more of their conversation.

"I'm horny, you know?" Katherine said. "But I don't want to fool around with anyone else!"

"Then you have to wait for Darren!" said Kevin.

"But I get bored, I can't help it!"

"You just have to convince him to have sex with you! He will eventually!"

"I'm scared! I'm scared of something serious with him!"

"Just have fun with it! Why are you scared?"

"Because I get bored! I'm trying to follow my lust and feelings! He's the one putting the wall up!"

"You have to stay consistent! Have fun and stay consistent!"

"But I'm never consistent! I can't be consistent!"

"You have to play the fucking game! Play the fucking game!"

"Ok! Ok! Thank you! I will!"

Just as their conversation was coming to a close, Darren walked ten steps away, turned around, then walked ten steps back toward Kevin and Katherine as if he had been somewhere else the whole time. Now they noticed him.

"Darren!" they yelled.

"I'm drunk!" Darren yelled back.

In unison, Kevin and Katherine yelled, "Me too!"

That was the end of it. A few beers later, Darren also appeared back to full health. (Kevin would eventually tell me that Darren and Katherine had sex a few weeks later.)

With these conflicts out of the way, Kevin and Darren could now enjoy the party. In a short time, we all became very drunk.

Later in the night, I joined Darren on the beer pong table. Darren was now extremely drunk. When the other teams were shooting, he would turn around, bend forward, and shake his ass near our cups as a distraction. I was drunk enough also that I thought it was a good idea to mimic Darren. Our challengers for one game were two girls who didn't know anybody else at the party. They were attractive, but not so attractive that I was afraid of them. As we were playing against them, Darren yelled out, "This guy's writing a book! He's a badass!" This was Darren doing his part in trying to get me laid, so I now felt tasked with trying to charm these girls. They asked about my book, and I explained it to them across the table.

When the game was over, I stayed talking with them. The conversation was an embarrassing mixture of me talking about myself interspersed with asking interview-style questions to pretend like I was doing some sort of journalism. "So how many students go to Baylor? Ok, ok, very interesting." Whatever I was doing seemed to be working, because the girls hadn't walked away yet, which is what I was used to. And not only had they not walked away, they both seemed extremely into me. Whenever there was a pause in the conversation, they would smile nervously, trade loaded glances with each other, then look back at me while still smiling.

The other accountants were also trying to help me out while this was going on. Occasionally one of them would walk by, pat me on the back, and say to the girls, "This guy's a badass," then walk away. I didn't want to disappoint them, so I kept talking and talking.

I knew that if I wanted to move things forward, we would have to leave the party to go somewhere private. But I had nowhere to take them. Unsure of what to do next, I took a slight risk and lied, telling the girls that my host had already left the party, and that I had no ride back to his apartment. Then I asked if I could sleep at their place instead. To my surprise, they agreed. (The girls later told me that they knew I was lying; they could see Kevin on the other side of the room the whole time.) They said they lived in a girl-only dorm and would have to sneak me in through the window. I quickly texted Kevin to tell him what was unfolding, happy that I might have a story for him and the accountants.

The girls called a friend to pick us up from the party and drive us to their dorms. When we arrived, one of the girls went inside to unlock the window while the other led me through a maze of alleyways outside.

"Do you do this often?" I asked.

"We've never had a boy in our room," she said.

The window opened from the inside, and we hoisted ourselves over the ledge. When I stood up inside their dorm room, the girls looked extremely embarrassed. They were both standing with their hands over their mouths, holding in laughter. I quickly realized why: the room was decorated like they were ten years old. One half of the room was decorated with princess posters, princess pillows, and princess bed sheets. The other half was covered in posters of boy bands. I started laughing.

"This needs an explanation," I said.

They started laughing too, so hard that they were barely able to speak.

"Neither of us had girly rooms growing up," one of them said.

"So we wanted to do it for college," said the other.

At this point we were all cracking up at the awkward situation, but I was still trying to stay calm and charming. I changed the subject.

"What year are you two?" I asked.

"Freshmen," one said.

We talked for a few more minutes until one of them asked me to close my eyes while they changed clothes. I turned around, and they both changed into pajamas.

"Ok, do you just want to sleep on the floor?" one of them asked me. The floor was made of hard tile.

"Not a chance," I said. "I'm taking a bed." I sat down on the bed with the princess sheets.

The girl who owned the bed quickly joined me on it. "You better not take up too much room," she said. She looked pleased.

I took off my shoes, and she lifted up the covers for us to get under.

"I think I'm going to take a shower," said the other girl shortly after. "I'll be gone for about 15 minutes." It was clear that she was leaving in order to give us some alone time. Once she grabbed her towel and was about leave the room, she asked us, "Do you want the lights on or off?"

"You can turn them off," said the girl next to me.

The lights switched off, and the room faded to black as the door closed. We were now alone.

The main appeal of casual sex for me was not the sex itself. What interested me most was the psychosocial aspect of it, the etiquette, and the communication. It was an exciting new realm of life to explore and to learn about. It was something I was supposed to be good at, despite inexperience. I wanted to know how it goes down. I wanted to know what she would say and how she would say it, and what I would say and how I would say it. I wanted to know what we'd talk about right before and right after. I wanted to know if we would cuddle afterward like boyfriend and girlfriend, or if we'd go back to acting like strangers. The fact that I might enjoy the sex itself had little to do with why I wanted to do it. Sex was just a perk that came along with the exciting feeling of exploration, which was the real thing I was after.

The girl with the princess sheets lay next to me, facing the other way in the darkness. After a moment's silence, I put my hand on her shoulder and gently turned her toward me. She turned the rest of the way herself so that we were now facing each other. I leaned forward to kiss her, and she returned the kiss. I pulled her body close to mine.

A few moments later, she pulled her head away and whispered, "I barely know you."

"I barely know you," I whispered back.

My response was apparently satisfactory. We went back to kissing. I started to slide my fingers beneath the elastic band of her pajama pants.

"Wait," she whispered again.

I paused.

"My roommate will do more with you," she said.

"What do you mean?"

"My roommate will go further with you than I will."

"I don't want her, I want you," I said.

"Ok. You don't care?"

"No."

While making out, I reached my hand under her pajama pants and she reached her hand under my shorts.

"This is all I'm going to do," she said. "Is that ok?"

"It's great," I said, taking my shorts the rest of the way off.

A little while later, I tried to reciprocate, but she didn't want me to. Her body had turned somewhat lifeless, and there was no longer as much of a sense of warmth or closeness between us. We kissed a little while longer until her roommate came back in the room, then we pretended like nothing had happened. I wasn't sure what to think.

The three of us stayed up talking and laughing for another

hour before falling asleep. I woke up the next day at noon. The girls told me they had been up all morning, not sure how they should wake me. No longer drunk, the entire situation seemed bizarre and uncomfortable. Even so, I tried my best to keep up a little bit of my charm from the previous night, so they wouldn't feel deceived. I thanked them politely for their hospitality, climbed out of their window, then headed back toward Kevin's apartment on foot.

Two weeks later, the girls both friend-requested me on Facebook. According to her Facebook page, the girl whose bed I shared had a boyfriend. Perhaps that's why her body had turned lifeless—some mix of regret and guilt. They had been together for a long time, and her profile showed lots of happy photos of the two of them. She also frequently posted Bible verses. This all came as quite a shock to me. Until that moment, I never thought I might have to ask a girl if she had a boyfriend before hooking up with her. I'd always figured that she would tell me first. In movies and television when someone cheats, there's usually a vibe of sinfulness or wrongdoing, but that girl seemed sweet and innocent to me, so I wasn't sure what to make of it. I chalked it up to a strange coincidence and didn't let it cause me much grief.

When I returned to Kevin's apartment, Kevin, Darren, and TJ were sprawled across the couches nursing their hangovers and watching television.

"There he is!" Darren said as I entered.

"How'd it go?" Kevin asked me.

"Good," I said.

"What happened?"

"Handjob," I said.

"Well done. Which girl?"

"The taller one."

"Good choice."

The guys sat there smiling and nodding in approval. They were impressed, and the atmosphere was congratulatory. As a 20-year-old, their approval meant a whole lot to me, and my desire for it had perhaps been the main thing motivating my actions the previous night. Having now received it, I felt deeply satisfied.

For a young or immature man, the best part of sexual activity is the male approval. The sexual activity itself is often so emotionally confusing and intimate that he is unable to derive much pleasure from it. The real pleasure comes when he reports the story to his friends. To young men, sexuality is a magical and mysterious realm. He who journeys into this realm and returns with a story is celebrated as a hero by other young men who have not yet journeyed as far or as deep. As he tells the story to his friends, he can edit out the insecurity, the shame, and the doubt. He tells his story as one composed purely of pride and accomplishment. Fortunately, this stage of life only lasts a short time. By age 25, most men have lost their fascination with other men's sex lives. If you try to tell a man older than 25 about your sex life, he will probably just feel annoyed that you're still seeking his approval for something so mundane. (If I find myself boasting about sexual activity at 25, it's usually about something I would have been ashamed of at 20. "Dude, I got erectile dysfunction last night, but we were able to have a mature discussion about it, and neither of us got our feelings hurt. It was awesome, dude!")

Before I left Baylor, Kevin and I sat down together to have some coffee. During this conversation, Kevin was reminded of a passage in Ecclesiastes that he liked. He went to his bedroom and grabbed his Bible so he could read it to me. Surprised by Kevin's interest in the Bible, I asked him if he believed in God, and he said that he did. Kevin's appreciation for Nietzsche, his study of evolutionary biology, and his cynicism about human relationships—all of these things made me assume that Kevin didn't believe in God, but my assumption was incorrect. Kevin even went on to say he believed that human existence had purpose and meaning. Again I was surprised, so I checked another one of my assumptions.

"What about love?" I asked. "Do you believe there's some kind of love beyond just chemical addictions and the desire to reproduce?"

"Yeah, I think I do," Kevin said. I expected him to give a long explanation like he usually did, but this time his answer was brief.

"What about your fish?" I asked. "Aren't you trying to prove that everything is just genetics?"

"No," Kevin said, "I'm trying to prove it's not."

3

UNIVERSITY OF OKLAHOMA

I left Baylor feeling somewhat bad, almost dirty. I didn't like the way Kevin saw the world, and I wanted to forget what I learned there. I drove five hours north to Oklahoma ready to experience something completely different.

For the second week of the trip, I would be writing about a girl in one of the top sororities at the University of Oklahoma. This was a huge accomplishment for the book, since I wasn't sure that I'd ever find a girl in a sorority who would let me write about her. I would stay with her during the day, then at night, since I wasn't allowed to sleep at the sorority house, I would be sleeping at a nearby fraternity house with the person who connected me with Kelsey. All week I was nervous and shy—both at the fraternity house and the sorority house —but the beauty of being there as a writer, I learned, was that I could be a little bit unusual compared to everyone else and my behavior would still be socially acceptable.

When I arrived, it was already 10pm, so instead of meeting Kelsey on my first day, I went straight to the fraternity house to go to sleep. My host Dylan met me outside by my car to help me carry my things inside.

"Just a heads-up," Dylan said, "but I told my roommates about your book, and one of them said, 'What the fuck? He doesn't go to college?' And also, this might be kind of awkward, but we're hazing tonight. If anyone sees you, you should just pretend like you don't notice anything."

Walking into the fraternity house, we could hear loud noises coming from the basement—mostly chanting and occasionally what sounded like loud stomping. Dylan told me the hazing was not so bad when he went through it, but he was now ashamed of some of the things that he was made to do. For instance, the pledges were once made to chant, "Pound booze! Rail sluts! Pound booze! Rail sluts!" As an 18-year-old, the chant seemed cool, Dylan said, but one year later he had reconsidered, and he now resented the pledge trainers who made them do it. The process was repeating itself below us as he told me the story. (Oddly enough, this fraternity had the reputation around campus of being nice and respectful, so I wondered what the other fraternities were doing during their hazing rituals.)

We went straight to Dylan's bedroom so nobody would see me. Before we went to sleep, Dylan told me what he knew about my host Kelsey, who I had never met. Kelsey was well known around campus for being extremely involved. This meant that she was a member of many of the prestigious organizations at OU, and that she always applied for the leadership positions. Kelsey's sorority was known for its campus involvement, and Kelsey was one of its most respected members. The reason that she was allowing me to write about her, Dylan said, was probably because she was the ideal student who didn't do anything wrong.

In the morning, I met Kelsey and some of her friends for break-fast at a bagel shop. Kelsey was so busy with her campus and sorority involvement that she had little time to see her closest friends. This breakfast was a rare opportunity for them to see each other and catch up. When Kelsey came inside, she greeted me with a big hug and an excited smile. I did my best to match her enthusiasm, but I don't think I came close.

Once the rest of the girls arrived, we all ordered bagels and took seats. I was amazed by the way the girls so comfortably allowed me to witness their unfiltered conversation. It was the six of us sitting in chairs around a circular table, except I was one foot farther away from the table than anyone else, and I barely spoke for the entire hour.

The first topic of conversation was spring break diets. Spring break was about eight weeks away, and it was commonplace for girls in sororities to go on diets in preparation. (You're on the beach, probably wearing a bikini, and lots of people are taking pictures of you to share on social media.) However, some of the girls—not the girls here, other girls—were going on unhealthy crash diets that were stressing out everybody else. "If she loses any more weight, she'll snap in two," someone said about one girl who was trying to eat only one piece of bread and ten almonds a day. "I haven't seen Kendall eat anything in days," someone said of another girl. Kelsey was on a small diet—no sweets and none of the garlic bread that was frequently served at the sorority house.

Next they discussed the status of a bunch of other people's relationships—who was beginning to date, and whether a couple's relationship was strong or if they were currently fighting. I learned that it is common for a girl in a sorority to group text her sorority to ask for advice while she's with a guy. For example, one girl was recently with her boyfriend in his hometown, and he was playing video games with some of his guy friends. The girl sent a group text to her sorority that said, "I'm sitting on the couch next to him and he's just playing video games with his friends. What should I do?" Everyone in the sorority began collectively criticizing him, saying, "He's disrespecting you," and, "Girl, you should just get up and leave!"

Finally, since the girls hadn't seen each other in a long time, the conversation ended with an informal shower of compliments. The highest compliment seemed to be that someone's hair looked healthy, or that it was the perfect length. There was a great deal of warmth to the compliments—a girl would lean forward, touch another girl's forearm, and say, "By the way, your hair looks amazing right now." The content of the compliment wasn't as important as the warmth.

Although this part of the conversation was unusual to me at first, I quickly found myself wishing that my friends and I would end our conversations with a similar shower of compliments.

As we were leaving, I noticed for the first time that the bagel shop had been deathly silent except for our table, which had been quite loud for morning time. The other patrons were watching us walk out the door with what appeared to be a great sense of relief.

(By the way, I support the general effort to call women "women" and not "girls," as "girls" can be infantilizing if used inappropriately. However, most of the young women in this book are about the same age as Britney Spears when she released her classic, "I'm Not a Girl, Not Yet a Woman," which many people don't realize is actually a brilliant song about the difficulties of copyediting. Is a 19-year-old a girl or woman? She's most accurately a young woman, but you can't say that every time. In my personal life I often use the word "gal" to solve this problem, but that would sound ridiculous if used throughout this book. My rule of thumb, then, was to choose the word most used by the young women themselves at that particular school. Most of the time the word they used to refer to themselves was "girl," though there are some exceptions later in the book.)

After Kelsey said goodbye to her friends, we went together to her office hours for the President's Leadership Class, known as PLC. PLC is a highly selective student leadership organization at OU. In Kelsey's class, 7,500 freshmen applied to be a part of the organization, and only 125 were selected. Kelsey was selected to be one of the 125, and she was also one of the leaders. One of her duties as a leader of PLC was that she had to be available in the PLC office for ten hours a week so that freshmen in PLC could talk to her.

When we entered the office, there were already a few freshmen sitting on the couches, presumably waiting for Kelsey. Anyone in PLC was allowed to visit Kelsey for as long as they wanted, but over the course of the week, it became apparent that it was mostly a handful of regulars who would hang out in the office. Kelsey's job was to be available for conversations with the freshmen, but in practice she seemed more like the leader of group therapy. A freshman student would come in with a complaint—"I'm nervous about my Spanish quiz," or, "I'm worried that my professor doesn't like me,"—and Kelsey would do her best to console him or her. This was a nice system most of the time, but sometimes it seemed like a lonely freshman with nobody to talk to would invent or exaggerate a personal problem in order to have an excuse to hang out in the office. Since the personal problems were rarely very serious, Kelsey would usually offer them a simple platitude like, "Well, it'll all be better in the end!" Perhaps, similar to Kelsey's conversation with her friends, it was not about the content but the warmth. Kelsey was always the leader of the conversation. If she spoke about herself, she'd place her hands over her heart, and everybody would lean toward her. If any students came in who seemed shy, she'd say, "You don't have to stand there, you can come in closer with everybody else!"

At one point, one of the campus administrators came by the office and told me about Kelsey. Apparently Kelsey, as a high schooler, set up a meeting with him and said, "When you get my application, know who I am." He described Kelsey as the "activator" of PLC—the central ingredient that brings everybody together. As he walked away, Kelsey complimented him—"Charles, your scent is spot on today."

During a lull in the conversation, Kelsey got on Facebook. She had 4,500 friends and 292 pending friend requests. In her inbox were a bunch of messages, mostly from PLC members asking what they should wear to a ballroom dance lesson that night. One message from a guy, not a PLC member, said, "Hey what's up you are very pretty can I get your number?" She didn't respond. Kelsey said that most of her work for PLC takes place outside of office hours—things like people calling her at midnight to talk about a breakup.

Near the end of office hours, a family walked in—two parents and two high school kids—to ask about PLC. Kelsey jumped to her feet, greeted the high schoolers with great enthusiasm, and started asking them about their high school experience and what they wanted to do in college. The high schoolers were seniors who had been accepted to OU, but they hadn't committed to attending yet. After Kelsey told them about some of the things that happen in PLC—a dinner with the Oklahoma governor, hearing a talk from the OU football coach about leadership, a trip to Italy, parties, and charity events—the entire family seemed extremely impressed. The mom said that she's sending her first kid to college, and she's so excited to get him involved in something so great like PLC. (This statement seemed at least partially political: her son had not been accepted into PLC yet, but since Kelsey and the PLC administrator—who was also present— had the power to choose who was accepted, it might have helped his chances.) By the end of the conversation, the kids said that they were for sure going to go to OU now, and the mom said, "I already feel good about OU, but now I feel so much better." Kelsey had done her job well.

One PLC administrator, Jill, was an important figure in Kelsey's life. Kelsey, as a PLC leader, was expected to be a role model for freshmen at OU, and Jill seemed to be an enforcer of Kelsey's good behavior. Jill told me that leaders need to be good people outside of PLC too, and that Kelsey doesn't do anything she wouldn't want a freshman doing. (I think this mostly meant that Kelsey didn't drink alcohol or do anything inappropriate.) Jill also wanted Kelsey to make a 4.0 GPA, and she was worried that all of Kelsey's other obligations might get in the way of her school work.

After PLC office hours, we went to a few classes and then were picked up by Kelsey's roommate Tina. Tina was holding a piece of chocolate, and since she had a pact with Kelsey not to eat any sweets, Kelsey hit the chocolate out of her hand. We were headed to their sorority house, which was a rather nerve-racking experience for me at first. The sorority house was essentially a huge mansion, and the parking lot was full of expensive cars—mostly large, high-end SUVs. Inside the main room of the house—the only place I was allowed to go—there were rows of long tables where girls were studying, eating, or talking with each other. Kelsey and Tina took seats and started working on homework.

Most men, when in the company of attractive women, go out of their way to display their positive qualities. They're extra outgoing, extra friendly, and extra charming. When I am in the company of

attractive women, I go out of my way to avoid humiliation. I slow
down, become very quiet, and try not to make any social errors. That
was my protocol all week as I sat among Kelsey and her friends at the
sorority house. When I did speak up, I did so strictly as a writer
seeking information to write a book. Accordingly, I learned a great
deal about sorority life.

Sororities are in constant competition with one another. Among
Greek students, there is a never-ending debate about whether a
sorority is considered top tier, middle tier, or bottom tier. Since there
is no formal ranking of sororities, each sorority's social status is determined by popular opinion, and the outcome is never settled. When I
asked Kelsey and her friends what makes a sorority considered a top
sorority, they told me that it is based on community service, campus
involvement, leadership positions, winning the President's Trophy (an
award given by the OU president to one sorority and one fraternity
each year), and winning Scandals (a theatre competition). One girl
jokingly added, "And having the prettiest girls!" She said it as a joke,
but it seemed self-evident to me that having pretty girls was one of
the more important factors in a sorority's rank.

Much of my confusion about sorority ranking was clarified when
I later found a website called GreekRank.com, which hosts a fairly
active community of anonymous members of fraternities and sororities who rate and debate the perceived reputations of houses on
campus. On the website, sorority houses are rated on the following
categories: looks, popularity, classiness, involvement, social life, and
sisterhood. If you read the comments, it's clear that physical appearance is important. One comment about Kelsey's sorority said, "If you
look at their last pledge class, you'll notice that they have a few that
need to spend more time in the gym." Other comments talk about
whether the girls are nice and sweet or if they're stuck up, and
whether or not they're fun to party with.

Many Americans who value freedom and autonomy would hate
to be in a system like this. Sorority reputation management follows
the same social logic as North Korean concentration camps. Apparently in North Korea if you are a political dissident, they throw not

just you but three generations of your relatives into a concentration camp. If you try to escape from the concentration camp, they kill not just you but your entire family. (Imagine if your uncle's political tweets could get you thrown into prison.) This leads to a paranoid social style where individuals must constantly monitor each other and discourage any possible bad behavior. Sorority dieting follows the same social logic. If a girl in a sorority wants to skip the gym and eat an entire pizza, not only does she risk being mad at herself, she also has to consider the possibility that her friends might be mad at her. If she makes this decision repeatedly and begins to gain weight visibly, she lowers the status of her sorority and worsens the reputations of her friends. So she goes to the gym. In addition to this, she is also incentivized to monitor her friends' eating and exercise habits, and to pressure them to make healthy choices and to shame them if they don't. When viewed this way, small things like Kelsey hitting the chocolate out of Tina's hand because they had a pact to not eat any sweets start to seem sinister and terrifying.

When I was at OU, I couldn't comprehend how Kelsey was motivated to be a leader of so many groups. In addition to being the leader of PLC, she was also preparing to be a director of a high school leadership camp, she was competing to become an orientation guide for next year's freshman orientation, and she was the lead actress in her sorority's play for the Scandals theatre competition. She was by far the busiest student I met on the whole trip. For a long time, I couldn't understand where she found the energy and motivation to do so many things, but it started to make sense when I considered it in context with her membership in her sorority. If sororities were judged in part based on their campus involvement and leadership positions, then Kelsey's activities can be seen as her working hard on behalf of her sorority. In a collectivist group like a sorority, the individuals are supposed to subordinate their own values to the group, then derive a sense of self-worth from the health of the group. Once you are accepted into a top sorority, you're expected to compete to maintain its status as a top sorority.

The University of Oklahoma tells its incoming freshmen at orientation that the most important thing they can do in college is to find a community. The idea is that a new student can make the most of her college experience by finding a group of students to be a part of, a group where she can belong. But this advice comes too late, because by the time most freshmen arrive for orientation, the sorting of insider and outsider has already begun. Two weeks before the first day of school is sorority rush, the week-long recruitment process during which incoming freshmen compete for acceptance into one of many sorority houses. Girls who are rushing move into their dorm rooms at the start of rush week, which means that everyone who rushes a sorority has two weeks to become friends with each other before the non-Greek girls arrive. Even though the non-Greek student population is the majority of the student body, non-Greek girls arrive on campus in the wake of a massive social competition where the Greek girls—who tend to be the most socially well-connected to begin with—have already found their communities. I imagine that the non-Greek girls arrive feeling anonymous and left out.

Sorority rush is a two-way process where sorority houses try to impress the girls rushing in order to recruit the most appealing girls, and the girls rushing try to impress the active members of sororities in order to be accepted by the most appealing houses. The process plays out in a series of short meet-and-greet events throughout the week (there's also some singing and dancing somewhere in the mix). The girls rushing are expected to make pleasant small talk with active members and form connections so that they can pass successive rounds of cuts. While it is most important that the rushees form connections with active members, a good deal of importance is also placed on other concerns. For example, the high school you attended may play a role in your acceptance (private schools from wealthy areas are preferred), your high school reputation may matter, your clothes and your car may matter, and I even heard stories where active members asked rushees how much money their parents make. Rush week can accordingly be very high-pressure and stressful. When my cousins rushed their sororities, our entire extended family was kept up-to-date on their successes and failures throughout the week.

Not everyone who rushes is accepted into a sorority. Girls start out competing for acceptance into a top sorority, but the sororities have to weed out all the girls they don't want. Kelsey's sorority, for instance, had to reject 500 girls on the first day of rush. Once a girl is cut from all the top sororities, she will try to gain acceptance into a middle tier or bottom tier sorority. If a girl has already cut the bottom sororities, and then is herself cut from the middle and top sororities, it's possible that she won't be accepted anywhere.

The final day is Bid Day, where girls are told which house they are accepted to. At Oklahoma, there's a big tradition that plays out. The rushee will return to her dorm room to find a sign on her door indicating which sorority she was accepted to, and then she will sprint across campus wearing a dress and heels to her new sorority house. The girls all sprint across campus at the same time in a sort of running-of-the-bulls spectacle, some of them crying from happiness, while their fraternity counterparts sit outside cheering them on. While many of the girls are crying from the happiness of acceptance, some others are in their bedrooms crying from the sadness of rejection. It's not uncommon for these girls to begin their plans to transfer to a different college.

Although a lot of this seemed strange to me, I nevertheless felt that if I were an 18-year-old girl going to a Greek-dominated university, and if I were pretty enough and wealthy enough to have a good chance at making it into a sorority, I would find it very hard not to join. To give an example of how important sorority status is for some people, I met a girl who was a senior in the Chi Omega sorority at Oklahoma, and by senior year she was so tired of sorority life that she wanted to quit. The only thing keeping her from quitting was the fact that if she quit, her future daughter would no longer have legacy status. She said, "I would quit, but I want my daughter to be a Chi-O."

Kevin from Baylor, based on his knowledge of evolutionary psychology, would tell you that men are more interested in physical beauty in their mates, whereas women are more interested in social status. However, that received wisdom does not apply to Greek life at Oklahoma. It is apparently far more common for a girl in a top sorority to date a guy who is non-Greek or in a low-ranking fraternity than it is for a guy in a top fraternity to date a girl who is non-Greek or in a low-ranking sorority. Here, the guys are the ones who are more sensitive to their mates' social status, and the girls respond accordingly.

During my week with Kelsey, I witnessed her having success after success. Her first success was becoming an orientation guide. One day when I was there, she had an interview for the position. She wore a nice dress, heels, and gave herself big, Oklahoma-style hair. The following day, we were sitting in the sorority house when a group of girls came in yelling, "Oh my God, Kelsey, did you hear? You got it!" Kelsey launched to her feet, joined the girls, and they all screamed in a fit of excitement. At first, I thought Kelsey wanted to become an orientation guide entirely for its own sake, but I later learned that this too was a part of sorority competition. As soon as the initial excitement died down, the girls checked the list of orientation guides (nine in total) to see how many of the orientation guides were representing other top sororities. It was considered bad news if any girls from the other top sororities had been accepted as orientation guides, and it was considered good news if their own sorority filled most of the positions. By becoming an orientation guide, Kelsey had effectively scored her sorority one point in the battle for sorority status.

Kelsey's next success was passing the first round of the Scandals theatre competition. Scandals is a theatre competition where sororities are matched with fraternities, and then they have to write and perform a play together. This sounds like it might be all fun and games, but winning and losing Scandals has a large influence over a sorority's reputation, so it's taken quite seriously. The first night of Kelsey's Scandals practice, I sat in the corner of the room observing, but afterward, the director of the play told Kelsey that I wouldn't be allowed back again for their next practice. Apparently people were nervous that I was a spy from another fraternity.

The pairing of fraternities and sororities for Scandals is another interesting phenomenon. Fraternities will go around to different sororities and sing them a song as an invitation to be partners for Scandals, and the sororities will have to accept or reject the entire fraternity. Scandals is not as big of a deal for fraternities, and mostly the guys are doing it in order to meet women (my fraternity hosts said that if they were single, they would do Scandals for that reason). For sororities, Scandals is more important, so they choose a fraternity based on its reputation and their belief about whether or not the guys will make good partners.

Kelsey had been telling me all week how nervous she was over whether or not they would pass the first round of Scandals, but once they passed, she didn't seem surprised. As a top sorority, it would have been a huge shock if they hadn't.

Kelsey seemed so busy meeting external pressures—the pressure to stay thin, to be a role model, to make a 4.0 GPA, to help freshmen in PLC, and to work on behalf of her sorority—that she seemed to have little time to consider her own needs. In some sense, she seemed so busy with these tasks that it almost appeared that she had no needs, and it was hard for me to feel close to her a lot of the time. (For the majority of the colleges I visited, I felt like I developed a surprisingly deep degree of intimacy with my hosts, but this didn't happen with Kelsey; Kelsey stayed in public-relations mode the entire week, and I was not a good enough writer yet to learn about her more private thoughts.) One moment of closeness, however, occurred when Kelsey told me that although she spends so much time consoling other people, she has few people to turn to when she needs consoling. The most egregious example of this that I witnessed was one day when Kelsey had a bad cold. She was asleep on the couch in her office, and a freshman walked in. I told him, "Kelsey's sick," which I intended to mean, "don't wake her up," but he still proceeded to tap her on the shoulder, wake her up, and say, "I'm nervous that I won't be able to finish my homework before class." Kelsey, with sleepy eyes and a scratchy voice, told him that he should try his best and that she was sure it would all be fine in the end.

I heard one year later that Kelsey ran for president of her sorority and lost. Kelsey seemed to have been living her life on a constant ascent from achievement to achievement, but after this disappointment she apparently went through a brief depressed phase (according to her friend Tina), after which she never again put as much effort into acting on behalf of her sorority. Although it shouldn't normally be considered a happy ending to hear that somebody lost faith in an organization they had exhausted themselves to support, I felt strangely happy for Kelsey when I heard the news. If Kelsey became a little bit disillusioned with the values of her group, and if she gave herself some slack from trying to be a perfect role model at all times, I think that these are only positive developments.

(And I fear that I might have made Kelsey's sorority life sound too stressful and difficult. Sorority competition and the battle to be a top sorority is probably pretty fun most of the time, and if you're winning —as Kelsey's sorority was—it would be even more fun. From what I could tell, Kelsey and her sorority sisters were some of the happiest students I met on this trip. Also, I've met many girls in sororities who don't take sorority life very seriously and have a healthy sense of humor about the whole thing, so the comparison to North Korea is a bit extreme.)

My last day at Oklahoma happened to be Valentine's Day. Since I had spent the preceding week surrounded by girls who cared a lot about Valentine's Day, I admit that I got into the spirit. It seemed self-evident that Valentine's Day was an important and special time. My week at Baylor had left me feeling cynical and dejected about relationships, so I thought I might do something utterly wholesome and romantic to cleanse my palate. I tagged along with my fraternity host to a flower shop where he was buying his girlfriend flowers, and I decided to buy yellow flowers for Kelsey as a platonic gesture of thanks. (I think the flowers were carnations. I later learned that yellow carnations symbolize disappointment and rejection, which means I made a huge mistake in my selection for Kelsey. Why would a flower shop even sell yellow carnations on Valentine's Day? Fortunately, I think Kelsey knew what I was intending.) I also bought red carnations for another girl, Autumn.

I met Autumn one day in the sorority house while Kelsey was studying in a back room. The sorority house had a room with a piano, and I was in there playing by myself when a girl walked in and sat down next to me. (When I was about 12, I desperately wanted to quit piano lessons, but my mom convinced me to stick with it because it would be a better extracurricular activity to put on college applications. I'm very grateful for this fact.) Afterward, we sat talking for a while. The fact that I was supposedly there to write a book emboldened me to ask her a long series of personal questions, and in short time we were having a rather intimate conversation. Autumn was studying to be an eye doctor so that she could do medical missionary work. She told me that she had recently experienced some profound spiritual growth, and she now wanted to dedicate her life to helping other people. I was smitten right away. Most of the girls I met at Oklahoma were extroverted, talkative, and loud, but Autumn seemed one step removed from ordinary life, and she had a certain depth and intensity about her. We sat talking with soft voices and almost never looked away from each other's eyes. For the rest of the week, whenever I would see Autumn, I would walk over and talk to her for a few minutes. On one of these occasions I was a bit drunk—I was at the fraternity house beforehand, my hosts were chugging boxed wine straight from the bag, and I had joined them. On that occasion, I had the courage to ask Autumn if she had a Valentine's date, and she said no. I then asked if she wanted to go on a date with me for Valentine's Day, and she said yes (though she insisted that the date be just for fun).

Shortly after Autumn agreed to go on the date with me, I made an intellectual decision that I was going to try to kiss her on the cheek at the end of the date. By "try" to kiss her on the cheek, I meant that I would try to convince myself to do it. Obviously the physical act of kissing someone on the cheek is easy; it would be the internal, psychological aspect of kissing her that would be a challenge. What was probably going to happen, based on my lifetime history of cowardice, was that I would think about kissing her all night, and then when the precise moment came when I should do it, I would say goodbye with no kiss, walk away in shame, and then quickly add the experience to my list of lifelong regrets.

Our plan was to go out to eat dinner with her friends, then split off for one-on-one time at a place that serves cupcakes and coffee. The friends we ate dinner with were a mixture of guys and girls, and I got the feeling that they were Autumn's friends from church. Before eating in the crowded restaurant, we held hands and prayed together —the first time in my life I had done such a thing in public. When we split up from her friends, Autumn drove us to the cupcake place. I gave her the flowers in the car, which seemed to go over well as part of our just-for-fun Valentine's date. My highest ambition for the night was still only to kiss her on the cheek, but even so, the thought of the kiss was making me incredibly nervous. Once I started to think about the kiss, I could think of nothing else.

I'd always thought that blushing was something that happened momentarily—your cheeks turn red for a couple minutes and then return to normal—but no, once I sat down across from Autumn, my cheeks went red hot and stayed that way for two excruciating hours.

While sitting across from each other, eating cupcakes and drinking coffee, Autumn asked me a sudden question. "Are you a Christian?"

My answer to this question was more complex than a simple yes or no, and yet I wanted to say yes. Autumn was very pretty—she was perhaps the prettiest girl to have ever given me her undivided atten- tion—and I didn't want to disappoint her in any way. I chewed over her question and tried to think of a way that I could answer 'yes' while still telling her the truth. Perhaps I was a cultural Christian, or perhaps I believed in the message of Christianity without believing in the literal truth of the Bible. But I was taking too long to think of an answer, so she asked me a second, more pointed ques- tion, as if to help me out. "Do you accept Jesus Christ as your lord and savior?"

She had me stumped. "I don't really know," I said.

As soon as I said this, I saw the sparkle in her eye fade away. If Autumn had been entertaining the fantasy that she might presently be talking to the boy who would become the future love of her life, I watched that fantasy abruptly die.

And yet I still had ambitions to kiss her on the cheek. On the drive back to campus, I felt the tension in my chest increase in opposite proportion to the time left remaining before our separation. I kept envisioning the worst-case scenario—that I would say goodbye without attempting to kiss her. And based on the way I was feeling, it didn't seem like I was going to have the courage to do it. I played all sorts of mind games with myself to try to build courage. (If I was having a conversation with Autumn during this period of time, I was only using about 5% of my attention to do it.) Eventually I thought of something that worked. I promised myself that if I didn't kiss her on the cheek, I would give each of my three fraternity hosts $20. The thought of losing $60 gave me something concrete to think about and to fear. When Autumn parked the car, I told her I had a good time, then I leaned across the seat and kissed her on the cheek.

I felt far more pride than my small accomplishment deserved. We sat there smiling nervously for a minute or two as we said our goodbyes. This was as far as things were ever going to go between us, but I was extremely glad that it had happened. The date with Autumn filled me with a warm, romantic, innocent feeling that stayed with me through the night and left me feeling optimistic and excited for the future. If my goal had been to do something utterly wholesome to forget about Baylor, I had succeeded.

I was leaving for Auburn that same night. When I grabbed my things from the fraternity house, I was practically boasting to my three hosts about kissing Autumn on the cheek. Instead of thinking I was pathetic for being excited about this, they agreed that it's also hard for them to make moves while sober. This was an odd truth I learned around the country: guys were having lots of casual sex while under the influence of alcohol, but many of them still struggled to kiss a girl if they'd had nothing to drink. I thanked the guys for their hospitality, then said goodbye.

(By the way, this fraternity house was a dreamland for a college guy. A couple nights a week, the fraternity would host a mixer, which just meant that they'd put two big thermoses of alcoholic punch on the second-floor hallway where all their bedrooms were. Girls would show up in small dresses, fill up the hallway, drink the punch, and then wander into the guys' bedrooms where the guys were hanging out. The guys who lived there treated it like it was no big deal; I was incredibly jealous.)

One year later when by chance I was passing through Oklahoma again, I contacted Autumn to see if she wanted to meet up, but she said she was busy. Another year later she was married.

4

AUBURN UNIVERSITY

"Put on something fratty," said Randy. His breath smelled of alcohol and he was in some sort of hurry. "We're going to the bars."

"Is this not fratty?" I asked. I was wearing a red sweater, dark jeans, and loafers.

He eyed my outfit, presumably thinking 'no' but then said, "Ok, that's fine, just wear that."

Randy was meeting me at my car, which I parked somewhere near downtown Auburn so that I could join him at the bars. My drive from Oklahoma to Alabama took 14 hours, and I had only stopped for a couple short naps in the back of my car. But I was there to write about Randy, so I wouldn't be able to sleep just yet. He led the way to the bars, so eager to arrive that his walk was almost a jog.

"Drink specials end in an hour, so we need to get there quick," he said. "You get these huge mixed drinks for $2 until 9pm."

"You've already had a few?" I asked.

"Yeah, I've had a few. I had to leave the bar so I could come find you."

As we walked into the nightlife part of town, Randy pointed out each bar—the freshman bar, the GDI bar, the country dancing bar, and then, finally, his bar, called 17/16 and named after the score of a classic Auburn vs. Alabama football game.

"This is my bar," he said. "Don't say anything weird, ok? Just be cool."

"Yeah, ok, I plan to try," I said.

He realized his rudeness and waved off the thought with his hand. "Yeah yeah yeah yeah, no, you'll be good. You're good."

I hadn't been nervous about meeting Randy's friends until Randy told me not to say anything weird. Now I was nervous. The first impression I made as the strange visitor was extremely important for what kind of week it would be, whether or not I would be invited to things, and whether or not anybody would tell me anything interesting. (I also just wanted to be liked.)

Inside 17/16, Randy and I each ordered three of the big mixed drinks so we could enjoy the cheaper prices before drink specials ended, then we carried them wedged in our hands outside to a table of Randy's fraternity brothers sitting on the patio. On Tuesday nights, Randy and some of his fraternity brothers come to the bar for drink specials before their chapter meeting. They were all wearing white-wash jeans and cowboy boots. There was loud country music playing, and the guys all had their stockpiles of drinks in front of them at the table. I shook hands with each of them briefly, then Randy and I pulled up chairs.

The guys started asking me about my book, and I gave them the usual answers.

"So, do you just watch what goes on, or do you get to party?" someone asked me.

His phrasing was funny—do I 'get' to party?

"I pretty much do whatever Randy does," I told him. By this point in the trip, I had given up my plan to be an objective observer.

"You're gonna try to keep up with me, huh?" Randy said. "You better get drinkin' then." He raised one of his big styrofoam cups in a ritualistic "ready to drink?" gesture. I picked mine up and matched him as he gulped down about half of its contents.

"Good luck writin' about Randy, he's a real shithead," one guy said.

"Oh, get that shit out of here!" Randy snapped back.

"Fuck you, Mississippi bitch!"

"Oh, fuck you, Tennessee!"

The guys started insulting each other, the verbal equivalent of roughhousing. That took the attention off of me, so I sat back and watched as a spectator of their pastime as I tried to finish the three massive mixed drinks. There was a brief conversation about whether the actives were abusing the pledges that semester, but mostly they stuck to insulting each other's home states. It was quickly apparent that my host Randy was the runt of the group—the lovable one who nevertheless gets picked on the most.

A little later, Randy's fraternity brothers left the bar to go to their chapter meeting. Randy was going to skip it that week because I wouldn't be allowed in. After we finished our three drinks, we each ordered two more, then sat side by side on the back patio. For me, this was an incredible amount of alcohol, especially on an empty stomach.

"I am fucked up," Randy said.

"Me too," I said.

"You didn't do too bad back there."

"What do you mean?"

"You weren't weird. I was worried you'd be weird."

"Thanks, I've had a few weeks now to warm up. Also, drink specials help."

"Good, good. Hey, I'm gonna tell you something, ok?"

"Go for it."

He turned to face me and opened his eyes wide with a sudden drunken seriousness. "My goal for the end of this week is for you to be able to say my name and be proud of it."

I matched his seriousness and looked back in his eyes.

"Ok?" he asked.

"Ok," I said.

We left the patio and went back inside the bar. As we entered,

Randy scanned the room as he had many times before. He was looking for a girl, one girl, his girl. And there she was. He turned to me over his shoulder.

"My girl is here," he said. "Keep walking, don't look." Randy sat on a stool at the bar and I joined. "If you nag me, I might go talk to her."

"Your girl?" I asked.

"Don't look," he said again. "She's across from us right now. She's kind of my dream girl."

17/16 had a wraparound bar. The bartenders were in the middle of the bar and the patrons sat around it facing inward. I looked across the bar to a group of girls facing our direction from the opposite side.

"Which one?" I asked.

"She's blonde. It should be obvious."

"In the red dress?"

"Yes. Stop looking."

"Dream Girl, huh?"

"Yeah, I mean, whatever you call it." Randy nodded along to the country music as he pivoted his head toward Dream Girl, trying to appear innocuous, until his eyes reached her. He let them linger for a moment, then turned back to me and said through his teeth, "Goddamn." To Randy, she was ethereal, so beautiful and alluring that she could have only been conceived in his dreams.

"I have a confession," he said. "I've never talked to her."

"What? Go right now."

"No way. I am way too fucked up."

"You don't seem it."

"I am fucking smashed."

"Does Dream Girl know you exist?" I asked.

"She has to," Randy said. "We always make eyes across the bar. We're always here on the same nights. She must know who I am."

"So go talk to her. You told me to nag you."

"Dude, I am so fucked up. You gotta understand."

"You have to at least talk to her before I leave, ok?"

"Fine."

We ordered more drinks. Then as the bar filled up with more people, we lost each other for the rest of the night. Randy's phone died, so I couldn't contact him, and I forgot where I parked my car. I hadn't been to Randy's apartment yet, so I had no idea where to go or what to do. I was also a lot more drunk than it was responsible to be. I did a lot of humiliating things over the next couple of hours, the last of which was lying down to sleep in an alleyway. That lasted until a guy who was taking out the trash told me that I couldn't stay there. Desperate, I started making phone calls and was able to reach an acquaintance from high school who went to Auburn. My call woke her up in the middle of the night. She said I could sleep on her couch, so I took Auburn's student bus there and went to sleep right away. (Thanks again, Erica.)

In the morning I called Randy, and this time he answered.

"I got fucking blitzed last night," Randy said. "Where the hell did you go?"

I told him the whole story.

"Damn," he said, "on your first night in town. We'll see if we can't beat that tonight."

The good thing about being a 20-year-old and embarrassing yourself by drinking too much is that it's usually a badge of honor instead of a source of shame. When Randy picked me up at Erica's apartment, he looked at me with an odd sense of pride. He was proud of me for getting that drunk, and he was proud of himself for facilitating it.

Now we were on the way to Randy's accounting class. When we arrived, we were late and had to walk across the front of the room and interrupt class before sitting down. Randy was wearing sweatpants and flip-flops; I was still wearing the red sweater and loafers from the previous night. The professor smiled, as if to say, "Oh, you boys."

After we took our seats, Randy turned to me and said, "She can't say a damn thing—I just got a 96 on her test."

He turned to his friend on his other side. "Chad. What are you doing for spring break?"

Chad didn't answer and kept listening to the professor.

"Chad! What are you doing for spring break?" Randy repeated.

"Randy," Chad whispered. "Dude, she's teaching. She's literally talking to us right now."

"Oh, right," Randy said. He turned to me, laughed, and shrugged.

———

One of Randy's roommates and fraternity brothers, Nick, had just been released from the hospital. Three days earlier, his esophagus had randomly constricted and blocked his air flow, nearly killing him. Randy and I waited for him to pick us up so we could get margaritas with more of Randy's fraternity brothers before a party.

"Hop in, man!" Nick yelled over the loud rap music.

Randy asked him about his throat. They hadn't seen each other since the incident.

"It was scary, man," said Nick while driving, "but I got some awesome pain killers out of it! I'm supposed to take one but I just took four! Feels crazy, man! And I ripped my bong too before I left!"

Randy grinned back at me from the front seat, knowing I'd be nervous to ride with an intoxicated driver.

"Hey, does this truck have seatbelts?" I yelled over the music.

"Nah, man!" said Nick. "Alabama doesn't have a seatbelt law for the back seat!"

"Interesting!" I said, clutching the door.

We sped through winding roads, bouncing and rattling as the driver's drugs kicked in. He must have been sober enough, though, because we made it to the restaurant without an accident. Inside we joined a long table of Randy's fraternity brothers who were eating chips and drinking margaritas. On the far ends of the table were the pledges—younger guys undergoing the process of initiation into the fraternity. During pledgeship, a pledge must remain sober, aside from when he's being hazed, so that he is always available to drive active members from place to place. These pledges were only there because they had given the actives rides, so now they had to sit on the edges of the table as subordinates until the actives were finished eating.

Throughout the meal, the pledges were timid about dipping their chips into the queso if an active's hand was anywhere near the vicinity of the bowl. It was currently spring semester, which meant that there was a small pledge class—eight guys compared to the usual 40 in the fall. This meant that eight pledges had to do the same workload of pledge rides as 40 pledges. The pledge next to me at the table was jumpy, even around me, monitoring my chip-dipping to make sure he didn't encroach on my territory by trying to dip his chip at the same time—and all this because I had arrived with an active member.

Randy, who was 20 years old, had lost his fake ID a few weeks earlier on a trip to Atlanta. During margaritas, Randy convinced a pledge to let him borrow his fake ID until he could get a new one. The pledge was upset, because that meant he couldn't go to the bars himself, but he had no choice.

After margaritas, a pledge dropped us off at a fraternity brother's apartment to keep drinking. At the apartment we drank whiskey and became fairly drunk. Our plan was to go to a house party hosted by the freshmen in Randy's fraternity, then go to the bars. As we drank the whiskey, I noticed that there was a huge shift in Randy's behavior when he started to drink, more of a shift than normal people. During the day when he was sober, he was kind of lethargic—he'd wear sweatpants, have messy hair, and would keep a bit of an unamused air about him. Then when he started to drink, he'd get a twinkle in his eye, a spark of vitality and optimism. I don't think it was just the alcohol though, but also what the alcohol symbolized, which was that nighttime was beginning.

Nighttime was the best part of Randy's day, perhaps the only good part. He worked 25 hours a week stocking vegetables at a grocery store and did all of his studying alone in his bedroom. A lot of his peers studied in groups at the library and made their studying into a social activity, but Randy always studied alone. His typical day began with a commute to a few accounting classes, followed by five or six hours at the grocery store, then followed by a few hours studying from an accounting textbook in his room. At that point it was either time to get ready for bed or to start drinking. If it was an off night, which meant that his friends weren't doing anything, he'd spend the evening alone or with his roommates in his usual lethargic state. But if it was an on night, he would have dreamt about it all day—during class, work, and while he studied—and then when nighttime finally came, he'd give it his full dedication.

"I hope these fuckers have something fun," said Randy. "I'm about to get blitzed." On the way out the door of the apartment, he took two cold beers and shoved one into the front of each cowboy boot, then he took a third beer and put it in his pants pocket.

We took off to the party, about eight of us down the sidewalk. Randy's pace was quick, like when I first met him. The pledge who sat next to me earlier was still with us. He spoke to me when we were separate from the group.

"I know it's hard and it's gonna get harder, but I'm not gonna drop," he said about pledgeship.

"Why do you want to join?" I asked.

"I don't really know."

"I'm not from here, so I don't know what the point is of joining," I said, acting dumb. "What's the appeal of a fraternity?"

"I don't know. I don't really get it either."

We could hear music from the party before we reached the apartment. Before going inside, Randy and his friends went to the side yard and pissed shoulder-to-shoulder into some bushes. Only the pledge and I didn't join in. (For some reason, guys from the same fraternity often ritualistically piss in front of each other; I don't know why, but I have a few guesses.) I followed Randy inside the apartment. The walls were covered in Christmas lights, which illuminated many dozens of students packed into the apartment and spilling outside into a courtyard area. Randy's group agreed that it looked like the freshmen had thrown an impressively good party. We passed by a keg and a few big thermoses of punch, but we didn't need new drinks yet. As I scanned the faces of the students, I began to understand at least one reason why that pledge didn't want to drop out: among the faces in the crowd were a large number of good-looking girls smiling at us as we walked by. At a bar you're always arriving as another anonymous face, and you have to charm a girl from scratch if you want her to be interested in you. Here it felt different, almost like the girls were already halfway charmed.

(For the record, I have a plain face and a large, curved nose; for a girl to be attracted to me, I really have to earn it—perhaps with a rare burst of charisma or a well-timed display of talent. But here, since the girls mistook me for a member of Randy's fraternity, it was as if I had already earned it. Girls would make eye contact with me then give a warm, inviting smile. Such smiles were foreign to me, and I didn't know what to do about them.)

I followed Randy to the courtyard behind the house and then up a ladder leaning onto the rooftop. There were some students on the roof already, but Randy and I sat alone. We had arrived too mellow for the party, according to Randy, so he wanted to drink more to catch up. We lay back on the roof with our heads to the sky, drinking without conversation. From below us, the party noises blurred and wrapped us with the sensation of being in the center of everything. We were in the right place and could finally relax. After a few more beers, Randy pushed his hair to the side and wiped the beer suds off his lips.

"Something about the rooftop, man," he sighed. "It's gonna be one of those nights."

I agreed with Randy, thinking that by "one of those nights," Randy was referring to the peaceful, relaxed, contented feeling that we were experiencing on the rooftop. But no, Randy had something entirely different in mind.

I had no reason to expect what Randy did next. When we climbed down from the rooftop, he headed inside to the big thermos of punch and told me he needed help because he planned to chug the rest of it. I agreed. We unscrewed the top and lifted the thermos up to his head. He put his mouth on the rim then started to tilt back the jug. As Randy began to chug, shouts of "CHUG!" and "OH, SHIT!" could be heard throughout the room, and this encouragement led Randy to tilt faster and faster. The punch began spilling down his neck and onto his shirt, and as the jug got more vertical, more students turned to watch, so as the noise crescendoed, Randy lifted the jug up and away from his mouth so that the last remaining contents poured down all over him, soaking his hair, face, and shirt just as the cheering reached max volume. Across the room, girls' eyes were beaming—if not with romantic interest, then with sheer amusement—although Randy acted nonchalant afterward by never acknowledging the crowd, instead turning his back to them to deny that his act was in any way a performance. It had been a huge success.

"I am fucked up," Randy told me with another intense stare. When Randy told you that he was drunk, it was always with life-or-death intensity.

"I am fucked up too," I said, trying to mirror him.

"I didn't think you'd be such a shithead."

"I knew you'd be a shithead."

Randy smiled and said, "Fuck you." I took this as a sign of affection.

Then Randy disappeared into the crowd, leaving me alone. I didn't really know what to do now that I was by myself. I wasn't emotionally mature enough to just stand alone for a minute, to maybe make eye contact with a guy or girl, give a friendly smile, make a small comment about something trivial, then perhaps get into a longer conversation or perhaps not. Instead I'd start to feel anxious about the fact that I was doing nothing, and I'd rush to get involved in something new. Parties were hard work.

One of my go-to maneuvers during these situations was to play wingman. Playing wingman is a great way to stay busy at a party, to do something useful that your friends will appreciate you for, and to talk to girls without having your own ego at risk.

I went to some cute girls and yelled, "Holy shit! Did you see the guy who chugged that punch? Who was that?"

The girls glanced at each other and shrugged.

I continued, "Oh my God! That's the coolest guy I've ever met! What the fuck!"

(This sounds extremely obnoxious, I agree, but I was just matching the energy level that already existed in the room.)

And it was working. The girls were getting more interested. One of them smiled and asked, "Really? Who is he?"

"I think his name is Randy," I said. "Do you want me to introduce you?"

The girls glanced at each other again. One of them nervously said, "Yeah, ok," with a smile.

"Hold there," I told the girls. "I'll go get him." I pushed through the room and went out onto the patio to find Randy. "Randy! C'mere! These girls want to meet you!"

He had a new beer already. "Ah, what the fuck! Alright! I am fucked up!"

I pulled him back through the room to the girls and introduced him with my arms like a magician introducing a sidekick—"This is Randy."

The punch that Randy chugged must have taken him across a new threshold of drunkenness. The twinkly-eyed, charismatic Randy from the start of the night had shifted into something new. He stood there peering under heavy eyelids as he looked at each girl. He took a sip of his beer and then muttered, "Man, I am fucking hammered." Then he walked away.

The girls hadn't said anything to Randy, and Randy hadn't said anything to the girls. With Randy now gone, they looked to me for an explanation.

"I'm really sorry," I said, shrugging. "I guess he's not interested. You can't force these things."

Randy's group of guy friends was rounding up by the door to head to 17/16. Randy and I took more beers in our pockets before we left. On our five-minute walk, Randy tried to keep alive whatever recklessness he had displayed when he chugged the punch. First, he punched a pedestrian crossing sign, and then a telephone box—the latter so hard that another guy said, "that's a broken hand for sure," to which Randy replied, "You wanna see a broken hand? I'll show you this broken hand flipping you off all night!" as he flicked him off.

Next, Randy chugged a warm beer that was sitting on the sidewalk and threw the empty can at a different group of students in front of us, then ran ahead to kick the can but missed it completely and fell back onto his ass. Once on his feet again, he stood defiantly on the edge of the road with both middle fingers in the air and yelled, "Suck my fucking dick!" to the next two passing cars. Calming down from this act, he noticed his knuckles were bleeding from having punched the telephone box. He tasted the blood, then asked me to taste it too. I declined. For the rest of the walk, he hobbled along, muttering and yelling to no one in particular, flipping people off, and kicking or punching whatever objects we happened across. Oddly enough, despite all of this, Randy's friends still weren't paying any attention to him.

17/16 was a lot more crowded this time, and I lost Randy in the crowd for much of the night. He had a habit of making laps around the bar, though, so every now and then we'd bump into each other while he was going for a lap. (He actually called it a lap. When he was done talking to you, he'd say he was going to make a lap and he'd see you later.) Each time he came around on a lap, he'd tell me with his intense stare just how drunk he was, each time with a new word: hammered, smashed, stupid-drunk, obliterated. On one lap, he told me that he just ripped a $20 bill in half, on another he told me that he punched a hole in the wall and re-bloodied his knuckles, and on another he told me that he just helped his friend get into the bar by handing him a fake ID from the patio and then retrieving it once his friend was let inside. He described this last move as "some Martin Scorsese shit."

I spent most of these nights at the bars standing by myself but trying to look like I wasn't. I was there to write about Randy, but I had to keep a balance between following him around and not annoying him. At one point, I saw another guy standing alone who looked a little uptight because his shirt was buttoned too high.

I said to him, "Freshman?"

He said, "How'd you know?"

I pointed to his shirt collar and said, "One button too many."

He smiled, unbuttoned the extra button, and said, "Thanks."

He probably thought I was some sort of badass, when in reality my brief interaction with him was one of the coolest things I did all year.

I also tried my hand at hitting on women at the bar, but I was getting nowhere. Auburn girls were particularly harsh about the fact that I didn't go to college. I tried to make my book sound as cool as possible, but nothing seemed to make up for the fact that I had no higher education.

Eventually Randy found me on another lap and said, "Let's go." I didn't know how much more he'd had to drink, but he was nearly unresponsive at that point.

We went to get pizza from a place across the street. Randy cut the line of customers and went straight to the large man who was handing out boxes of pizza to those who had already ordered and paid. Randy walked up to him and said, "I'm just tryin' to get some fuckin' pepperoni."

The large man serving the pizza said, "I swear, if you keep running your mouth, you're not gonna get a fucking thing," so Randy backed away and sat down while I waited in line.

As soon as I ordered pizza for myself, Randy walked up to me suspiciously and admitted that he just tried to steal pizza, but they caught him in the act. "Let's get out of here," he said, "I'm fucking belligerent."

"Nah, man, I just ordered," I said. "Wait until I get my food, I already paid."

"'Nah?'" Randy said. He clenched his fists and stepped aggressively toward me. "You tell me 'nah'?"

This pizza shop was tiny. I looked around and realized we were standing up in the dead center of the place, and everybody was silently watching us. The whole restaurant had seen Randy try to steal the pizza, so everyone was still observing him as the scene developed. Randy continued toward me with his fists ready.

When he got too close, I pushed him in the chest, but not very hard. I didn't think we would actually fight—neither of us were the type. Randy bit his lip and came toward me again. Again I pushed him back. This time two grown men, roughly 45 years old, stood up from their booths next to us, ready to intervene and break up a fight.

Randy looked at me and said, "Fuck you."

"Back up," I said.

"Fuck you!"

"Randy, back the fuck up!"

The two men stepped closer to us, keeping the peace by threatening violence. Randy looked at them, realized he stood no chance, then put his hands up in submission and stepped back.

Now my pizza was ready. I had ordered two slices, so I offered one of the slices to Randy as a truce. As soon as he took the slice from off my paper plate, he dropped it onto the muddy tile floor below us, cheese-side-down. Randy bent down to pick up the slice. Everybody was still watching us. "Oh my God," a woman gasped, "he's gonna eat it."

Randy did. He shoved the pizza into his mouth without thought and chewed it like a zombie eating brains. The woman groaned. The two men who had prevented our fight shook their heads in disgust and sat back down. Randy wasn't a violent threat anymore, just a drunk moron.

"Let's go," said Randy.

We left out the back door into an alleyway. Randy leaned his hands against the brick wall, took a deep breath, then forced out a belly full of vomit that splashed across the concrete. "Fuck," he said. He leaned his back on the wall and let his head hang limp. His blonde hair glowed orange in the street light while his puke glistened between his cowboy boots. He spit onto the puddle of vomit and wiped his mouth. He was calm for a second, as if maybe he had vomited away his troubles. Without lifting his head to look at me, he said, "Dream Girl was there tonight."

"Did anything happen?" I asked.

"Nothing at all," he said, defeated. "Nothing at all." He lifted himself off the wall. "C'mon, we gotta walk back."

I thought he had calmed down, but on the street Randy's aggression returned. When another guy would pass us, Randy would raise his arms and say, "What? What?" and when a girl would pass, Randy would say in falsetto, "Sup, girl? Sup?" He was on auto-pilot, and nobody indulged him. It was around 3am now, and the people out on the streets were all headed home like us.

Randy's recklessness was coming back in full force. When we passed by a clothing store with nobody around, Randy walked up to the big display windows, faced away from them, leaned forward, then donkey-kicked the glass with the bottom of his boot. The glass flexed and rattled but didn't shatter. It could have been a serious crime for vandalism if he'd kicked just a bit harder.

"Oh, shit!" Randy yelled as if it had been somebody other than himself who had just kicked the glass. "We need to get the fuck outta here!"

I sprinted behind Randy. We took a left, right, then left until we were suddenly wedged between two apartment buildings, stuck in dense shrubs. Randy led the way, pushing, tripping, and getting tangled up in the sticks.

"Ah, fuck these branches!" he yelled. "Fuck this! Goddamnit!" Randy's shirt sleeve was caught up in a small limb, and he tried to flail his arms while tackling the bush, but this only made him lose his footing and fall over with his arm still stuck in the bush.

I couldn't help but laugh.

He heard me laugh and said, "You think I'm a pussy?"

"Yeah, I do," I said.

"Oh, you wanna see pussy?" Randy said. "I'll show you pussy."

Randy stood up and went next to the window of one of the apartment rooms that faced into the alleyway.

"I'm gonna punch this fucking window out."

"No you're not."

"Wanna see?"

"You won't."

He did. He clenched his fist, wound it around his body, then in one quick motion, unwound, letting the side of his hand fly into the glass, which, this time, did shatter. Glass poured into the dark room next to us. It was almost certainly somebody's bedroom, and since it was around 3am, they were almost certainly asleep before the crash.

Randy yelled, "RUN!"

We took off again through the alleyway, this time unfazed by the shrubs, then down a small street, through a wooded area, across a parking lot, down another alleyway, and across another street. At one point we could hear sirens, but we weren't sure if they were for us.

Our stupid escape ended when the road opened into a sweeping panoramic view of Auburn campus. We stopped running and caught our breaths, figuring we were safe for now.

"Holy fuck," Randy said as he gasped for air.

"I know," I said.

"I just smashed a fucking window."

"Yes, Randy. Take it easy. Jesus."

He looked out across campus and raised his chin a little.

"You see that?" he asked. He pointed to a big bronze statue, far away in the middle of campus. "Someday there'll be a statue of me. None of these fuckers know it, but someday there'll be a statue of me."

We continued on. Randy tried to jump a fence at one point but only managed to sit on top of it until it was too wobbly for him to hold himself up. He looked at me for sympathy, but I gave him none. The only way for him to get back down was to fall off the fence onto his ass. When he stood back up, he kicked the fence and said, "Fuck this fence." But that fence must have humbled Randy, because finally his aggression was subsiding. He walked ahead of me with his head hung low. He started to unbutton his shirt. A half mile later he muttered some words to himself: "I can do all that, but I can't even talk to her. I waited for her all night, but I can't even talk to her."

(This line sounds like something I made up, because it seems too good to be true, but Randy really said it.)

I asked, "Dream Girl?" but he didn't reply.

His shirt, now fully unbuttoned, clung with sweat to his shoulders. His hair had lost its swoop and instead fell across his forehead without design. His head, shoulders, and feet were heavy—the physical body he occupied was now a burden for him to transport. Ahead of me, he slowed to a stop. I stopped too, leaving him some room.

He tilted his head back, took in a deep breath, then screamed, "I'M THE BIGGEST PUSSY IN THIS TOWN!"

His body drooped, and he took off his shirt. He turned back to me and gave me the saddest look I'd ever seen. It was a plea for my sympathy and for my silence. I nodded. He tossed his shirt over his naked shoulder and carried on toward home. And with that, the night was finished.

―――――

Randy stood above me as I lay in my sleeping bag. He was showered, dressed, and had already gone to two classes that morning without me. Now it was 2pm and I was just waking up with a terrible headache.

"I made a lot of mistakes last night," Randy said. "I'm not proud."

Randy had a 3.83 GPA, among the highest in Auburn's accounting program. A scholarship paid for 75% of his tuition, and he was on track to graduate with honors, leaving him likely to receive scholarships that fully pay for his tuition in grad school.

"I can't believe I did that," he said. "That's just straight vandalism. That's not even ok. I punched someone's window out. They're going to have to get that fixed. I would be livid. That's just unacceptable."

"Yeah, man, that was pretty violent behavior."

He smirked. "Still, that was one hell of a night." Randy checked his bank account from his phone to see how much money he spent. "Fuck. Holy shit I spent $67 last night. How the fuck did I do that? We are not going out tonight." He smirked again. "Well, maybe."

Randy stepped into the next room to call a friend who went to another university to tell him last night's story. His retelling had more a mood of fascination than of regret.

"...then I just hammer-fisted the fuck out of the window..."

"...just sprinted off..."

"...I have no idea..."

"...yeah, I think there were sirens..."

"...now my hand's all scabbed..."

It was as if he had been a witness to his own actions and not the perpetrator. The conversation included no mention of Dream Girl, or any discussion of his possible motivation.

(Randy thought the person who lived in the apartment would be "livid," but I don't think that's necessarily true. The older I get, the more I realize that the person might be less angry and more terrified. If someone smashes your window in the middle of the night, you don't know who did it or why. You don't know if they're going to come back. It would be reasonable to assume that the act was committed by a force aimed directly at you, and you wouldn't know how ominous of a force it was. You might become unable to fall asleep in your own apartment. You might go out and buy a gun. You might be traumatized for months or years. That's the worst-case scenario. The best-case scenario is that the person sleeping in their apartment heard Randy yell, "RUN!" like a dumbass and realized it was a drunk college kid committing a random act of vandalism. But we'll never find out.)

Later, Randy and his fraternity brothers reconvened at Cracker Barrel for lunch and to discuss the previous night. Randy told them all the story as if it had been a war story that he survived. ("The window goes BAM! and glass shatters everywhere.") The other guys told stories too—the worse the outcome, the better—"Dude, the chick I was with had to get her stomach pumped." ... "Did you see Big Johnny smash Tony's head on the bar? Tony's in jail now, public intox, while he was just passed out on the road." Even I told a story, a dramatic reenactment of the standoff between Randy and me at the pizza shop. Somehow during lunch with these guys, I actually started to wish that I was the one who smashed the window. I was actually jealous that it was Randy and not me. After all the stories had been told, when we'd pieced together our collective narrative, we all sighed, and then one guy summed it up by saying, "I hope tonight is as fun as last night."

"Let's get fucked up tonight," said Randy.

We had planned not to drink at all after the chaos and financial expense of the previous night, but Randy's tedious day of stocking fruits and vegetables led him to a change of heart. When the sun dipped below the horizon, we bought a 12-pack and headed over to the fraternity house.

"Sometimes after two beers, I'm like, 'Whoa, head rush,'" he said on our walk. "Then at six, I'm like, 'Ok we're in business,' then at 12, I'm like, 'Oh shit,' then around 15+ is when I turn into what I was last night."

"What is your typical pregame count?" I asked.

"I usually drink eight or so before the bars."

"Eight drinks before you leave for the bars. So you still feel pretty normal at that point?"

"Pretty much."

"And then at the bar you lose count of your drinks?"

"Correct."

The entryway to the fraternity house was a small room with polished wooden furniture and composite photos of each class of fraternity brothers dating back many decades. It exuded refinement and legacy, some sense of belonging to history. Through a set of doors we entered the main downstairs area, which was fluorescent-lit and had tile floors, some couches around a big television, a pool table, and a large empty space where the guys who live there typically eat, but instead of the usual dining tables there were just a couple long beer pong tables. There were a few dozen guys standing around, many of them with a personal 6- or 12-pack by their side, as they waited to leave for the bars. Randy joined in a game of beer pong and got talking to an older fraternity brother about what he missed at the last chapter meeting. The fraternity members, together with the alumni, were working out plans for six-figure renovations on the house. The house was starting to look worse and needed some updating to keep it looking nice, they thought.

The guys who were headed to the bars called cabs or pledges and left to continue their nights. Randy and I had not consumed our required eight beers yet, so it was too soon for us to leave. We stayed behind, the only two guys in that part of the house, and played a game of pool.

"I need to get my life back in order," Randy said.

As Randy lined up a shot, he lost focus from the cue ball to something over my shoulder. His arm fired reflexively and took a lousy shot. When I turned to see what had caught his attention, I had the same stunned reaction. Walking in was one of Randy's fraternity brothers—a guy who went by his last name, Powell—and he was choking back a big grin because of who was accompanying him. Next to him was a girl who in another context could have been pretty or beautiful, but who right now seemed to be just purely hot without any of the softer qualities. She wore heels that clicked on the tiles as she walked confidently toward us, a thin sweater that draped over her breasts and then cut off to reveal all of her stomach, and jeans that were sitting so low on her waist that we could almost see the exposed curve of her pelvic bone. In her hand was a case of the infamous drink that had to be banned because of its deadly mix of caffeine and alcohol. Randy and I were standing there, frozen, as she walked in a straight line toward us.

"Hi, I'm Christina," she said to Randy.

"Hey, I'm Randy. What house are you in?" I was impressed that Randy could even speak.

"I'm not in a sorority, so I don't have any rules," she said, smiling seductively. "My two girlfriends are coming. You guys might like them. One of them is a petite whore. She's a spinner."

I was shocked that she said that. She seemed to take pleasure in how intimidatingly hot she was. She was already way out of our leagues, but instead of trying to tone down the sexiness to be less intimidating, she was ramping it up. Christina was playing the role of the femme fatale, and she was doing an extraordinarily good job. I was powerless before her, just a stupid mess of fear and awe.

"Cool," said Randy.

"Yeah, cool," I said.

She walked away to make a phone call, and the three of us guys stood watching her until she was out of earshot.

Randy tugged on his collar and whispered, "Holy fuck."

"I know," said Powell.

Randy gave him a high five. "How'd you make that happen?"

"I don't know, I met her at work."

"Dear Lord. Don't mess that up."

"What's a spinner?" I asked in a whisper.

Randy and Powell didn't know either, so I looked it up on Urban Dictionary and read the definition out loud: "A woman so thin she is able to be mounted and spun in a circle on an erect penis."

"Fair enough," said Randy. He slurped his beer.

(This "spinner" thing, to me, was more frightening than enticing. For some reason, I was imagining extremely fast spinning. The act, I thought, might cause what as children we used to inappropriately call an "Indian sunburn," which involved someone grabbing your arm with both hands and twisting the skin in opposite directions.)

Christina's friends arrived soon, bringing with them another case of beer to share. Her friends weren't anything like Christina, either looks-wise or behavior, and the one who had been described as a "petite whore" probably would have been mortified if she had heard that Christina told us that. Shortly after they arrived, loud music came on through the house speakers, and the girls removed their heels to climb onto the pool table. Us guys grabbed new beers then took seats on the couch as the girls began dancing. We sat together in a kind of trance, watching Christina's body as we rapidly consumed alcohol. Randy and I had completely forgotten about our plan to leave for the bars. This part of the night lasted long enough for us to become very drunk.

An empty bottle hit the floor, broke, and sprinkled shards of glass across the tiles. Christina had chugged a drink and thrown the empty bottle across the room. This seemed to give her great pleasure, so Randy hopped up, chugged another drink in front of Christina, then handed her the bottle to throw again. She tossed it, but this time it didn't break, so I ran to retrieve it, brought it behind my head in a baseball windup, then threw a fastball into the same open tile area, where it smashed and broke into clear sandy glass across the ground. We all died of laughter, and the collective enthusiasm quickly led to a big ritual of chaos. Randy chugged another drink to throw himself. Smash! Christina's friend threw one. Smash! Now Powell. Smash! Everyone was laughing uncontrollably. It was clear now that we were going to shatter every glass bottle we had. Smash! Smash! We needed more bottles, and I found a big glass liquor bottle, which I side-armed across the room. Smash! We were destroying this fraternity house. At this point, anything was fair game to throw. People were yelling, "Throw it! Do it! Go! Do another!" We started taking pool balls and throwing them as hard as we could at the walls, which would leave big craters behind. The floor was completely covered in glass. Randy started running around yelling, "FUCK THIS SHIT!" He jumped up and punched an 'exit' sign, which fell to the ground. He kept running around yelling the same thing, "FUCK THIS SHIT! I SAID, 'FUCK THIS SHIT!'" We were all laughing so hard that our cheeks were sore. It was around that time that Randy and I both blacked out.

Randy was usually able to wake up for class despite any severity of hangover, but the next morning was too much for him. He skipped his classes, and we both slept in until mid-afternoon. After that we moved out into the common area of their apartment, each lay on a couch, and kept napping. We hadn't said a word about the previous night. In the evening, one of Randy's roommates, Jim, came home and was cooking himself dinner. He was tall, well-mannered, and was also one of Randy's fraternity brothers.

"Hey, did you break the coffee table at the house?" Jim asked Randy.

"No," Randy said.

"I'm pretty sure you did."

"I'm pretty sure I didn't. I don't remember it."

"Apparently Bill came back from the bars, and you like, grabbed his hat, jumped on the couch for some reason, punched the composite a few times, then just jumped onto the coffee table and shattered it."

"What the fuck? I wasn't even that drunk."

"Well, that's what happened."

It was silent for a moment.

"Wait," Randy said. "I remember breaking it."

"It's all coming back," said Jim.

"It's vague, but I think I remember."

"You're a moron."

"It's collateral damage. It's a fucking fraternity house. I'm not proud."

"You're fucked. Just pay for it and you'll be fine."

"I'm not fucked, and I'm not paying for it."

"You just gotta own up, and quit being a five-year-old when you're drunk."

Jim decided to make a trip to the fraternity house to do some "recon" for Randy. He would assess the damage and then inform Randy of what he should do. After Jim left, Randy turned to me.

"Gonna be honest," he said. "I do have a memory, though it's very, very hazy, of me smashing the table. I didn't do it on purpose, but I do remember jumping on it."

"I don't remember that at all," I said. "How much did we drink?"

"It was fucking Powell's girl. She just kept dropping drinks in my hand. I probably had 15 drinks in not much time."

"It's hard to say no to a girl like her," I said.

"Exactly. This is all Powell's fault. Dude, that's gonna be fucked up —the pledges are going to have to clean up all that glass. And probably do pushups on it too."

Jim called Randy from the fraternity house. His report was that the front table was upside down and one of its wooden legs had snapped off. But the composite photo, which was harder to replace, was ok. Jim recommended that Randy lie low for a few days and offer to pay for the table. He added, "We've kind of been trying to change the way the house is treated."

Randy and I took an "off night" that night, which meant that we stayed at the apartment and shared only a six-pack of beer. At one point, Randy called me over to his laptop.

"C'mere," he said.

"What?"

"C'mere." On his laptop was a photo of a girl wearing a bikini. "Pretty good, huh?"

"Who is this?" I asked.

"Dream Girl."

"Oh yeah. Pretty good."

"I'm not her friend, but these photos are public."

Before sleeping, I lay in my sleeping bag next to Randy's bed. The room was dark and we were each on our backs staring toward the ceiling like at a 3rd grade sleepover.

"I gotta think more about my drunk behavior," said Randy. "I've been doing some damage."

"I wonder who lives in the apartment whose window you smashed," I said.

"I don't even care about that as much as the table. I guess because I actually have consequences with the table. Is that fucked up?"

"It's a little fucked up, yeah."

"Maybe it'll take some bigger consequences before I change my ways."

"You're just waiting for some extreme consequence to force you to change."

"No, not exactly. I just mean, that might be the only way."

"Do you ever get that feeling when you're incredibly drunk and happy," I said, "but deep down, you feel an overwhelming sadness?"

"I don't think so."

"It's like, you're screaming with your fist in the air, but in your head you're going, 'What the hell am I doing? Am I just pretending? I could stop in an instant. Does everyone feel this way?'"

"Yeah, I guess I've felt that. It's like you don't even know who you are. That must be what it's like all the time if you're an alcoholic. I just need to stop getting so belligerent."

"And if you stop getting so drunk, maybe you'll talk to Dream Girl."

"We gotta stop calling her Dream Girl. It makes the whole thing harder."

"You're the one making it a big deal. Look, next time you're at the bar, limit your drinks. What's the fewest number of drinks you need to feel comfortable?"

"Maybe eight or so."

"Jesus. Eight? Well, ok. Pregame with four and then drink four more at the bar."

"I'd be so sober."

"You'd be able to form sentences. That's more important."

"Good point. Ok, I will try. Dream Girl will be at the bar on Friday. I will try to pace myself."

"Good. This will be good for you."

"There's something wrong about this though. I was always the guy in high school who drank too much, and now in college I've become more of that guy. I honestly don't know if I can stop. But it's normal to drink this much right now. Or, well is it? Because I mean, everybody has their nights, but do all my friends get blackout like I do? I don't know. Maybe I'm just blind to it all. What I need to realize is that somebody actually has to wake up to what I do. When somebody spills a drink at work and I have to clean it up, I'm legitimately pissed. And there are tons of people who have had to wake up to what I do when I'm belligerent. Friday will be interesting—if I can talk to Dream Girl and not get belligerent as fuck, that'd be a hell of a night."

Randy saw me writing notes.

"Oh, fuck you!" he said. "You just want to see me change for your goddamn book."

"Yeah, it's going to be great," I said. "This is mutualism at its best."

"Son of a bitch. Well, maybe this is why I wanted you here in the first place. But I'm still pissed. Put that on the record: I'm still pissed, and you're an asshole."

We still had one night before Randy expected to see Dream Girl.

Randy was going to "lie low" and avoid his fraternity until he figured out what to do about the broken table, so we went to 17/16 on the night that was unofficially the night when only graduate students went there. Our plan was only to have a few drinks, but we ended up sitting at the bar in a melancholy sort of way, having one drink after another, until the lights came on at 2am. When we stood from our barstools, we were both hammered again, and Randy wanted to get some cigarettes for the walk back. After he'd smoked one, he started to feel sick to his stomach, so we looked for a place to sit. Since we didn't want the police to see us, we took our seats behind a dumpster.

"I feel like ass," Randy said. He leaned over and vomited. "Uggggh."

"Get it all out. You're good," I said.

He sat up and leaned back against the dumpster, wiping his face off with his shirt sleeve. "Goddamnit, dude. What am I doing? I didn't even want to drink tonight."

"That seems to be our pattern," I said.

"No, I'm serious now. What the fuck is this?"

"You're just hammered."

"No, I don't know if that's it."

"What is it?"

Randy told me a story about his friend from high school who was in a drinking-and-driving accident. One passenger in the car died, and Randy's friend suffered serious brain injuries.

"I was here in Auburn, and he was back home," Randy said. "I was in my room studying and my mom called me. There was nothing I could do. I bawled my eyes out when I heard. I just bawled my eyes out. My mom had never heard me like that. I just bawled my eyes out and didn't know what to do. I was actually gonna go to the bar that night but I stayed home."

We were shoulder to shoulder, each leaned against the cold dumpster. It smelled like garbage and vomit and cigarettes. Randy's voice shook a little as he spoke.

"I just don't know when this is all going to stop," Randy continued. "I don't know why I do this, get so fucked up all the time. I didn't even want to drink tonight, and I just vommed behind a dumpster."

"You're talking like drinking is something that happens to you. You can stop or drink less if you choose."

"But it's like I can't. Drinking is what everyone knows me for. It's just who I am now." Randy leaned over again to vomit but nothing came out. "Fuck, we need to go."

That night our walk back was somber and professional. No smashing, kicking, or fighting. I didn't know what Randy was thinking about. On a walk home like that he could have been thinking about anything, but I imagined that he was working to straighten things out, to give himself some kind of direction, and hoping that somehow because of it all he would wake up a new man.

The next day began in high spirits. The first thing Randy wanted to do was to email his fraternity president about the broken table. Randy read his email aloud to Nick and me for feedback.

"People in my pledge class have been talking today about my actions at the house on Saturday. I woke up Sunday with no recollection of breaking the coffee table in the foyer, but I guess word got around that I broke it, and people finally started talking to me about it. I have no idea what I was thinking, and I know this comes at a bad time when we are really trying to turn things around with the house. I just wanted to apologize to you directly, because I know you have to figuratively deal with a lot of people's messes all the time. I would be more than happy to clean it up if it is still broken up there. Also, if necessary, I can definitely replace the table or figure something out. I hope this isn't too big of a problem, and I will definitely make sure to be more respectful of the property next time I'm up there."

"Yeah, that's literally perfect," said Nick. "You can't do anything more than send him an email like that, and now he knows that you actually give a fuck. It's not even a big deal."

"Fuck it. Collateral damage, dude," said Randy. "What if that table's like a grand or something?"

"Dude, it's gonna be a couple hundred dollars, easily."

"What did it even look like?"

"You don't remember? It was pretty fucking big."

"And I just stepped up on it?"

"Yeah, you like hopped up on it, hopped from the couch. I don't know why the fuck you were punching the composite, trying to break it."

"I'm glad that shit didn't break."

"And then you hopped onto the coffee table and it shattered."

"That's literally just the dumbest shit. Completely no reason to do that, whatsoever. I just like seeing things break I guess. I actually need to learn how to control myself. That's real fucked up. I didn't used to be destructive like this, I really didn't. That's fucked up dude, I'm kinda pissed. Fuck Powell, dude. This all comes back to Powell."

"How does this come back to Powell?"

"Because if he hadn't shown up, we would have had six beers and gone to the bars. Instead, we had 15 drinks. I had had seven beers. We were about to leave. Powell shows up, starts dropping drinks into my hand. I had three or four, maybe more. Then a girl shows up with a case of beer, hands me like five more. I'm at like 15 drinks, and this is when I start doing this. This is so fucked up. I swear, if I have to pay…"

"Just get ready because you're going to have to."

"I don't think so. If we're about to drop $90,000 on renovations."

"Dude, they just dropped like $100,000 on that one room," said Nick.

"What room?"

"The fucking foyer. That's why they had the nice ass shit in there right now!"

"Like what?"

"The new couches and the new coffee tables and shit!"

"In the foyer there?"

"Yes! You can fuck shit up anywhere but the foyer, and that's the room that you ruined. The foyer is like the centerpiece of our fucking house right now, and that coffee table made it look nice."

"I might not show up for a while at the house."

.   .   .

It was my last day at Auburn, Friday, the day Randy was going to talk to Dream Girl. I even said this to him—"today's the day." But when Randy returned from work that night, he was drooped over and depressed. There had been an incident at the grocery store, and it didn't seem like he wanted to go out drinking anymore. I would have to convince him.

"Just don't provoke me tonight, ok?" Randy said. "It's not good to drink when you're pissed off."

"So, you still want to go out? You gotta talk to Dream Girl."

While Randy thought, I went to the fridge and took out two beers.

"I guess we're going to," he said, accepting one.

Randy went through the motions of cracking his beer open, but his heart wasn't in it as usual. He sipped it hesitantly, without trust. But a few sips later, a little smirk came to his face.

"Attaboy," I said, smiling back. As long as I drank no more than Randy, I was not the one with the drinking problem.

I opened my beer and took a big swig. I tilted back the can and eyed Randy out the side. He did the same. Somehow this eye contact initiated a chugging race. We each slurped our icy beers as suds spilled down our chins and necks. Randy beat me and crushed the empty metal can in his hand.

"Ah," he exhaled. "You're one hell of a shithead."

"You too," I said when I was done.

Hope was back in Randy's face. Randy was the kind of guy who you always wanted to cheer up if he was looking melancholy.

"Two more?" he asked.

"Of course."

"I figure this period is the most drinking I'll ever do in my life. I cannot possibly sustain this. I am at the peak of my drinking life. I literally treat every weekend like it's my 21st birthday. What am I even going to do on my 21st birthday?"

"I don't wanna be around."

"But I think you're supposed to be a shithead in college. I bet my dad was, even though he says he wasn't. But I think being a shithead is a good thing. I hope my son is a shithead too."

The end of this chapter is a huge disappointment. It was Friday night, my last night in Auburn, the night that Randy was supposed to talk to Dream Girl. We went to 17/16 again, expecting to see Dream Girl, but she never showed up. Somehow the idea that Dream Girl would be at the bar on Friday felt like a complete certainty. But she never came, so Randy never talked to her.

There is good news, however. I don't want to give anything away, but I'll tell you now that the story between Randy and Dream Girl doesn't end here.

Since Dream Girl never showed up, Randy gave up trying to only have eight beers. Instead he became incredibly drunk, as was customary. It was just like any other night.

My night, however, took a surprising turn. I was ordering Randy a drink, and I asked him what was the cheapest beer at 17/16. Randy named a beer that probably wasn't the cheapest.

"He's lyin' to you," said a young woman standing next to us.

"What?" I asked.

"He's lyin' to you. That one's expensive."

"Thanks for warning me," I said.

I ordered the drink for Randy anyway, but then I stayed talking to her. She was named Molly. She was a 25-year-old Methodist from Georgia, in town for a wedding. I was raised as a Methodist as well, but when I told her this, she rightfully didn't believe me, so we looked up my childhood church on her phone, and I sang her Methodist hymns until she did. When I told her I was writing a book, she smiled and said, "Wow, I've never met a writer before." She had the accent of a Southern belle, which I found amusing and endearing. I still didn't identify as a writer, and I felt like a huge imposter, but I played along and tried to act the part. Molly bet me that I wouldn't kiss her on the cheek, so I did, then she bet me that I wouldn't kiss her on the lips, so I did, then she bet me that I wouldn't make out with her, so I did. At the time I thought I was the one seducing her, but in hindsight it was the other way around.

She was staying at a nearby hotel, so I told her in a cheeky way that I had never been in a hotel in Alabama before. She told me that I could walk her back to her hotel, but I was only allowed to look at the hotel from the outside. We left the bar together, and I gave her a piggy-back ride through the streets to the hotel. When we reached the hotel, we walked straight up to her room. Inside her hotel room, she told me that we could only make out. "Of course," I said. Once we started making out, she asked me if I had any condoms, and I told her I had two.

Randy would tell me the next day that I must have had beer goggles to go home with this girl, but she was cute to me, and either way I didn't care. The recipe for a successful romantic or sexual encounter is not just who I'm attracted to, but also who is attracted to me. Randy's standards for women were so high that the only girls he was attracted to were so attractive that he was unable to speak to them. By contrast, I knew who was in my league.

This was the first time I'd ever slept with a stranger, but I tried to act like I'd done it dozens of times and that the night was nothing special for me. I could have had a much better time and achieved a deeper degree of intimacy if I had told her the truth, but I was too caught up in my performance as a cool, sexually experienced guy for there to be any honesty. After sleeping together, Molly told me that I was the fourth guy she had had sex with, and that the first three guys were boyfriends. It was the first time she had had casual sex as well. I was just as inexperienced, but I wasn't willing to share that with her. We spooned through the night, then in the morning I woke up feeling hungover and awkward. I didn't have the strength to keep performing my persona from the previous night. I got dressed and told her goodbye with no parting kiss—something I would later come to regret. (You never know what you mean to someone else.)

Back at Randy's apartment, he told me about his night. He almost got into a fist fight with a senior from his fraternity, then he went to his roommate Nick's girlfriend's apartment and woke them up at 3am. Nick and his girlfriend had to console the drunk Randy for an hour before convincing him to walk back to his own apartment. None of this was very amusing to me anymore. I had badly wanted to see

Randy face his fears and talk to Dream Girl, but he didn't have the opportunity, and I had to leave Auburn feeling disappointed.

At the start of the week, Randy told me that his goal was for me to say his name and be proud of it, but Randy never again brought up the question of whether or not I was proud of him. I don't think he bothered to ask.

5

UNIVERSITY OF SOUTH CAROLINA

My car was a Honda Element, one of those small, boxy SUVs. The back seats could recline parallel with the ground to form a makeshift bed, and that's where I planned to sleep overnight when I was between two colleges, or whenever I visited schools where my host had no place for me to sleep. The car had blankets and pillows to make it comfortable, and I also had a warm sleeping bag for when it was cold outside.

South Carolina was one such week where I would be sleeping in my car, because my host lived in a girl-only dorm. Males had to leave each night before 11pm, so my plan was to shadow Louise during the daytime, and then as night approached, I would leave to sleep in my car until the next morning.

Louise and Alexa picked me up off the street headed to a fast food place called Cookout. Louise was who I'd be writing about that week, and Alexa was one of her suitemates. I got in their car and introduced myself. They were both freshmen who had only been at college for one semester. So far, all of my hosts had been the same age as me or older, but Louise and Alexa were a year younger than me. I didn't know what Louise and her friends were going to look like before I met them, but I admit I was delighted to discover that

Louise and Alexa were both quite attractive—the kind of girls who I'd never find myself hanging around in normal life; and yet, here I was. Theoretically, the fact that they were attractive should not have mattered to me, but I couldn't help it. My attraction was involuntary, and as soon as I was attracted, it became a large part of my experience.

"We should take Drew to Pav's this week," said Alexa. "It's this bar in the city, and all the guys come up to you and hit on you in like, really obvious ways. So it's fun to turn them down."

"You don't turn them down," Louise said, "you lead them on."

Alexa giggled.

"I did a lot of drinking last week, but I guess I'm down for more," I said.

"Drinking is pretty much all we do here," Alexa said.

"That's not true," said Louise.

Alexa started telling me about their lives at University. Louise was the one I was supposed to be writing about, but Alexa had a way of always shifting the focus back on herself, and I sensed that it was annoying Louise. That dynamic never changed for the length of my stay—Alexa fighting for attention, Louise getting annoyed.

My original plan for this project was that I would not participate in college life, but instead observe the proceedings from afar in order to stay objective, and even though the plan had clearly failed by this point in the trip, I did have some renewed intentions at the start of this week to act more responsibly and to treat my work with more respect.

However, there's some relevant backstory here. While I was driving to South Carolina, the guy who connected me to Louise for the purpose of writing this book told me that I should "think of my stay at USC like it's spring break," and that I could "probably have some fun" with my host's friends. Basically, he meant that I could probably hook up with one of Louise's friends if I wanted to. I tried to laugh this off, saying, "Nah, man, that's not really what I'm out to do," but his comment did somehow set the tone for the week. Somehow I had the idea that if I didn't manage to hook up with someone, I would be a disappointment. This stupid idea would end up getting me kicked out of USC after only two days.

At Cookout, a fast-food restaurant that's only in the Carolinas, the girls ordered distinctly Southern food—chicken tenders, bacon wraps, and sweet tea. Back on campus, I moved my car to a parking garage where I'd be sleeping in a few hours, then walked to their dorm building. It was a huge dorm that looked more like big-city condos than the dorms I'd seen so far. Since it was an all-girls dorm, I had to sign in with a security guard and tell him that I would check out by 11pm. Then Louise, Alexa, and I stepped into the elevators.

"They call this the Pussy Palace," Alexa said after the doors closed.

Louise's cheeks turned bright red. "Who calls it that?" she asked.

"The boys," said Alexa.

"I don't think that's true," said Louise.

"Well, that's what they call it. The boys who get to come in here are the lucky ones." Alexa said all of this without looking at me, but it was clear that I was her audience.

If this exchange had happened in front of me only a few weeks earlier, I would have likely let out an involuntary high-pitched squeal of laughter, which would have quickly indicated to the girls that I was uncomfortable with anything sexual—which was still basically true —but because of my sheer exposure to women over the preceding weeks, I had learned to be comfortable enough with this sort of thing that I managed to internalize my nervousness, and instead I stood perfectly still with no reaction.

I also started to get the feeling that the guy who connected me to Louise had put in a good word for me—as if he told them I was some sort of badass or something. Louise and Alexa seemed to be trying to impress me from the very beginning, instead of the other way around. I found this bizarre and unwarranted, but I welcomed it anyway. In order to not disappoint them, I slowed down, became very quiet, and tried not to make any social errors.

The elevator doors opened, and we continued into their suite. Louise's and Alexa's rooms were separated by a bathroom, and each girl had another roommate. On Alexa's half of the suite, she and her roommate had shoved their beds together to make one large, shared bed in the center of the room. We sat in Louise's room—me on the futon, the two girls on the beds. As soon as we sat down, Alexa took out her phone and asked Siri if it liked to have sex. Then she asked Siri its favorite sex position. This seemed to be Alexa's way of injecting the idea of sex into the conversation again. Louise rolled her eyes.

"Are you really going to sleep in your car?" Alexa asked me a moment later.

"Yeah, it's not so bad," I said.

She turned to Louise. "Why don't we let him stay here?"

"Alexa, we can't," said Louise. "He has to sign out."

"We can sign him out then sneak him back in."

"No, it's too risky."

"It's fine, the car's not bad at all," I said, though I think I was secretly rooting for Alexa. (Who am I kidding, I was definitely rooting for Alexa.)

"It's 100 hours of community service if I'm caught," said Louise.

"Don't worry. I'll take the blame if we get caught," said Alexa.

Louise hung her head and said, "Fine."

We spent the next hour scheming about how we would sneak me inside for the night. First I went downstairs with Louise and signed out. Then we walked to my car, where she took my sleeping bag and brought it back to her room. Next I stood near a back entrance of their dorms and pretended to use a pay phone while waiting for Alexa to open the door from inside. The risk was that one of the security guards who patrolled the place would see me on the way in and chase after us. If that happened, we would have to outrun him and make it back to their suite without him seeing which room we entered.

The door behind me opened, and Alexa popped her head out. "C'mon!" she whispered. I hung up the phone and walked inconspicuously to the door. When we stepped inside, we turned and bolted up four flights of stairs while our giggles reverberated in the concrete, then ran down a long hall past a dozen or so posters about safe sex and how to prevent sexually transmitted diseases. When we turned into Louise's room, we were out of breath and both had big smiles on our faces. Louise, however, did not share our same feeling of relief. Alexa finally noticed that Louise seemed bothered.

"Did Jeff text you or something?" Alexa asked her.

"Everything's fine," said Louise.

"Jeff's her boyfriend," Alexa said to me.

"He is not!" said Louise.

"Louise doesn't want to make it official with him, but he wants to."

Louise ignored Alexa, then, clearly miffed, said she needed to study and asked us to go to the other side of the suite. There I met the third suitemate, Sophia. She was the girl who grew up with Alexa in a town nearby.

"I feel like we didn't do anything at all in high school," said Alexa. "Like on a Friday night the thing to do was just go sit in a fast-food parking lot. College is so different."

"Neither of us had ever partied in high school," said Sophia. "And here that goes on all the time. So it's still all so new to us."

"But you learn quickly," said Alexa. "Has Louise told you about Jeff?"

"No," I said.

"Louise has this tendency to meet boys that get obsessed with her. She likes to tease then leave."

"Jeff got her flowers on Valentine's Day and asked if she wanted to be his girlfriend, and she got mad at him," said Sophia.

"Why would Louise be mad about that?" I asked.

"It's dumb," said Alexa. "They're basically in love, but Louise doesn't want to make it official."

"She wants her mountain man," said Sophia, "some guy who likes the outdoors, is smart, and isn't clingy. But she isn't going to get that here."

"Jeff is older than her, so he wants to settle down or something."

"Older guys want to settle down?" I asked.

"Yeah, they become babies as they get older," said Alexa.

"Freshmen are easier because all they want is sex. My boyfriend is two years older than me, and he used to get needy all the time. Freshmen guys just want to go have fun and get laid."

I was a little disappointed to hear that Alexa had a boyfriend. But she was quick to withdraw the statement.

"Actually, I mean, he's my ex-boyfriend," she said. "We broke up, but we still hang out and talk and stuff. We just decided to be completely honest with each other, you know, about whatever we do with other people."

So she was single, I thought.

A little later, I left to Louise's side of the suite since it was now late and she had finished studying. I unrolled my sleeping bag and went to sleep on her futon. Somehow the thought never occurred to me that maybe Louise did not want me there. She had been pressured by Alexa to sneak me in and had submitted to the pressure. It didn't occur to me that I probably should have been sleeping in my car like I had said I would.

It was morning now, and I was alone with Louise for the school day. She wore boots, a somewhat formal shirt, and a silk scarf. Around campus, other students also dressed more formally than I was used to seeing—girls in flowery dresses, guys wearing pastel shirts tucked into khaki pants. The guys here often wear bowties, Louise told me. Each year, students here attend an event called the Carolina Cup, a weekend at a horse track where girls wear big sun hats and sun dresses, and guys wear pastel shirts, colorful pants and bowties. The fashion of the Carolina Cup seemed to spill into campus all year.

"How was first coming to school?" I asked Louise.

"I loved it. Well, I loved a lot of it. Actually, at first I was pretty upset because the school part of it was really bad. I tried really hard in high school and when I got here it seemed even easier than high school. I called my mom on the third day of school crying. I was like, 'Ah, I worked so hard in high school, and now college is so easy!'"

"Has it gotten any better?"

"A little bit. It's still freshman year, so I'm hoping it gets harder. People here don't really spend much effort on the school part."

We went to her English literature class, where the professor screened a Ken Burns documentary about Mark Twain. Afterward, we went back to Louise's room so she could change into workout clothes and pick up the fourth roommate, Joan, who was very polite and somewhat meek, the opposite of Alexa. Now we were headed to a class on self-defense.

Inside the gym sat a row of 30 girls leaned against the wall, most of them wearing giant t-shirts and leggings and running shoes. The teacher—a tall, middle-aged man in a black sweat suit with a shiny martial arts dragon on the back—sat in a small plastic chair facing the girls. It wasn't a girl-only class, it just happened to have no boys.

"Today we're going to continue our journey into self-defense," the teacher said while leaning back in his chair. He had an extremely serious and dramatic tone. "We'll be talking about how to turn everyday objects into self-defense weapons."

As a 20-year-old I was all Rousseau, no Hobbes. I thought the world was fundamentally safe and that instances of violence were strange anomalies. Accordingly, this self-defense class had the tone of comedy for me. I was on the edge of laughter throughout class.

He continued. "What's one object you keep with you all the time?"

"Keys," a girl answered.

"Precisely," he said. "Car keys: sharp, strong, always in your pocket. Keys make a great weapon in a pinch. Not the best, but they work." He stood up and removed his keys from his pocket. "Keys don't have much force behind them, but they'll slice through skin with ease."

He held one of his keys like the tip of a pencil and swung it through the air, paced to the other end of the girls, then swung the keys through the air again. He looked up, scanned the girls' faces as a sort of dramatic pause, nodded, then returned to his chair.

"So keys are a good weapon," he concluded.

His favorite weapon, he told us later, is the bow staff, but unfortunately he's unable to carry one with him all the time.

After his lecture, he had the girls practice heel-smashing the imaginary foot of an attacker on the ground of the gym. That was the end of class.

"So is self-defense something that is often on your minds?" I asked Louise and Joan on the way out.

"I think so," said Louise.

"All the time," said Joan. "Columbia is a really poor city, so we get a lot of crime and muggings here."

"It's not that uncommon for a girl to get assaulted here."

"We always walk in groups, especially at night."

"I know a lot of girls who won't walk around at night, not even in groups."

"We usually have to plan out what routes we take and stuff like that."

After hearing how important self-defense was to Louise and Joan, I felt bad for having chuckled through self-defense class. But I actually learned something from the class: after I left USC, whenever I pulled my car over at a rest stop along the highway at night, I would carry my keys with me into the bathroom, the same way their self-defense teacher taught us.

After lunch, we went to Louise's statistics class, then to British Literature—both classes where she was the only freshman. Away from Alexa, Louise seemed smart, thoughtful, and driven. Unfortunately, I only spent one day with her, so I wasn't able to learn much more.

After class, Louise was called by Jeff, the guy who Alexa said was Louise's boyfriend, but who Louise said wasn't. She walked a few steps ahead of me and spoke quietly. I heard my name at one point.

"He's being a jerk," she said after she hung up.

"How so?" I asked.

"He wanted me to come over, and I said, 'Good, so you can meet Drew!' and he said he didn't want you over. Anyway, he called me a bitch, so I called him a dick."

"I don't need to follow you over there, if that's what the argument was about. I wouldn't want me over either."

"I know. No, you're fine, he's just... I don't know."

I hadn't yet considered the implications of writing about a girl who had a boyfriend. It would be a lot to stomach for the guy. I was spending every waking hour with her, and now I had somehow weaseled my way into sleeping in her bedroom. Men know other men; if his girlfriend is attractive, then he knows that I am also attracted to her. Somehow I was ignoring all of this. Conflict and tension seemed to be unfolding all around me, but I didn't sense that I was its source.

Louise's dorm glowed orange from the setting sun. The day had been long and filled with classes, but it was not nearly over. We were joined again by Alexa in Louise's room. There, the girls tried to figure out what plans they should make for the night—a process that was rather enlightening for me. The plan was still to go to "Monday night Pav's," but the question was, with whom? Both of the guys who were their sort-of boyfriends had been annoying them during the day by being too needy, so Alexa said that she was considering texting another guy who had messaged her about studying together, and Louise said that she might also text a different guy. I felt bad for every guy involved: first for the sort-of boyfriends, for obvious reasons, but more so for the backup guys who were likely to misunderstand the intentions of the girls. I wondered how many times in my life I had been a backup like that.

"So what's the situation with Jeff?" I asked Louise.

"I don't know," she said. "I guess I'm just not very into him and didn't want it to get as serious as it has. But he's good company, and he brings me to a lot of functions, and knows a lot of people, and those things. He's sort of a frat daddy."

Louise left to go to a sorority officer's meeting that I wasn't allowed to attend. I'd be meeting her afterward. In the meantime, I had some alone time with Alexa. When Louise left the room, she told Alexa to "keep Drew entertained," a phrase I found rather amusing.

The door shut and seemed to vacuum the air from the room, and all was quiet as I sat on the futon, Alexa standing in front of me. I had not been alone with Alexa before, so I was curious to see how it would go.

"So you're supposed to keep me entertained," I said.

"Hmmm," she said. "It's hard to think of something entertaining."

"Louise told me you're the crazy one of the group. Is that true?"

"Maybe."

"What makes her say that?"

She pushed her mouth to the side. "Drinking, maybe," she said while taking a seat next to me, "and boys."

"Drinking and boys," I repeated.

I kept a toy ukulele with me in my backpack. Alexa saw it, picked it up, and started to strum it. (I absolutely despise it when guys use instruments in any way to impress women, and yet I'm a huge hypocrite because I try to do it all the time.)

"Is this entertaining?" she asked.

"It's not bad," I said.

I taught her how to play two chords. To do so, I touched her fingers a lot more than necessary in order to make the situation more intimate. It was like a cliché scene from a bad movie, and I cringe now when I think about it, but there was no audience at the time, so I did it shamelessly. Then Alexa sat and played as I watched. When she set the ukulele down, her body relaxed and she spoke in a whisper.

"How was that?" she asked.

"Lovely," I said. "I think you're a natural."

The room fell silent again as Alexa and I looked at each other with nothing to say. After a moment, the door to the room swung open, and Louise's sorority sister walked in to pick me up. I had only been alone with Alexa for ten minutes, but I felt that a lot had happened.

I was now heading to Louise's sorority chapter meeting. Louise had already been there for an hour, since she was an officer, but the other 300 girls in the sorority would only be attending for the final hour. I planned to wait outside for Louise while all this took place, but on the walk across campus with a group of Louise's sorority sisters, one of them, a tomboy-ish girl in a basketball jersey and sneakers, assured me she would be able to sneak me into the meeting.

Louise's sorority's chapter meetings take place in one of the school's lecture halls. As the officers' meeting concluded inside the lecture hall, the rest of the girls—hundreds of them—waited outside. I sat far away from the door to the lecture hall and planned to stay there, but as the doors opened and the girls began filing in, the tomboy-ish girl waved me forward and yelled, "C'mon!" so I stood and followed her, then stood at the back of the line of girls like an idiot.

I was hoping that the door to the lecture hall would lead to the back of the room so I could sit on the back row and go unnoticed. That was not the case. When I finally reached the door, a girl standing by the door flung her arm out to block my path. Instead of opening to the back of the room, the door opened to the front and center of the room, and all 300 girls were already quietly seated, waiting for the meeting to begin. I looked up and realized that I was standing in front of all of them as they waited to find out why some strange dude was trying to get inside their chapter meeting.

The girl who was blocking my path said, aggressively, "What are you doing?"

I searched the crowd ahead of me for the tomboy-ish girl—she was the one who told me it was okay—but she was facing the other way looking for a seat.

"Oh," I said. "Well, I'm—"

She cut me off. "Are you a freshman or something?" she asked.

"No, I... I can leave," I said. I looked at my feet then back to her and said, "I'm writing a book about college. She..." I pointed to the tomboy-ish girl, "...she said it was ok."

The girl looked toward who I was pointing at, and unfortunately so did everybody else in the room. Somebody got the tomboy-ish girl's attention, who then turned, saw me, and shouted, "He's writing a book!" At that moment, I had never felt like more of a phony in my life. I had no reason to be there—no agent, no editor, no publisher, no authority supporting the project in any way to lend credibility. The longest thing I had ever written was a two-page essay for high school English, and I got a B.

"Ok..." the door girl said to me with the tone of having said, "Why should I give a shit?"

I had about five seconds to answer her question, but I didn't know how to explain what I was doing in five seconds. I should have said, "I'm writing a book about student social life at college. Can I come in?" Instead, I started mumbling and explaining that I didn't go to college myself, and how the experience of everyone telling me I'd made a mistake made me want to discover the meaning of the college experience, so now I was on this trip to write this book, etc. I talked for way too long of a time.

She paid attention only to the first thing I said. "You don't go to college?" she asked.

"No," I said.

"Anywhere?"

"No."

"Ok. I'll have to ask."

She walked over to another girl and spoke to her quietly, then that girl spoke to another, and so on, until a chain of five conversations reached a middle-aged woman in the corner who was the sorority advisor, all the while I stood there trying to look innocent and hoping my knees wouldn't buckle under the pressure of having 300 blonde girls staring at me. The advisor eventually nodded, and the command traveled back down through the link of girls.

"You can come in," the door girl said.

I couldn't believe it. "Thanks," I said.

I walked up an aisle to the back row, never in my life more aware of my gait, and took a seat next to the tomboy-ish girl, who was named Emily. Still at least 60 girls were turned around in their seats watching me.

"That was intense," I whispered to Emily.

"I can't believe you got in," Emily said.

"What? You're the one who said it was ok."

"No, I didn't think there was a chance," she laughed.

"Goddamnit."

I sunk into my seat and took handwritten notes to appear official and professional. As one of the officers, Louise was up front taking roll call, and fortunately she had been calling out names during the previous incident and didn't see most of what happened. She would call out a name and each girl would respond with "Nu," short for their sorority name Chi Nu. (This is a made-up sorority name.) Emily kindly whispered to me supplemental information throughout the meeting, so I would know what was going on. This particular chapter meeting was a "dress down" meeting since it was the last meeting of the month, in contrast to all other meetings, which are semi-formal. Sometimes if a girl is rewarded for good behavior, she will receive a "dress down pass" to dress casually at the semi-formal meetings.

The girls stood to recite their Chi Nu motto. Next, a girl stood up front and read a short passage about spring break and togetherness, which proclaimed that even when things derail, Chi Nus stay together. Spring break was the following week, so this meeting was dedicated to discussing travel safety.

But first there were two slideshows for senior girls who would be graduating at the end of the semester. The slideshows were made by their respective mothers with pictures starting at childhood and continuing to their lives at college. As one slideshow played, one of the Chi Nus read a letter aloud written by the girl's mom: "...you were such a spunky and honest kid..." "...when you went off to college your dad and I were so proud..." "...you were going off on an adventure that promised new friends, new experiences, new challenges..." "...being a Chi Nu has been such an amazing time for you..." After the slideshow ended, the mom surprised everyone by showing up in the flesh to greet her daughter with a bouquet of flowers, and the two shared a long tear-filled hug as everybody else awwwed, and then they waved and left the room—off to eat dinner or something—while the girls applauded and cheered like a daytime talk show's studio audience. If there is a singular modern-day coming-of-age ritual for sorority girls, I suspect that senior slideshow day is it.

The tone shifted dramatically after the moms left. One of the sorority sisters stood up front and announced that some of the girls would be fined (not money but "demerits") for poorly written letters on behalf of their sorority charity. Some of the girls were caught copy-pasting the same letter to all of their donors. Emily thought this was hilarious.

Next, about 40 girls walked to the front of the room to begin a presentation on spring break safety. These were girls who had gotten in trouble for drinking alcohol when they weren't supposed to, and their punishment had been to each create one slide for the Power-Point we were about to view about the dangers of spring break week. The presentation's title was "Risk Management Presentation." The slides were:

-Effects of sun on aging
-Effects of alcohol on aging
-Drinking in the sun
-Rohypnol: Roofies
-What Not to Keep in Your Hotel Room
-Drinking Day to Night (This one included the advice, "Don't forget to eat dinner," and "Don't get ready while you're wasted.")
-Drinking Games on Spring Break ("You may binge drink without realizing it")
-Telling People Where You're Staying (The advice was simply, "Don't.")
-Balcony Danger with Hotels
-When to Call 9/11
-Why Not to Take Drinks from Strangers
-How to Avoid Attack ("Don't go back even if you have been with him all night." Emily told me during this slide, while laughing, that her mom made her get pepper spray for spring break.)
-Alcohol-Related Deaths
-Don't Go Back to His Place

There were a few chuckles in the crowd throughout the slideshow, but most girls appeared to treat it with seriousness (Emily not included). Afterward, the room was opened for discussion of additional advice. A sorority sister stood and said, "Girls, really be careful. I've had friends who were raped before at spring break." Another stood and reiterated that same advice. Another said, "Sometimes a frat guy loses sight of how to treat a woman and gets pushy." One stood and simply said, "Don't bring guy friends to Mexico."

Then a small girl stood and began, "Hey guys, most of you know I transferred here from North Carolina this year." Her voice was weak and shaky, and she was asked twice to speak up. "Well, the reason is because last year at spring break, something happened to my best friend. We drank all day and really weren't paying attention. She seemed fine all day." Her voice was becoming even softer.

Emily buried her head in her hands.

The small girl continued, "Well, the next day she didn't wake up. She died with a .4 BAC."

Emily's shoulders trembled slightly, and I wondered if she was crying—maybe she had experienced something similar or even knew the girl who had died.

Nobody responded for a few moments, so one of the officers spoke up and said, "Girls, that's why we're having this presentation. This is all very important."

Emily took a deep breath, then finally lifted her head and revealed that she had actually been choking back laughter the whole time. She wore a foolish grin that she tried to hide with her hand. Then she leaned over to me and said, "God, that was so awkward."

I smiled and said, "You're a terrible person."

"It was just funny, man, that's all."

Finally, the girls stood and held hands to sing their sorority anthem, which brought the meeting to a close.

Afterward, Louise and I walked back to her dorm room. Similar to my sleeping on Louise's futon without her complete agreement, I also barged into her sorority chapter meeting without her agreement. She had told me earlier that I would have to wait outside for the meeting to end, but I didn't listen. Emily told me I should follow her in, so I followed her in. I tried to smooth things over by explaining the story to her, but I could tell that I was causing her some stress.

When we got inside her dorm room, Alexa was there. Something odd was unfolding, and I couldn't figure out what it was. Louise and Alexa were involved in some heavy drama that I didn't know about. They were both rapidly texting on their phones, pacing around the room, sometimes stepping outside for a few minutes at a time, and whispering to each other in the other room. Meanwhile, I sat on the futon with an innocent look on my face, trying to pretend like everything was fine. Eventually Louise spoke up to tell me her situation.

"So, Jeff's getting mad," she said.

"Is it me?" I asked.

"Kind of," she said, "but it's not your fault. He said you're taking all his time with me before spring break. He's just being stupid."

"Well, do what you need to do. I don't mind," I said.

"Yeah, I might need to leave tonight," she said.

Louise stepped outside again. Alexa was now changing clothes and putting on makeup in the other room, still planning to go out drinking for what she called "Monday Night Pav's." She came into Louise's room and made herself a mixed drink of soda and pineapple rum.

"If she leaves, I still want to have fun," Alexa said to me. "What about you?"

"Of course," I said.

Louise returned and told me that Jeff, the so-called frat daddy, was going to drive over, and that he wanted to meet me outside. I had been permanently nervous since I had arrived at USC, so meeting this guy was just going to be more of the same. On our walk outside, Louise was not her usual self. She was somber and she wasn't speaking, so I prepared myself for some sort of serious confrontation with Jeff. I was mostly just confused.

Jeff arrived in a pickup truck and stepped out wearing a backward baseball cap. He was about my size, my height. Louise didn't introduce us. She apparently couldn't handle the tension, because she faced the opposite direction while looking down at her phone.

"Hey, I'm Drew," I said, sticking out my hand.

"I'm Jeff." He shook my hand and searched my eyes for a long while.

He seemed to be sizing me up and making a snap judgment of me. Louise still couldn't watch, and I still barely knew what was going on.

"Hey, man, you can just come over and watch a movie if you want," he said, "so you don't have to keep sneaking into dorms."

I thought of Alexa back in the room, still ready to have fun. "I appreciate it," I said. "I'm fine though, it's actually pretty easy to do."

"You sure?" he asked.

"Yeah, definitely. Thanks."

"Alright," he sighed. He got Louise's attention and motioned to her with his head. That was the whole exchange.

"I'll let you back in," Louise said to me.

She snuck me in through the back door of the dorm the same way as the first night, except this time it was neither fun nor thrilling.

"I'm going to stay over at Jeff's!" Louise told Alexa. She had a cheery voice now, all tension gone. I didn't understand why.

"Alright!" said Alexa.

"Will you two be able to entertain yourselves?"

Alexa looked at me and said, "I think so."

Then Louise, on her way out, turned back to us, and in a sing-song voice said, "You two have fun!" making two syllables out of the word "fun" in a way that seemed to me rather suggestive. The words echoed in my head, and I tried to make sense of all the layers: the first layer was just simple politeness; another layer was her attempt to mask whatever issues were going on between her and Jeff; and the final layer of her phrase seemed to say, "If you're going to hook up, this is your opportunity." I liked this interpretation. It reminded me of the girl at Baylor who asked me and her roommate if we wanted the lights on or off while she stepped outside for a shower. Because of this similarity, I thought that Louise was purposely giving us alone time, and I felt that I had to take the opportunity, otherwise I'd be letting everybody down. As Louise closed the door behind her, again a vacuum seemed to suck the air from the room.

Alexa stood before me in a small black dress, mixed drink in hand, while her eyes moved in a big circle, unsure of where to settle.

"You should make me one of those drinks," I said.

It happened soon. We had each poured only one drink—more for the ritual than for reasons of intoxication. We were sitting side by side on her futon while she showed me photos of her from the Carolina Cup. When Alexa sat down next to me, she sat cross-legged with the full weight of her knee on my thigh. I then rested the full weight of my hand on her knee. After I did this, when Alexa didn't flinch or adjust her knee, I finally believed that I'd accumulated enough evidence to think that if I kissed her, she'd kiss me back. I can't remember who was the first one to sexualize the conversation, but after a little while, we got to trading sex stories back and forth. Alexa told me story after story—getting caught having sex in the bushes, sex with older men, random sex at fraternity parties. I had an extremely small number of stories about casual sexual experiences to share, but I shared each story as if I were choosing at random from an inexhaustible reservoir of erotic memories. And my trick worked—at some point Alexa said, "Oh my God, I thought you were cute, but I had no idea you'd be so experienced."

Eventually Alexa told me she had never had sex in her own room. I asked, "You mean this room right here?" She said yes. A minute later I kissed her, and she returned the kiss.

Before long, we were naked in her bed, fooling around. During a blowjob I asked, "Is this on the record?" and Alexa said, "Yes." A little while later, my leg kicked and bumped one of the glasses that we had been drinking from, and it fell off the bedside table and shattered across the floor. We stopped what we were doing so Alexa could go into the other room to search for a broom and pan to clean up the glass. While she was out, her phone buzzed and lit up in the dark room. I was sitting right next to it and couldn't resist looking at the screen. When I looked, I saw that she had eight texts from her ex-boyfriend. There were eight texts, but the only text visible to me was the last one. It said, "You have no idea how much pain you are causing me right now."

Shit, I thought, how horrible. Was his text somehow about me? I wasn't sure.

I moved to the other side of the bed and pretended not to have seen her phone. Alexa came back in with a broom and swept up all the little shards of glass. Afterward, she walked over to the bedside table and checked her phone. The room was still dark, so the phone's light illuminated her face cold and blue. As she read the text, "You have no idea how much pain you are causing me right now," something strange happened. As she read the text, a satisfied smile came to her face. It had made her happy—pleasure at his pain. She sent no text back to him and laid the phone back on the table, this time face down.

"Let's have sex now," she said as she crawled into bed.

I felt extremely disturbed. I replied "Ok," but I was still trying to process how I felt about what I had just witnessed. I didn't know if I wanted to have sex with someone who was sadistic like that. Did Alexa only want to have sex with me as a way of causing pain to her ex-boyfriend? I wasn't sure if I wanted to play that role. We went back to making out, although the whole time I was deep in thought.

(I don't want to make myself out to be some kind of saint here. In addition to feeling disturbed by her apparent sadism, I was also dealing with some performance anxiety. I had made myself out to be some kind of sex god, and Alexa believed every bit of it. But what if I underperformed? This fear also slowed down my sexual initiative.)

Whatever I was thinking about wouldn't have mattered anyway, because within minutes the door opened and the two roommates I didn't know very well walked in on us while we were still just making out. We were in Alexa's bed, which, as you recall, also belonged to her roommate. They had pushed their two twin beds together to make one large bed, and that's the bed we were using. None of this had occurred to me until then. Alexa and I covered our exposed body parts.

"Hi," the roommates said, giggling in the doorway, again turning "hi" into a sing-song, two-syllable word.

I said nothing. Alexa jumped out of bed, put her clothes back on, and went into the hallway with them. I got dressed while I waited for her to come back in. Ten long minutes later, she came in and assured me everything was fine.

"Are you sure?" I asked.

"Yeah, they're going to sleep next door."

But things clearly were not fine, because Alexa immediately lay down on her futon to go to sleep, which reminded me of a scolded dog. It was clear that we were not going to continue hooking up. I remained on the bed, but I soon felt a small bit of clarity return to my thoughts. I was in a bed that belonged to somebody I didn't know. What the hell was I doing? How was I planning to hook up with Alexa while not frightening her roommates? Was I really planning to continue writing about Louise for the rest of the week as if nothing had happened?

I made Alexa switch spots with me so I wouldn't be the one in the bed. Before we fell asleep, Alexa checked Twitter and saw that her roommates had tweeted something about "Deer in the headlights!" referring to the two of us. Some intense text message drama would surely unfold before the morning. I wondered how much damage I had done. The only solace I took was remembering something Alexa told me. Apparently before Louise left for the night, she told Alexa, "Go easy on Drew." That must have meant she condoned us hooking up, right? I hoped so.

Louise returned late the next morning. I was a complete moron: I acted as if nothing had happened and sat there ready to go with her to another day of classes. She sat on her bed without looking at me while she was busily texting. Eventually she spoke, but still she didn't look up from her phone.

"So, things are a little awkward right now," she said.

I waited.

She continued. "Jeff is in James's fraternity."

"James, Alexa's ex-boyfriend?"

"No— James, Alexa's boyfriend."

"Boyfriend?" I asked.

"Yes."

"Currently?"

"Yes."

"Oh. I don't—Alexa said..."

"When Joan and Sophia walked in on you two, they called me, and I was with Jeff, and he told James. Anyway, things are pretty tense right now."

"I thought they had broken up."

"No. And it's not the first time this has happened. Or the second. Or the third." She looked up at me dramatically. "Or the fourth. Or the fifth."

My ego had been inflated by the belief that I had done something special to seduce Alexa, but as Louise spoke, my self-esteem plummeted on an exponential decline in exact proportion to each of her words—first, second, third, fourth, fifth.

"I see," I said.

I sat and actually twiddled my thumbs while Louise tried to solve the conflict one text message at a time. Alexa was in the other room out of earshot folding a shirt on her bed. After a little while I stood up and walked over to her.

"So, you and James are dating. Is that true?" I asked. My voice was soft and non-confrontational. In hindsight, I shouldn't have said anything at all. It was only going to make things worse.

"What? That's not true," Alexa said, getting louder. "I'm not together with him. I mean we talk and everything, but he's not my boyfriend!"

She dropped her shirt and rushed across the suite to Louise on the other side. I didn't think she'd react so abruptly. I tried to stop her, but I was too late.

"Louise! What's going on?" Alexa asked.

Louise didn't look up at her, just stayed focused on her phone.

"Louise!" Alexa yelled. "If something's going on, I need to know! Now!"

Louise ignored her again.

"Somebody tell me what's going on!"

I stood there wide-eyed like a moron. When situations are tense, I become mellow and almost sleepy.

Louise eventually stood up and walked with Alexa into the other room. They shut the door behind them and remained there for 30 minutes. Meanwhile, I sat and tried to do some breathing exercises to relax, but they did not work. The only support I could think of was to text the guy who first connected me with Louise and tell him what happened. It turned out that he had already heard the entire story from Louise as it developed over the past two days. He found it hilarious.

"This is like Tucker Max," he said. "Awesome. I'm glad you're getting good material."

Goddamnit, that was the exact opposite of the person I wanted to emulate. I told him the truth: "It's not very awesome right now."

Louise left for lunch without inviting me, which was good evidence that I would probably be leaving USC soon. Sure enough, a few minutes later she texted me: "I'm not sure what you came here to do, but you've crossed the line. I know Alexa had a part in it too, but you've made my roommates feel very uncomfortable. Sophia had to sleep in the library last night. I think you need to leave."

Reading that text hurt, but I deserved it. Louise really stuck her neck out to allow me to write about her, and I completely disrespected her effort. Alexa had told me the previous night that everything was fine with her roommates, but it turned out that it wasn't fine at all. I replied to Louise, "I understand, I hope I haven't caused too much trouble. Maybe it'll make sense later. I will head out now."

I found a pen and some paper and wrote a note. I addressed it to Louise, Joan, and Sophia (all the roommates, minus Alexa). It read, "Thank you all so much for letting me stay here. It seems you were such good hosts that I started to feel a little too comfortable! I wish you all the best. You have a good thing going here. Thanks, Drew."

I took my sleeping bag, backpack, and pillow, and headed out. Alexa was still in her room, and I saw her through the doorway as I left. I didn't say anything as I walked out. She must not have known Louise would be asking me to leave, because when she saw me carrying my things, her eyebrows pinched tightly together with a sudden realization of concern and confusion. Then the doorframe swiped across her face and she was gone.

I stepped into the midmorning sun heading prematurely toward my next college. The experience at USC left me feeling vaguely predatory. I worried about my own intentions and wondered if I would give off the impression that I was just traveling around trying to get laid. That was not my plan, and I didn't like to think of myself as someone who would do that, and yet, that's what I seemed to be doing—not just here, but everywhere I went. I worried especially about the shy roommate, Joan, who took self-defense classes and said that she worried for her safety at all times. How had I made her feel? I wasn't sure. I looked up toward the sky and let a big grin wash over my face, trying in vain to laugh off the pain I felt in my chest.

6

CHARLTON UNIVERSITY

(Note: Charlton is a fake name for this school, because it is difficult to keep these people anonymous if I mention their school. Charlton is a well-respected school in the Deep South.)

I took two days to make the half-day drive to Charlton. Along the way, I took a detour and stopped at Great Smoky Mountains National Park, turning off at different trailheads, beginning to hike, then turning back toward my car after only a couple of minutes. It seemed the idea of hiking was more appealing than actual hiking. My mood was low, my thoughts were cynical. I dwelled on the selfish notion that the communities I had passed through continued on without me. What was still significant for me no longer mattered to the people I met. Friendships that did last were now only text messages —Randy might text me if he saw Dream Girl at the bar (he still hadn't spoken to her), or Kevin might ask my location. It occurred to me that a person was more likely to create false intimacy with me because I was just passing through. I was also struck by the thought that everybody I met was influenced by varying degrees of observer bias; that is, the fact I was writing a book would dramatically change how people acted around me. I wanted people to like me as a person outside the context of my book project. I wondered, would anybody have actually wanted to spend time with me if I weren't writing a book? Would women have liked me? What vanity! My mission was to write a book, not to meet friends or lovers, so I shouldn't have had those expectations. But I couldn't help it—I just felt sad and lonely.

Christian played baseball for Charlton. He was also the guy who had connected me with Louise at USC, so he knew the story of why I had to arrive at Charlton five days early. I met him the evening after one of their baseball games. The team had lost.

"Just a fair warning," Christian said, "a lot of the guys are pretty pissed right now. We're usually a winning team, but we've had a terrible season, like 1-8, so if any of the guys are short with you tonight, that's why. Some of them are probably going to get blackout drunk too. Just a heads-up."

"That's fine," I said.

We were headed to his dorm room.

"You're going to have to meet my buddy Billy," he said. "He's totally Tucker Max. He basically just pounds booze and rails sluts. He's probably my best friend here. He's from Bumfuck Nowhere, Iowa."

I tossed my sleeping bag down on Christian's couch, and he tossed me a beer.

"Lots of the guys here are total studs," Christian continued. "Bunch of em turned down huge signing bonuses to play for Charlton, like half a million to a million. One guy you'll meet turned down millions to play here."

"Is the losing season going to make it harder for them to be drafted?" I asked.

"Not really. Baseball is a sport of individuals. To get drafted, it only matters how well you do, not the team."

Christian spoke with the voice of a salesman. If he told you a story, you got the impression that he'd told it before.

"I'll tell you a secret if you don't tell the team," he said. "I'm thinking about quitting baseball next year. I've got some business stuff I'm trying to work on, and baseball really isn't in my future. I'm not good enough."

"The other guys don't know?" I asked.

"No, not yet. I don't want to mess with morale mid-season. When I came to college, I thought baseball would be even bigger of a game, more important of a game, but what I've learned, at least for me, is that it's just a game. It's just a game, and for me it's going to end at the end of these four years. So I need to plan for the future."

Christian's story was cut short when one of the other players entered the room. He was short, bulky, and dense, like if you shoved him he wouldn't move. He was unshaven and had a buzz cut.

"This is who I was talking about!" said Christian. "Billy, meet Drew."

Billy shook my hand quickly then turned back to Christian to say what he'd come into the room to say. "I feel like getting fucked up tonight and just saying, 'Fuck the midterm.'" He looked back at me. "Oh, is this the book guy?"

I said, "Yep."

"Well, goddamnit, we'll get you some stories! I'm tellin' you, you haven't seen anything."

After my unprofessional visit to South Carolina, I wanted to establish myself as a more serious writer, so I asked him the boring question, "What's something you've learned so far at college?" I was looking for an answer about the importance of hard work or of managing time effectively.

But Billy blew my plan and said, "I've learned that I'd fuck anything. Well, anything that'd fuck me."

"He's not lying," said Christian.

"I might skip class to get some ass tomorrow," said Billy.

"Let me know how that goes," I said. Oh well, I tried.

We headed down the hall to meet more of the team. The baseball team lived in dorms, and on this particular hallway there were three dorm rooms in a row where only baseball players lived, so the middle room of the three served as their central hangout location. Some other baseball players, eight of them, were gathered around a TV playing a baseball video game.

"Fuck all the Blacks, fuck all the Jews, and fuck everybody in the state of Louisiana!" Billy said as he entered. The Louisiana bit was a reference to the team that beat them that night, Louisiana State.

Nobody responded to him, both because it seemed a normal thing for Billy to say, and because everybody was preoccupied with the video game. Those who weren't holding controllers sat with school papers in their laps, but they still seemed more interested in the Xbox than their work.

"Somebody got the tests, right?" asked Christian.

"Julie straight up hooked us up, dude," said one of the players. In his hands was a stack of papers.

"Are those old tests?" asked Christian.

"Yeah, six of 'em."

"Good, we'll go through those later."

What was happening was that a few of the baseball guys acquired from Julie six old tests from previous years for a class they were taking. Later they would figure out which questions had appeared multiple times over the past six versions of that test. The "studying" that took place after this was to memorize those answers.

As they played Xbox baseball, the guys traded stories—all of them sexual. It was clear that everybody in the room had already heard all the stories, but they enjoyed listening again anyway. The next story and storyteller would be elected by random outbursts of enthusiasm like, "Oh! Tell the one about the bitch from the burger place!" or "Oh! Tell the one about that slut you fucked in the closet at the frat party!"

I listened and laughed along with the team, not planning to participate in the storytelling, but Christian surprised me by electing me for the next story.

"Dude, Drew, you gotta tell the guys what happened last week," he said, letting out a hearty laugh. "Guys, this is hilarious."

I did not want to tell the story. The girls at USC had successfully shamed me for my inappropriate behavior, and I felt sincere remorse for my actions. But the team was looking at me with anticipation, so I had to tell it. This would be my first impression with all of them. If I won their respect, I'd be welcomed into their world for the week. If I lost it, I'd spend the week as an awkward tag-a-long.

"Well, I was at South Carolina writing about this girl," I said. I could hear the regret in my voice, despite trying my best to hide it.

The team listened intently.

"And so, the girl I was writing about had this roommate," I continued. "And so the second night, I was alone with her, and she had been giving off sort of sexual vibes since I got there."

My demeanor made me sound like I was confessing before a jury. It didn't sound like a fun story, it sounded like a sad story. I was killing the mood. Some of the guys got nervous for me and looked over at Christian, who raised his pointer finger and smiled as if to say, "Wait for it... trust me... wait for it..."

But my enthusiasm had died, and I was trailing off. "Yeah, and so, basically this girl's kind of into me and stuff, and uh—"

Just as I was about to lose the crowd, Christian jumped in to save me: "Basically he fucked the shit out of her!" he said. Christian knew that wasn't the real story and that we never had sex, but he also knew that the story required that ending.

The team looked back at me and eagerly awaited some form of confirmation. I scanned their eyes.

"And the next morning, I found out she had a boyfriend," I said. "So her roommates kicked me out, and that's why I'm here a week early."

They burst out with a big roar of laughter and a bunch of 'attaboys' and 'fuck yeahs.' I chuckled and let go of some of the tension in my chest.

"Was she hot?" one guy asked.

"Yeah," I said.

"How were her tits?" asked another.

"Big," I said. "Big and nice."

I was supposedly there as a writer, but the only two words I could come up with to describe her breasts were "big" and "nice"? I probably could have done better than that. But these guys clearly didn't care about my writing ability. In this entire hallway of baseball players, I counted a grand total of one book, and it was written by Tucker Max.

I joined in with the laughter and let their approval wash over me. Perhaps I hadn't misbehaved at USC. Perhaps my behavior was just fine.

Everybody needs a role model. The guy who entered the room next would soon become Billy's. He played baseball at another school and was just visiting for the weekend, but he used to go to Charlton, so he still knew some of the guys on the team. He was a few years older than these guys, who were mostly sophomores, and was something of a legend to them. Until he entered, Billy had ruled the room with the best stories. But Billy's reign soon ended. As this guy spoke, everybody stopped what they were doing (even the Xbox was paused, which I never saw happen again). He told stories about prostitutes in Japan, about having sex with an army wife by accident, about being walked in on by his girlfriend while having sex with another girl, and more. All of the stories were two to three years old, however. Now he was monogamous with a new girl and was planning to marry her soon. That aspect of his life wasn't wild or crazy, so in order to not disappoint the crowd, he passed around a photo on his phone of her naked breasts—just a closeup shot of two breasts. The polite thing to do was to compliment his fiancé's breasts before passing the phone.

"Goddamn," one player said.

"Those are some bombs," said another.

"Some big titties right there," said a third.

When the phone reached me, I said, "Very nice," which seemed to be good enough.

And then he was gone. He left at the peak of our interest. The team then slumped back into homework and Xbox. Billy, however, stared up in wonderment. He didn't go back to work. These dorms were laid out like apartments, so there was a communal room and two bedrooms, but each dorm had three roommates, which forced one roommate to sleep in the communal area. Billy was the roommate who slept in the communal room of this dorm, so he was lying across his bed in the back of the room. With all the guys facing the

TV on the opposite side of the room, Billy seemed sort of lonely behind them. He was loud, talkative, and offensive, but somehow he never had anybody's full attention.

"Oh my God," Billy said. "I'm so glad he doesn't go here. I would be finished."

"What do you mean you'd be finished?" I asked.

"I'd just be done. His stories are better than mine. I'm seriously wondering if I'll ever live up to that." He kept staring at the ceiling, alone in the back of the room. None of the players responded.

Sometime later, one player asked the first serious question of the night.

"You guys think there are going to be cuts next year?"

"There have to be. There are 15 recruits."

"Who might get cut?"

Names were suggested, and some of the guys in the room were candidates to be cut. Nobody took it personally.

"What sort of cuts?" I asked the group.

"A team can only have 37 players," said Chris, the guy who had turned down the million-dollar signing bonus. "Our coach recruited 15 freshmen to come play next year, so they'll have to cut from the older guys, and that's us."

Chris didn't talk much. He was the team's best player and kind of a strong, silent type. But he was talking now.

"What happens if you get cut?" I asked.

"Well, you probably either go to Junior College or just bang it," he said. (Bang it meant to quit.) "But the thing about baseball is that most people can't quit. So if you get cut, you'll either go to JC or take a year off and try again."

"They can't quit because they love it so much?" I asked.

The question seemed sort of obvious or dumb after I'd asked it, but the team didn't take it that way. They nodded or said, "Yep," though more to themselves than to me. The Xbox soon was shut off and the guys stood to collect their things; it seemed that I had prompted the end of the night. Nobody was drunk or aggressive like Christian had warned. Practice was early in the morning.

"Most guys who are still playing baseball started off incredibly young," said Chris, "and they basically played all day, every day from that point on. It's all they know. How could you quit?"

In the morning, I walked to class with Christian and Billy. Both of them were too busy with baseball to put much focus into academics. Billy repeated the old "C's and D's get degrees" adage. It was the last day of classes before the Charlton students would leave for spring break, but not the baseball players, who had games scheduled throughout the week. Christian explained that fraternities and athletes don't get along at Charlton. The fraternities think the athletes are stupid; the athletes think the fraternity members are "pieces of shit." Fraternities, however, rule the school, and most of the students wouldn't recognize the names of the superstar athletes, although they would certainly recognize the name of a fraternity president. He said a girl will ask, "What house are you in?" and if a guy is in the same fraternity that her dad was in, it is a good sign she will like him. Girls here are looking for guys like their dads, Christian said. Charlton is a school run by elitists who accept mainly the children of elitists, Christian said. The long point he was making was that college sports were so time consuming that the athletes had no time to capitalize on what little glory that being an athlete gave them.

After their financial accounting class, Christian and Billy saw a girl they knew who was headed the other direction.

"Coming to our game?" Christian asked.

"I'm heading home!" she said.

"She's a fair weather fan," Billy joked.

"Yeah, support us when we're up," said Christian," but when we stop producing, you leave us in the dust!"

Afterward, they left for baseball practice, and I split up with them. Their coach, who the players refer to simply as Coach, was mad at Christian for missing a tutoring session for one of his classes. Coach stays involved in the players' lives and calls and texts them frequently. Christian told me that freshman year, Coach would call him early in the morning, saying, "How are you? Are you awake?

Have you showered and brushed your teeth? Eaten breakfast? Good," then hang up.

When practice had ended, the guys were exhausted and said they had their asses beat by Coach. They were chewed out for 30 minutes then spent the rest of practice doing brutally exhausting defensive drills.

"I need to rail some pussy," said Billy. We were headed to the cafeteria. "I need to rail pussy about twice a week to stay satisfied."

"Spring break is coming up, right?" I asked. "All the girls are about to leave, what are you going to do?"

"I know," he said. "I have 24 hours before one girl leaves." It was the same girl he said he might skip class for in order to "rail some ass."

At the cafeteria, we met with Julie, the girl who gave all the old tests to the baseball team. She was one of the team's managers. According to Billy, she didn't often sleep with the baseball players but she had "fucked the whole basketball team." Billy didn't filter his language around her, and our conversation about Billy's sexual habits continued.

"I end up boning way fewer girls during the baseball season," said Billy.

"Me too," said Christian.

"Why's that?" I asked.

"We're too busy to go to parties and we're not really supposed to drink," said Billy.

"Why don't you guys just get girlfriends?" Julie asked.

"I'm not good enough," said Billy. "Girls don't see me as a boyfriend type. I don't like having sex too much during the season anyway. I can't get sucked off or fuck within about ten hours of pitching or I lose my competitive spirit."

"I hooked up with a guy on the team," Julie said, "and the next game, he hit two homeruns."

Billy ignored her. "I just need to get out of my slump," he said. "I'm paying like $45,000 a year to go to this school, I better have some awesome stories to tell my son. My dad called me freshman year to ask if I was getting any pussy."

"What'd you tell him?" I asked.

"I said, 'Yeah.' He said I'll never have a better time to score so much pussy."

"And are you taking advantage of that?"

"Oh yeah," he said.

"Billy has no standards," said Christian. "On the quantity vs. quality spectrum, Billy is entirely on the quantity side."

"It's true," said Billy. "I get fucked up and don't really care who I'm sleeping with. And I won't wear condoms, so I'm usually only with the sluts who don't make me wear condoms."

"The girls don't stop you?" I asked.

"No. I don't ever ask if they want me to wear one, and they never bring it up."

"You ever been tested?"

"For STDs?"

"Yeah, for STDs."

"Honestly," he said, "I don't want to know."

That night the group that usually gathered to play Xbox instead gathered for the first meeting of an unofficial fraternity they were forming: Beta Alpha Sigma, 'BAS' for short, as in 'baseball.' Christian and Billy were the president and vice president, respectively. (By the way, this "fraternity" did not last for more than a week after I left Charlton.)

Billy kicked off the meeting. "Alright, alright everybody! Quiet down! First thing's first— no Blacks, and no Jews!"

"Fuck you!" one of the black guys yelled.

About 15 baseball players were sitting and listening to Billy, who stood elevated on a chair. Some of the guys in the room were black, and it was obvious that they'd be accepted into the fraternity. They were also apparently used to Billy's racist jokes.

"Ok, second," he continued, "I'm the vice president. Christian is the president. Nolan is treasurer. Neal's in too, but I don't know what he is yet. Anyone else who wants to join has to watch gay porn while he drinks six beers without getting a boner."

"Oh, fuck you!" another guy yelled.

"No, no," said Christian, "to get in you just need to buy a case of beer. Also, if anybody gets too drunk at one of our meetings, they have to pay $5 to sleep on the couch, and that goes to beer funds."

"I'm in charge of the money, right?" asked Nolan.

"Yes," said Christian. "You'll run things. Me and Billy basically just sit back and oversee everything, and you will take care of all the operations."

Nolan nodded, not quite understanding that he was accepting all of the responsibility and none of the power.

"Ok, and on to parties," Christian said. "We're going to throw some cool parties, but we need girls. So me and Nolan will be quality and Billy will be quantity. Got it?"

The guys nodded.

"Cool," one player said, "So, what do we do now?"

Christian thought for a moment, then said, "Now we just hang out like usual."

I knew that Christian would be quitting the team soon, so I thought that maybe this was his attempt to keep a formal bond of friendship with the rest of the guys after he quit. The baseball team spent all of their time together, so not only would the sport be hard to quit, Christian would also be separating himself from his only friends.

"Hey man, could you wake up?" Christian said. "We might have to go to the ER."

I scratched my eyes. "What?"

It was morning now.

"Birch—you haven't met him yet—is in the ER," said Christian. "I'm not sure what happened. He got fucked up last night and assaulted some girls then passed out and got arrested."

Christian called Birch in the ER and put the phone on speaker for me to hear.

"I was pouring drinks out havin' a good time," said Birch from the hospital, "and it was time to walk back to my dorm, and I somehow woke up in the ER. They said I was walking back, and they found me passed out, and so they took me to the ER."

Birch didn't need a ride quite yet, so Christian and I walked to the cafeteria for breakfast. All the usual guys were there, minus Billy. The team was having a big discussion about Birch.

"Fuck! He's definitely going to be kicked off the team," said Christian. "Damnit. All I know is that this is the last thing we need."

"Why wasn't he with us last night?" Nolan asked. "We should have had him there with us so this couldn't happen."

"He was Code 139— belligerently shoving two girls and aggressively hitting on another."

"My parents were alcoholics, so I know what's up," said Neal. "We shouldn't have let him keep drinking like that. We should have talked to him."

One of the guys turned to me and explained, "Birch came from a super sheltered family with really strict parents. He hadn't done anything before he got to college, and he started drinking and just started getting fucked up all the time. He was opened to a whole new world and became a straight alcoholic."

"We should have talked to him," said Christian. "All I know is that we're fucked if he gets kicked off the team."

"If Birch gets kicked off the team, it'll be the end of his life," said Neal.

"How so?" I asked.

"He's one of our best pitchers. So he'll go to the Junior Leagues, and they don't drug test in the Junior Leagues. He can't control himself after only one drink, so the pressure would just be too much for him."

Billy was not at breakfast—he was still sleeping. Christian and I went to his room to wake him up.

"I heard Birch got in trouble?" Billy asked.

"Yeah, no shit," said Christian. "We might have to get him from the ER."

"Coach called me and asked if I was with him."

Christian explained the story to Billy, who sat on his bed with his head in his hands, occasionally saying, "Goddamnit." Birch getting kicked off the team meant he'd leave Charlton, and the guys would never see him again.

Billy said, "It's gonna be different, man. I guess it hasn't really hit me yet. I guess it'll hit me when I just stop seeing him."

Then Birch texted Christian from the ER: "I think I'm just going to pack my things and head back to Knoxville."

Christian told him, "At least talk to Coach first."

By now it was lunch time, and nobody had spoken of anything but Birch. Everybody shared some sense of responsibility. The consensus was that they should have had an intervention with him before it happened, since they had all recognized his problem.

Then around 1pm, Christian got another text from Birch: "Still here, baby."

Christian stepped out and called him. Birch would stay at Charlton and remain officially part of the team, but he wouldn't practice or play until he went to Alcoholics Anonymous to get healthy. "You can play once you're healthy," is what Coach told Birch. This was great news for the team, but it would still be a struggle for Birch.

The guys in Billy's room sat around playing Xbox, still taking blame for his behaviors.

"I wonder how he ever let himself get that way," Christian said. "How could he get so fucked up before a game day?"

"That's the thing about being an athlete," Billy said from the back of the room. "Everyone says, 'Oh, you're an athlete, you get to do what you love,' but really you're not doing what you love. You're doing what you're good at."

That morning I had received a text from my mom that said, "Hey Drew, just making sure you're ok. Are you in Charlton yet? I heard there might be tornados in that area. Just be careful!"

That day there were tornadoes near Charlton. It was the last day before spring break, as well as a game day for the baseball team. The team had left for their game while I was still in Christian's room.

Outside, tornado sirens blared. Some sort of horrible storm was about to pass by.

I walked outside to look around. A few groups of students were running inside covering their heads with books. A security guard yelled at me to go back inside, so I turned back into the dorms. The students who had just gone inside waited at the elevator, headed down, so I joined them. The elevator opened into a long basement hallway, an underground tunnel. It was a passage between two dorms that was currently serving as a tornado shelter. Lined up along the walls were hundreds of students sitting with laptops, cell phones, and books. At the end of the hall, you could see outside through an upstairs window. Heavy rain now fell, and violent, snapping wind howled. New students, progressively more wet with each new load, came out of the elevator to join us. With nobody to talk to, I paced up and down the halls, stepping over the outstretched legs of the students.

Nearly everybody was on the phone with their parents. The calls were littered with the words "mom" and "dad" and "scary." My impression then shifted from viewing us as mature adults to recognizing the truth: we were just kids. When there was danger, we thought of our parents first, even if they were back across the country and couldn't help. I was too stubborn to contact my parents first, but they would still contact me, and I'd respond. You can run away from home, but you still have to ignore your mom's texts.

The storm eventually passed, and the students returned to ground level. Outside there was hail on the ground, but no tornado had been anywhere near us. I eavesdropped on one girl's frantic phone call:

"Hi Dad we had a tornado it was so scary. Meredith came into my room and we were like walking and then it was hailing and it got really really windy, like really really bad, so we were like, 'Maybe we should go to the basement,' and like everyone was in the basement and it was really really scary."

She was quiet for a moment as she listened to her father's voice.

"Dad," she said, "you're not being very sympathetic."

The baseball game had been canceled due to the weather, so I met with some of the baseball team at a burrito place.

"Did your parents call you guys about the tornado?" I asked.

All of them had received calls from their parents telling them to be safe and stay inside. Billy walked in a minute later, and I asked the same question.

"Nah, my parents don't give a shit," Billy said. He was the only one who hadn't received a call.

For the rest of the day, the guys played more Xbox baseball. They played video game baseball just like real baseball, making frequent player substitutions, almost never stealing bases, and hitting conservatively. There was a lot of bunting; the game was oddly serious. Billy was in the back of the room on his bed. He never played the whole week I was there. Instead he always sat alone.

"So what went wrong on Monday with Cassandra?" Christian asked Billy. Cassandra was the girl Billy was going to skip class for so he could sleep with her. He had in fact skipped class and met up with her, but they did not have sex.

"I don't even know," said Billy.

"Tell me about Cassandra," I said.

"Cassandra is the girl Billy's in love with," said Christian.

"I'm not in love with her," said Billy.

"Oh, yes you are."

"You're in love with Liz."

"I am definitely not in love with Liz."

"Yeah, and I'm not in love with Cassandra."

"Ok, then neither of us are in love." Christian looked at me. "Billy just wants to fuck Cassandra."

"And Christian just likes to fuck Liz."

"Good."

"Good."

"What happened on Monday, then?" I asked Billy.

Christian answered. "She wanted to fuck, but he couldn't do it."

"I don't know how to push the boundaries when I'm sober," said Billy.

"She said she wanted to fuck, and you said, 'No'?" I asked.

"No, but I could tell she was down to fuck—I just couldn't make it happen sober."

"Have you had sex before while sober?"

"No, I guess not," Billy said.

Billy had had a lot of sex, but never once had he done it sober. It was sad in a way.

"You could have had sex with her if you wanted," said Christian.

"I know. I don't know why I didn't. I guess I was just scared to," said Billy.

The conversation ended as Christian's attention shifted back to the TV. The Xbox game had gone into extra innings, and the guys were particularly animated—screaming, jumping up and down, hitting each other. Billy didn't let the game excite him though. He lay on his bed behind the action with his fingers interlocked behind his head, his eyes wistfully searching for answers on the ceiling.

The volume in the room dropped between each pitch. Billy sat up and continued talking.

"You know what my biggest fear is?" he said to nobody in particular. "When rich girls take guys home to meet their parents, what do they expect them to do? Like, if Cassandra takes me to meet her parents, and they try to ask about my socioeconomic class or whatever, what do I say?"

The room stayed quiet for a few heartbeats. Then somebody hit a line drive and scored a run off third base. The room exploded into jovial cheers. High fives were given all around, except for Billy, who again put his hands behind his head and lay on his back. The loser of the game gave his controller to the next guy waiting to play, and another game started. Billy let out a long breath. Nobody said anything.

Old folks with blankets sat scattered across the seats of the Charlton baseball field. The Charlton students had left campus for spring break, so the game had one of the smallest crowds of the year, primarily made up of the elderly. Charlton played a double-header and won both games with ease. The first game was 6-0 after only the first inning. Each player has his own "walk out song," which plays for a few seconds as he walks from the on-deck circle to the plate. I'd heard some of the guys take their songs very seriously, like, "Hey man, I'm thinking about going with Drake this week. What do you think?" I had never much cared for baseball, but the games were exciting to watch since I'd met many of the players.

Afterward we went out to eat. The guys made a ruckus and played around by shooting spit balls at each other. That night the BAS fraternity had their first chapter meeting to celebrate the win. Campus was a ghost town. Despite their lofty ambitions for the night (which involved all trying to get laid), there were no girls for miles, and even so, the team had practice early the next morning. What took place was not much different from their typical nights. Here's a rundown of what they did to celebrate:

They bought two cases of beer. Nolan, the treasurer, tried to collect $10 from everybody, but nobody gave him any money. Neal, who gets picked on the most, was "Iced" with a pint of Smirnoff Ice, so he chugged it until he was teary eyed and had to quit without finishing, so everybody punched him. One guy had another guy pop a zit on his ass, and everybody cheered. Billy shoved the end of his penis into a shot glass and left it hanging there. Xbox baseball was on the whole night. One guy said he doesn't understand lesbians because "girls need dick to be happy." Everybody disagreed with him. Once Neal was a little bit drunk, he looked at pictures of his ex-girlfriend and said, "I miss her more than anything. She's my best friend." He was notorious for his sensitivity, and everyone teased him. Eventually Christian said, "Well guys, I feel like a brotherhood now," then left for bed. I followed behind. It was 10:30pm.

The following day was a lazy one. We lounged around, ate big meals, played more Xbox. Christian and I went to a barber for haircuts, and we both asked for "the George Clooney." In the evening, we drove to see a movie, then went out to eat again. It was Christian, Billy, Nolan, and Neal.

"What are your goals?" Nolan asked me between bites of his burger.

"My goals? I'm not sure."

"Like, you're not going to college. Why?"

"Well, I guess right now I'm working on this book. If I were in college, I couldn't be here."

"But what about success? Don't you need success first before your passions? If you go to college and do well, you're guaranteed success. For you, it's like you're putting your passion before your success."

"What do you mean by success?"

"I know success isn't money, but that's part of it. You need to be stable before you can go after your passion. You have one life to live, how can you take that risk?"

A few years later I would agree with Nolan, but at the time I was filled with naive optimism and a touch of grandiosity.

"I see it the opposite way," I said. "I'd say, you have one life to live, how can you not take that risk?"

"So, you should chase your passions, even if it means you don't get success?"

"I don't think it's one way or the other," I said.

Christian chimed in. "My dad would always say, 'How big is your sack?' I have my quarter life crisis coming up. I'll have to decide between trying to get a big consulting job—success—or trying to start my own business—passion. The question is, how big is my sack? Right now Drew already made his big-sack decision, but who knows, he might get fucked by it."

"There's a huge chance I get fucked by it," I said, "or at least waste a ton of time. But I try not to think about it."

"That's like baseball," Christian said. "Baseball is about being relaxed and confident. It's not about being successful, it's about being the least unsuccessful. So a .300 batting average is great, but you're still missing 7/10 times. So when you're on a losing streak, you think, 'We need to hit more,' but you really need to think, 'We need to miss less.'"

"Baseball is a great metaphor for life," said Nolan.

"Oh yeah, it's the best one," said Christian. "How about this one: baseball can lull you to sleep; it's routine and monotonous; run to the same base each time, first, second, third; but in that routine there are a lot of variables, like the ball hits a different way, a funny hop; in life's routine you have to constantly make little adjustments; so the key to life is to look for the variables and recognize them."

"Or how you have to break the routine sometimes to take big opportunities," said Nolan. "Or another is that you can do everything right, like hit a line drive right up the middle, but it can still be caught by a center fielder."

"Or the opposite of that, where you can screw up, and sometimes it still works out," said Christian.

"Exactly," said Nolan. "I used to worry a lot about scouts and sometimes choke up for a game. My dad looked at me and said, 'Nolan, don't worry about things that are out of your control. That will be your demise.'"

"Another thing my dad says is, 'Often times in business and in life it's better to be lucky than good.'"

"How often do you think of your personal lives in the context of baseball?" I asked.

"Always," said Nolan.

"Yeah, pretty much always," said Christian.

The next morning a group of players ate at a local diner. Most of them took a big handful of pain pills along with their breakfasts. Chris's pills filled up his palm, and he dumped them into his mouth all at once before washing them down with a quick swallow of water. Christian had many pills of his own; he had told me that part of his wanting to quit baseball was because it was too hard on his body, which had been injured in one way or another for as long as he could remember.

"So, how many people are going to get cut?" one player asked.

"Probably seven or eight," another said.

"Coach, I swear to God," said Nelson, the guy who had been elected the social chair of their fraternity, "if you cut me off the team my senior year, I will burn down the field, burn down your house, fuck your daughters, and fuck your wife."

"Do you guys pay tuition here?" I asked.

Christian gave me a look that told me it was an inappropriate question to ask.

"There are 11 full scholarships to give out for baseball players," Christian said.

I understood the message: 37 players and 11 scholarships meant that the majority of the guys I met were paying full tuition to play baseball, even though most of them had no future in it after college.

"Got it," I said.

Near the end of the week, Christian and I were sitting alone in his dorm room.

"I learned more in a year of college than in my entire high school life," Christian said. "It wasn't a total 180, but it was a severe adjustment. You're exposed to a lot more of your flaws in college, because in high school, there's always a place to go home to where people love you unconditionally, but in college, everything is conditional. You're only as good as you were the previous night."

"Even among the guys on the baseball team?" I asked.

"What do you mean?"

"Your friends here might not love you unconditionally like your parents do, but it's not like they're going to start hating you if you're less than awesome one night."

"Yeah, that's true."

"Do you have many friends here outside baseball?"

"Actually, not really. I guess you just spend all your time with the guys, so that's how it goes."

"What are they going to think when you quit? Will they understand?"

"I hope so."

Something unfortunate and mildly traumatic happened to me at the end of the week. For years, I had omitted this story from the book —Christian practically begged me not to write about it—but ultimately, I decided to include it. In a week full of overwhelming male sexuality, I found myself one night on the receiving end of its harmful aspects.

My host Christian thought of himself as some sort of businessman, and he was always trying to network. He had become acquainted with a recently divorced middle-aged man in Charlton who was apparently a big-shot music producer, and he wanted to deepen the connection. We spent two nights of my stay at Charlton over at this man's house. I think Christian's motive was two-fold: he wanted to impress the music producer by showing him that he had a writer writing about his life, and he wanted to impress me and the readers of this book by showing us that he was hanging around a big-shot music producer.

The first night was fine. We sat for a couple hours drinking some nice liquor and having a normal conversation. The big-shot music producer, named Joey, was not exactly the spitting image of a great success: he was short, overweight, bald, a bit awkward, and sloppily dressed, but he was an inviting and charismatic host, and Christian and I tried our best to impress him. At one point, Joey asked me how I would direct a particular music video for a band who was his client. I thought for a few minutes, then gave him the best answer I possibly could. He appeared to be moved and inspired by my response. Since he knew that I was an aspiring writer who also did work as a free-lance videographer, he gave some vague hints that he might actually hire me to direct the music video. It was as if I had given such a good answer and displayed such a profound vision that I was now his number one choice. I didn't think this was very likely, but neverthe-less I felt myself warm to him, thinking that I might someday become an important and valued person because of this new connection. Christian even seemed to be proud of himself that he was the person facilitating our meeting. Joey suggested that we come back to his house later in the week when it would be his 44th birthday, and we told him we would. (By comparison, Christian was only 19, and I was 20.) When we left for the night, Joey shook my hand with his right hand, then put his left hand on my shoulder and slid it down to my lower back for a brief moment. I had a glimmer of thought that he might be gay, which of course was fine, and then I thought nothing more of it. Christian and I drove back to campus with boosted self-esteems: we had just rubbed shoulders with a successful music producer, he liked us, and we both had the happy feeling that we were going to become successful one day. Christian kept the details of what we were doing hidden from the baseball team, as if we were engaging in some top-secret business deal-making or something.

The next time we saw Joey, the night had a different ending. This time the three of us watched a movie, again while drinking nice liquor. Throughout the movie, Joey would ask us if we were ready for new drinks, we'd say yes, then he'd grab our glasses, take them to the kitchen, and come back with them filled. Christian and I were existing in a reality where we were three businessmen engaging in the manly custom of trying to out-drink one another—some sort of power game where we were supposed to display our alcohol toler-ance like we had seen in movies and TV. One of the times when Joey went into the kitchen, I glanced behind me and saw that when he was making our drinks, two of the glasses were filled to the brim with whiskey and only had a splash of soda, whereas one of the glasses just had a splash of whiskey and mostly soda. At the time, I found this almost endearing—it meant that Joey was a light-weight, and he was embarrassed that he couldn't drink as much as us kids. But again, I didn't put much thought into this; I was busy watching the movie. I was also used to drinking cheap whiskey, so I always knew how strong a drink was by how awful it tasted; but these drinks were going down smooth, and I couldn't judge how strong they were. Also during the movie, Christian and I would step outside into Joey's backyard to piss. I found out from Christian the next day that the reason he was doing this was so he could pour out the whiskey, since the drinks were so strong. But at the time, Christian gave me no hint that he was doing this. Instead of pouring my drinks out like Christian, I was taking advantage of the free alcohol and drinking my whole drink each time. I remember one of these times in Joey's backyard, I was dying of laughter with Christian about how drunk I was. We were both very happy. I paid no attention to how I was going to drive us home. Since there was an adult present, I felt protected from danger.

When the movie ended, I stood up, walked over to Joey's piano, and tried to play. I could usually play the piano while drunk, but this time, I had absolutely no finger coordination. My vision was blurry, and I could hardly see anything. I remember bashing the piano keys with my hands, and even laying my head on the keys. When I tried to speak, my lips felt huge and blubbery, and I couldn't form articulate words. I'd been extremely drunk before, but this was never a symptom.

I lost consciousness and woke up in a new place. I was lying on my back on top of a bed in a dark room. Joey was sitting upright next to me, and his hand was rubbing my upper thigh through my jeans. He'd rub my thigh for a while, then move his hand over to my limp penis for a while, then move back to my thigh. It's not exactly that I was conscious while this was happening—it was more like I woke up and gradually became aware that this had been going on for at least a few minutes. As soon as I became aware of what was happening, I used all the energy I had to mutter the word, "No," then I rolled over onto my side. Joey stood up and walked to the doorway, where he stood menacingly for a long 15 minutes while facing my direction. I didn't know why he was standing there, but I desperately wanted him to leave. I didn't have any strength to move, but I stayed awake to see if he would come back toward me. Eventually he walked away, and I fell back asleep.

I jolted awake sometime later in the night, and this time I was as clear-headed and lucid as I had ever been. I was now willing to become violent, if necessary. The previous memory was extremely blurry, but I remembered it. I needed to find out what was going on. I walked down the stairs, went out the front door toward my car, and saw that it was gone. I reached into my pocket and noticed that my keys were also missing. I went back into the house and went looking for Christian, but I couldn't find him anywhere. Joey was sleeping on the couch in the living room. I'd never called a taxi before, and this was a couple years before ridesharing apps became popular, so I wasn't sure how I would get back to Charlton campus. I felt stuck at Joey's house.

I sent Christian a barrage of texts in panicky all-caps. I've since lost the exact texts, but they were something like, "WHAT THE

FUCK DUDE I THINK JOEY JUST TOUCHED MY DICK. WHERE ARE YOU DUDE I THINK JOEY JUST TOUCHED MY FUCKING DICK DUDE."

But it was 4am, so Christian never answered my texts. Here's what had happened (I learned this from Christian the next day): Once I started trying to play the piano, Joey convinced Christian that I was so drunk that I needed to stay at his house while Christian drove back to campus, and he said that he would drive me home in the morning. This didn't make any sense, but Christian went along with it. Joey reached into my pocket, pulled out my car keys, and gave them to Christian so he could drive himself home in my car (Christian was extremely drunk, too, but this didn't seem to matter to anyone). This left me alone with Joey, unconscious in his house.

At one point in the night, when I was still looking for Christian, Joey was sitting upright on the couch.

"What's going on?" I asked.

"You were very drunk," Joey said.

"Where's Christian?"

"He left."

"Why didn't I go with him?"

Joey didn't answer the question. Instead he said, "It must feel weird, waking up in a strange place."

Joey told me that he'd drive me back to Charlton campus in the morning. Unfortunately, I felt forced by circumstances to accept his offer. I never confronted him about what happened—I was too confused, and I didn't think there was a point. At no point did I fear for my safety—mostly it was just awkward. I got the feeling that Joey didn't think I would remember what happened. I went back to the bedroom and sat awake on the bed until the sun rose. During this time, I sent Christian a surprisingly reasonable text, which I still agree with: "In the grand scheme of unwanted sexual contact, this was not that bad."

In the morning, Joey gave me a ride back to campus. In the car, the full weight of my consciousness was directed out the window as I eagerly awaited what felt like my freedom. I did have a sense of humor about the whole thing, even as it was going on. Near the end of this car ride—the most uncomfortable car ride of my life, by a wide margin—I found myself choking back laughter as I imagined just how unamused my face was going to look the next time someone suggested that they introduce me to a supposed "big-shot."

Christian and I spent the morning trying to figure out what happened. Was I roofied, or was it just alcohol? We never figured it out. We were both in shock about the whole thing—alternating between fits of laughter and head-in-hands despair. Christian was not exactly apologetic, but he did seem extremely embarrassed for himself, and he kept laughing while saying, "Dude, you definitely can't write about this. No way, man, no way." At some point that day, Joey texted Christian and told him not to ask me about the previous night. According to Joey, I vomited on his carpet, and I might be embarrassed about it, so it was best that Christian doesn't ask me any questions about what happened that night. I feel fairly certain that I didn't vomit, so I think this was just a bad attempt by Joey to protect himself.

In the end, having my penis fondled for a minute was not so big of a deal. What was harder to cope with was the fact that my model of reality had been so wrong. I thought one thing was happening at this man's house, when in reality something else entirely was going on. As a 20-year-old, I thought that only other people were naive, and that I had a particularly high degree of wisdom and life experience. But I had to learn that that wasn't true. I was fooled, tricked, duped, and I had to accept that. Today I approach similar situations with more caution and less alcohol. I also have no trust whatsoever for anyone who makes vague promises of future glory, and I don't allow myself to warm to them the way I did with Joey. "Maybe we'll hire you to direct this famous band's music video." "Maybe we'll invest money in your company." Yeah, I'll believe it after we sign the paperwork.

(I should add here that my experience wasn't nearly as bad as it could have been, and even so, I still experienced it as traumatic, and it took me years to process and accept what happened. I did not fear for my physical safety, Joey stopped immediately when I said, "No," and everyone I told the story to believed me immediately. Some people are assaulted or raped by others who are physically intimidating and dangerous, the assailant doesn't stop when the victim says, 'No,' and they don't just merely graze the outside of a person's genitals through their clothes—they forcibly remove their clothes and penetrate them —and then, when the victim tells their story, people don't believe that it really happened that way—they say, "Are you sure you didn't want it? Are you sure it wasn't consensual, and you're just changing your mind later?" I can't begin to imagine how terrible this would feel, and I know that these experiences are utterly common. By comparison, what happened to me was not a very big deal.)

Another interesting thing to note is that for a few years after this happened, I was completely convinced that this would be a secret that I'd keep for the rest of my life. It seemed profoundly shameful and emasculating to be the recipient of unwanted sexual contact from another man. I was even convinced that if this story got out, women would no longer be willing to sleep with me. I only started to change my mind years later after I told a therapist, and she didn't shame me in any way. She didn't even flinch—I guess therapists hear stories like this all the time. I then wrote the story down in this chapter and sent it to a few women friends. I was fearful that they would laugh at me or see me as weak and pathetic after they read it. But to my surprise, the next time I met up with each of them in person, they seemed to like me more, not less, than before. "Hm, I guess it's ok!" I thought.

That same morning, a few hours before I was going to leave town, I was told that I absolutely had to come hear about Billy's night. He had been talking about it all morning with the team during practice, and it was decided among them that the "book guy" had to come document it to share it with posterity. So I met them again at the burrito place and joined Billy, Christian, Neal, and Nolan in a booth. I used my phone's audio recorder, so this is his long story, transcribed verbatim:

"You're not going to fucking believe a goddamn word I say. I'm gonna say that right now. This story is so fucked up that it can't be made up. Ok? So, me and Porter were like, 'Hey, let's go downtown and hang out for a while and do our thing.' Everyone's getting turned down for their fakes and stuff. So we're like, 'Fuck.' So we try one more place, and they're the toughest on IDs in Charlton. So everyone gets turned down, but we get in. So we're like, 'Ok, let's party, then we'll go home.' And we fuckin' get shitfaced."

Everyone else had already heard the story earlier that morning. They all sat listening with big smiles, glancing back and forth between Billy and me so they could see how I was reacting.

"So, we go back outside, and there was this guy with all these roses on the street, and we get a bunch of roses. And we see these two girls, and I start talking to one, and I was like, 'Hey, you want a rose?' or whatever, like hitting on her, and I look over, and Porter's talking to this girl trying to give her a rose, and she's, like, feeling him up through his shirt and shit, and we're talking or whatever, and I'm like, 'What are you doing tonight?' and anyway, she's like, 'Well, let's go back to your place,' and I say, 'Naw, let's go back to your place, I have too many roommates,' and she's like, 'I have roommates too,' and I go, 'Who is it?' and she looks over at the exact same girl who's feeling up Porter, and she's like, 'That's my roommate,' and I'm like, 'That's really funny, that's my best friend, I think we should go back with you,' and she was like, 'Alright, fine,' so we go back to their place. $27 in the cab. I didn't pay a goddamn dime. Me and Porter look at each other, watching the thing like roll up, and we look at each other, and we're like, 'Dude, we're not paying a goddamn dime for this fucking cab,' and we just walk out of the cab. She pays $27 for the fucking cab. And we get to talking like, 'Oh, what do you do?' and she's like, 'I'm a Charlton nurse.' We kept our identities on the down low."

"So, we get to her place and instantly start fucking, just fucking. Like, we fuck in the living room, her bedroom, the bathroom, her shower, the fucking bathroom floor, kitchen floor, kitchen table, just fucking going at it for like an hour and a half. Anyway, so all the sudden we get up and go to the shower. We're fucking butt-ass naked.

We go into the room where Porter is, and literally all four of us were just fucking each other. It was like a gang bang on this small twin bed. Like, Porter was literally—I'm fucking pounding this girl like this, and Porter was pounding the girl like this, and we're just looking at each other like, 'What the fuck's going on?' and then, we're just like pounding like, 'What the fuck's going on?' and then, that's when we went to the shower. And like, this bitch, I was fucking her in so many different positions, it wasn't even funny. Like, I couldn't get off, she'd gotten off like six fucking times, and she's like, 'Are you gonna go?' and I'm like, 'I'm fucking working on it, quit fucking talking to me and ride my dick,' and so we go back to her room and start fucking again."

It had only been about two hours since the music producer had dropped me off at the Charlton campus. After my experience the previous night, Billy's story took on a bizarre, unreal quality. I tried to be a good sport and act like I was entertained, but really this was the last thing I wanted to listen to.

"Porter fucking walks into the room and lays down on top of me, rolls over, and me and this girl start making out, and he starts fucking sucking on her nipple while I'm making out with her, and I was like, 'We might as well just have a three-way,' and she's like, 'I'm down,' and Porter's like, 'I'm down,' and I'm like, 'I'm more than down.' Dude, we had this fucking look in our eye like we are going to fucking rail the shit out of this bitch. Like, 'We're doing this.' And next thing I know, we're not doing it, he just fucking leaves. And then she's like, 'Ok, well you need to hurry and get off because I'm starting to get dry,' and I'm like, 'Yeah, I fucking know,' and she's like, 'Ok, I have an idea,' and she fucking whips out—this is how much of a slut this bitch was —she had a shit ton of fucking lubes just laying by her bed. So A) either this bitch fingers the shit out of herself all the fucking time, or B) this bitch likes to fuck. So I'm like, 'Alright, whatever,' and that's the first time I've ever used lube, so I just lube my cock, and we start fucking. She gets off again, and I still haven't even gotten off. So I'm like, 'Fuck this shit, dude,' and I just go to pound town. So I fucking put her legs up by her fucking head and just start railing the shit out of her, hard. So, when I finally bust, I just bust this streak all the way up her fucking chest, like this. And like, I just leave it, and like, literally, bust it, then roll over and go to sleep."

"Ok so, morning, my alarm goes off. Porter calls me, and I miss the call. I'm like, 'Fuck, we have shit to do today, I gotta go lift,' and I'm like, 'Where the fuck are you? Where am I?' and he's like, 'I don't know where I am,' and I'm like, 'Where the fuck am I?' and he's like, 'I'm with those girls we went home with,' and I'm like, 'So am I!" and I'm like, 'Where are you?' and he's like, 'I'm in the living room,' so I walk in there, and Porter is laying on the fucking floor just sprawled out. The girl that I was with walks in there and starts laughing, and he's sprawled out and I'm like, 'Holy fuck,' and she's talking or whatever and Porter's like, 'We gotta get the fuck out of here,' so we walk out the door, and all the sudden this bitch, that I was fucking all night, walks out and was like, 'Hey, do you guys need a ride?' and I'm like, 'Well, this is awkward,' but I'm like, 'Yeah, we do need a ride.' And so, we get in her car, and this bitch was being a complete fucking bitch the whole time, so me and Porter were just being complete assholes, like, 'Where the fuck are we?' like, 'How close are we?' like, 'Learn to drive,' just being complete fucking assholes to her. So anyway, here's the best part of the whole fucking night. This is the epitome of what fucking happened. So we're getting out of the car, and all the sudden Porter's getting out, and as soon as Porter's getting out, his ass is facing in the car, and I just hear him—" Billy made a loud fart noise. "Fucking straight rips ass in her car, fucking shuts the car, I shut my door, and just fucking walk off. And this bitch just drives off. Fucking just shit on her bro, it was awesome. It was unbelievable."

Everybody looked at me to await my reaction. Billy had learned to view sex as an adversarial relationship between men and women, and the farting into her car was the final blow—the coup de grâce—at the end of that night's long battle. Billy told us the ending of the story with some belief that we as fellow men would be proud of them for scoring our team one point. I went ahead and gave him the laugh that he wanted. My laughter was a mixture of social politeness, sincere disbelief, and, I admit—even though it was rude and inappropriate behavior that I do not condone—that the whole thing was so ridiculous that I found it a little bit funny.

"I think you've just changed the way I see the world," I said.

They all laughed.

To complicate Billy's sexual behavior slightly, in addition to wanting to conquer and/or humiliate women through the sex act so that he could report the story to the boys, he also had an obsession with cunnilingus, which he called "eating box." (Of all the slang words I've ever heard for vulva or vagina, "box" must be the strangest.) Billy made constant remarks throughout the week about how much he loved to "eat box," which didn't fit neatly into the picture of Billy as a selfish lover only trying to get the better of women for his own satisfaction. It interests me now to know how Billy gives oral sex—whether it's aggressive and combative, or if it's tender and loving—and I think the answer is the key to understanding Billy's character and his real attitude toward women. Unfortunately at the time I did not think to ask.

"Billy, weren't you talking about meeting that girl's parents?" I asked.

"Cassandra?" he asked.

"Yeah, Cassandra. It's just funny to me—like, out of curiosity, when do you think you'll slow down with fucking these random girls and go after, you know, only girls like Cassandra?"

"I have no fucking clue," he said.

"Do you want to get married?"

"Someday, I guess. Not for a long time."

"What's the ideal age? 25? 35? 45?"

"Maybe 30s."

Nolan nodded in agreement.

"What about you, Christian?" I asked.

"Probably younger, mid to late 20s. You know, get out while you're ahead."

Christian had the same philosophy about women as he did with baseball—quit while you're ahead. Even the guy from the first night,

Billy's role model, had eventually given up his lifestyle of reckless sexual pursuits in favor of settling down. I wondered if that would ever happen for Billy, if he would slowly outgrow his current way of life.

After all the talk about marriage, Billy, referring to his story, sighed and said, "You know, I think I told it better earlier."

He would keep retelling this one until he had it all talked out, or until the team quit listening. It wouldn't last forever, but it'd last a good while.

I didn't tell anyone about what had happened with the music producer until years later. Since I was traveling, I just told myself that it was something that happened to me in Charlton, and that once I was out of Charlton, it was behind me. I got into my car, drove away, and didn't think about it anymore.

7

UNIVERSITY OF TENNESSEE

My visit to the University of Tennessee happened by accident. I started to get tired while I was driving through Knoxville, Tennessee, so I pulled into a Walmart parking lot to sleep in my car for the night. As I was falling asleep, I received a text from Randy from Auburn.

"Where you at?" he asked.

"Knoxville," I said.

"You going to the University of Tennessee?"

"Is it in Knoxville?"

"Yeah. My buddy says it's Boxing Weekend. You should check it out."

I googled Boxing Weekend. It was some sort of fraternity boxing tournament, supposedly a huge college event. Damnit, I thought, I guess I have to go.

My hair was gross, so I bought shampoo at the Walmart then left toward campus. I parked along a strip of bars, walked into the bathroom at a fast food fried chicken place, then washed my hair in the bathroom sink. Next I bought two 24oz beers. I hunched down in the back of my car, drank both beers, then changed into nicer clothes.

A little drunk, I walked up and down the strip of bars and got talking to a bouncer about Boxing Weekend. He told me that Boxing

Weekend is a Greek event where each fraternity sends their best fighter to a three-day boxing tournament. Around 5,000 people attend each year, and it's held away from campus at a convention center. The night I was there was the second of the three nights, and I had unfortunately already missed the boxing that night. However, all the Greek guys and girls should be headed back to campus for their after-parties.

"Are they usually open parties?" I asked. "How does it work?"

"You probably need to know someone or be a part of the fraternity," he said.

"Do you know if Tennessee has the fraternity called PBT?" (This is a made-up fraternity name, so they can stay anonymous.)

"Yeah, it does."

The reason I asked about PBT was because a close family friend of mine who is much older than me was once a member of PBT at The University of Texas. I figured he might know how to get into their party, so I gave him a call. He answered drunk.

"Yo, buddy, what's going on?" he asked.

"So I'm in Tennessee, and PBT is having a party here I want to write about. How would I get in?"

"Dude, just tell them you're a PBT."

"Do I need to know anything? Any passwords?"

He tried to explain the secret handshake, but it was extremely difficult to understand over the phone.

"What do you mean the index finger slips *behind* the thumb?" I asked.

"Are you fucking stupid, Drew? *Your* pointer finger goes *behind* his thumb."

"Around his thumb, or over it?"

"Goddamnit, dude, *behind* it!"

"No, no, *behind* it doesn't mean shit if I don't know which way I'm looking from. Anyway, what should I say I'm doing here if they ask? Why would I be in Tennessee?"

"They don't give a shit, but just say you're on spring break or something. Nobody's going to ask you shit at the door. They don't want to talk to you."

"But why would I be showing up alone?"

"I don't know, your friends got lost or something. Nobody cares, you're going to walk right in without talking to anybody."

"Alright, alright. Thanks."

I found my way across campus to Greek Row. The streets were quiet except for the occasional group of students walking past. I walked around looking for the PBT house. Then, nestled on the back end of the street, the PBT house sat waiting for me to enter. The alcohol still in my system soothed my nerves just enough for me to walk up and go to their party. I knocked on the door.

A guy poked his head out without opening the door all the way.

"Hey man, what's up?" I asked.

"Hello?"

"Yo man, I'm a PBT from Texas."

"Cool, what's up?" He opened the door a little wider, and I could see inside the house. I saw no people and heard no music. It was empty.

"Not too much, man, I'm just hanging out," I said.

"Well, you wanna come in?" he asked.

A possibility I hadn't considered had occurred: there was no party at all.

"Cool, man, yeah, sure," I said. I didn't want to go in, but I felt powerless to eject myself from the social context that I had established.

He closed the door behind us. The reality of the situation was setting in: I would either have to tell him the complete truth right now, or lie like hell. Another option was to calmly walk out the front door and then immediately sprint away, but I didn't have the guts to do that.

"So what are you doing here at UT?" he asked.

"The only real UT is Texas," I joked. I had learned at South Carolina that there's a chummy rivalry between USC South Carolina and USC Southern California about who is the 'real USC,' so I figured the same joke might exist between Tennessee and Texas.

"Yeah, yeah," he laughed politely. He wore a big Hawaiian shirt and khaki shorts that cut off at mid-thigh.

"I'm on spring break right now, so I thought I'd check out Boxing Weekend and stuff," I said.

"Cool," he nodded.

Another PBT walked down a distant hallway. The first guy yelled to him.

"Frank! C'mere, this is a PBT from Texas."

Frank walked over, and I traded names with both of them. The first guy was Chuck. Then Frank introduced himself as one of the fraternity's officers, one of the worst people I could meet. He seemed to have a lot of respect.

"What're you doing in Tennessee?" Frank asked.

This was getting more intense, so as a precaution, I started to feign a slur in my speech and speak with extra excitement to indicate being more drunk than I was. If I said something that didn't make sense, I could blame the alcohol.

"We're on spring break, man," I said, "just checking things out."

"I thought you guys go to South Padre for spring break."

"Oh yeah, we do. I'm not going this year though. Fuck it, man."

"Who're you with?" he asked.

"Oh, right. Yeah, my friends got drunk at the bar, so they're all still there. I was trying to come check out some Boxing Weekend stuff."

"Are they PBTs too?"

"Yeah, man, we're all PBTs."

"How many of you guys?"

"Eight." Shit, why did I say eight?

"Big group," he said.

"Yep. Had to caravan. Two cars."

"And you decided to come here for spring break?"

"Nah, we're headed to Panama City Beach."

"Through Tennessee?"

"Yeah, big loop. We picked up a buddy at Oklahoma, now comin' through here, then gonna head down."

"Oh cool, is he a PBT at OU?" Frank asked. He had a tone that made me think he knew the PBTs at Oklahoma pretty well, so I would have to say that my buddy wasn't a PBT at OU.

"Nah, he transferred from Texas," I said. "He was a PBT at Texas but didn't stay active when he went to OU."

"Why would he do that?" Frank asked.

"Shit, man, that's what we said. He's a dumbass."

"Fair enough," he smiled. "What other schools are headed to PCB?"

"Whoever's there, man. We just heard it was wild, wanted to see what it's all about."

There was a lull in the conversation. The guys weren't intentionally interrogating me, just curious to meet another PBT and to figure out why I showed up drunk and alone at their front door at midnight.

"How many guys are in your chapter down there?" asked Chuck.

"It's about 200 or so," I said.

"About?"

"Yeah, something like that, the exact number just changed."

"That's fucking huge. I had no idea you guys were so big. Is that the biggest in the country?"

I had no idea how big fraternities were. "Yeah, we're pretty damn big," I said. "Not sure if we have the most."

Frank nodded. "So what do you guys think of your athletes down there?"

This one I especially had no idea how to answer. I said, "Ah, you know, it's kind of a love/hate relationship."

"Yeah. Same here," said Frank.

Chuck asked the next question with the exact kind of casual tone as all the other questions:

"Are there any black guys in PBT at Texas?"

Again I had no idea, so I took a guess. I said, "Nope."

"Good," he said. "Same here."

I was shocked, but I had to hide how I felt. I pursed my lips and nodded. I would have to reserve my judgment for later.

"There's a half-black legacy here who's rushing," he continued. "We're trying to keep him out."

I was amazed by how easily those words came out. Chuck seemed to have no fear that I might not also be a racist. I had no idea how to respond.

Frank noticed my discomfort and changed the subject. "What's your president's name again? I know I met him at Nationals."

I was glad to move on to a new topic, but this was an extremely tough question. I had no choice but to name a name. "Kyle," I said.

"Hm. No, it wasn't Kyle. I can't think of his name right now."

"Well, it's Kyle."

"He's sort of tall and lanky, right?"

"Nah, I sure wouldn't call him lanky," I laughed.

"You sure?" asked Frank.

Chuck laughed. "Is he a fatass?"

"He's a big guy, yeah," I laughed.

Frank searched his memory. "Weird, because I met him at Nationals, and then I was actually in Austin last year and hung out with him again."

"I don't know, man, you must have met somebody else."

Frank's eyes went wide. "Oh my God, and when I was there they showed me your basement. Jesus."

I had no idea what he was talking about, but I played along. "Oh man, don't even bring up that fucking basement!"

"I can imagine," he said. "How was pledgeship down there?"

"Pretty good, pretty good," I said.

"Pretty good?" he asked, confused. It was clear now that his question really meant, "Tell me, just how awful was pledgeship?"

I corrected myself. "Ah, well, you know, pledgeship. It is what it is, you know? You just do it."

"Yeah, yeah, I feel you."

The front door opened. Both PBTs lost track of our conversation and instead shifted focus to the guy who walked in. It was their boxer, Jonathan, who had won his fight that night and would be fighting in the final rounds tomorrow. He said he needed to sleep early but first wanted to eat, so we all hopped in a car to grab some fast food. I attempted to talk a lot whenever the conversation was about something other than PBT so that my silence would not seem odd when they were discussing the fraternity. I was wearing dark jeans (fraternities are all about white wash jeans), a sports coat, and some brown suede shoes, so I preemptively told them that I'm referred to as the 'hipster' of the fraternity. Eventually the guys invited me to boxing the following night and told me to bring all my PBT buddies for their pregame in the afternoon. I said, "For sure. We'll all be there."

Back at PBT, they let me sleep on one of their couches in the main room. Guys were coming and going from the room all night, and I heard a few ask, "Who's that on the couch?" with the reply, "Some PBT from Texas who stumbled in." It seemed I had done a good enough job with my lying.

That night the fire alarm went off. Everybody had to stand outside on the porch until the police came by and gave us the ok to return. The back window had been smashed, and the police found fresh blood on the glass. But this wasn't of any concern to anybody and appeared to be a regular occurrence. One of the other fraternities, they figured, had smashed the window as an act of boxing rivalry.

In the morning, I awoke on their couch, came to my senses, then bolted out of there before I had to answer any more questions. There was only a slight relief in leaving, however. It all felt unreal. I realized that I had told them I'd be back that afternoon with seven other PBTs from Texas to get drunk at the pregame, then ride on their buses to the boxing tournament. This was, of course, impossible, unless I rounded up seven professional actors, and going back undercover with more lies seemed ridiculous. I just needed to get out of Tennessee.

Sitting in my car, parked far from campus, I called my family friend and told him what happened.

"Dude, you should have gotten your ass kicked," he said with the groggy voice of a whiskey hangover.

"I know, I don't know how I didn't," I said. "Should I go back tonight, or is that suicide?"

"Well, you're writing that book, right? It sounds like you have to go back."

"What am I supposed to say? I told them I'm traveling with a bunch of PBTs."

"Dude, I don't know. If they ask, tell them your buddies met some swampdonks at the bar last night and one of your friends is a total pussy and he's trying to get his dick wet because he hasn't gotten laid in over a year."

"What's a swampdonk?"

"A swamp donkey—an ugly girl. Be like, 'Yeah, my buddies met some DGs and they're trying to get one of my buddies laid because he's a total pussy and hasn't gotten his dick wet in over a year but the chick is a total swampdonk and I wanted to get the fuck away from that situation."

"What's a DG?"

"Jesus, Drew. A girl from Delta Gamma, a sorority. I'm pretty sure your mom was a DG. How do you not know this?"

I took a deep breath. "Fuck."

"Or, you can just get really drunk and avoid all of that conversation," he said.

"What if those guys have looked up the name of the current PBT president at Texas?"

"I don't know, just say you were super wasted last night."

"Yeah, I might have to use that one."

All day as I stayed in Knoxville, I felt terribly paranoid about running into the guys I met the previous night. I ate breakfast at a really expensive diner, figuring it would be the least likely place to see them. I looked online for the list of active PBT members at Texas and tried to memorize a few names in case somehow I was quizzed. I read the "PBT Creed" online and tried to memorize at least the beginning of it. I paced in circles around my car, reciting little segments of speech I might have to use that night: "He was trying to get his dick wet, but she was a swamp donk." "He's tryin' to get his fuckin' dick wet, but she was a total swamp donk." "Fuckin' get his dick wet." "Bitch was a total swamp donk."

I had no conviction. It wasn't working. No amount of preparation settled my anxieties about showing up again at the fraternity house. I drove around the city and wanted to leave, thinking I might drive right then and there to the next school and skip this stupid plan.

But just as I was about to give up, it hit me. Randy's voice echoed in my head—"Put on something fratty." Yes, yes. Put on something fratty. I just needed to look the part. What was the frattiest thing a guy could wear? What one piece of clothing was only ever worn by the badasses of the Greek system? There was only one option. A baseball cap of the specific brand everyone knows, worn backwards. (I won't mention the brand for fear of being sued for associating the brand with racism.) Absolutely everyone in fraternities was wearing this exact hat while I was writing this book. And you had to wear it backwards. Instead of referring to this hat by its brand name, as everyone else did, I will refer to it as a "fraternity hat."

I did a metaphorical fishtail and drove straight to the nearest retail shopping mall. Inside I wandered through the department store looking for the fraternity hats. I couldn't settle for mediocrity here—I had to take this to the max. Across the store, I saw the display case for the hats. As I approached it, a bright yellow hat with a navy logo seemed just a touch brighter than all the rest. I picked it up. Standing in front of a full-body mirror, I held the hat in my hands with the brim sticking back behind me then put it on top of my head and slid it down until it locked into place. My head tilted back, my shoulders relaxed, and my chest reflexively puffed itself out. My hip joints seemed well-oiled, my fingers settled comfortably by my sides with no nervous fidgeting, and I even looked a few inches taller.

I gave myself a smug smile, then said, "Nah, man, I tried to bring 'em to Boxing but one of my buddies is back at the bars tryin' to get laid, which I support, but I didn't want to have anything to do with it."

It was horribly embarrassing, but I thought it might work. I bought the hat.

Now I looked the part, but I would still have to act the part. I bought four beers and a small bottle of whiskey, parked near campus, crawled into the back of my car, then drank all four beers as fast as I could. I wasn't proud of my need to get drunk in order to show up, but I had to do whatever it took to get me to that party. While drinking alone in the back of my car, I sent the same depressing text to two different people. I wrote, "Do we drink to seek pleasure or to avoid pain?" Both people wrote back and said, "Seek pleasure," but I felt I knew the truth.

The pregame had started 30 minutes earlier. As I walked up to the house again, I made sure my shirttail wasn't covering up my whiskey, which stuck fashionably out my back pocket. I would be putting everything I had learned so far on this trip to the test.

The noise from the party came out of the backyard, so I entered through the side gate. I saw lots of other backwards fraternity hats that matched mine. Perfect. A group of guys was standing, beers in hand, in a large semicircle around a few tables set up for beer pong and a few trash cans full of ice and beer. On the opposite side of the yard, some girls were talking amongst themselves. I couldn't find any of the guys I met the previous night, so I walked up to a random guy in a backwards fraternity hat and gave him an upward head nod.

"Hey man, you a PBT?" I asked.

"Yeah, what are you?" he asked.

"I'm a PBT from the real UT."

"Oh shit, Texas?"

"Yeah, man."

As he shook my hand, I could see his estimation of me growing.

I discovered, over the course of many similar conversations, that not only was the University of Texas considered a cool school in general, its PBT chapter in particular was much more respected than the PBT chapter at Tennessee. The guys here were quick to inform me that all the other fraternities at Tennessee looked down on them. The effect of this difference in fraternity status also meant that as an individual I was cooler than them as individuals. I didn't originally expect this, but I embraced it wholeheartedly. I was a badass in their eyes, so I played the part.

"You must throw wild parties down there," one guy said to me.

"Pretty wild," I said, squinting into the sun while taking a little sip of whiskey as if I were parched and it would soothe my throat.

"Damn. And you guys throw a foam party, right?"

"Yep."

"How is it?"

All I did was shoot him a mischievous grin.

"Shiiit," he said, shaking his head in jealousy.

(Let me make one thing clear. None of this was fun in any traditional sense. All I originally aimed to do at Tennessee was to find out about Boxing Weekend, lie briefly about being a PBT just to look inside and observe the party for a few minutes, then leave. I do believe this situation unfolded on its own, and never before or after have I attempted to lie about my identity to get into parties. Every moment of this night was full of stress and the fear of being caught.)

The PBTs were asking me too many questions I didn't know the answers to, so I switched to the other side of the party and talked to the girls. I was already incredibly drunk—I had been so nervous upon arrival that I was practically chugging beer after beer. The backyard had a basketball goal in its center, and after some small talk, I started shooting baskets with one of the girls. Somehow over time, the other girls joined us, and I would rebound their shots and pass the ball back to them. This grew into a rather obnoxious display, where I'd pass one girl the ball and then loudly ask, "What's your name? Karen! I bet you've got a good shot, Karen! Let's see! Oooh, no good!" Meanwhile the semi-circle of guys sipping beer had shifted their attention toward me, looking at the yellow fraternity hat on my head, the whiskey in my hand, and the girls around me. Something occurred to me suddenly: I was playing my role too well—I was the biggest douchebag in the backyard.

While this was going on, Frank, the officer, came into the backyard and walked onto the court.

"Hey man, good to see you," he said. "Where are your buddies?"

"They're meetin' us at Boxing, man! They're with some DGs trying to get laid right now!"

"Ah, good!" he said. He patted me on the back and carried on. The crisis was averted, or at least delayed.

I continued drinking the whiskey with a few intermittent beers. The sky darkened, which meant boxing was soon. But I was drinking too much, too quickly, and I blacked out for yet another time on this trip. I have no memory of the next hour or so.

My memory picked back up as we were boarding the PBT school bus to ride to the convention center where the boxers would be boxing. I was getting on the bus at the same time as four of the girls with whom I was playing basketball. On the bus, the girls sat two to a seat across from each other. Without hesitation, I sat down next to one of them, making us three to a seat, and squashing one of the girls against the window. I was essentially brain-dead from the beer and whiskey—social etiquette was foreign to me. The girls looked at each other, confused by what I was doing, except the girl next to me. She was pretty, and she smiled at me. She closed her eyes, then opened them slowly. I leaned in and kissed her. She kissed back. I cupped her face in my hands. We made out with heavy, sloppy kissing and lots of tongue. It was probably disgusting to watch, but for me, the pleasure was dizzying. I pulled back for a second and saw that all the girl's friends were in fact watching us. The girl who was smashed between the window and us looked mortified. Irrelevant, I thought. I dove back in for more. The bus began to move, and we remained embraced and making out for the entire ride.

(One thing did not occur to me until I returned home from this trip. If this fraternity didn't want black guys to join, were the women who partied with this fraternity aware of that? Did they condone it? This thought never crossed my mind while I was there. At the time, I treated the girls at this party as completely separate people, and I really hope they were.)

When the bus dropped us off, we stumbled toward the arena. The event was no joke—there were police and ticket booths with security guards, and, to my surprise, plenty of people who were not even close to college aged. Old men, in fact, made up a sizeable minority of attendees. Thousands of people were there. Inside the convention center, my vision was engulfed in a sea of Greek neon. The students stood atop bleachers that circled the ring. Each fraternity had their own set of bleachers, and the girls who rode with them were mixed in. A fight was already underway. Screams echoed and multiplied into one sustained roar. The boxers wore tank tops and shorts, with gloves and face masks and belts. The boxing was tournament-style, so if two fraternities were fighting each other, most of the yelling during that fight came from their corresponding sets of bleachers.

I joined in with the PBT bleachers and somehow lost the girl from the bus ride. With her gone, that dizzying pleasure was shifting into an equal and opposite sadness. I didn't remember her name or face, but if I didn't find her again, I was going to slip into a real sour mood. I scanned the crowd in vain for the source of that pleasure. The students around me strained their lungs, screaming at the fight. The neon everyone was wearing was hurting my eyes. I was beginning to feel very depressed. My whole soul was fixated on finding that girl again, but probably not for healthy reasons. Instead my fixation seemed to have a compulsive quality born of desperation and loneliness.

My search was interrupted by a PBT I met earlier that night, who was standing next to me. I snapped back to reality.

"A fight broke out last night!" he screamed.

"Between who?" I screamed back.

"It was us and the Fiji's when our boxers were fighting!"

"Fuck them! Fuck Fiji!"

"I know! And our guys are boxing each other again tonight!"

"I'll have my fuckin' fists ready!" I yelled.

But no fight broke out that night. In a daze, I walked laps around the outside of the bleachers. The fighters were in the middle, surrounded by a circle of judges—middle-aged folks taking the whole event very seriously—who were surrounded by the fraternities, who were surrounded by the old men in the corners with arms crossed. In this social environment, I felt like a little dot somehow lost outside of it all. I was a hornet in a bee hive; I did not belong. What was I doing? I wanted to be a part of it somehow, but it was never going to happen. Where was the girl from the bus? I was desperate to kiss her again. My sour mood, my drunken sadness, was building.

A fist smashed the jaw of one boxer. His face snapped right. He dropped. The arena volume dipped for a heartbeat then shot up higher than ever. My circling, by chance, had me standing next to the PBT bleachers again. I threw my fist in the air and screamed. I jumped up into the bleachers, back with my pretend brothers, whose fists were up too, their screams blasting.

And there she was. Maybe she'd been in the PBT bleachers all along. I pushed my way through the guys and kissed her. There it was again, that intoxication. That was all I needed to rid me of my depression. In her bra she had hidden five single-shot bottles of vodka, and she handed one to me. We bent down out of view of the police and each took a shot, hidden inside a circle of PBTs. We stood up and made out some more. I learned that her name was Katie.

The PBT boxer didn't win in the end. We took the bus back to the PBT house, and this time I actually spoke to Katie instead of just making out with her. Katie was a sophomore, and the girl I'd smashed into the window earlier was her friend visiting from another school. When we were dropped off again at the PBT house, there was no official after-party, but a few dozen students stayed around sipping beers inside. It was getting late, and I could think of only three possible places for me to sleep that night: the back of my car, on a couch at the PBT house, or with Katie. I figured that if I wanted to go home with Katie, I would need to find another guy to pair up with her visiting friend.

"Do you want me to help you find a guy here?" I asked Katie's friend.

"Sure," she said.

"Ok, point out who you're interested in."

She pointed to a guy in khaki shorts, blue t-shirt, and a bright red fraternity hat, worn backwards.

"I'll see what I can do," I said.

The girls stepped outside, and I walked over to the guy.

"Hey man, I'm trying to hook up with some girl, and she's with her friend," I said, "so I wanted to hook her friend up with a dude too."

"Alright," he said.

"So I told her I'd help her out and told her to choose a guy. She pointed at you."

He nodded. "Where is she?"

"Did you see the girl over there in the green shirt?"

"No, I don't think so."

"They just walked outside."

"Ok. I don't know who the girl is, but I'm down if she is. You can all come to my room. I have some vodka and a bunch of condoms. My room is 221, just come up when you find the girls."

He really said that. It was that simple.

"Sounds good, dude," I said.

"And my name is John."

"Drew," I said.

We shook hands and split up. I went outside. Katie and her friend were out by the curb, phones in hand.

"I talked to the guy, and he's into you," I told Katie's friend.

"Our other friend is throwing up now. We have to go," said Katie.

"Ok. Are you coming back?" I asked.

"No, but you can come over later, maybe."

Maybe. Maybe is almost never a yes. Katie gave me her phone number, and then one of their friends picked them up and drove them away.

Back inside I told John the bad news: the girls were gone.

"Ah, no worries," he said. "Was she hot?"

"She was alright," I said.

"No biggie, then. Thanks for trying."

Easy as that. Now I had to sit and wait for the text from Katie that would let me know where she lived, and if I could come over. The battery on my phone was low, and it had been an hour without a word from her. At the time this was intensely dramatic.

Eventually she texted me the word, "Laurel." Just the word "Laurel" with no additional information.

I sprung up from the couch, found Frank the officer, and asked where Laurel was.

"It's pretty far, you couldn't walk there," he said.

"How could I get there?" I asked.

"I don't know, man. Why are you heading there?"

"I'm trying to hook up with a girl who lives there."

"Oh shit, you should have said something. We'll get you a pledge ride."

Frank called a pledge to pick me up and drive me to the Laurel dorms. Within minutes, the pledge was waiting for me outside. These were the perks of brotherhood, the perks of being an insider and not an outsider. These guys were treating me very well. In my drunken state, I had almost forgotten that they didn't allow black people into their club.

"You're staying with some chick at Laurel?" the pledge asked me.

"Hopefully, dude, hopefully," I said.

"I hear ya."

The ride was silent.

"We're here," he said. "Good luck."

The wind outside Laurel was violent, and leaves were blowing in little tornadoes down the street. I called Katie. No answer. Called again. No answer. I texted her that I was outside. No response. My phone, meanwhile, was at 2% battery life. She still hadn't actually said that I could come over, she'd only texted me the word 'Laurel.' Then my phone died. I sat and waited. I decided I would give her ten minutes to come outside, otherwise I'd accept defeat and head back to my car for the night.

I thought over the course of events that had brought me there. I was alone, my actions not propelled in any way by the shadowing of any student or in the name of participatory journalism. There was nothing new inside those dorms for me to learn about. This was not research. I enjoyed the world of college so much that I was attempting to join it fully, and I'd lost all objectivity in the process. Upon recognizing how far off course I'd gone, I regained my wits and resolved to call it a night and get some much-needed rest before the drive to my next real school where I would be doing actual work. I decided that was actually the best outcome for the night.

But I was bullshitting myself, because through the door and down a distant hallway, I could see Katie headed my way, and I was instantly back to Plan A.

She opened the door. "My friend is still vomiting a lot," she said.

"I don't mind," I said. "Can I come in?"

She said, "Ok."

This was another all-girl's dorm where I was not allowed inside. We walked up a flight of stairs and into her dorm room, which was apartment-style with a kitchenette, small communal area, and a hallway that led back to two rooms, both of which were occupied— one by Katie's friend from out of town, the other by the vomiting roommate—leaving us only the common room and the couch. As Katie filled herself a glass of water, I walked up from behind her, put my hands on her shoulders and kissed her neck. She set her glass down without having had a sip, then spun toward me. We kissed our way over to the couch and lay down. I took my shirt off, then helped take off hers. Katie unbuttoned my jeans. I kissed the warm skin of her neck and collar bone. Her chest rose and fell as she let out heavy breaths in my ear.

"Why is your hat still on?" she whispered.

"I don't know," I said.

I took off the hat and saw my reflection in a mirror. Ah shit, I thought, so that's who I really am. I had the bizarre fear that when I took off the hat, my whole persona would come off along with it.

I kissed my way down Katie's body until I reached her waist line, then started to peel off her pants. She had already unzipped my pants, so I thought this was appropriate. But before I could get very far, she stopped me.

"Uh uh, nope!" she said playfully, shaking her head and, oddly, smiling.

I kissed my way back up her body. When I reached her lips, she kissed back more aggressively than before and grinded against me. Things were getting more heated. I took this as a sign of encourage- ment to try again with her pants, but I did it very slowly this time.

"Nuh, uh, uh!" she said again, sounding like a patronizing mother warning a child not to take any cookies.

She seemed to be teasing or taunting me, and I couldn't figure out how to respond. I knew that under no circumstances should I proceed if a woman is telling me "no," and yet I also felt fairly confident in my ability to read body language and interpret tonal inflection, and I believed that she had been giving me non-verbal encouragement to try again with her pants. You might think I'm wrong, but that's how it felt at the time. How was I supposed to respond to this teasing? What should I have done to pass this test?

When a woman desires a man and he is persistent, he becomes extra sexy—it is the stuff of romance novels. But when a woman does not desire a man and he is persistent, she experiences him as ranging from annoying to creepy to terrifying. When you are an inexperienced young man, it can be difficult to know whether you are being the sexy kind of persistent or the annoying, creepy, or terrifying kind of persistent. As an inexperienced drunk 20-year-old with an erection, this was too confusing for me to handle, so I pulled away and stopped what we were doing.

"What's the deal?" I asked in a straightforward way.

"I'm very hard to get," she said, still flirting.

"Ok," I said plainly.

"I don't let just anyone have sex with me."

"That's fine."

"It better be."

"Well, I'm not going to keep trying if you keep telling me no," I said.

"Well that's just too bad then," she said.

A more seductive man would have been a lot more patient and a lot less goal-oriented. Perhaps he would have also played along with her hard-to-get scenario instead of abruptly killing the mood. I didn't know how to do this, so instead I shrugged and sat up on the edge of the couch.

"And anyway," she said, "I have to take my friend to the airport in like two hours, so I need to sleep. You can sleep here." She put her shirt back on and went to her bedroom for the night.

And there I slept, confused by Katie but delighted to not have to sleep in my car.

It pains me to share this story because I would never try to have sex this way anymore. This night took place way back in the distant, forgotten past, back during the Wild West of sexuality when the law of the land for sexual consent was "no means no," and the new standard of enthusiastic verbal consent had not yet achieved widespread adoption. I had never heard of enthusiastic verbal consent, and I'm pretty sure Katie hadn't either. No one had thought of that yet! My high school taught us abstinence-only sex education, so the topic of consent was never discussed. "Just wait until you're married and everything will be fine," they told us. The first time I had sex, my girlfriend and I had discussed whether or not to do it for six months ahead of time; now that I was out in the world of casual sex, I was trying to have sex right away, but nobody had ever talked to me about how to do it, what to say, or whether I needed to say anything at all.

I learned about enthusiastic verbal consent about halfway through this trip, and I adopted it immediately. A lot has changed in five years. People older than 35 would find the sex that young people are having today to be extremely polite. "May I take your shirt off? Would you like it if I sucked on your nipples? May I stick it in your butt?" and so forth. Having lived through the shift from "no means no" consent to "yes means yes" consent, I believe that this is not a small change, but a full Kuhnian structural revolution in sexuality. In "no means no" consent, there was often someone pushing forward and someone pushing back, someone being sexually assertive and someone being sexually modest, someone seducing and someone being seduced. Today no such dynamic can exist, because both parties have to affirm with enthusiasm that they want the sex to happen at every step of the process. Today a person cannot make a display of modesty and still consent to sex. If Person A says, "Do you want to have sex?" and Person B shows any sign of hesitation or caution, Person B no longer meets the requirement for enthusiasm and therefore cannot consent to sex. With "no means no" sex, seduction was often like a battle of wills, whereas with "yes means yes" sex, seduction is more like two people playing on the same team. Psychologically it is a whole new experience.

Enthusiastic verbal consent is extremely important because it defends against the terrible and all-too-common scenario where Person A is so aggressive and frightening that they cause Person B to exhibit a freeze response. When someone is terrified, they can exhibit a fight, flight, or freeze response. I exhibited a freeze response, I think, when the music producer was standing in the doorway in Charlton. Some people have such low social intelligence and are so determined to get laid that they cannot distinguish between a person exhibiting a freeze response and a person wanting to have sex. Person A might think that since Person B hasn't said "no" or hasn't resisted, that they are consenting to sex. Clearly if Person A has sex with Person B while they are exhibiting a freeze response, that is rape, but the old standard of "no means no" had no way to address this scenario. With "no means no" consent, Person A could claim that Person B never said "no." Today Person B can only consent if they say "yes" and have some enthusiasm about it, so they are protected from this terrible scenario.

While this is extremely important, a downside is that now two people with high social intelligence, empathy, and communication skill can no longer legally have the kind of hot, old-fashioned sex where they rip each other's clothes off and move straight to intercourse without having a polite discourse along the way. I strongly prefer the new standard—it's safer and less confusing—but I'm also still holding out hope that somebody figures out how to make the new way more erotic. Today if I am sleeping with somebody new, I am thinking mostly about the law.

(Although I don't mean to say that eroticism is dead. The way to handle this dilemma is to have the new style of polite sex the first few times you sleep with someone new, and then have a conversation with your partner about what degree of verbal consent is necessary for future sex.)

I told the story of Katie teasing me with "nuh, uh, uh!" to a guy from another school, later in this trip. At the end of the story he said, "I would have just done it."

"Done what?" I asked.

"Fucked her."

"You mean raped her?"

"No, fucked her. She didn't know your name. Just use a condom."

This was an otherwise nice, respectful guy, who seemed so stupid that he couldn't comprehend why that would be rape (he also went to one of the best colleges in the country). I had to slowly and deliberately explain to him why forcefully having sex with someone after she says "no" would be rape, and in the end he only vaguely seemed to comprehend it. In debates about consent, the phrase "teach men not to rape," used to offend me—men were not natural rapists, I thought. But unfortunately, I now think that some small percentage of young men are so stupid that they do need this explained to them. What was so disturbing about this conversation was that the guy didn't seem sadistic or cruel, he seemed to be mostly suffering from narcissism—a complete inability to step into the hypothetical girl's mind and imagine what psychological experience she might have had if he had "just done it." In this particular case, I believe that if he realized he would be causing extreme trauma, he wouldn't have said this or considered doing it, and that's why education—"teaching men not to rape"—is unfortunately necessary for some. (I should add here that every other guy I've told this story to has been completely appalled by what this one guy said.)

When I woke up the next morning, I was extremely disappointed with myself for just about everything I had done the previous night. I couldn't comprehend how I kept getting myself involved in such ridiculous situations. In my normal life, my demeanor was calm and mellow, plain and boring. And yet, I kept finding myself acting like a reckless, insane moron. I couldn't understand it. But I did feel glad that I hadn't slept with Katie, since I might have been lying about my identity. This is at the very least unethical, and possibly also illegal. I couldn't remember exactly what I told her about myself—whether I was an undercover writer or that I was a PBT from Texas—but I was too scared to find out, so I left quickly without much conversation. All I can say is this: thank God I was not more charming or better looking. (Update: Five years later I decided to ask Katie how she felt about me being an undercover writer. She said, "Lol I think it's weird that you did that, but I don't really care." Phew.)

I don't feel like I'm the right person to make a speech here about the racism in this chapter. All I feel qualified to do is to share my own experience I've had while thinking about it. For a couple years after my visit to Tennessee, I was delighted that I was able to document some real racism—not just the subtle, unconscious racial biases of the typical person, but real, overt racism. (To be clear, I was disgusted by the racism itself, but as a writer I knew this was a juicy story, so I was delighted that I was the one to capture it.) These guys actually didn't allow black people into their fraternity. I thought this would make a shocking story for my book that people would talk about. That's all the thought I gave it. But then, the first time I read this chapter aloud, when I came to the words, "Are there any black guys in PBT at Texas? Good, same here. There's a half-black legacy here who's rushing, and we're trying to keep him out," I started to cry and couldn't speak the words. It is extremely painful to feel real empathy, so the mind defends against it. (If you felt real empathy for everybody all the time, you would quickly lose your mind and spend the rest of your life in tortured agony.) But for a brief window of time, I was able to feel a bit of real empathy for this half-black legacy who was rushing PBT at Tennessee. It seemed so terribly sad to me, for the first time, to think of the experience of that single guy who was rushing their fraternity but who was not going to be allowed in, the guy whose whole life had been directed toward college, the guy who dreamt of finding a group of friends who understood him, a place where he belonged, and who had gone looking for it in the same fraternity that had accepted his white father, but who on account of having a black mother would not be accepted, would not even be given a chance. I felt sad for him, and I felt sad for all the guys in the fraternity who were going to miss the opportunity to make a new friend.

8

FURMAN UNIVERSITY

Culture exists based on the solidarity of many individuals in support of a shared system of values. This is why traveling is so often recommended to young people: the individual is subjected to the influence of values that are different from the ones she felt growing up. Until you travel between cultures with different values, you can't feel culture as a force, because it's invisible.

Until I reached Furman, college culture had pulled me mostly in one direction without me being quite aware of it. Culture can be a pernicious force, because if you aren't cognizant of your natural urge to be liked by those around you, you can be swept along and taught to value whatever your peers value. Ideally, then, an individual would explore different cultural values for a time, decide what is important, then settle on a framework of the world, after which she would stick to that framework and those values despite future influence from peers (though you can always revise your values as you mature).

If we take psychologist Erik Erikson's model of psychosocial development, wherein the period of adolescence is defined by the individual asking, "Who am I?" then I would claim that today, adolescence continues through college. That is, a college student is still trying to figure out who she is and how she fits into society at large.

Therefore, a college student will decide what is important in life based in large part on the social influence of her peers.

Sociologist Max Weber once contrasted German students with American students based on their higher education systems' respective differences in educational philosophy. In Germany, Weber wrote, students arrived ready to inherit the worldview of their professors, so they were both harder working and knew more than their American counterparts. In contrast, American students arrived seeking the skills and knowledge needed to advance professionally but were not interested in acquiring the specific worldviews of their professors. Weber intended to criticize the American students, although personally I'm not sure that either model is necessarily superior. American students are effectively left to fend for themselves and must create their own identities, which may lead to more identity uncertainty but also more identity creativity. The American college experience, then, is a time for malleable students to live among other malleable students and together explore what is important or not important. The results of these explorations will then serve as their adult worldview. American students create their own worldviews, for better or for worse.

Because of this, the most important decision in choosing a university, at least regarding the subject of identity, is its culture and the values supported by its students. Since over time a student will learn to view the world through the same paradigm as her peers, it's her fellow students who will have the most impact on her future.

All this is to say that Furman existed as a refreshing counterexample of what students were doing with their lives. The school was apparently ranked as the second most rigorous college in the country, and the students accordingly admitted that they didn't have lives outside of studying. The social climate that had developed was one that valued education, productivity, and work ethic.

Until Furman, I hadn't encountered a social climate that I would describe as even vaguely intellectual, except for, perhaps, Kevin's at Baylor. Students so far never talked about what they were learning in class when they were outside of class. It was almost a social foul to bring up anything school-related at a party. It took me visiting Furman to realize that I had felt a little depressed, thinking everybody else seemed so apathetic in regard to learning. What I had internalized before Furman was that higher learning was just kind of dull, that nobody cared about it. But Furman showed me that there were students who cared, and that there really were great professors out there trying to get through to whoever would listen.

I stayed at Furman for only three days. In that time, nothing wild or crazy happened. The students at Furman occasionally have wine parties, but none occurred during my visit. The idea of drinking wine and conversing was infinitely appealing in comparison to the parties I had been attending. What I witnessed instead of partying was the classes, the studying, and the work. It may seem like students wouldn't enjoy themselves if this is all that goes on, but here there was simple pleasure in collective academic progress.

I met Alaina in the morning while she was on the way to her job at the campus print shop. She had short hair and wore an old brown leather jacket. Spring time was beginning to show itself on our walk to the inside of campus. The sun shone golden orange through dark green leaves overhead, and flowers bloomed the same golden orange alongside our feet. We passed a picturesque pond full of swans, which, according to Alaina, costs the school roughly $50,000 a year to maintain. Long ago, students also used to swim in the pond, but ever since an E. coli contamination the swans have had the pond to themselves. The campus had the feel of a country club, and the students had already named it Club Furman. The grass was lush and recently edged, the sidewalks clean, the flowers and shrubs planted and maintained with geometric elegance.

Two students, Sean and Theo, were already in the campus print shop looking over some pie charts and bar graphs of Furman's budget. They weren't employees like Alaina, they just used the room to hang out. Before I was introduced to them, I overheard them each mention their intentions of becoming CFOs one day. Alaina told them I was there as a journalist, then she went to the far side of the room to work.

"Where are you from?" Sean asked me. "Whoops, I ended that sentence with a preposition. I should have said, 'What was your prior location?'"

I answered him, "Texas," then added, "I'll try to be careful with my grammar."

"I'll catch you up on what we were talking about," Sean said. "Two years ago our school president started a big environmental initiative, like, for example, the sustainability program had a rule where they couldn't drive their cars before 3pm. But we have a new president now who is scaling back, because many of the students found the whole program wasteful. Apparently the sustainability program did a whole lot of printing themselves. So we've been looking at the financial records of the program."

"The whole program was overfunded," said Theo, "which was ironic considering their central purpose."

"But you want to know about student life, right?" Sean asked rhetorically. "You want to know about student life at Furman? It doesn't exist."

"He's right," said Theo. "There's probably more social life in this room than on the rest of campus."

"I'm sure you've heard we're the second most rigorous school, right?" asked Sean.

"I was told that on the way here," I said.

"People here are either very studious or very social. It's hard to find anybody in the middle," said Theo.

"But I feel like nobody else really knows how hard Furman is. Most people haven't even heard of Furman," said Sean.

"I feel like I'm overworked and under-respected," said Theo. "Furman's education is just harder than people across the nation realize."

Alaina was still across the room. She was talking with a student who had come in to make copies of a poster with roller coasters on it. They were now chatting about theme parks.

Theo overheard Alaina's conversation and said, "Yeah, you'll probably need spring break at a theme park after spending about 24 hours here. But it's not awful. The top 5% of students here are very involved, very type-A. Most students have a similar personality type. Hard working, driven."

"Most people, after college, they're done," said Sean. "They want to move on with their lives. Here, people want to do more once they leave, and college is just one of those steps. They want to go save the world or study abroad or go to grad school."

The guys then named a long list of clubs they were both in. Theo was part of a conservative student group called CSPT, as well as the NRA club. Theo, who is white, had recently been going with Sean, who is black, to the NAACP club, in order to show that CSPT isn't racist. Sean was a member of CSPT and NAACP, but not the NRA club.

Another girl, Claire, walked in and stuck around with us, eager as well to share with me information about Furman. She was part of the tiny group of students who hung out in the print shop despite not having actual jobs there. The boss of the print shop, on busy days, would sometimes tell Sean, Theo, and Claire to go away unless they had some real printing to do.

"There's something we refer to as the Furman Game," Claire said, "where basically people compete personally with how rigorous their workload is. Somebody will be like, 'Oh man, I haven't slept in three days!' and somebody else will say, 'Man, I haven't slept in a week!' It's kind of like one big shit show."

For most college students, a "shit show" is a party where everyone gets especially intoxicated and reckless. For instance, ten guys like Randy from Auburn getting drunk together might turn into a "shit show" if the circumstances were right. Claire's use of the term to refer to excessive studying—staying up all night to do school work—was peculiar and revealing.

"Furman gets painted as a socially awkward school," she continued, "but we're actually pretty socially affluent. We work during the week and save it for the weekend."

"Being ADD, it's really nice to have the enforcement of knowing so many people are studying," Sean added.

"Studying is kind of a social thing," said Claire.

"Yeah, we'll definitely shoot the breeze while we study," said Sean.

"Shoot the breeze," Claire repeated. "So sophisticated."

"But then there's that natural progression into silence when we all start to get the work done," said Sean, "and the closer to the deadline, the less fun it is."

"We do have a pretty big Greek life though," Theo said, "but there are no houses, so there aren't any of those huge parties. Though if you want to party, you'll be able to find that niche. We still have fun, but it's not like, 'Party hard!'"

"There's kind of an air of efficiency and responsibility," said Sean. "No, that sounds too judgey."

"It's just that we don't see studying as a hindrance," added Claire. "Some kids might think of needing to study as something that gets in the way. We are always looking for ways to fit it in."

"Some of my friends make fun of me and say I go to a brain factory," said Sean.

"And yeah, the professors here really expect you to be doing the work," said Theo. "At class, you're basically defending your studying. Teachers will give you a hard time and ask you why you missed class if you skip."

"The workload here kind of breaks you down then builds you back up," said Sean. "We're challenged to approach a concept in multiple ways. I was able to reinforce something from Economics with something completely unrelated from English."

"And does everyone here feel like this?" I asked.

"Not necessarily," said Sean. "Lots of people are involved, but I'd say there's a particular small group of people who are hyper-involved. They're a little bit obsessed with joining as many clubs as they can and take everything a little too seriously."

"Who makes up that group?" I asked.

Alaina was listening from across the room, and she smiled to herself as she heard me ask this question. She would later tell me that it was precisely people like Sean, Theo, and Claire who made up that group.

"Oh, I don't know," said Sean. "Maybe we're a part of that."

Alaina and I went back to her on-campus apartment so she could study for a health test. All students at Furman live on campus in different apartment complexes based on their school year. Alaina and the three women she lived with were seniors and had met in the dorms as freshmen. Alaina's roommate Amanda had the same health test to study for and sat next to Alaina with books in hand. They both disliked their professor and said they should have looked harder on Rate My Professor before deciding to take his class. A running joke that I joined in on was to say his first name with disdain at random times. Alaina and Amanda studied mostly in silence, except for occasionally saying little comments aloud without expecting a response. None of these comments seem funny when written down, but the general vibe was humorous and maybe even fun. I was actually having a great time just sitting and listening to Alaina and Amanda study.

"I keep wanting to write CVS when I write CPD," said Amanda.

"African Americans are sensitive to salts?" Alaina asked a little later.

Later they brought out flash cards and quizzed each other.

"Myofibrils cause..."

"Hypertrophy."

"Yes."

"Boom shaka-laka. I should probably never say that again."

"Ok, now chlamydia."

"Ew, I don't know. Flu-like symptoms?"

"No, that's AIDS."

"How many students have HIV?"

"All of them?"

"No, 1 in 500."

"All firetrucks are red but not all red is firetrucks."

"Wait, no. Ok, wait. How?"

"Wait, were you the one who hates Descartes?"

"Uh, yes."

"Name three ways to ask your partner about STDs."

"Excuse me, but before we engage in coitus, might you have any diseases of the sexually transmitted kind?"

"I suddenly really want to paint my nails green."

"What does that urge feel like?"

"Like procrastination."

Alaina drank a Dr Pepper. Her dad went to Baylor, and it seemed the Dr. Pepper Hours at Baylor ~30 years ago had done their job, for Alaina drank it daily, the same as her father. She would be going to law school at Baylor the following year.

"I'm mainly just excited for Dr. Pepper Hours," she said. "I feel like that's just one of those things."

Amanda's boyfriend Joe, a white guy who was also in the NAACP club, came by later in the night. He walked in laughing because he had just seen Sean and Theo together at the NAACP meeting.

"The CSPT is going to every club to prove they aren't racist," he said.

"Are they racist?" I asked.

"I don't know," he said, smiling, "probably."

For the next hour, Joe told me about a school nearby called Bob Jones University. I'll omit the conversation here because it's the subject of the next chapter. Joe convinced me then that I should visit.

Joe left, and Alaina and Amanda went back to studying until bed time. Eventually, they went into their bedroom to sleep, and I crawled into my sleeping bag on the sofa in the main room. Through the wall, I could hear them laughing together for at least another hour.

The next morning, we arrived at Alaina's communication law class, her favorite. The style of this class was a question-and-answer format. The students had to read a few legal case studies as home-work then email the professor questions or comments. The professor would choose questions, read them aloud, then use those questions to inform and direct his lecture. The student who submitted the particular question or comment would be called upon afterward to comment further, which would in turn spur an in-depth class discussion. This class format was far more engaging than the copy-notes-from-the-PowerPoint style lecture I had seen so much of elsewhere.

After class, we met Amanda and Joe in the dining hall. Everybody at Furman eats in the on-campus cafeteria, since it's too far of a drive anywhere else. This meant that the cafeteria operated like middle school or high school, at least socially. Students sat grouped at tables of cliques that could easily be identified. From the second level of the cafeteria, where we ate, Alaina pointed down and labeled some of the tables.

"That's the NAACP table," she said, "there's the Eros table, there are all the Greek kids, and those are the Drama people."

I turned to Joe. "What got you into the NAACP?"

"Black people," he said with a smile. "I was the only white guy in it for a few years, and now I'm on the advisory board. There are more white people now. I was in one club, and some people from the NAACP were in it too. They told me I should come to an NAACP meeting once, so I did. They had done the same thing with some people in the Eros club, and then from the NAACP meetings we started going to Eros meetings too. It's all pretty mixed up now."

During lunch, two girls walked past us wearing sorority t-shirts. One of them said to the other, "I think I'm going to sit at the Sigma Chi table," with a voice that sounded kind of like a stereotypical cheerleader from a bad movie about high school. Alaina overheard the girl and repeated the line out loud to us a moment later, mocking her and emphasizing the cheerleader voice. I had been spending a lot of time in and around Greek life over the past few weeks, and it had started to feel normal to me, but sitting next to Alaina and Amanda, I saw Greek life through their eyes and couldn't help but see it as completely stupid. I was amazed by how easily my thoughts and feelings could shift based on who I was around.

Next we went to a class on world politics.

"I usually let you guys talk and ask questions, but today I'm just going to talk," said the professor. "Out of all the lectures I give throughout the year, this one is the most important. So I just want you guys to sit and listen. This is the most important thing I have to teach you."

He turned on the overhead and put up a few lines of text. Some papers rustled, and students reached for pens.

"No, no," he said. "I don't want you to take notes. I can send you guys the slides later if you want. But today, just sit and listen. No notes."

He sat on top of his desk and crossed his legs under him. His lecture began with a story from his childhood and adolescence. He grew up in Germany with parents who were Macedonian and Turkish. Germans, he said, hated Turks, so he told people he was Yugoslavian. Then Yugoslavia committed mass genocide, so he began to tell people he was a Turk, since the Turkish had started to look better by comparison in the eyes of the Germans he surrounded himself with.

"Whatever identity you take," he said, "is not stable. Identities are volatile. They change."

He put up more words on the overhead. Some students flipped pages.

"No. No notes. Please." He stood from the desk and continued his lecture while pacing from one side of the room to the other.

"There are two psychological processes related to our selves. There is the conception of 'us' and the conception of 'them,' and the two have a constant interplay. One of the processes is to see 'us' as good, to promote positive self-esteem. The other process is to see 'them' as bad, negativizing them. This is also aiming for self-esteem."

It's a rare chance that a person shares with you what they believe is the most important lesson in all of life. This was one of those moments.

"The big question," he continued, "is how we relate to others of difference. This will shape your daily interactions and also lead to how we try to tackle the questions like peace on Earth. I'm going to read for you the words I know to be the most beautiful, which are written by Aimé Césaire. I used to read these words and get teary-eyed each time, but I have read them enough that it doesn't happen anymore."

He slid a new sheet into his overhead projector and read the words, loud and slow, repeating each line a couple times with different emphasis before continuing.

"But the work of man is only just the beginning," he read, "and it remains to conquer all the violence entrenched in the recesses of our passion, for no race possesses the monopoly of beauty, or intelligence, or force. And there is a place for all at the rendezvous of victory."

He must have repeated "rendezvous of victory" five or six times.

He sat back down on top of his desk, crossing his legs under him once again. He took a deep breath.

"What's my answer? To lead yourself outside of yourself. To the rendezvous of victory. You can forget everything I ever tell you in this class as long as you remember this. Not because I'm the one who said it, but because it's for the good of humanity, and we have to get this right."

He paused again as he made eye contact with each student in the room.

"It's up to you guys how we understand difference, and what we do with it. You guys are the authors of the world we'll be walking in tomorrow."

He stood up. "Class is over."

As a 20-year-old, I had utopian sensibilities. I thought that humans had the ability to create a world of everlasting peace, so the lecture resonated deeply with me, and I even got chill bumps. Unfortunately, at age 25 I have read enough history to know that one person's "rendezvous of victory" is often another person's genocide, so a lecture like this would be slightly less inspiring to me now.

Still, at the time I felt moved and inspired, so I said to Alaina after class, "Man, that was a good lecture."

She laughed and said, "He always gets like that."

We went to another of Alaina's shifts at the Furman Digital Express, the print shop. It was busier this time with more actual work to be done, so there was less socializing. Alaina told me on the way there that Sean was different from the other students because he took mainly night classes and wasn't officially enrolled there at Furman.

He lived off campus with his mother, was a few years older than most of the other students, and had to work at a clothing store to pay for his classes (which also explained why he was so sharply dressed).

"Most kids here are already privileged," Sean told me during a break. "There's a kind of rivalry with status and money. When it was rush week for the sororities, there's this store that all the girls are supposed to get shoes from." He found a photo of the shoes for me. "So it's sort of a class system around here for the clothes you wear. Like, if you're a KA, you have to wear Vineyard Vines."

"So is everyone competing?" I asked.

"No one is explicitly peer pressured into anything, but everyone still wants to fit in somewhat. Before I came to Furman, I probably didn't wear as many pastel colors. But I saw it on campus and liked it, and it's part of the culture."

"Would you consider the 'class system' a good or bad thing?"

"I don't know if it's either, but either way you're forced to play along."

That night Alaina and Amanda studied more for their health test back at the apartment. Their study session was filled with so much laughter that I almost wished I had to take the test too.

After they went to sleep, I again lay on the couch listening through the wall to their giggling. That night I fell asleep easily and wasn't sure when their laughter stopped, or if it ever did.

9

BOB JONES UNIVERSITY

I spent only one afternoon at Bob Jones University. That afternoon was supposed to be my final day at Furman, but my hosts encouraged me to investigate Bob Jones instead. Bob Jones is a strict Evangelical Christian university. Before I visited, I went to their website and read through their rulebook. These are just some of the rules that students must follow:

-On and off campus, physical contact between men and women is not allowed.

-Male and female students should guard their testimonies; they are not to be alone together in a classroom, rehearsal room, or other room.

-Mixed groups of brothers, sisters, and first cousins may go to public places together.

(The odd part about specifying "first" cousins, instead of just cousins, is the implication that second cousins should not be left alone.)

-With Dean's approval, residence hall male students may date a female day student or non-student in town. To date a non-student or day student off campus, residence hall women students are to have an approved chaperone.

-Because of the sensual nature of many of its forms, dancing is not permitted.

-Students are not to watch movies on campus. In private homes, students may view G-rated movies and movie trailers. In faculty/staff homes, students may view certain PG movies when the faculty or staff member watches with students and objectionable elements are discussed.

-Students are not to play video games rated above E10 or games that contain graphic blood or gore, sensual or demonic themes, violent first-person shooting, suggestive dress, bad language, or rock music.

-BJU encourages students to use the Internet as the valuable tool that it is but also expects students to be good stewards of their time while on the Internet and to avoid objectionable sites such as celebrity home pages.

-Gambling—or risking the material provisions of God on chance —is poor stewardship and caters to covetousness and the love of money. It is based on the false premise of "luck" and is a portal for exploitation. Therefore, gambling of any kind is unacceptable for any student. Because face cards are associated with gambling, students may not play games with face cards.

Bob Jones requires that men's sideburns are trimmed to above the inner ear, that shirts are tucked in, and that hair is neatly combed. To prepare for my visit, I showered, shaved, and put on the nicest clothes I had with me. To enter campus, one has to drive through a security gate and talk to a security guard. Students aren't allowed to leave campus without permission, but anybody is allowed to enter campus.

Campus was sparsely populated when I first arrived, and I had to walk for ten minutes before I saw anybody. Eventually classes were let out, and the sidewalks filled with students. I observed the students from afar, wondering if their behaviors would be unusual, but I noticed nothing unusual except for some differences in clothing. The girls, as I should have expected after having studied the student handbook, wore long skirts down to their ankles with loose blouses tucked in. Many of them carried their books the old-fashioned way—

flat against their chests with their arms crossed over them. The guys wore dress shirts tucked into slacks. The clothes were modern-looking, not decades or centuries out of date like I had anticipated. I had expected Bob Jones to look like an Amish village, but instead, my first impression was that it was a typical campus.

I walked past some students and scanned their faces. Nobody seemed to notice me as an outsider, which was a relief. The girls kept their eyes pointed down as they walked on the sidewalks, though most of them had permanent little smiles on their lips. My hosts from Furman told me that up until a few years ago, Bob Jones had separate sidewalks for men and women, which meant that these sidewalks were newly desegregated. I wondered how a student could eventually break through all the rules. How does a guy meet a girl if he's not allowed to talk to her without a chaperone? How do you maintain a relationship if you're not allowed to touch?

The school handbook states that men may talk to women underneath a specific gazebo on campus without a chaperone between 10am and 5pm. I found my way to this gazebo before 5pm, not to try to talk to girls, but to eavesdrop on the conversations already taking place. There were about ten tables there, all of them filled with students, except for one, which was where I took my seat. A guy and girl who had been sitting together stood up to leave and walked past me in a leisurely, romantic stroll.

"Ok, I'll see you tonight," he said. "Maybe 7:15, so we can get a seat up front?" He was setting up a church date. His hands clutched his backpack straps.

They came to a stop and faced each other. The textbooks she carried were shielding her heart.

"Ok, 7:15 it is," she said with a sweet smile.

They stood there looking at each other for a long while. It was the moment when two people would typically make some physical parting gesture, like a hug, but since touching was not allowed, they didn't touch. The parting gesture was the touching of their eyes, and during the brief pause that they took to look at each other, it seemed like they were sharing in a recognition of the absence of touch. That subtle gesture—the mutual moment where the denial of touch was recognized—kept all the tension that had accumulated from their gazebo date and left it there without releasing any of it.

There was something rather sweet about the moment. If a typical date—one taking place far away from Bob Jones University—has gone well, then the couple would physicalize their feelings in one way or another at its conclusion with a hug, a kiss, or sex—sex being the ultimate relief of tension. If the relationship loses its sexual tension before any secondary driving force, like emotional connection, has been created, then both parties end up satisfied and have no more need to see each other, at least until their sexual appetites return. The model here at Bob Jones circumvents that risk by preventing every chance of satisfying those physical desires, at least until marriage. Also, if everyone is following the rules, then presumably nobody is masturbating. That means that everyone is tremendously horny with no outlet other than talking under the gazebo and sitting next to each other at church. I imagined that with desire so intense, and with so few outlets, that even eye contact could be sweet, intense, and pleasurable.

After those two students left, I switched my attention to a table next to me where four students sat—two handsome guys and two cute girls. They had just made plans for a picnic a few days from now and were seated in male/female pairs. The pair farthest from me shared a textbook and spoke quietly to each other. The closer pair did the same while sharing a laptop. Their group had been unremarkable until I witnessed the guy in the pair nearer to me do something unbelievable. If he did this anywhere else in the country, I would have never noticed, but at Bob Jones his action took on new and profound meaning. As I watched the scene unfold, I sat rubbing my eyes in disbelief.

Here's what happened: The guy and the girl were sitting next to each other. She was in front of the laptop, and he stood up next to her. He took a step closer to her then put his hand on the back of her chair such that his arm was around her but not touching her, although it was only inches away. He then leaned down one inch at a time until his head was level with hers. She was meanwhile typing something on the laptop and not reacting to how close he was to touching her, which was very close. But still they did not touch. He then looked across the table to see if their friends were watching, and when he saw that they weren't, he went for it. He pushed the side of his shoulder into hers, nudging her just enough that she moved along with the contact. He touched her! I was amazed. He stood back up, removed his arm from around her, and sat back down in his chair.

Soon after that, I saw even more subtle touching at another table, and this was even more risqué than the first couple. It was a guy and girl sitting together on the other side of the gazebo. His posture was slumped and his shirt was halfway untucked, giving him a rebellious vibe compared to other guys at Bob Jones. He sat facing her with his knees spread apart around hers so that her legs were sandwiched between his. They were sitting so close that her knees almost jutted into his crotch, and yet they were not touching at all. Neither one looked at the other, for they were both preoccupied by their cell phones. Meanwhile his legs swayed in and out rhythmically, first spreading far apart, then closing, such that they almost, almost touched hers, but then did not, and then spreading back out again. This also had me rubbing my eyes in disbelief. Next he began to slowly move his foot closer until the outside of his shoe touched the outside of hers. He wore sneakers and she wore black slip-ons, and their shoes were without-a-doubt touching. My vision was binocu-lared in on their feet, and I could see that his toes were moving up and down, as if he were trying to rub the exterior of her shoe from the inside of his own shoe in a way that she might be able to feel. Meanwhile his knees continued to sway in and out, almost as if he were fanning her legs to keep them cool, his legs spreading wide, then narrow, wide, then narrow. I'd never seen anything like it. Even-tually, the cumulative effect of the footsie and the strange swaying of the knees gave me the impression that their mating ritual was far less decent and civilized than if they were just groping each other and making out.

All the intense sexual tension under the gazebo had made my

hands and forehead perspire, so I had to leave to dry off and catch my breath—plus, sitting alone in that gazebo designed for courtship wasn't unlike somebody eating at a restaurant alone on Valentine's Day, crying into his soup while dozens of couples wait outside for a table to open up. So I found my way to the main visitor's building and browsed around reading some pamphlets about the school. A man who worked behind the front desk approached me and asked if I was waiting for a tour. I told him that I would like a tour, so he called over a girl named Samantha, who was working as the school's tour guide.

"So are you a prospective student here?" Samantha asked.

I didn't want to tell her that I was writing a book, so I lied and said yes.

"What grade are you in right now?" she asked.

"I'm a junior," I said. As a 20-year-old, I could still pass for 17.

"Are your parents here?" she asked.

"They're checking out the city right now. We looked at Furman yesterday, but I wanted to check out Bob Jones too." I didn't enjoy lying, but I was good at it.

"Well, that's great," she said. "We have a pretty cool place here, so let's go look."

We began our stroll around campus, me pretending to be a 17-year-old prospective student to one of the nation's most strict Evangelical Christian schools.

"Just ask me any questions you might have as they come to you, and I'll do my best to answer you," Samantha said.

"Ok," I said. "I heard you guys have pretty strict rules. I don't know much about them. What are they like?"

"We do have some rules here, and there are a lot of rumors and stories out there about our rules that aren't true, but I can get you a copy of our rules, and you can look over them."

Everything I had heard about Bob Jones so far had come directly from the Bob Jones website. I wasn't sure what additional rumors there could possibly be. Samantha had a squeaky, optimistic voice and a face that fluctuated between either a half smile or a full smile.

She was a senior at Bob Jones and gave tours as part of her campus involvement.

"What do most students think of the rules here?" I asked.

"Well, the rules we have here are all meant to help keep the students focused. The rules are pretty particular, but they're there to keep students on track. So it's really about the attitude of the students when they show up. If they want to be kept on that track and have a good attitude, the rules will help them, and they'll appreciate the rules. I guess a few people might show up with a bad attitude and not like them, but almost everybody supports what the rules aim to do, and they're really happy with them."

I nodded my head and stuck out my lower lip. In order to seem younger and more wholesome, I blinked a lot and scanned the campus with wide, innocent eyes like a child.

"The faculty here is really great," Samantha said. "I'm from Michigan, so I don't see my family all the time while I'm here, and I became really close with one of my professors and his wife. They would let me do laundry at their house if I wanted, and drive their car sometimes. I'd go over and eat dinner there too. They really became like grandparents. A lot of the students have relationships like that with the faculty. It's kind of like one big family. They really make you feel like home."

"That's really nice," I said.

"So what kind of high school did you go to?" she asked.

"What do you mean?"

"Was it Christian, private, secular..."

"...oh, right. I've only been to public school, so secular, but I thought I might enjoy a private Christian school for college."

"I couldn't imagine going to secular school myself, but my fiancé, who I really love and respect, handled secular school really well. I don't mean to say anything bad about it, but I've heard of some people who have gone to secular school and lost their faith."

"Yeah, it has been pretty tough. So your fiancé didn't go to Bob Jones?"

"He goes to Indiana University right now, and we're going to get married once we both graduate."

"Oh, that's nice. What is it like dating somebody while you're a student at Bob Jones?"

"Well, it's actually a really great place to meet someone," she said, "and you might have heard some of the rules about that too, but it's really pretty easy actually. Like, right now since I'm a senior and I'm engaged, I get more privileges, so my fiancé and I can go off campus together for up to three hours at a time as long as there's a chaperone with us, but the easy part is that the chaperone can be anyone at all, like my little brother, so that lets us do wedding planning or go out for lunch, or all sorts of things."

Samantha was using the fact that she was allowed to leave campus for up to three hours with a chaperone, now that she was an engaged senior, as an example of how lenient Bob Jones was.

"Oh, that's neat," I said.

We walked inside one of the school buildings, where Samantha let me peek into some classrooms that were empty. These were small rooms, about the size of a high school classroom, with desks and chairs and a chalkboard. Everything looked normal, except for some quotes written on the walls. Perhaps the quotes were meant to be instructive or helpful, but to me they were nothing but ominous. One said, "You have the power to do anything you ought to." Another said, "There's nothing you can truly get away with."

"Let's go check out the science building," Samantha said. "Our science classes are really good. They're some of my favorites. We teach both creation and evolution."

"Evolution, really? I didn't expect that."

"Yeah, it's great. Our evolution classes teach you all about how to talk to people who believe in evolution, and how to understand the way they think. I never learned evolution growing up but college has taught me how secular students think, so I can talk to them about it in a way they understand."

So the evolution classes were actually anti-evolution classes.

I said, "That's good."

"We also teach how to understand things in the news in a Biblical way, you know, things like, 'Don't eat this!' or 'Don't do this!' and how to filter them through a Biblical context. It's really useful."

Once inside the science building, we peeked into an active lecture hall. The students there turned around in their seats, waved, and smiled to us. Along the walls down the hallway were taxidermized birds and rats of many different species, as well as a collection of rodent skulls. Somewhere among those animals and skeletons must have been definitive proof of divine creation, or, if not, at the very least they aided the Bob Jones science department's illusion of credibility for its students.

"Do you want to see some dorm rooms?" Samantha asked.

"Sure," I said.

Women aren't allowed in the men's dorms, so Samantha knocked on the door and talked to a security guard through a cracked door, asking if he could let me in to show me one of the rooms. I followed the guard inside and up some stairs. He pointed out the largest room on the floor, which belonged to the hall advisor—the adult in charge of supervising and mentoring students on the floor. Next he knocked on one of the dorm rooms so I could look inside. The two students inside told me I could come in and look around. They appeared like they had just been sitting in their rooms doing nothing at all before I arrived. Perhaps they had been silently ruminating over their condition.

"Any questions?" one of the guys asked me.

"How do you guys like it here?" I asked.

"In our room or at Bob Jones?"

"At Bob Jones."

"It's great," he smiled.

I looked at the other guy for his answer. He nodded and gave me an unconvincing smile. He said, "It's good." The second guy almost seemed like he was trying to say, "Help me! I'm trapped! I'm a prisoner!" but I wasn't sure.

I met back with Samantha and continued walking around campus. "So how about stuff like making friends here?" I asked.

"It's really easy," she said. "Your best bet is your roommate. My roommate freshman year is my best friend now. And from there you just branch off and meet people through all the social activities and clubs and those sorts of things. At a lot of secular schools it's all about study, study, study, but here the social is really well integrated."

"Ok. That makes sense. How about things like meeting girls? How does that happen within the rules?"

"It's really easy and not awkward," she said. "You might see a girl around and ask her to eat lunch with you or to go with you to church. Or maybe the group knows her and you see her and people set you up saying, 'Oh, maybe you two would like each other.' It's very casual and people find each other often."

Samantha walked me back to the front office where I met her. Along the way, she told me some stories about her family back home, her little brother, the brownies her mom sends her, and about fun times on campus. Attending Bob Jones may sound like torture to most people, but Samantha said she enjoyed it, and I believed her. If you already follow the teachings at Bob Jones and impose its rules on yourself anyway, then submerging yourself in a village of likeminded people who are also following its rules might be quite nice. (With that said, it's also probably true that most people trapped in cults believe they're enjoying it while they're inside, even though they're often deprived of essential human needs such as freedom and autonomy. I don't know if Bob Jones could be described as a cult, but it certainly shared some similarities.)

I said farewell to Samantha then finished my tour by heading to the campus book store. I passed by a section of anti-evolution books with titles like, *The Dark Side of Darwin: Darwin Exposes His Own Secret*, and then I wandered to a section of books on dating and relationships. I thumbed through a book called, *Boy Meets Girl: A Return to Courtship*, and felt curious enough to buy it. In the book, the author relays the story of how he mentioned marriage to his wife on their first date. He had met her through church and already asked the church elders if they thought she would make a good wife, and then he took her to dinner and mentioned the idea that he would like to pursue the possibility of marrying her someday—not proposing right then, not stating that he was already willing to marry her, but letting her know that he wasn't just seeing her because it felt enjoyable in the present moment. I had deceived myself into believing that I was reading the book only because it was "funny," but by the time I finished it, I had to admit to myself that it was somewhat compelling —not because I wanted to follow his ideas, but because it had expanded my understanding of what was possible. As a 20-year-old, I had never considered pursuing someone based on lifelong compatibility—someone to raise children, get cancer, and die with.

As I left campus, I felt like I had just been in some horrible alternate reality, and I was now glad to be back in the real world. But the further I drove away, the more I felt that the place had been charming in its own way, and eventually as I drove further, I began to feel a nagging disappointment that the real world wasn't just a tiny, tiny bit more like Bob Jones.

10

SPRING BREAK

Throughout the trip thus far, one of the questions most asked of me was, "Are you going to write about spring break?" Originally I didn't care to write about it, but after I had been asked so many times, I decided that I probably should. Panama City Beach, Florida is rumored to be the trashiest, most stereotypical college spring break destination in America. If I were going to write about spring break, Panama City Beach was where I would have to go.

I didn't know anybody who was going to Panama City Beach for spring break, and I couldn't find a connection through friends-of-friends, so I'd been spamming spring break Facebook groups for a few weeks, asking if there was anybody who would like to have their week documented by an aspiring writer in a book about college. Only one person responded—a girl who would be flying down to Florida from Montana State University to meet with three of her friends from around the country. The girl, Hannah, told me that she was "looking forward to Tucker Max Part 2." I still hated that comparison, but in this case I had to embrace it. I told her, "Hell yeah!"

I left South Carolina in the middle of the night and crossed the Florida state line at sunrise. For some unknown reason, I cried for the entire drive while listening to Johnny Cash's rendition of "Danny

Boy" on repeat, weeping hundreds of joyful tears onto my steering wheel. I hadn't cried in years, and when I was done, I felt renewed and full of hope. It was the nicest drive of my life.

The four girls I would be meeting in Panama City Beach were my Facebook friends at this point, and they had been posting so many moment-by-moment photos of their trip onto Facebook that I wondered if my physical presence was even necessary to write about their week. So far they had taken a group photo next to the "Welcome to Florida," sign, then they went to Walmart to buy pink cowboy hats and alcohol, then they went to the beach for a photo session of them wearing the hats. I texted Hannah to see where she was, but she didn't respond. That was ok—I figured I'd give them a few more hours to check into their hotel before trying again.

In the meantime, I stocked up on liquor for the long weekend, assuming my ability to socialize with the girls would otherwise be limited. I bought a handle of cupcake-flavored vodka for them and a small bottle of whiskey for me. Having driven all night, I pulled over on the side of the road to take a nap, hoping to wake up with a response from the girls.

I awoke much later in the day than planned, around 6pm, still with no text from Hannah. By the time I made it to the beach, it was already nighttime. I needed no map or sign to tell me where I was when I arrived; the main street of Panama City Beach was like a lesser Las Vegas, with its towering hotels brightly lit, and on either side of the road for three or four miles were crowds of young people dressed in post-beach attire out for drunken strolls. The traffic was terrible—the cars were moving at the same speed as the people traveling by foot. The only people not stuck in the gridlock traffic were those who were lane-splitting on their rented scooters.

I parked my car for a few hours while waiting for Hannah to contact me, meanwhile watching the masses of young people pass by on the street. I projected my frustration with Hannah onto them and felt universal hatred. Not everyone appeared to be a college student; in fact, plenty of them looked to be in their late 20s or 30s. I later learned that Panama City Beach is a spring break destination not especially sought out by college students, so these people were mostly just uneducated degenerates like myself. I decided to call Hannah, but she didn't answer. A few minutes later, she finally texted me back.

"Henry's!" she texted.

"Is that where you are?" I asked.

"Yeeeeah!!!" she wrote.

I drove to Henry's. When I arrived, she texted me again.

"Club McNamara!!!" she said.

"Are you there now?" I asked.

She didn't respond.

I looked up Club McNamara and saw that it was supposedly one of the craziest nightclubs in North America. I drove there through the stop-and-go traffic at approximately one mile per hour, hating the pedestrians even more than before. The club had a giant parking lot, which was full, surrounded by many small sandy streets zigzagging away in all directions. At the end of one street, I found a spot for my car and parked with my wheels submerged in the sand. I knew I had to be drunk before meeting these girls, so I climbed into the back of my car and kept my head low to begin my tragic one-person pregame. I felt angsty, rebellious, and tough despite drinking the girls' cupcake-flavored vodka. After chugging down as much of the warm, sugary liquor as I could manage, I sat out on my tailgate, which faced the street, and waited for the effects to set in. Along the streets, spring breakers flocked toward the distant thumping of Club McNamara. As the liquor hit, the hordes of partiers who I had previously eyed with disdain were now becoming potential friends, each with their own troubles, histories, and ambitions. I understood them and sympathized with their plight. The night was fresh and electric. We were all just looking for a good time. How beautiful, how serene!

"Ayyyyy!" one guy hollered out.

I matched his hoot with my own. "Ow! Ow!"

"Ooooooh!" another partier shot back from across the street.

This was spring break solidarity, real human connection. I was feeling drunk.

As cars drove slowly by—usually with their windows rolled down and deafening rap music blasting—I smiled to the passengers, pointed friendly fingers, and sent back all the good vibes I could. When groups passed by on foot, I'd respectfully stand to my feet and wish them a pleasant evening, offering them swigs of my liquor in exchange for their warm positivity and sometimes liquor of their own. I played host to the city.

"'Ey 'ey! Welcome to Panama City Beach, motha fuckas! You guys havin' a good night? Good then, good to hear! Let's get fucked up!" I toasted my handle of vodka to the stars and took another swig.

The night was young, it was spring break, and I needed to stay exactly this drunk if I wanted to fit in with Hannah and her friends.

Eventually I followed a crowd of people over to the club. At the entrance, the line to get inside stretched around the building. I asked the guy in front of me if there was a cover charge.

"It's fifty," he said.

"Holy shit! Fifty?" I simply could not afford $50—even $15 would have seemed absurdly high for me—but I had to make it inside to meet these Montana State girls. I needed a plan.

As I got close to the front of the line, I could see a second entrance guarded by a bouncer holding a few sheets of paper. Occasionally I'd see a person walk up, talk to him, then get to walk straight inside without paying. It was the VIP entrance. I quickly formulated a plan so stupid that it might be evidence of clinically diagnosable levels of grandiosity. I walked right up to him like I'd seen the other people do.

"What party are you with?" he asked. He started looking down the list of names on the VIP list.

"My name's Bryan Ott," I said. "I might not be on the list yet."

Not only was I not on the list of VIPs, I was not even 21 years old. I handed him my fake ID, which was my brother's old expired ID. My brother and I look related but not similar enough for the ID to always work.

"You have to be on the list," the bouncer said. He had huge trapezius muscles that curved upward from his shoulders to just below his earlobes.

"I talked with the club earlier today, and they told me to come in through the VIP line," I said. "My name's Bryan Ott. I'm writing a book about student social life at college. They told me I could just come in through the VIP line."

"No, man. It doesn't work that way." He looked down at the ID. "Take off your hat."

I was wearing the yellow fraternity hat, backwards. I took it off.

"Ok, now stand up straight," he said.

I did.

He scanned my face while looking at the ID. "And this isn't even you. Get out of here." He put the ID in a stack of about 20 other IDs on a table near him, crossed his arms, and quit making eye contact with me.

My plan was utter garbage; I realized that immediately. I thought I might get rejected, but I didn't think he'd take my ID from me. Now I was facing a real predicament. The two most important tools for me to write this book were a car and a fake ID. If I lost my fake ID, my whole project might be ruined. I had to get it back.

"No, that ID is mine," I said. "I don't know what to tell you."

"You want to test that?" he asked. "I'll call the cops right now, and they can let me know if this is you." He raised his eyebrows aggressively high. "It's a third-degree felony. Want me to call them?"

The trick to lying is to believe your own lie. I had spent more time living as fake identities than real ones in the weeks leading up to this, so my lie came with ease. I said, "Yeah, go ahead and call them if that's what I need to do to get in. That's my real ID."

"Ok? Ok? You want me to call them? Ok, then. Stand right there, I'll call them."

He pointed to a lamp post and told me to stand next to it while he called the police. I went and stood there while watching the bouncer out of the corner of my eye to see if he made any phone calls. In the meantime, I took my debit card, which said my real name, and hid it in a crack between two bricks, in case they were going to search me. I desperately needed my ID back. While I stood waiting, I tried to figure out how far I was going to take my lie. Would I even lie to the police? Wouldn't they have to fingerprint me to assure themselves that my ID wasn't me?

The bouncer hadn't made a phone call yet, from what I could tell, so I walked back up to him.

"Hey man, are the cops on their way yet?" I asked.

"Yeah, the cops are on their way. Get out of here."

My logic was that no police would bother with such a small issue when the rest of the city was so overrun with debauchery. I was nonthreatening, friendless, pathetic. I played up all these attributes as I stood back by the lamp post looking as sad as I could. There was another bouncer closer to me who was younger and smaller than the first, and I kept making sympathetic eye contact with him until he eventually gave me a "What is it?" look. I shrugged, put my palms up, and walked up to him.

"That guy doesn't think my ID is me," I said. "I don't know what to do. He took it."

"Is it you?" he asked.

"Yeah, it's me. I don't know what to say. I'm waiting for the police to come verify it for me, but it's been like 30 minutes."

"One second," he said. He walked over to the first bouncer and talked to him. The first bouncer bit his lip in anger and shook his head. Then they both went inside. I waited outside with a stupid, innocent look on my face.

Three huge bouncers came out headed straight for me. None of them were the concerned, friendly one I had just talked to. One of the bouncers grabbed me by the arm and pulled me around the corner of the building. I was alone now with three of them, out of sight and earshot from anyone else. They stood shoulder to shoulder with my ID held up next to my face.

"This isn't you," the big one in the middle said.

"It's me," I said. "I don't know what to tell you."

"You want a third-degree felony?" he asked.

"No," I said truthfully.

"Then tell us the truth."

"I don't know what to tell you. I'm here alone, and I'm trying to meet some girls who I don't really know. I'm not drunk, and I don't even really feel like partying. But that ID is real."

"You're lying to us."

"I don't know what to tell you."

"Tell us you're lying."

I started to think about the third-degree felony and/or prospect of the three of them kicking my ass. The thought was horrifying. I started to realize that I wasn't acting very intelligently and that I might be making a terrible decision by doing what I was doing. I was staring into the bouncer's eyes without speaking, but I could feel the truth bubbling up in my throat. I was about to tell him the truth, but a split second before my confession, he spoke again.

"Flip out your pockets," he said.

I did.

They took everything out of my pockets—my wallet, phone, and keys. They took the case off my phone and checked behind it to look for other forms of ID. That's where I had been keeping my debit card, which would have given me away. I tried not to eye the crack between the bricks where my debit card was hidden. One bouncer shook his head in frustration and walked off, leaving only two. The big guy who had been holding my ID passed it off to the last guy.

"See what you think," he said to him.

The last guy held it up and looked back and forth between me and the ID.

"Hm," he said after some time. "I can see how they thought it didn't look like you. Something about the nose."

He raised his arm to call over yet another bouncer by the doors. This person walked over with a wrist band and put it around my wrist. I couldn't believe it—the wristband said "Club McNamara VIP." While they had been concerning themselves with whether my ID was real or fake, they must have forgotten the part about me not even being on the VIP list, so now I was able to get inside for free. More importantly, I had my ID back.

"Thanks, guys," I said. "Sorry about the confusion."

As I walked inside, the original bouncer gave me a death stare when I passed him. I pursed my lip and nodded to him politely. I felt like a Zen master floating two inches above the ground.

Once inside, the scale of the club hit me. The club seemed more like 15 clubs jammed together with hallways in between, each with different themes. I stood in a roofless section that was covered in the remnant suds of a foam party and called Hannah three times. No answer. Goddamnit. I walked all around the club looking for her. The music and lighting in the club overwhelmed my senses. Everybody's skin was dark red and flashing and I couldn't hear my own voice when I hummed, but if I stopped and really looked around, it seemed that everybody else was also just there to watch. We were all passive observers, waiting to see what the big deal was all about, a crowd gathered for our own show. The only people dancing were the hired go-go dancers in one room on stripper poles. The patrons mostly just wandered around like tourists. I imagined that if the lights turned on and the music turned off, we could have been in a conference room at a low-key networking event.

There was a small room with no music playing where a few groups of young people sat in booths next to open windows. I asked if I could join them for a couple minutes. They all seemed dejected like me and therefore easy to talk to.

"Man, I can't believe we paid $50 to get in here," one of them said.

"Are you guys on your spring breaks?" I asked.

"Yeah."

"Why'd you come to Panama City Beach?"

"We thought it would be fun, but we were stupid."

"Me too," I said.

This was apparently a wild and crazy nightclub worth checking out, but not on the night I was there.

After a couple hours with no word from Hannah, I left the club and actually sprinted past the bouncers, grabbed my debit card from between the two bricks, then ran back to my car. My absurd fear was that the bouncers would chase me down, but nothing ever came of it. I figured I'd have to meet Hannah the next day for something beach-related, so I wanted to get some rest. A girl parked next to me needed help backing her car out of the sand, so she offered me a bag of grapes to help, which I accepted. She was a local from Panama City Beach.

"What's it like living here?" I asked.

"Nothing happens all year, and then spring break comes and ruins the city," she told me.

"That's too bad. Thanks for the grapes."

I took my ukulele and the grapes and sat again on the tailgate of my car. After some time, a group of fraternity guys stopped their walk to listen while I played. My music was no good, but they were drunk and friendly.

"Bet that little guitar gets you a ton of pussy, right?" one of them asked.

"It's endless," I lied.

"Goddamnit," he said, turning to his friends, "we shoulda brought us one of those!"

"Hey bro, you'll get 'em next year," I said as they left.

I tossed the ukulele inside my car and crawled in after it. That was enough nonsense for one night. Soon the bass from the passing cars would rattle me to sleep.

Unfortunately, my incredible good luck with getting into the club didn't translate into any luck at all with contacting Hannah. I spent three depressing days trying to find her somewhere in Panama City Beach, to no avail. She wouldn't answer her phone, and the texts she sent me were only the names of whichever bar or club she was at. For three days, I wandered in and out of clubs, looking around for Hannah, trying to call her so we could meet up, then hearing nothing from her until she would text me the name of yet another bar or club.

But life has a way of turning bad circumstances into good ones, because just 30 minutes away was the town of Destin, and there I witnessed one of the most amazing stories in this book.

I was still in Panama City Beach after three days of trying to track down Hannah. Weak and in need of sympathy, I texted Randy from Auburn about my dilemma, figuring he would know about spring break and possibly have some suggestions for what I could write about instead of the Montana State girls. He responded immediately with a pleasant surprise.

"Ok, here's a plan," he texted. "I'm only 30 minutes away from you in Destin. It's my last night here, so I don't think anybody in our house would mind if you came since you wouldn't really be squatting. There's a party around 9pm so you can come around then. Can you pick up a 12-pack for you and me if you come?"

"Goddamnit," I texted him. "Yes, that sounds awesome."

What happened by the end of the night was unbelievable and could only have occurred by some sort of journalistic miracle.

I hadn't showered in three days, so I first stopped at a gas station, snuck into the bathroom with my towel and Dopp kit, washed my hair in the sink, and splashed water under my arms. Next I bought a 12-pack and headed toward Destin full of renewed hope and happy to see my old friend. Destin was also a good opportunity for me to keep wearing the fraternity hat, backwards of course, so I put it on and tried to get myself into a mood where I would fit in. Wearing the hat is embarrassing in hindsight, but at the time I took great pleasure in the feeling of going undercover. (Or, maybe I was just desperate to fit in, and I told myself I was going undercover as a rationalization.)

Randy was staying with members of the SigEp fraternity instead of his own fraternity for spring break, because one of his friends was a SigEp. This was a big social foul, apparently, but Randy said he didn't care. Destin is a Greek spring break destination, more upscale and expensive, whereas Panama City Beach was decidedly not. Students going to Destin rent big houses by the beach for the week. The routine is to get daytime drunk on the beach, then take a nap, then get nighttime drunk at a house. Repeat all week.

I drove there leaned forward with excitement over the steering wheel. Seeing Randy again could not come soon enough.

He met me outside by my car.

"Didn't think I'd be seeing you so soon," he said. He wore a loose white shirt halfway unbuttoned, and he had a nice tan. His cheeks looked sandy at first, but it was really just his bright blonde peach fuzz from not shaving all week.

"Neither did I," I said. I noticed his red eyes and said, "You were drunk the first time I met you, are you drunk tonight, too?"

"No sir, no sir, not tonight."

But he clearly was. "You sure about that?" I asked.

"Alright, I admit I've had a few," he said.

"Well I brought us a few more," I said, taking the 12-pack out of my car.

Cops patrolled the streets in the area, so we had to bring the beer into Randy's house in a backpack. (We were still both 20 years old so it was illegal for us to be drinking at all.) The party we were headed to wasn't for a couple more hours, and Randy wanted to get a few additional beers in him before we left. We walked toward his house.

"Just play it cool while we're at our house," he said.

"Dude, I know. What the fuck."

"I know, I know. It's just there's this squatter at our house who nobody likes. He's some military kid, and he brought a ton of the liquor he gets on discount the first night, and now he thinks he's like been accepted and can stay here, but nobody likes him."

"Ok dude, I'm not about to do that. Jesus. How has spring break been?"

"Absolutely brutal. Pretty much getting smashed twice a day all week."

"Very nice."

"Oh, there's one more thing I need to warn you about. Have you heard about pancake breakfast?"

"No?"

We stopped our walk so Randy could tell me about pancake breakfast before going inside.

"Ok, so it's this game we're playing," he said. "Basically, if you're fucking a girl in the house, you're not allowed to lock the door. And there's this thing where apparently if you're fucking a girl and someone scares you, you just come right away. I don't even know if that happens."

"Interesting."

"Yeah, but ok, so if someone walks in on you and you finish right away, you owe the guy a pancake breakfast. If you are able to keep fucking the chick without blowing, the guy who walked in on you owes you the pancake breakfast."

(I hate to kill the suspense so soon, but unfortunately, no—nobody had to buy anybody a pancake breakfast that night.)

We walked up the stairs into the front door. The house was rented by the sophomore class of Auburn's SigEp fraternity for the week and was much nicer than my parents' house. Inside there were ten guys and girls sitting around a dining table, a few people lying on couches and chairs, and a few people standing in the kitchen sipping on beers. Some of them were wearing backwards fraternity hats, so I felt like I blended in reasonably well. The energy in the room was low, so it must have been the off-period between the two phases of partying each day.

"There's the fucking squatter," Randy said, pointing. "I hate that kid. We all hate him."

The squatter was out on the porch. He had red hair and strange posture—sort of held his arms out too wide.

"Goddamn, I already hate him," I joked. "That guy sucks."

Shared hatred is one of the strongest forces of bonding.

"There you go, there you go," said Randy as he patted me on the back.

After a few more beers, we headed for the party, Randy and I walking together along the empty beach where cops couldn't see us so we could keep drinking on the way. The stars and moon lit up the white sand under our feet—Randy in cowboy boots—and the gentle tide provided the musical soundtrack as the night took its lovely shape.

"Goddamnit, this is the life," Randy said.

"Ain't it?"

He knocked his beer against mine for the third or fourth time and tilted it way back to suck out its last drops. "Need another?" he asked.

I shook my empty can.

He grabbed two more beers from the 12-pack, handed me one, then turned out to the water. "Look at this shit," he said.

"My God," I said sincerely. "The fucking ocean."

Randy cracked open his new beer and put his arm around me. The ocean was calm enough to paint a perfect reflection of the sky above. I cracked open my beer, too, and put my arm around Randy.

"Is this America?" Randy asked, "or is this fucking America?"

I looked out over the water and knew exactly what Randy was saying.

"Is this college?" he asked, "or is this fucking college?"

I felt a little bit sad at this idea, but I tried to ignore the feeling. We knocked back hearty chugs of our beer.

Typically with Randy, a moment like this would be the high point in the night, just before his sudden lapse into drunken aggression or sadness. But not this night. We were still climbing and had a long way to go before the crash.

To find the party, we had to get off the beach, which involved jumping a few fences and sneaking through private backyards. The beach was lined with fancy homes, tall and skinny, with casually perfect yards and a Range Rover or two in each driveway. The party was at one of those houses, which had been rented by Auburn sophomores.

Before we knocked on the door, Randy said, "If anyone asks, say you know Dave Collard. Say it."

"Dave Collard."

"Yes, Dave Collard."

Randy knocked on the door, and a girl opened it, telling us to hurry inside; the party had to be hidden from the neighbors. Inside, the party was nearly dead, just a few people milling around in hushed little circles of conversation. But that wasn't the real party, we learned. The party was upstairs. The girl led us to a tiny spiral staircase where we had to hunch our bodies over in order to walk up. The stairs were metal and hard to see because no lights were on, and each stair was covered in a few inches of sand. We reached the second floor and saw more people sitting around talking, but the stairs continued on past the second floor, so we kept going. Now we could hear music coming more clearly and loudly from above, and some voices too. There was a third floor now, also with lights turned off and just a little hallway with more people sitting with beer. The stairs still continued on past the third floor. How tall was this place? Our heads were hunched down so we wouldn't smash them on the stairs above us as they spiraled upward. Now we could hear chanting, too, and it sounded like the kind of chanting you would hear entering a sports arena. The chants grew louder, and as we kept climbing, we could start to make out the words.

"U-S-A! U-S-A! U-S-A!"

Randy was ahead of me, and he turned back from above and yelled, "What the fuck!" The fourth floor blasted light into the stairwell, the shaft of light illuminating Randy's head as his eyes opened wide and a big grin spread across his face. I couldn't yet see what was causing his surprise. The chanting had become deafening and sounded like it was coming from at least a hundred people.

"U-S-A! U-S-A! U-S-A!" the voices rang out.

I could see it now as my head rose from out of the stairwell. It was a giant room packed wall-to-wall with over a hundred students, the air full of clenched fists as everybody punched upward in a 1-2-3 rhythm along to the syllables of "U-S-A! U-S-A!" Bright fluorescent lights overhead lit up the guys' fraternity hats and the girls' long blonde hair. Everyone wore neon or pastel. We were smashed together with no room to move at all. The tile floor was covered in sand. Everyone's bodies were tanned and nicely sculpted—their spring break diets over the past weeks and months had culminated in this moment right here. I had never seen a party with this much energy. I followed Randy as he slowly made his way through the crowd, pushing aside some people and high-fiving others. As we were walking, another chant spontaneously began. This time the chant was coming entirely from the guys.

"Tits! Out! Tits out for the boys! Tits! Out! Tits out for the boys!"

Randy later told me that someone at Auburn heard some Australians chanting this one time, so they brought it back to America. (By the way, even though this was being chanted, there was no chance that any of the women were about to undress. We were in the

Deep South, where modesty was still a virtue. Also, the chanting did have a satirical quality—or at least that's what I hoped.)

The chanting eventually stopped, and people were back to yelling and drinking. We passed one group of guys who would pour a beer into a paint stick and then, in less than two seconds, force the whole beer down one of their throats with the pressure of the paint stick. Randy was amazed. Finally we made it to the edge of the room where we could step outside onto the patio to catch our breaths.

"Oh my God," Randy said. "This is the wildest party I've ever seen."

"Me too."

"It's like a fucking movie party."

"No, it's even better."

"Dude, I don't know how they threw this party. There are like, all our best football and basketball players here. And there are so many girls. I've never seen this many hot girls at Auburn. I'm pretty sure this is the fucking place to be. Do I hook it up or what?"

"This is ridiculous. You hook it up, dude."

"I feel like, I feel like this is just the absolute best place to be right now."

"That fun thing that people across the world are imagining they might be missing out on right now? We're literally at that thing."

"We're the people actually at that thing."

"Incredible."

"Incredible."

We took deep breaths of fresh air then dove back into the ocean of bodies.

Inside we each pumped a cup of beer from the keg then split up. At a party like this, you have to either be engaged in a conversation or very conspicuously and rapidly consuming alcohol. Since the only person I knew was Randy, this put me in a stressful predicament. Randy was gone, and I didn't want to just stand there by myself. I touched my head to make sure I still had my magical hat on, then walked up to the first group of girls I saw. It was a group of three talking amongst themselves.

"You look like you don't know anybody here," I said to them, interrupting their conversation. "Am I right?" This, of course, was actually my own situation.

"Yeah, not really," one of them said.

"Well, I'm Drew. Now you can fit in." (This is cringeworthy, but I really said it.)

"Thanks," they smiled. They were all short and cute.

"Freshmen, right?" I asked, taking a guess.

"Yeah, from Ole Miss."

"Aw man, fuck Ole Miss!" I yelled. I'd learned on this trip that it was appropriate to make fun of another person's school. I was basically mimicking something I'd heard a cool guy say one time.

"What's wrong with Ole Miss?" one of them asked. They were still smiling at me, so I knew I hadn't crossed the line.

"Everyone who goes to Ole Miss is a piece of shit," I said, "and your football team sucks."

The girls continued smiling at this and seemed to think I was cool for saying it. The girls must have thought that I was from a respected fraternity, because everything I said was golden to them. I could say nothing wrong. I offered to get them drinks, and then we moved out to the balcony overlooking the ocean, where I continued my bullshitting. After some time, Randy stumbled out the door in a drunken hurry and whispered at me.

"Drew."

"What," I said.

"Drew, c'mere."

"No, come over here." I started introducing him to the girls. "This is Randy right here, probably the biggest badass at—"

"—no, no, cut the bullshit and c'mere. I need to tell you something."

"What the fuck?" I said. I walked over to him.

"Dude," he said, staring at me.

"What the fuck is it?"

"Dream Girl is here."

Oh my God, I thought, impossible.

"Where?" I asked.

He pointed inside. Through the crowd and across the room, Dream Girl was sitting on a countertop. She was at the party—I couldn't believe it. I didn't personally feel the same all-consuming euphoria over Dream Girl that Randy felt, but I could certainly appreciate her beauty.

"I don't know what she's even doing here," Randy said. "How the fuck? She doesn't know any of the people throwing this party." He looked at me for some direction and guidance.

"Talk to her," I said. "Right now."

"I don't know," Randy said. He tried to walk away.

I grabbed him and pulled him back. I placed my hands on his shoulders and stared through his eyes, deep into his drunken soul. "Listen, motherfucker. You're going to talk to her. You're fucking Randy, do you know what that means? Go talk to her. Fucking go."

He stared back at me so intensely that his brain seemed to vibrate inside his skull. "Alright," he said. "Alright."

Then he went inside.

I was so amazed by what was happening that I had to run over to the three Ole Miss girls and tell them the entire story. I told them about how Randy had been obsessed with Dream Girl forever and had always "made eyes" with her from across the bar, and how he never had the courage to talk to her, and how I had been in Auburn to write about him, and how the whole climax of that chapter was supposed to be that he would finally talk to her at the bar, but she wasn't at the bar on the final night, which was a huge disappointment, and how it was an insane coincidence that I was even in Destin at all on this night, and how it was an even greater coincidence that Dream Girl was also here now, how she was right there, at that very moment, through the crowd and across the room, and how Randy was just about to talk to her for the very first time.

In order to explain things, I also had to briefly explain that I wasn't actually a college student, that I was just there as a writer. I even took off my fraternity hat and said, "See? This isn't even my real hat."

The girls had been completely engrossed in the story about Randy, so I thought that they would still accept me. But instead, one of them asked, "So you don't go to college?"

"No," I said.

"Not at all?" she asked.

"That's correct," I said.

The girls traded looks with one another. "Well, good luck to your friend and with the book," one said. "We're gonna go back inside."

The girls did just as they said, leaving me alone. I watched them go inside, then I slowly turned out toward the ocean. I took a big swig of beer and watched the waves. At least I was honest, I thought. Out of the corner of my eye, I noticed a guy leaning over the railing the very same way as me. He looked over at me and smiled.

"I thought you had 'em, man," he said as he toasted his beer.

"Hey buddy, can't win 'em all," I said, toasting him back. "Cheers."

Back inside, I watched Randy make his way across the room toward Dream Girl. He ended up standing in a circle of people that was directly next to Dream Girl, such that Randy and Dream Girl were standing back-to-back while each of them was engaged in separate conversations. Then after about ten minutes, Randy somehow managed to switch conversations, so that he was now in Dream Girl's conversation circle. He was right next to her, speaking words, and she was listening.

I ran over near them, hidden out of view, and eavesdropped with my full attention. I couldn't hear much of what anybody said, but I could see Randy clutching his beer up by his chest with a goofy smile on his face. I could tell he was incredibly nervous, but he was nervous in a way that could pass as confident. He kind of just looked like a friendly, happy guy.

Over time, their conversation circle shrunk to only three people. It was just Randy, Dream Girl, and one other guy standing and talking. This would have been great news, except that the other guy was also interested in Dream Girl, and he was a huge threat.

"C'mon, just give me a kiss," the guy said to Dream Girl. He was wearing an orange sleeveless shirt, which exposed huge biceps that looked like tennis balls.

"Why?" Dream Girl asked.

"'Cause I want you to," said Biceps.

"Well, that's too bad," she said. Dream Girl had a cute Southern accent—it was the first time I'd ever heard her speak.

"Ah, just do it!" said Randy, for some reason. "Get it over with!"

Dream Girl called Randy's bluff, turned to Biceps, and leaned in. Their lips touched, then their tongues. It was an exaggerated, showy kiss. Randy craned his neck and drank a big mouthful of beer.

After their kiss, Dream Girl and Biceps were speaking softly to each other as Randy simply watched them. He was about to lose her, and he was watching it happen. I felt like I had to do something.

I walked over and hit Biceps on the arm. "Yo man, whatcha drinkin'?" I asked.

"Oh, it's some punch," he said.

"Badass, brotha! Nothin' like a lil bit of punch, eh?"

"Hah, I guess so!" he said.

I was trying to distract him. It was completely obnoxious, but necessary.

"Where you from, bud?" I asked.

"FSU, how about you?"

"Florida State— what are they, the Gators? Crocodiles? Is it still Seminoles? Am I thinking of the right school?"

Biceps turned toward me, forced to be polite as I interrupted his conversation with Dream Girl. Meanwhile I could see over his shoulder that now Randy was talking with her. If I could keep this up, maybe Randy could make some progress on his end.

Suddenly there was a loud noise like a gunshot. Everyone quit talking to look around. The noise in the room dropped. Bam! Bam! I turned and saw that it was a girl hitting a pan—some angry girl with a frying pan and a spatula. Bam! Bam! The noise dropped even more.

"EVERYBODY GET OUT! IF YOU DON'T KNOW ANYBODY HERE, GET OUT!" she screamed.

The party was over. The girl was going around the room, group by group, and either letting people stay because they knew the host, or forcing them to leave because they didn't know the host.

I continued spewing my nonsense to Biceps, distracting him, until I noticed that the three Ole Miss girls from earlier were pointing toward me from across the room while talking to the angry girl with the spatula. I got the feeling that they were trying to tell Spatula Girl that they knew me, thinking that it would allow them to stay at the party. I walked over to them immediately.

"What's going on?" I asked.

"Are these girls with you?" asked Spatula Girl.

"Oh, these girls?" I looked at each of them and thought about our conversation from earlier. I said, "Nope."

"Who do you know?" she asked me.

The name. The golden name. "Dave Collard," I said.

Spatula Girl nodded in approval—Dave Collard was the guy to know. That meant I was in, and the Ole Miss girls were out.

Spatula Girl pointed to the stairs. "Ok girls, get out! Get out right now!"

The three of them lowered their heads and left down the stairs. As I watched them leave, I felt full of guilty pleasure.

"We have to have this place clean by 9am tomorrow morning," Spatula Girl said to me. "We're fucked. Look at all this fucking sand. Just look at it."

She was right—the floor was completely covered in sand. I had no idea how anyone would be able to clean it by morning time. But that wasn't my problem. My problem was Randy and Dream Girl and Biceps.

"I'll try to help you clear people out," I said to Spatula Girl. Then I had a brilliant idea. "See that guy right there?" I asked.

"Who?" she asked.

I pointed at Biceps. "Him. He goes to Florida State."

The crowd was thinning out now. Biceps was back in the three-way conversation with Randy and Dream Girl. I brought Spatula Girl over with me to the three of them.

"You go to Florida State, right?" I asked Biceps.

"Yeah?" he said.

Spatula Girl interrupted. "Alright, get out! Go!"

"Wait, wait, it's cool!" he pleaded.

"NOPE!" she yelled. "Get out!"

Spatula Girl started to physically push him away, but he remained looking at Dream Girl while he reached his hands out for her like someone who had fallen off a cliff and was still reaching up for the ledge.

"Hold up, just wait!" he said. "Give me just one second!"

"No! You have to get the fuck out!" said Spatula Girl.

"Get out, man," I added unnecessarily. "This isn't your house."

Biceps was still pleading with Dream Girl, who now appeared entirely disinterested in him—it's simply unattractive to get kicked out of a party. He was finally pushed to the stairwell and forced to go home. The whole thing was a little bit cruel, but my friend was Randy, not Biceps. And now Randy was alone with Dream Girl. The knowledge that I had orchestrated some of it made me feel euphoric. Everything was coming together perfectly, and I couldn't believe any of it was really happening.

But the party was mellowing out. Not wanting the night to slow down, I decided to have another drink. Dream Girl was carrying a pitcher full of a bright orange liquid, and I asked her what it was.

"It's shots," she said. "You can have it."

"It's 'shots'? What do you mean?"

"Yeah, these are shots."

"Ok, just pour it in my cup," I said.

She did, filling my cup to the brim. In my giddiness, I made the poor decision to drink all of it, and I blacked out a couple of minutes later. I remember nothing else from the night. I would have to find out what happened with Randy and Dream Girl in the morning.

I woke up in my sleeping bag in the back of my car. I was naked except for my socks, and I was soaking wet because I'd pissed myself. It was 12:30pm, and with the sun coming in through the windows, it felt like it was about 120 degrees in the car. I checked my phone and saw that I had missed 24 texts from Randy. My vision was blurry from my hangover, so I couldn't read all of his texts, but as I scrolled through them, I saw some phrases like, "biggest mistake of my life," and, "I'm going to raise my son differently." I called him. He didn't answer, but within a minute he was standing outside by my car.

"I was knocking on your car all morning," he said. "You wouldn't wake the fuck up."

"Careful," I warned. "I'm naked under here and I pissed myself."

"You piece of shit." Randy stood outside the car, talking to me through the vent in the window.

"How'd I get back here?" I asked. My car was in the lot next to Randy's house, at least a mile's walk from where the party had been.

"Dude, you fell down a staircase and then you vommed. Do you remember that?"

"Fuck. No, I don't."

"My buddy drove you back."

"Was he drunk?"

"Yeah, but not as drunk as you. Did you see my texts?"

"I haven't read them yet."

"Good. Don't ever, ever read them. I sent that shit to you from the lobby bathroom of a random ass hotel. I have no idea how I got in there."

"What happened?"

Before Randy could answer, he did a double take. "Oh shit, what happened to your face?"

"What? What is it?"

"You have a bunch of cuts and a big scrape."

"Ah fuck, my hand hurts like shit too." My wrist was dark purple and brown.

"Probably because you fell down a fucking staircase," Randy said.

Randy stepped away so I could climb out of the sleeping bag, dry off with my towel, and put some clothes on. I was by no means clean, but that level of hygiene would have to suffice until I could find a shower. In the meantime, I piled my wet clothes and sleeping bag into the back corner of my car, knowing I'd need to wash every single thing in the car as soon as I could.

We took a walk to eat some fast food for breakfast. We sat in a booth in the corner with our heads hung low. It was there that Randy began his long story. We were both still drunk at 1pm.

"Last night could have been the best night of my life, ok?" he said. "I don't know, I don't know what happened. We left the party, you were back behind us when we left, do you remember?"

"No."

"Well, we got split up from you. She and I went out onto the beach to walk so the cops wouldn't stop us along the road."

"You and Dream girl?"

"Yes," he said impatiently, probably wanting to not refer to her as Dream Girl anymore. "Actually, there was another guy with us, but you yelled at him and told him to come back with you."

"Hell yeah. I think I remember that. I told him he was cock blocking."

"So we were walking along the beach, and we were like walking along the water part, and I started carrying her in my arms."

"Bride style?"

"What do you mean?"

"The way a groom carries a bride."

"Yeah, I guess so, yeah. I don't know how it started, but yeah, we walked along, and I was carrying her in my arms."

So Randy and Dream Girl were walking along the beach, Dream Girl in his arms, smiling up at him in the moonlight on the last night of spring break. Randy remembered none of the conversation that took place between them—he said he was just yammering on about something unimportant, but that she was laughing and enjoying it. I could hardly believe it, the thought of Randy carrying Dream Girl in his arms along the empty beach in the middle of the night.

They continued along the edge of the water, headed up the beach toward their respective houses, as waves splashed Randy's boots. He knew which sorority Dream Girl was in, and he knew where she was supposed to be sleeping that night, yet he had carried her up the beach far past where she needed to be dropped off if she were going back to her own house. That was a great sign—Dream Girl not saying anything when they walked past her house. But Randy still hadn't kissed her or discussed anything about where they would be staying, or if they would be staying together at all. Dream Girl must have been waiting for Randy to make a move. According to Randy, absolutely no thoughts were going through his head this entire time—not fear, not desire, not disbelief, just nothingness. When enough time had elapsed since they had passed Dream Girl's house, she finally spoke up and said, "We've already passed my house."

Randy, still carrying her in his arms, set her down in the sand and asked, "Really?"

Then she asked him, "Where are you staying?"

He told her that he was staying with the SigEps, and that he was going there.

She told him the sorority she was staying with. "It's back that way," she said, pointing.

He faced her and she faced him. The tide rose, then it fell.

Kissing a girl can be a weird thing to do if you're out of practice. You have to invade her personal space, put your mouth onto her mouth, and then just cross your fingers in hopes that her mouth kisses yours back. If she doesn't kiss you back, it feels really bad, because it means that she doesn't like you in the same way that you like her. It's reasonable to be scared of kissing someone. Unfortunately, Randy didn't even try.

Dream Girl told him that her house was back behind them. She stood there pointing, presumably waiting for Randy to either make a move or to invite her to his house. But Randy didn't.

"Alright. See you later, I guess?" Randy said.

"Yeah, ok. Bye?" Dream Girl said, starting to turn away from him.

"See ya," Randy said, also turning away from her.

And then, in the moonlight, along the sandy coast, as the water rose and fell at their feet, on the last night of spring break, Randy and Dream Girl departed toward their separate houses, never to speak again.

"I don't understand," I said, "how did... So you just set her down and walked away? Why didn't you do anything?"

Randy chewed his burger and took a sip of soda. "I don't know," he muttered.

"How did you... Why didn't you call back to her or chase her down or something?"

"I don't know. I just walked back toward the house and somehow stumbled into some hotel lobby bathroom. That's where I texted you."

"Why didn't you kiss her when you set her down? You were just scared?"

"I don't know. I have no clue. I just stood there."

"Jesus, dude. Well you don't need me to beat you up over it. You already know."

Randy nodded and ingested another large mouthful of burger. He was in the beginning stages of grief.

Randy's story was one of the most unbelievable and painful things I had ever heard. In romantic comedies, the woman says to the nervous man, "Aren't you gonna to kiss me, silly?" then he kisses her, and then they fall in love. But real life is harsh, I was learning, and it doesn't reward cowardice. I was almost as devastated as Randy.

"When do you go back to class?" I asked.

"Monday. We could actually stay one more night," Randy smirked.

"Oh my God. Maybe we should. I'd need to take a long-ass nap today, and maybe an ocean swim to get this dried piss off me."

"You and me are what's wrong with the youth of America."

We finished our burgers and made a plan. Randy and the SigEps no longer had their rental house, so we had nowhere to shower or hang out. We would buy some disinfectant spray for the urine, clean out my car, both crawl into the back of my car to take a long nap, then wake up and party for one more night. When we agreed to this, I was still drunk from the previous night, so the full extent of the hangover had not hit me yet. We pulled into the parking lot of a Winn Dixie to buy the disinfectant spray.

"There's a liquor store across the street," said Randy, "for later."

We bought the spray and some trash bags, sprayed down my car, then put my sleeping bag, clothes, and towels into the trash bag. We picked spots in my car and climbed in, lying shoulder to shoulder as the hot sun shone onto our faces.

"I feel... I just don't even know what to feel anymore," said Randy.

"Imagine if you had even just made out with Dream Girl. You two, rolling around in the sand."

"Fuck off, please. I'm serious."

"Sorry."

My hangover was starting to creep up on me as Randy hunted like a dog for a comfortable position to lie.

"This is uncomfortable as shit, how do you sleep back here?" he asked.

"There's usually a sleeping bag, and it's usually just me."

"There's no fucking room."

"I don't care, shut up."

"What the fuck, dude, my head's resting on this goddamn plastic."

"Yeah, that's because the pillows are covered in piss."

"Dude, I don't fit. We're not spooning. Can you turn over or something?"

"No."

"Fuck, dude, c'mon, this sucks."

"I know it does. Just relax."

Randy was still a moment. "What would our parents think of us?"

"Not much, man."

"We could get some beers to help us sleep."

"Fuck you."

"I'm kidding. I don't want to drink ever again."

"Neither do I. We should just go back to Auburn."

"Dude, can we? I don't want to party tonight."

"Thank God," I said. "Drinking sounds so awful. My hangover is coming on. Can you drive back?"

We changed plans. I handed Randy my keys so he could drive, and I stayed lying in the back of the car while trying to survive my hangover. We blasted air conditioning and played one particularly soothing Coldplay song on repeat for the three-hour ride back to Alabama.

"Dude, would you sit up?" Randy asked.

"No, man. Fuck you. My head's killing me."

"Just sit up, c'mon. I'm drowning in my sorrows up here."

"You'll manage."

"I'm going to turn your song off."

"Do not turn off the fucking song."

"Fine."

We drove with the music playing for another 30 miles without talking until Randy broke the silence and verbalized what must have been circling through his mind the whole time.

"Spring break is attached to the biggest high and the biggest low," he said. "When school first gets out, you're like, 'Fuck yeah, it's spring break,' but then it's over and you have to go back and you won't have it again for another year. Going back is the most depressing thing I can think of. Especially in my case with what happened. Anyway, I've never been more upset going back to Auburn."

It appeared that Randy and I could think of nothing else to do for our last night together other than to drink. Although we had skipped out on one more night at the beach on account of not wanting to drink anymore, after we arrived in Auburn we felt up for it again. We stopped at a department store to buy a paint stick, hoping to imitate the guys we saw at the party the previous night. One of the employees asked us why we were so particular about the kind of paint stick we were buying, and we told her the truth that we hoped to drink beer with it. Once we bought the paint stick, we couldn't make it work, but the trial-and-error process filled our afternoon. Afterward, Randy grabbed a bottle of whiskey from his refrigerator, and we left toward his friends' apartment.

At the apartment, the usual crew of Randy's fraternity brothers sat around on the couches. Everybody had been away to different beaches for spring break, and they were now returning together to share stories.

"Hey! Look who it is!" Barnes said to me. "He couldn't get enough of us."

"You guys do have a certain appeal," I said.

"Yo Randy," Nick said, "did you get your tip wet over spring break? Tug job? Maybe a sandjob?"

Randy ignored the question. "Hey, tell Drew about the table I bought."

"It fucking sucks," said Barnes. "He got a total bitch table."

This was the table Randy broke and had to replace for the fraternity house. During my time away, Randy had settled his debts by buying a new side-table for the entryway.

"I spent 20 bucks at the thrift store," Randy said. "It's a little short, but it looks just fine."

"It's a bitch table and everyone knows it," said Barnes.

"How were your spring breaks?" I asked the guys in the room.

"One thing I learned," said Nick, "is that I will NEVER let my daughter go to Destin."

"Ah, fuck that!" said Randy. "I'll go with her!"

The guys shared their stories—getting daytime blackout drunk, run-ins with cops, falling in love. Randy listened but didn't share any stories. He took the whiskey and poured it into a tall plastic cup to make a mixed drink for himself, then looked at me sheepishly.

"I'm not trying to get real fucked up," he said.

"Of course not," I said.

"I probably just shouldn't say anything. We know what this means. I can't win."

"Want to make me one of those too?"

"I knew I loved you."

"I only join in because I know I'm free to leave at any time."

"That's what you like to think."

Randy wanted to go to 17/16 one last time for my final night in Auburn. Randy's fraternity brothers weren't joining us that night, and none of Randy's other friends would be there. It was a night of the week when none of the college students went out to bars. We sat at the bar and spent a few hours chatting easily, drinking a couple beers, then a couple more, and so on, until we became just as drunk as every other night.

"The thing about Auburn, the thing about Auburn," Randy said. "Everything's a memory. Everything is one big fucking memory. I love it."

"Last night already feels like a distant memory."

"That's one memory I hope does not last."

"You'll look back fondly someday. Maybe after you graduate and never see Dream Girl again."

"That's going to be a shitty day, the day I have to throw in the towel. And the paint stick."

"I wonder if that's how it works," I said, "like if there's one day where you throw in the towel, or if you gradually throw in lots and lots of smaller towels until you eventually run out."

"I'm keeping the paint stick either way."

For the next round of drinks, I ordered us each a beer and a shot of whiskey.

"It's my last night, I had to do it," I said.

"I hope you never, never come back," Randy said.

"Me too."

"I swear, I can't walk into this bar without getting just straight fucking hammered. It's awful. And kinda cool."

"Think you'll ever talk to Dream Girl again? I think you could. Maybe she thinks you just didn't want her for some reason."

"If I had hooked up with that girl it might have been the best night of my life."

I looked around and noticed the crowd was much older that night. It was an "off night" for college students, and still I couldn't help but see the patrons as old students. They were in their 30s and 40s, but I couldn't see them as anything but old versions of former students.

"You know," I said, "someday we won't fit in at a place like this. There'll be new 20-year-olds filling in our places, and we'll be the old ones."

"Fuck off," said Randy. "I don't want to think about that. I'm never getting old."

"Sometimes I want to be old. Old and content at the end of a long life." I took a swig of beer. "When do you graduate?"

"Two more years. I can't do it. I don't know how I'm ever going to leave." Randy stared into the mouth of his beer but didn't take a drink. He moved his fingertip around the lip of his can, collecting all the little droplets of condensation. "Ah, that's what grad school is for."

11

UNIVERSITY OF LONG ISLAND POST

There is a moment in every young man's life when he takes off his fraternity hat and never puts it back on. I took off my fraternity hat somewhere in Florida and retired it forever; it would do me no good in the Northeast. Today the hat lives on in infamy at my parents' house, where my dad sometimes wears it—forward, not backward—as he mows the grass.

For the first time on the trip, the next campus was farther away than the distance of the drive back home. That meant that after each subsequent week, it would be a shorter drive to visit a new school than to give up and return to Texas. Once I drove to the Northeast, I was in a sense stuck there, because I would be so far from home. Along the way, I had to ask myself if I thought there was more to learn about college life. Had I seen everything that there was to see, or had I only seen a tiny portion? A person is supposed to go on a journey and come out the other side better off. Unfortunately, I was feeling worse off than when I started. I felt my values eroding and my sense of self fragmenting into incoherent parts.

Long Island University has two campuses—one in Brooklyn and one on Long Island. Noah went to the one on Long Island, which was called Long Island Post. He met me at my car as he was heading to the cafeteria to eat.

"I sort of feel like I was tricked into coming here," he told me. "The advertising for Post makes it sound like people are coming here from all over the world, so I thought it was for people who wanted to go far from home to be independent, but it turns out that something like three out of four kids don't even live on campus and just drive in from around Long Island. It's mostly a commuter school."

"Interesting," I said.

"But anyway, I heard there were 10,000 students who went here when I visited, so I thought campus would be packed, but somehow I never found out that most people don't live on campus. In the evenings there just aren't a lot of people here."

We went inside the cafeteria, called Winnick.

"Be careful with Winnick," Noah said. "I'm 80-90% sure they put a little bit of laxatives in the food in case people get sick."

I burst out with laughter, but Noah was serious.

"I'm pretty sure there's a legal amount of laxatives you can put in food at a cafeteria like this," he continued. "If I were you, I'd pick something safe to eat, because you'll probably get the shits as you adjust to Winnick."

I was teary-eyed with laughter, mostly because Noah was entirely sincere. He introduced me to two girls he knew while my eyes were still full of tears.

"Sorry," I told them. "Noah's cracking me up by saying the food is full of laxatives."

"No, it is," one of them told me. "Last year like 40 people got food poisoning at the exact same time, so this year we're pretty sure they started putting laxatives in the food."

(Disclaimer: Apparently this is not true. It's a common myth around college campuses that the cafeterias put laxatives in the food.)

Noah and I sat eating by ourselves.

"I'll just go ahead and tell you what's going on for me," he said. "This year I'm really getting things together, trying to be a better student and more involved and all that. I figure there's a lot to accomplish at college. But yeah, last year I sort of sat in my room a lot and didn't do much. I made this gravity bong that I kept in my room, and so, yeah, I pretty much didn't leave. But it turns out I'm one of the smartest kids here, I guess. I have a 3.9 GPA, and that's way better than in high school. People around here actually respect me for my grades, but I sort of wish I was more challenged and picked a better school. Like, a teacher shot himself in the leg while teaching a class on gun safety. Just saying. That was last year, and I wasn't in the class, but it's just an example."

After dinner, we headed toward Noah's dorm.

"It's really stupid, but I don't talk to my roommate anymore," Noah said. "We started fighting over Facebook."

Noah went on to tell me a long story about how he called his roommate, Jeffrey, "Captain Fucking America," so then Jeffrey made a cake with letters "CFA" written on it, the abbreviation for Captain Fucking America. Then Jeffrey's girlfriend prank called Noah on spring break, so Noah called Jeffrey a douchebag in front of their group of friends. Then Jeffrey ate some of Noah's cookies that Noah's girlfriend's mom baked.

"It's so middle school of us," Noah continued, "doing little things to piss each other off like that. But it's kind of nice now, actually. I walk into our room and don't even have to look at him. But yeah, everyone in our group says we're being immature and need to apologize. And it's true. But I already tried to apologize to him, and he didn't say he was sorry back."

In Noah's dorm, his roommate Jeffrey and Jeffrey's girlfriend were watching TV. There were two small TVs set up side-by-side, so that no sharing would be necessary between Noah and Jeffrey. I introduced myself and acted like I knew nothing about their ongoing fight, meanwhile relishing the strange tension between them. Noah and Jeffrey did not speak to each other or even look at each other for the whole week.

Noah spent the rest of the night studying at his desk, so I took my first shower in three days and then sat quietly enjoying Noah's company.

In the morning, I went with Noah to a few of his classes. He liked to point out all the girls who were Scandinavian. Long Island Post didn't have as many international students as Noah had hoped, but it did have a large representation of attractive Scandinavian women.

"She's a Swede," Noah whispered to me during class. When another girl in the back spoke up, he said, "Turn around, look at her. Norwegian. She also has a really great ass."

After class, we kept walking and talking.

"I actually get noticed up here for my slight sense of manners," said Noah. "Like, it's really strange up here to hold open a door for a girl, so people notice. I try to say 'y'all' more than usual, because people think it's all exotic. I play up the Texas thing."

Noah was interrupted. Three blonde girls walked past us, and he whispered, "Swede, Swede, Danish."

He continued. "It's surprising that the people in the North really dislike the South. When I was in Texas, I would find myself defending the North. But up here, people actually say a lot of stupid shit about Texas. Like, people will still ask me the 'Do you ride horses?' shit. I figured the Northeast would be kind of more intellectual, but I've learned there are dumbasses everywhere."

I nodded.

"But what surprised me was to realize that I'm firmly from the upper middle class. I never knew too many people outside my economic background, so I was surprised to find a lot of these people's parents are blue collar workers. Around 85% of the students here are on government financial aid. My friends think I'm rich because my parents are paying for my college. So it's just a different experience coming here. I'm sure you've noticed how many minorities there are here. Is it more than you're used to seeing?"

"Yeah, I think so."

"It's weird, because here I have a pretty good academic scholarship and am almost a prized student. Someone from Jamaica, Queens would probably step onto campus and think it was a super-rich prestigious school, and to them it would be."

We sat through another class, then got into Noah's car to grab some food.

"The other thing up here," he said as he turned his keys, "is that the girls are way different. The first two to three months it was really hard for me to get laid. In the South, girls expect respect, so that's how I always did it. Up here, you have to be a big asshole. You ignore them as much as possible until they get close enough, then you go in for the kill. In the South, you show interest right away, talking and making jokes. Up here that's a turnoff. Up here you talk for a second then walk away. Except the Scandinavians."

"How do you get with the Scandinavians?" I asked.

"I've only fucked one Scandinavian. They're much more mild-mannered and take a lot more work."

The car was silent for a moment.

"Oh, and Long Island has a lot of STDs. So always bag it."

"Good to know."

We ate pizza in Long Island, then headed back to campus.

"I think I'm starting to hit a stage in life where I'm looking for more responsibility," Noah said. "For the longest time you try to avoid responsibility, you know? But I'm starting to welcome it. It's like hitting the next stage of growing up. There's a lot more satisfaction in that than I used to think when I was 17."

"You'll be surprised a lot in New York City," he continued. "You're taken aback a lot and humbled. My friend Dante lives on welfare in the city. He was shot when he was 3. He's a very intelligent person and a very rational person, and I was quite shocked to find that out about him. Sometimes you'll see the hood come out in him, just a bit, but he's raised the bar for his own neighborhood and the people in his neighborhood. He didn't go into drugs, didn't go into crime or violence. He coulda been making thousands a week—I talked to him about it—but he didn't. There's actually a black achievement award he just won for all Staten Island. And I was like, 'Where am I ever gonna meet an inspiring black guy who changes my idea of the hood and black people and poverty?' Not where I'm from."

In the center of campus at Long Island Post is a grassy field large enough to hold two American football games. On my fourth day with Noah, we headed there to play soccer with his friends. There were two or three soccer games taking place on one end of the field, while on the other end students sat together on blankets. Groups of students were gathered in large circles drinking beer and blasting music from speakers. Noah said it was the most alive he had ever seen campus. LIU Post is a wet campus, so students are allowed to openly drink alcohol if they are at least 21 years old. If you're under 21, you just put your beer in a brown bag, according to Noah. Although LIU Post might be one of the least well-known colleges in this book, its campus was one of the prettiest and the most active with social life.

"I've never seen it this packed," said Noah. "Everyone must want to have a good time. You came on the right week."

There were campus security guards at LIU Post, Noah informed me, but they're not affiliated with the police in any way. According to Noah, they have no license to use physical force, and the most they can do is hand out tickets. Noah recommended that if any of the campus security approached me for any reason, that I should just run away, since there are no consequences.

The students had just arrived back from spring break, the weather was perfect, and the flowers around campus were in full bloom. Something about the field radiated positivity, and I felt that no person there was unhappy. Noah and I stood along the sidelines of the soccer game waiting to jump in, and he took the opportunity to tell me another story.

In high school, his parents caught him getting drunk before school during his senior year, and as punishment they told him he couldn't go to college. In order to go, he had to beg and show proof that he would change his ways.

"I had really bad priorities," Noah said. "But now in college my priorities are straight and my motivation is high, and I take pride in the fact that I have good grades. This is going to sound bad, but it's almost more of a power thing. People now know I have good grades, and I'm able to get respect and pick up girls better because that's like an advantage I have. It makes me more well-rounded, admired. People respect me for it."

"So was it easy to straighten out your priorities?" I asked.

"That first semester, I didn't want to let my parents down, since obviously they let me go to college. But it's also kind of a spite thing, like, 'Fuck you, I'm gonna get amazing grades,' but then it turned into the pride thing."

We played a couple games of soccer with Noah's friends. When the sun set and it grew dark, the field remained just as active as it had been all afternoon. Most people there had been drinking the whole day, so since Noah and I were sober, that meant we were behind them. There was a rumor that a night party was going to happen on the field, so Noah and I left to buy liquor, then returned back to campus.

It was entirely dark as we hurried back to the field. Noah carried our whiskey and some paper cups to use as shot glasses. We passed some students heading the other way on the sidewalk.

"Are people still on the field?" Noah asked them.

"They all moved to the cove," one said.

We turned around to follow the group headed to the cove. The cove was a U-shaped area between three walls of a dorm building. The students had moved there from the field to continue their night. What was a pleasant, easygoing afternoon had turned into something of a rager. A big mob of students was packed together chugging from liquor bottles, smoking weed, yelling at each other, and getting into fights. As soon as Noah and I arrived, we saw the campus security guards on foot, approaching the students.

"Alright, everybody! Break it up! Clear it out!" yelled one of the guards. "Break it up, I said!"

Noah and I stayed back, making sure we wouldn't become the targets of the guards. They moved into the cove and tried to clear out the students with their yells, but like Noah had hinted at earlier, the guards had very little power. If a guard approached a student, the student would simply walk away. Each student only had to make sure he wasn't the closest person to the security guard at any one time.

"They have no authority!" someone yelled.

The crowd cheered.

Another group of security guards drove up in a pickup truck and parked with their headlights lighting up the cove. This caused the mob of students to spill out of the cove, and now that they were spread out, the guards were better able to corner one student at a time.

Noah echoed the student's yell, this time much louder. "THEY HAVE NO AUTHORITY!"

The crowd cheered again. Then somebody yelled out, "TIP THE TRUCK!"

Noah repeated it. "YEAH! TIP THE FUCKING TRUCK!"

"TIP THE TRUCK!" a student repeated.

Noah and a couple other students looked at each other wide-eyed to ask, "Are we doing this?" and then began in unison to start a slow chant.

"TIP THE TRUCK! TIP THE TRUCK! TIP THE TRUCK!"

The security guards kept yelling, "CLEAR OUT! CLEAR OUT OF THE COVE!"

The students' chants grew louder. "TIP! THE! TRUCK! TIP! THE! TRUCK!"

Noah leaned over to me and said, "Holy fuck, this is awesome," then hoisted his fist back up. "TIP THE TRUCK!"

Historians Will and Ariel Durant wrote that "revolt, of course, is an inborn right of youth; it is a mark of the ego becoming conscious of itself and demanding its place in the world." But this revolt? This was a useless revolt fueled by alcohol and nihilism. And I was chanting too! "Tip the truck! Tip the truck!"

But no students were making any real efforts to actually tip the truck, nor were they even gathering around the truck. It was a joke, a bluff. One of the security guards had managed to make one student stand still long enough to hand him a ticket, and the sight of that punishment worked as an effective deterrent for the rest of the students.

Now the crowd of students was marching out of the cove, away from the security truck, while still chanting "TIP THE TRUCK!" in unison.

"What the hell kind of mob is this?" I asked Noah.

"People got scared," he said.

Once we all rounded a corner away from the security guards, the chanting stopped, and we marched all the way back to the field. Along the way, students laughed with each other and said varieties of, "Oh my God, that was awesome!" about their chanting at the cove.

The party reestablished itself back in the middle of the field. The students stood around taking swigs of liquor or chugging beers. There I met one of Noah's friends, who told me that the key to college life is resourcefulness. He was incredibly drunk and must have said 'resourcefulness' a hundred times, each time using the 'A-OK' hand symbol—index finger and thumb making a circle with the other fingers sticking out.

"No, no, no," he said, "here's ALL you need to know about college: resourcefulness. Resourcefulness."

"I hear you," I said. "Resourcefulness, got it. But what resources?"

"You're not listening," he would say, "I'm already telling you all you need: resourcefulness."

We were interrupted by two guys having a dance-off. The crowd gathered in a big circle around them. After a few rounds of dancing, the two guys stepped close together and had a playful fight, which immediately escalated into a real fight. Everybody cheered as the real fight broke out. Eventually the winner of the fight pinned the loser and boxed his ears until he squealed in submission.

The security guards showed up again, but this time they parked their truck far away on the other side of the field and shined their lights at us. None of the guards ever stepped out of the truck to try to end the party. We raised our liquor bottles up in the air as taunts. Their lights actually helped us by lighting up the field to make it a better environment for partying.

In the middle of all the debauchery, I noticed that there was a girl, alone among a crowd of students, who was simply staring at me. She was staring at me in an almost frightening way, as if she'd been staring at me for five straight minutes. I walked over to her.

"Hi?" I said, suspiciously.

"You have very powerful eye contact," she said.

"You were the one staring at me," I said.

"Are you a spiritual person?" she asked.

"Not particularly, no."

"Do you believe in ghosts?"

"No. Do you?"

"Yes. I've always believed in ghosts, but only recently have I been able to communicate with the dead. I've been able to help some of the dead pass peacefully." She had dreadlocks and she was wearing a backpack.

"How much weed did you smoke?" I asked.

"None. I'm sober," she said.

"You must be stoned."

"Why would I need to be?"

"Give me one second."

I walked over to Noah. "See that girl there?" I pointed to her. "Is she crazy or something?"

Noah cracked up. "Not exactly."

"She told me she believes in ghosts."

The girl still stared as us from across the field, still standing alone, completely disengaged from the realm of social life around her.

Noah yelled over to her, "It's rude to stare!"

She took that as a cue to approach us, but she didn't speak.

"Noah said he doesn't believe in ghosts either," I told her.

"Why not?" she asked Noah.

"I don't know, I just don't," Noah said.

"I think you need to be honest about your deep emotional feelings. Tell me, how do you really feel right now?"

"Yeah, ok," said Noah, scratching his neck. "No thanks."

"No, really," she said. "You're a beautiful person. Tell me how you feel."

"I know I am," he laughed. "Thank you."

"Just be honest with yourself."

"Yeah, Noah," I joked, "just be honest about your deep emotional feelings."

"Ok, fuck this," Noah said before walking away from us.

"Sorry about Noah," I said. "He's just a little uptight."

"That's ok. Do you want to see a labyrinth?"

"What?"

"Would you like me to take you to a labyrinth?"

I couldn't say no to her offer. "Sure," I said.

We traded names. Her name was Olivia. Olivia led me across campus to a hidden spot that looked like an orchard of pear trees. I had no idea where we were. Behind an opening in the trees was a square patch of stones spiraling inward. This was the labyrinth.

"Get on my back," she said.

She was very short, but apparently she had strong legs. When I jumped up on her back, she could carry me with perfect balance. She started on the outside of the labyrinth and walked along the stones, finding her way to the center. Once we reached the center, she let me down.

"That was awesome," I said.

"It's nice, isn't it?"

"My spiritual energy is all maxed out right now."

"Are you making fun?"

"Sort of," I confessed.

"You shouldn't do that."

"You're right, I'm sorry."

"Why do you make so many jokes?"

"I don't know. This is a little unusual."

"Do things that are unusual make you uncomfortable?"

"Not always. Right now, maybe."

"You don't have to feel that way."

"You're right."

We stood in silence for a minute. After a few deep breaths I was able to feel an incredible sense of peace. We looked around at the leaves as they moved with the wind. I no longer felt drunk. Instead I felt entirely clear, like I had finally snapped out of a mood that had been with me for weeks. The LIU students were still partying on the field, but we were entirely separate from them.

"Do you want to meet my roommate?" she asked.

I said yes.

Their dorm room walls were covered in tie-dye sheets and peace signs and dream catchers. Olivia's roommate was sitting on her bed in the lotus position when we walked in. I took a seat on the floor and listened to them talk across their beds.

"Have you talked to your Pisces today?" asked Olivia.

"He felt cold in my thoughts," said the roommate.

"Maybe he just needs more space."

"But I'm giving my space to my Capricorn."

"I have a question," I interrupted. "How critical is somebody's astrological sign in your personal relationships?"

Both girls stared at me and didn't answer.

"Like, what if you get along with someone real well," I continued, "and then you find out their sign is incompatible for getting along?"

"It doesn't work that way. Everybody gets along."

"So it's more like the flavor of how you get along?"

"Yes."

"I have another question. How are my vibes? How is my energy?"

"You're open," said Olivia, "and you're warm toward people. But you're scrambled."

"Scrambled! I'm not scrambled!"

"Yes. You're sending yourself in too many directions. But you'll figure everything out." She turned toward her roommate. "Do you see it too?"

"Yes," the roommate said. "I can sense you're scrambled. But I've been scrambled before. You don't need to worry."

It was getting late, and the girls told me that I could sleep on their floor. Before bed, the girls saw a giant centipede on their floor. Instead of killing it and disposing of it like sensible people, the girls decided to let the thing roam freely in their room. They were concerned that it might be hungry or thirsty. Olivia even said, "I just want him to feel safe." Their empathy was commendable, but unfortunately I was the person who had to sleep on the floor next to it.

The girls were both asleep when I woke up, so I nudged Olivia's shoulder before I left. She jolted awake with huge eyes and let out a gasp.

"I'm taking off," I told her. "Thanks for letting me sleep here, and for showing me the labyrinth."

"Go safe in your journey," she said.

"You too."

I wasn't sure exactly what Olivia had taught me, but I left her dorm room that morning feeling like she had given me a wonderful gift.

———

On my last day at Long Island Post, Noah and his girlfriend Ellie were going to visit Noah's grandma, who lived on Long Island across the water from Manhattan. They invited me to tag along. We picked up sub sandwiches on the way.

"Thanks for coming along with me, both of you," said Noah. "It means a lot."

We took the elevator up eight floors to his grandma's apartment, which she had lived in for as long as Noah could remember. She lived there alone and had only her daughter—Noah's aunt—and Noah to come visit her. Noah and Ellie greeted her at the door with hugs, then we all took seats. His grandma had a thick New York accent and had an abrasive way of speaking.

"Did you bring food this time?" she asked Noah, looking at our sandwiches. She turned to me. "This one always brings food. He brings a pizza, eats the whole thing himself and takes a nap, then he wakes up and says he has to leave before traffic. That's what he calls a visit."

"Aw, that's not true Grandma," said Noah.

"How do you put up with these two, especially the big one?" she asked me. She was intending to call Noah fat, even though he wasn't.

"It's been difficult," I joked.

"Be nice, Grandma," said Noah.

"I raised him, but he was always grandpa's boy," she said.

"How did you deal with him?" I asked her.

"He moved to Texas."

"I can hear you, you know," said Noah. "Don't make me look bad."

Noah went over to her refrigerator and threw away a carton of expired milk.

"Did you remember to pour the milk out first?" his grandma asked. "It's a good thing I love you, otherwise I'd kill you."

"Thanks, Grandma," Noah said.

Noah's grandma stood from her chair, putting one foot down and then the other, gripping the arms of the chair and pushing herself up with the coordinated effort of each limb.

"Ah, old age is for the birds!" she said. She walked into the kitchen and told us for a long while about what her other grandchildren had been up to since Noah's last visit. We sat and listened, eating our sandwiches. Her daily life was focused on following along with the lives of her large family, however far away, with whatever news she was fortunate enough to have received. There didn't seem to be very many people in her life, so I sensed that her story for the next couple weeks would be that Noah and his friends came to visit one afternoon.

"Stop me if I'm talking too much," she eventually said.

"No, I like it," Ellie said sweetly.

"If your aunt asks you, I took my pills," she said.

"Grandma, take your pills," said Noah.

"I took my pills!" she said.

She walked over to Noah and asked, "Could you take me to the store?"

We left with her to the grocery store. Inside the store, Noah stayed close to her with his hand on her back, guiding and supporting her as she walked.

"I'm the one pushing the cart," she insisted.

"Ok, you can push it if you want," said Noah.

"Are these carts getting heavier, or am I getting weaker?"

"Both!" said Noah.

"You're not supposed to answer that," she said. "I should have drowned you in the bathtub while you were a baby!"

Noah smiled.

While we moved around between the aisles, Noah or Ellie would stay near her with a hand on her back and a hand on the cart to help push. Her grocery list only had milk, soda, coffee, and cheese on it, but we ended up with far more—cheesecake, cookies, and other sweets. Any time we passed something delicious that his grandma seemed interested in, one of us would toss it in her cart.

Afterward we stopped at a pizza shop because his grandma hadn't eaten any lunch yet. She cut up her pizza with a fork and knife and took her time. A herd of small children was let out of a school bus outside, and many of them came to eat some pizza, filling up the rest of the booths.

"My life-protector band has been going off sometimes at night when they have to test it, and it keeps me awake," said Noah's grandma.

I hadn't noticed until she mentioned it, but she was wearing a black plastic band around her wrist. She wasn't speaking in her usual abrasive, funny way, but instead sounded sincere.

"I wish your father would stop paying for it," she continued. "I'd rather be found dead in the chair than survive again."

"Don't say that, Grandma," said Noah.

Ellie lowered her eyes.

"Why not?" asked his grandma. She was still cutting her pizza as if she hadn't said anything other than small talk.

"Because then I wouldn't be here with you," said Noah.

Her fork and knife paused. Her eyes traced from her pizza to Noah's hands next to her, then up to his eyes.

"Well, alright," she said. "Ok then, I'll keep it."

The car ride was silent except for the sound of the breeze through cracked windows. The streets were lined with trees dotted with bursting pink blooms, their fallen petals piled up along the curb, and as our car rolled past, the petals would lift off the ground for a moment, then settle again. Noah's grandma sat low in the passenger seat, her head tilted back to see out the windows.

"Aren't the trees pretty?" she said. "But they never last long."

————

When I left LIU Post to go to NYU, I left my car behind at LIU Post and took a train into Manhattan. At the end of the week at NYU, I took a train back to LIU Post to pick up my car, and I stayed there for one extra night. Noah was staying at his girlfriend's dorm that night, and Noah's roommate was gone as well, so I had their dorm to myself. I took the opportunity to invite over a girl who I had met at LIU Post a week earlier.

The drunken night of students chugging liquor on the field actually took place three nights in a row. It was three straight nights of the exact same thing. On one of these nights, a girl ran up to me and grabbed my bottle of liquor, then sprinted into the woods with it. When I chased her down to take it back, we somehow started aggressively making out. As we were making out, she bit my lip extremely hard—hard enough that my lip was swollen for the next three days.

"Ow! Fuck!" I yelled.

"You're a baby," she said in a strong Long Island accent.

"That's bullshit," I said. "Here, let me show you how we kiss in Texas."

I didn't realize it at the time, but I guess I was heeding Noah's advice to emphasize my exotic Texan background. I cupped her face in my hands and kissed her as gently as I could. When I pulled away, she looked at me like she had just fallen in love—as if the only kissing she had ever done before was combative and adversarial.

That night we slept together on the futon in the common room of her suite, and we did the same thing the following night. Unfortunately, in between the two nights I learned that she had a boyfriend. I was innocent the first night, but guilty the second. My reaction was not surprise; instead, I thought, "Of course she has a boyfriend." He went to a nearby school, and Noah told me that she had cheated on him before.

(Actually, I knew she had a boyfriend the first time. I was lying about this for four drafts. Here's what really happened. After I made out with her a bit, I went to Noah to ask him about her. He told me then that she had a boyfriend, but she'd cheated on him before. I then asked a group of guys for their opinion on the ethics of hooking up with a girl who had a boyfriend. I asked, "What do you guys think about hooking up with a girl who has a boyfriend? Am I doing anything wrong?" The group vote was unanimous that she was the one cheating, not me, and that I should do it. The blogger The Last Psychiatrist calls this "outsourcing your superego." That's exactly what I did. Once I had group consensus that I was behaving ethically and morally, I did it.)

I never thought I would find myself willfully sleeping with a girl in a relationship, but I had reached a moral low. I had been shocked by the girl with the boyfriend at Baylor, and shocked again by the girl with the boyfriend at South Carolina. Both of those times, I thought the girls were single when I hooked up with them, so I didn't feel any guilt over it. This time, however, I knew Savannah had a boyfriend, but I just didn't care. I rationalized my behavior by telling myself that she was the one cheating, not me—I had made no commitments to anyone, so I wasn't at fault. I don't believe this anymore, but it's what I told myself at the time.

On my extra night at LIU Post, I invited Savannah over to Noah's dorm room, planning to sleep with her a third time. We had no alcohol to drink, so we sat on Noah's couch having a sober conversation. The unspoken assumption was that our conversation would lead to us sleeping together again. About ten minutes into our conversation, Savannah received a phone call. When her phone rang, a large photo of a guy's smiling face appeared on her phone. It was clear that the guy calling was her boyfriend. Savannah and I sat there in silence for the duration of the rings—which seemed to last much longer than normal—both of us staring at his smiling face. She didn't answer the call, and once the phone stopped ringing, she turned it over face-down.

"Tell me about your boyfriend," I said.

Savannah told me a bit about him, the story of how they met, and what their relationship was like now.

"Noah told me that you've cheated on him before, is that true?" I asked.

Savannah didn't seem defensive toward my line of questioning. She very comfortably told me the story about the first time she cheated on him. The first time she cheated on him, she called him and told him immediately afterward that she had cheated on him. He was riding on a plane at the time, and during the conversation, he began to cry. He ended the phone call by telling Savannah that he hoped his plane would crash, so he could die.

Savannah took a dramatic pause, then ended her story by saying, "That was the hardest day of my life."

If that was the hardest day of *your* life, I thought, then why are you still cheating on him?

I had once received that same phone call. My long-distance girlfriend cheated on me and then called me to tell me about it immediately afterward. I wept over the phone and then fell into a six-month depression. This was definitely an overreaction on my part, but I was young at the time and that's how I handled it. The worst part of the story is that I later met the guy she cheated with. I didn't know who he was, but he knew who I was, and I had to figure it out later. He walked up to me at a party, shook my hand and introduced himself, then laughed and walked away. While sitting next to Savannah, I was no longer upset that I was cheated on, but I was still disturbed by that guy's sadism. He apparently took pleasure in the knowledge that he had caused me that pain, and he even laughed at me for it. It felt terrible. And here I was, about to do something similar to somebody else.

Savannah and I changed the topic and began to discuss other things, but still I had a sick feeling. I could still picture the image of her boyfriend's smiling face, and now I knew that the thought of

Savannah's cheating made him want to die. I couldn't comprehend how Savannah could tell me that story and still sit talking with me like we were about to have sex. I began to feel nauseous.

"I'm really sorry," I said, "but I don't think I can do this again."

"Do what again?" she asked.

"What we're doing right now."

She sat in silence for a long time, then said, "I feel like you're judging me."

"I'm not judging you, I'm judging myself. I just don't feel right about this anymore. I'm really sorry."

Savannah and I stayed talking pleasantly for another hour before she went back to her dorm for the night. The whole time I felt proud of myself for making the difficult moral decision, and I felt like I'd chosen the proper direction for my life.

In the morning, Noah came back to his dorm and asked me how the night went with Savannah. I told him the story and mentioned how proud I was of myself.

"Do you think," Noah said, "do you think that maybe the first two times you hooked up, you were drunk, so you thought she was hot enough that it was worth it even if she had a boyfriend, but this time you weren't drunk, so you didn't think she was as hot anymore, so now it wasn't worth it?"

I thought for a moment. "Goddamnit," I said. "You might be right. And here I was thinking I was taking the high road."

This wasn't the end of the story with Savannah. A week after I left LIU Post, she texted me and told me that she was late for her period and thought she was pregnant. We had used condoms and they didn't break, so I thought the odds of this were extremely low. Nevertheless, I was paranoid for the next month about the possibility of becoming a new dad.

What would I have done if she were pregnant and decided to keep the child? This would have been a huge, huge change of plans for my life. This was not what I wanted to have happen. The whole point of casual sex is to not get anybody pregnant. Casual sex is supposed to be hijacking the pleasurable aspects of reproduction so you can enjoy them without any of the consequences. Existentially it is the equivalent of chewing a quesadilla then spitting it out. You are not supposed to swallow the quesadilla. And yet the low stakes of casual sex can quickly shift into the high stakes of reproductive sex with one small error of birth control. I was fairly certain that no semen could have escaped that latex barrier, but how would I know for sure until Savannah texted me and told me that she had finally started her period? This was not what I wanted to be thinking about, but these were the consequences of my behavior.

This experience caused me to seriously reconsider how I had been behaving on this trip. I had been taking every sexual opportunity that presented itself to me, and I seemed to have no restraint or caution. What had been driving me toward these sexual encounters was not an authentic desire to have pleasant intimate experiences with women. Instead my desire seemed to be more composed of other unrelated desires: the desire to impress my hosts, the desire to prove myself, the desire to entertain readers, the belief that this was what I was supposed to be doing.

I believe it is possible to have casual sex where both parties give and receive pleasure, have an enjoyable intimate connection, depart on good terms with mutual respect, and remember the experience fondly. But most of what I had been doing did not come close to meeting this standard.

What I was too inexperienced to know was that when looking back on these encounters, it would become important to me that the women I tried to sleep with would have good memories of me. Whether this is selfless or selfish is irrelevant; the result is the same. A good lover should care about the story his lover tells herself about their encounter, especially if it is a brief encounter—the only kind a traveler can have.

A good story needs a good beginning, middle, and end. The way a sexual or romantic encounter ends—the goodbye, the parting kiss— might be the most important part of the story. When Billy and his friend from Charlton farted into the woman's car after their one-night stand, they ruined the ending for her and forced her to change her story from "the time I had hot sex" to "the time I met that asshole who I should not have slept with," and the meaning of the night from something that might have been erotic and pleasurable into something that was shameful and gross. My endings were not as bad as that, but they were not as good as they could have been. So far my only good romantic ending was when I kissed Autumn on the cheek in Oklahoma, and perhaps that's why I still cherished the memory so much.

My real reaction to this pregnancy scare was not nearly as intellectual or ethical as I'm making it sound now. At the time my reaction was almost entirely visceral: I just really did not want to have any more sex.

At the beginning of this trip I had had a strong desire to explore sexuality, to journey into this magical and mysterious realm and return with new knowledge and experience and skill. But this pregnancy scare told me that I had gone far enough and learned plenty. If casual sex for me was once an exciting new realm of life to explore, I now felt like I had explored quite enough of it for a long while.

I am not exactly the best role model to say this, but here it is: sex, after all, is not the most important thing in life. At 20 I believed it was, but for me by 25 it has dropped way down to number two or three.

PART II

12

NEW YORK UNIVERSITY

This week I would be splitting my time between two students at New York University. Camille and Jonathan came to NYU from the same high school. They had been acquaintances in high school, but now at college they never saw each other. Camille studied finance, wore a suit and heels to class on most days, and as a sophomore was already starting her own business, the details of which I couldn't hear unless I wanted to sign a nondisclosure agreement. Jonathan studied history and journalism, cut his own hair, and ran a blog covering the Occupy Wall Street movement. The two students had come from the same suburban neighborhood and the same public high school, but now as college students they were pursuing different, almost opposite paths. I met with Jonathan first.

"Do you want to sneak on top of the business school?" he asked me. "It's a bit dangerous."

"How dangerous?" I asked.

"Well, I've done it before."

We were outside near NYU's business school building, which is called Stern. NYU does not have a typical college campus—the university is a collection of buildings spread out within the Greenwich Village part of Manhattan. The business school towered over the rest of the buildings in the area. Inside there were security guards stationed at the entrance. Jonathan leaned comfortably against one of the guards' desks.

"This is my friend," Jonathan said. "I work in the offices here, and I'm supposed to show him around."

"Does he have a guest pass?" the guard asked.

"No, he doesn't. But my boss is expecting him."

"What is your boss's name?"

"Marcia," he said.

Jonathan was lying. He didn't actually work there, so there was no boss named Marcia. The security guard must have known. He opened the electronic gate for us and said, "Go quick."

The business school was the most expensive-looking college building I had been inside so far on the trip. The textures were polished granite, clear glass, and shining stainless steel. We took the elevator to the 10th floor, then went to a tiny hidden stairwell to walk up the last few floors. At the top was a dirty window with an old rusty metal latch. Jonathan pried open the latch, stood on the stair railing, ducked his head under the window frame out into the sunlight, then hoisted the rest of his body through.

Outside we were greeted by what sounded like a waterfall coming from the building's air conditioning units, which rose up into giant pillars that spewed condensation. We weren't on the highest rooftop yet, so we still had more to climb. In front of us was a metal ladder that led up to some scaffolding. Jonathan climbed up and I followed. From the scaffolding platform, there was a long horizontal ladder that crossed onto another platform. There was nothing but air beneath the ladder for at least 50 feet down. As we crossed, the air conditioning thundered and rained mist onto us. Jonathan appeared to have no fear of the height and took casual steps as if the fall below wouldn't kill him; I took cautious steps as if it would.

"You're not scared of heights, are you?" he asked.

"Slightly," I said. "Mostly I'm scared of death."

Next we had to cross a long walkway of wooden planks laid sideways across more scaffolding. The planks weren't secured in any way, and some of them had disappeared, leaving gaps that allowed us to see all the way down to the sidewalk where we had first met. From above, the pedestrians were the size of ants. Once I had imagined falling through the cracks and splattering across the ground, I could think of nothing else. Jonathan was way ahead of me walking easily and without fear. He seemed to have a bit of a death wish; I got the feeling that if he fell, he wouldn't care very much.

We stepped out from the final walkway onto the rooftop at the very top of Stern. I relaxed now and tried to pretend like the journey up hadn't frightened me.

"So, here it is," Jonathan said with a shrug. "You been to New York before?"

"No," I said.

"Well, welcome," he said in a way that was purposefully anti-climactic.

Our view of the city was incredible, at least to me. Jonathan pointed to the Empire State building, to the new World Trade Center building that was under construction, and to the location of where the old World Trade Center buildings used to be.

"I didn't really like school until this year," he said. He was in the second semester of his sophomore year. "But I just had a short story published on a blog, and I'm working on getting a radio show."

"Why was last year bad?"

"I don't know. Campus is sort of weird. There's not really a campus. So you see people in classes, but I mean, I live over in China-town, and you don't really have people near you from school. So it's not really a campus or a school. The whole thing is just these build-ings you go to."

"And you don't like that?"

"I guess not, yeah. You're just kind of an anonymous person living in the city who happens to be a student at NYU. Outside of class there's nowhere you go where you're a part of anything. There are no real spaces outside of class, so it's kind of like, what is it?"

I nodded.

"NYU has so much money," Jonathan continued. "There are 40,000 students here paying over $50,000 a year each. So NYU just buys up buildings or builds their own because they can." He gestured down toward the Stern School of Business below our feet. "Like this. What is this?"

I felt like he was asking, "Why does this exist? What is happening here and what is the point?"

"Is it kind of hard to meet people since there's not really a campus?" I asked.

"I mean, I do know some people," he said. "I'll go ahead and tell you a story. I told myself before that I wasn't going to tell you this, but I guess I'm already saying it. I have two friends in Brooklyn and one of them is a big drug addict. They'd do everything. Lots of coke. And so, it's a long story, but essentially things were weird with his girlfriend and I ended up fucking her, fucking his girlfriend. So then he tried to kill himself. He was apparently in the bathtub with a toaster next to him, trying to call me on the phone right before he did it."

"Damn."

"But I was asleep, and so he didn't go through with it. It was a bluff. Now he just does a lot of coke. Have you seen a lot of coke on your trip?"

"Not really. Only once I think."

"There's a lot of it here. Coke is kind of like an initiation into the world of finance."

"I see. So do you still see those guys?"

"No, not really. At the end of last year I met this girl Maria. She was pretty much the only person I spent my time with."

"You still see her a lot?"

"Nah, she's away in China for the semester."

If the only person who Jonathan spent time with was away in China, that meant that he didn't really have any friends. After mentioning Maria, he turned his attention from me back to the skyline and seemed to concentrate deeply on the city. With so many people living there, it must have been strange to know so few of them.

He took a few breaths, maybe again thinking, "Why does this exist? What's happening here and what's the point?" Then he nodded and asked me if I had seen enough.

Later in the day, I met Camille outside the library, which is called Bobst. Camille didn't look like a regular student. She wore heels and a pea coat, which made her look more like a young, wealthy professional.

"I'm scared of that building," she said, referring to the library. "A lot of people have killed themselves by jumping off the top floor."

"Students?"

"Yeah, all NYU students."

Camille told me I should glance inside Bobst while she waited on the street. She didn't want to go inside because it frightened her. I took a quick look as she waited. The atrium was nine stories high, and by looking up you could see all nine floors of the library. Each floor had normal railings around the atrium except the ninth floor, which was enclosed by floor-to-ceiling reinforced glass. This was meant to prevent students from jumping off the ninth floor into the atrium. The glass was for suicide prevention. A student could otherwise throw her body over the rail and land on the polished granite below.

"There's apparently an optical illusion on the floor below, where from the top it looks like spikes," she said. "Somebody designed it so it looks extra scary from the top to help stop people from jumping. But I haven't seen it, because I never want to go in there."

"Why are so many people killing themselves here? Is the suicide rate here higher than at other schools?"

"It's higher, yeah. I don't really know why. There's not much community here. They sort of just throw you out there and expect you to find your way."

(Disclaimer: I am quoting the above dialogue because that was the actual exchange of words I had with Camille. However, it would be inaccurate to say that "so many" people are killing themselves at NYU. According to Washington Square News, there were 16 confirmed suicides of NYU students between 1990 and 2017. That is lower than the national suicide rate. It's difficult to know if the suicide rate is higher at NYU than other schools, because most schools— including NYU—do not publicize their suicide statistics. NYU takes the mental health of its students very seriously, and there are many counseling services available to students in need.)

We continued our walk to meet Camille's boyfriend for sushi.

"But yeah, I wouldn't say there's much culture," she continued. "Within specific schools, like at Stern, there's a bit of culture, but it's not really an overall thing. It's sort of just like living in the city."

"How has that been for you?"

"I think after high school people hone in on subtle differences— like, people were all pretty similar, but afterward the small things that made us individuals are what we focus on. For me, I found I like to stay really busy, and fortunately New York City has unlimited things to be doing, so I'm able to stay busy. I didn't know what to expect coming here and made up my mind super late."

"Why'd you choose it?"

"I thought it'd be a challenge, just something different than what I was used to."

"Was it?"

"Definitely. In downtown Manhattan you get exposed to a lot right out of high school, and you have to grow up real fast. You get through those growing pains. Yeah, so like, I have these stages for what it's like to move here. The first two months you just love it. Everything's new and you're all excited to be in a huge city. But then for the next year you hate it. It's dirty always, and stressful and it's too busy. But then stage three, you learn how to take care of yourself, and you get more comfortable staying here."

"And you're in the third stage now?"

"Yeah, I think so."

We took our seats at the sushi place where Camille's boyfriend Tim was waiting. He also studied finance and was wearing a pea coat.

"At NYU, you really don't know what you're getting into," said Tim. "I'm from LA, so I was used to a different type of big city."

"Freshmen usually get really hooked on night life," said Camille. "Or other people can get really sucked into competition, like in business school."

"Stern is considered really exclusive," said Tim, "and the people who go to Stern get a lot of advantages, or at least that's what people say. Most have internships or jobs, so they wear suits a lot. Other people have a joke, they'll make fun of us and say, 'Are those your uniforms?'"

"It's still cool to be wearing a suit though, right?" I asked.

Camille and Tim looked at each other and smiled, then Tim said, "Yeah, it's pretty cool."

After sushi, Camille and I left Tim to head back to her dorm, which was another random building in the city.

"People get stressed out by the academics here, but I think it's more the city," Camille said. "There's just no place in the city to relax, so it gets to them."

We walked through a revolving door into Camille's dorm building. The dorm had high security. There were electronic gates, and I had to show my ID, fill out some forms, and talk to a security guard in order to go with Camille to her room.

"Stern is a very competitive environment," she said. "There's an idea that says, 'Oh, you need to have a 4.0 so you can become an investment banker and be rich.' So some people come with a broader business perspective and then have it narrowed."

"What do you mean?" I asked.

"Well, don't tell Tim, but he has really had his business perspective narrowed—his whole methodology of what it means to be successful in business. He's very creative, and finance is a very results-oriented field. Whatever it takes to get the numbers is fine."

"So he became less creative and more interested in just the numbers?"

"I'd say so, but don't tell him I said that."

That night, Tim came back over to cook food with Camille for a 'diversity lunch' fundraiser that their co-ed professional development group was hosting the following day. Camille and Tim were the representatives of American food and were going to make chicken nuggets and macaroni. A lengthy, tense fight broke out between them over whether Tim should buy chicken nuggets from McDonald's or if they should be made from scratch.

That night, as usual, I slept on the couch in the common room. Camille was on the fourth floor, and there was a large window looking down onto the street. The fourth floor of a building is just high enough to have a nice view, and just low enough to still feel a part of the environment. The traffic flowed steadily all night, and I watched it for a long while, feeling excited to be in a huge city like Camille said. But later, when I thought of Jonathan and the idea of living there without knowing anybody, the traffic changed and started to seem a little sad, and before sleep I was lulled into a melancholy mood.

Camille and I woke up early for finance class. The class was about how to calculate the performance of an investment banker.

Afterward I went with Camille to a private lounge in the business building where students from her professional development group spent their free time. Camille swiped her ID card and the doors opened. Inside there were a dozen of her peers sitting around talking or doing work. Three girls were asleep on couches. A few of the students were carrying trays of food for the diversity lunch later that day. Two students were rubbing Bengay on their backs. Almost all of them were complaining that they had stayed up too late cooking their food for the diversity lunch. Camille had to leave without me, and as soon as she was gone, her friends gathered together to tell me about her.

"She's bubbly, delicate, passionate, and particular," one student said.

"Camille has her entire wedding planned to a T," another said. "She knows exactly when she wants to meet the right guy, when she wants to get married, and when she wants to have kids."

Camille had left her planner sitting next to me, opened to the current week. Her tiny handwriting filled the whole page, turning the white background gray when viewed from a distance. It was scheduling taken into the realm of art. With Camille out of the room, her friends all agreed that Tim and Camille already act like a married couple.

"I don't have my whole wedding planned out like Camille," one girl said, "but I know about my ring and my dress. Depending on the salary of my husband, I would want a diamond studded wedding band. And I would need at least 1.5 carats. My cousin just got married, and she wore Vera Wang."

The other girls gasped at this news.

"I need to meet more boys," one said. "All the guys in this group have girlfriends, and all the girls are single."

Two of the girls went on to discuss specific rich families whose sons they hoped to meet and marry. They didn't filter their conversation in front of me, either because they didn't think that marrying for money was a taboo, or because they didn't care what I thought.

"How much would you spend on a cake?" one asked the other.

"I don't know cake prices exactly, so I don't know."

"If my husband is loaded, the price of the cake won't matter."

"Obviously."

Camille came back to pick me up before she headed to the diversity lunch. I told her about the wedding conversation her friends were having.

"People often forget how privileged they are here," Camille said, "and around those people you don't watch what you say as much. The people here are really well off compared to others, because we're all paying so much to be here. I don't think it's any fault to those people, it's just the closed environment."

We arrived at the room where the diversity lunch was to be held. Camille, as the fundraising chair of the professional development group, set up a booth at the entrance to collect money. Five dollars got you two trips through the lineup of diverse foods. About 60 business students came to eat in total. Lots of the students kindly approached me, asked my name, shook my hand, and invited me to sit with them. Some of the conversations felt oddly formal, but it was nice to be included. The business students knew how to actually "make" conversation and force it forward if necessary. I sensed that some of these skills were learned in a class on networking, where you learn how you should approach people you don't know, give a good handshake, make small talk, memorize their name, and so on. Everyone in the business school seemed good at this.

"So how do you like Stern?" I asked one guy after our meal.

"It's really great," he said. "I just got back from a talk by this guy that was really inspiring. It was this guy who got arrested for insider trading. He's on bail right now. The crazy thing is that he was just a completely normal guy. By the way he made it sound, insider information is just floating around all the time. And that's what makes finance so interesting to me. It's always changing, you know?"

After lunch, Camille took the lock box of money to their advisor. Camille counted the money aloud, then the advisor counted the money aloud. Afterward, both signed off on the dollar amount and closed it in an envelope.

The next day began with a class on management, during which the students learned about intrinsic vs. extrinsic motivation. The professor shared a study that showed that employees work harder when money is not their primary incentive.

One student raised his hand and asked, "What if for some people money *is* the primary incentive?"

"Well," the professor said, "the studies I'm showing you have found that money is not a worker's primary incentive."

"Yeah," the student said, "but what if it is?"

Afterward we headed again to the professional development group's private lounge. The same students from the previous day were gathered around reading newspapers. The paper everybody read was the Financial Times, which they referred to as "FT," as in, "Have you read FT yet?"

One student who was reading the Financial Times was leaned way back with his legs crossed, and he would lick his finger every time he turned the page. "I was walking by the park on the way to class today," he said, referring to the location of the Occupy Wall Street protests. "And it smelled so bad."

The students laughed.

Camille had to work at her internship that day, so I met up again with Jonathan. He took me on a walking tour of Greenwich Village to show me NYU's faculty housing.

"NYU owns this too," he said. "It's basically Greenwich Village, brought to you by NYU. When you have so much money, you can sort of buy whatever you want."

"I didn't know so many people could afford tuition here. What is it, $50,000 a year?"

"$54,000 right now, and it's going up. I'm not sure how many scholarships they give, though. I'm here on a pretty good scholarship, otherwise I wouldn't have been able to come. Although I still regret it."

Jonathan wore dirty white sneakers and walked faster than the other pedestrians, and yet he also managed to seem more casual than the other pedestrians too. At intersections, he would move to the front of the people gathering to cross the street then begin to walk a second before the crosswalk signal told him he was allowed to. His arms swayed comfortably as he walked. Most of the other pedestrians looked in front of them as they walked, giving them a kind of robotic quality, but Jonathan looked all around. He looked like a stranger to the city. He existed within it but was not one of its members. When we got on the subway, he jumped over the arm of the pay booth without paying and then waited for me as I clumsily figured out how to buy a ticket.

"If you have a chance, you should ride the subway all the way through," he told me. "That way you can see all the diversity. In midtown you see lots of guys with man purses, then when you get out to the edges you start seeing more minorities and poor people."

We stepped out at Jonathan's stop in the heart of Chinatown, bought Vietnamese sandwiches and cheap beer, then headed to the roof of Jonathan's little apartment building with his ukulele and some folding chairs. The tall buildings of the Financial District loomed above us.

"The country was founded on being able to go out and make your living," Jonathan said. He gestured back to the Financial District. "And look what it's turned into."

"What do you do around here?" I asked.

"Well, last year I got into the labor movement. Because I was wondering if it was worth living here if you didn't have a ton of money. And I didn't think so. So I'm writing about the Occupy Wall Street protests. And I'm hoping to get published, but if I get published in New York I'd have to stay here, and I don't really want to, because I only know like five people here."

"Are those the coke guys?"

"Those are some of them. And also Maria. She'll be back next semester. We write letters sometimes, but that's it. I went on a date with this one girl last week. But I couldn't be with her. We were walking around, and she wanted to stop at a boutique. She was looking at $500 dresses. That's crazy. If I wanted to take her to dinner, she'd expect like $80 food, and I just can't do that."

"Not many people could," I said.

"It's not unheard of for girls at NYU to be dating guys in their late 20s. NYU is only about 40% guys, and probably half of those guys are gay. But that's not actually a good thing for straight guys, because there's no public forum to meet through, so in a lot of ways you're competing with the whole city."

"That's interesting," I said, "because at most colleges, the girls usually aren't willing to consider dating someone who doesn't go to their school."

"Man, that would be nice," Jonathan said.

Jonathan played "Sittin' on the Dock of the Bay," "Another Saturday Night," and "Me and Julio Down by the Schoolyard" on the ukulele. We sipped our beer and leaned back in our chairs. The air cooled as the sun was setting, so I borrowed an old knitted sweater from Jonathan. We sat there for another hour or so speaking easily and with many comfortable silences.

"NYU is a ridiculous carnival of extravagance and decadence, a never-ending spectacle. That's how it feels for me," Jonathan said. "For everyone else, it seems to be pretty much status quo."

Jonathan stomped flat his last beer can as we headed back downstairs.

"Maria and I used to cook dinner every night," he said as we walked through his kitchen. "We'd cook dinner then fuck. We did it every damn night. I miss the ritual of it."

"What was she like?" I asked.

"Real smart, thoughtful. I was her first boyfriend. She told me she loved me. It was nice."

"Bet so."

"Have you been in love?" he asked.

"I don't really know," I said. "How about you?"

"Yeah, I've been in love."

"Maria?" I asked.

"Yeah, Maria."

We walked to the subway so we could head back to NYU. In the subway, Jonathan told me about the third rail.

"See the red one?" he asked. "Don't touch that one. If you touch that one, it kills you right away. It's electrified. People kill themselves by jumping onto it."

"Lots of ways to kill yourself around here, huh?"

"Lots of ways to kill yourself anywhere. But this way makes a pretty big statement. It shuts down the subway and holds up thousands of people."

"Is it true that more students kill themselves at NYU than at some other schools?"

"That's what I've heard."

(Disclaimer again: There are no official statistics of suicide rates at NYU, so it is hard to prove or disprove whether or not NYU's suicide rate is higher or lower than average. NYU students seem to think that it has a high suicide rate, because that's what they kept telling me, but I make no claims that it is true.)

"Why do you think that is?"

"Lots of reasons. It's just kind of lonely, for one. And then you have lots of people trying to get rich, but not everybody can get rich. And then you have the normal reasons, like people just thinking life is shitty. I don't think anybody is really happy. How could you be?"

When Camille talked about suicide, you could tell that the topic was uncomfortable for her; the thought of suicide was not a place her mind was willing to stay for very long. When Jonathan talked about suicide, you could tell that he was comfortable thinking about it, that his mind had spent enough time ruminating on the thought that he had developed some familiarity with the subject.

Later that night, Camille and I headed to an apartment party, which was a pregame before going out to a bar. Camille and her friends wore black pea coats and heels that reverberated on the street during our walk. Regrettably, I was still wearing Jonathan's sweater, which had a big picture of an eagle on it. It was the type of sweater that would be cool if you were a bohemian artist, but it was definitely not cool if you were studying finance. When we arrived at the party, everyone else was also wearing pea coats and business attire with nice dress shoes and their shirts tucked in.

"Am I going to be underdressed at this bar?" I asked Camille.

She eyed my clothes with intense concentration. "What's under your sweater?" she asked.

I lifted up the sweater to show her what I was wearing.

"Ok," she said, "that might at least get you into the bar if you take off the sweater. But make sure you walk in with the group."

Fortunately, I didn't have to experience the shame of being underdressed. Camille couldn't get into the bar either, since she forgot her fake ID. Instead of going to the bar, we left with Tim to eat at a diner. As we ate, Tim comforted me and said that I could borrow one of his pea coats the next time we went out.

The following night, I went on a walk with Camille and Tim through Washington Square Park. I was borrowing one of Tim's pea coats, and I felt much better about my appearance. A man was playing Rachmaninoff and Debussy pieces on a grand piano in the middle of the park. Listeners stopped to drop money in his bucket, and children danced around in the music. We stood there transfixed through four of his songs, but as we left, none of us gave him any money.

As we were walking past Bobst, the library, Tim started to tell me what I'd already heard—that it is known for being a place where students have committed suicide.

"He already knows," said Camille. "I told him."

"Why do you think people have killed themselves there?" I asked Tim.

"NYU is sort of known for freshmen not really liking their experience the first year," he said. "And I can attest to that."

"Why's that?" I asked.

"It was sort of hard to make friends. I'm from LA, but my mom grew up in New York, so coming here was kind of my way of getting to understand the city and her background. I almost transferred somewhere else after freshman year."

"You like it here now, though?"

"Yeah, it's ok, now that I joined the professional development group and some other things. But I'm still real curious to know what the experience is like at a college that has a real campus."

I still had not seen the New York City skyline at nighttime, so Camille and Tim wanted to show me a good view. We headed to the top floor of an NYU building. We walked through the shiny halls into a ballroom with a 360-degree view out floor-to-ceiling windows. The city glowed with activity from all directions.

"I was here for a freshman orientation mixer," said Camille, "and I remember thinking, 'Man, I go to a cool school,' but I eventually realized I just go to a school in a cool city."

Whenever I was with Camille, I couldn't help but think about how Jonathan would have viewed things. The city at night was beautiful, but when I thought about how Jonathan would see it, it just seemed sad. For a finance student, the large city might inspire feelings of ambition and opportunity and power. For Jonathan, the same view might inspire feelings of isolation and meaninglessness.

After looking at the skyline, we headed to a club for the birthday party of a girl in finance. It was a private party in a hidden back room of an upscale night club. We walked through a series of hallways and down some dark staircases. The finance students had rented the room to celebrate the girl's birthday, and as we walked in, the song, "If I Was a Rich Girl" was blasting, and the birthday girl was in the center of the room wearing a tiara, hands in the air, and with her eyes drunkenly half-closed. I tried to join everybody with the dancing, but something in my body prevented me from letting loose. I was still seeing the world through Jonathan's eyes, and I could not help but think that what I was seeing was an "endless spectacle of decadence." Before long, I felt a flood of drunken depression, and I retreated to one of the dark booths in the corner to sit alone. Dance music still blasted. Now it was the song that goes, "Ass, ass ass; titties, titties, titties, titties." The song after that had lyrics that went, "Drink, drink, drink, drink, drink, drink."

I leaned back in my private booth and watched everyone dancing. There I had a really horrible and absurd thought where I imagined that everybody was actively fighting the urge to commit suicide. Externally they were smiling and dancing, but internally they were debating whether they should do it at Bobst or on the subway. I shivered at the thought.

After everyone had danced themselves tired, we left. When I rejoined Camille and Tim, I pretended like I had been dancing on the opposite side of the dance floor the whole time. We took a cab home with one of their friends. He was gay, and he came out at the end of his freshman year. At NYU there is a phrase, "gay by May," which means that freshmen guys who are gay realize that they are gay by May of their first year. He told me that he fit that stereotype perfectly. As soon as we stepped into Camille's dorm, she threw up in the bathroom. We all laughed at her; she apparently vomits every time she has even a couple drinks.

Camille had three other roommates. One was an acting major,

Lauren, who was also Camille's best friend at NYU. (I had an immediate crush on her, but I'd learned my lesson that I shouldn't act on it.) The other two roommates didn't speak much English, and they only communicated with Camille and Lauren through passive-aggressive post-it notes. Inside the dorm, Tim and I were still laughing about how Camille vomited.

"Shhh, don't wake them up," Camille said, referring to her two roommates who don't speak English.

"Are they really that light of sleepers?" Tim asked. "What the fuck do they do all day? Walk around at 5pm in pajamas? They have no lives."

"Shhhh," Camille repeated.

Tim told me that he also didn't have a pea coat when he first arrived at NYU. He had always worn skateboarder clothes in California, so it took him a while to get used to dressing fashionably according to NYU standards. I laughed and told him about my difficulty with wearing the right thing throughout the trip.

He shook his head and said, "That's so funny. Clothes are such bullshit. It really is the same all over."

It was comforting to think of Tim not as some rich kid who had come to NYU to study finance, but as a normal kid who had showed up in skateboarder clothes and realized that he had to dress better in order to fit in. I felt then that even Tim and Jonathan would get along, that students everywhere were basically the same, just wrapped up in different clothes.

In the morning, Camille and Lauren were in the kitchen talking about freezing eggs.

"Are you talking about chicken eggs or human eggs?" I asked.

"Human," said Lauren.

"Are you worried about becoming infertile?" I asked.

"It's scary," she said, "people getting married so late these days."

"You're only how old, 20?"

"I know, but I want to get married in my 30s and then have kids later. So maybe it'd be good to just have backup."

"What about you, Camille?" I asked.

"Ok," she smiled. "Here's my plan. Engaged at 24, married at 26, first kid at 28, second kid at 30. I might want to adopt, but my mom really doesn't want me to adopt, so I don't know."

"Camille is going to be super rich, so she'll be able to make whatever she wants happen," said Lauren. "That's super exciting for you Camille. Can I be your roommate forever?"

"Of course," said Camille.

"And you can sleep on our couch," Lauren said to me.

I laughed. "I might have to take you up on that."

Camille was helping to form a new club at NYU that aimed to promote women's financial literacy. She had to tune into a video conference with the other members that day, since their application to the national chapter was due. While she was on the video conference, I flipped through the Forbes magazine that was on her kitchen table. The cover story was about how women would soon be the breadwinners for the majority of American families. Sitting next to Camille, this made sense.

When her video conference ended, Camille and I had one last conversation.

"Did you hear about the Occupy Wall Street protests here?" Camille asked me. "They came and protested Stern. Basically, they trashed the school and disrupted class."

"What was that like?" I asked.

"Well, I was upset, because I didn't come to finance so I could learn how to be super rich."

"Why did you come?"

Camille told me that she wouldn't be able to give a short explanation. She took a deep breath, indicating that she had a long answer to my question. In a sense, she would be trying to separate herself from all the negativity surrounding finance. The country was still in a recession caused by a financial crisis, and it was commonly thought that the people in financial industries were becoming inordinately rich at the expense of everybody else. The distrust and disapproval of the people in those industries was high.

"Ok so, basically the way finance works," Camille said, "the reason why we actually have financial systems, is because when you accumulate a lot of money together, a lot of capital together, you can help mitigate the risk of small businesses failing and succeeding. If you put one entrepreneur out there, and he's only one person with $100 in his wallet, if he loses that $100, then he just totally fails. He's finished and he can't do anything about it. But say, if a lot of small businesses work together, and they all put their money together, then usually 50% of them will fail and 50% of them will succeed, but since they all work together, those huge differences in how much they're making and how much they're losing, they're kind of evened out. So that's why you're not as economically impacted. That actually helps everyone because everyone is working together. So that's a good reason why we have financial systems in general, and I think a lot of people don't understand the historical reason why we have financial systems. We need them because it actually helps our economy run better and it helps entrepreneurs. Now, obviously there are a lot of people in finance who abuse it. Because they know something, and other people don't know something, they're just going to take their money. A lot of the reason so many small business owners and individual home owners are losing a lot of money now, is because everything was going fine and they never took the effort to actually learn how things are happening. Just because they weren't aware of what was going on and how the system actually works, they didn't do the research or find enough information before getting loans or getting money to use financial intermediaries. That's why they got cheated out big time in the financial crisis. So, basically my whole deal is that in order for individual people to not be cheated out of money, the big thing is that people just need to be more financially literate. That's why I wanted to do finance. I personally want to be more financially literate before going into the system, and also I think it's important for other people to learn. I feel like people need to better understand the financial world, and that there needs to be better people in it. Just because an industry is corrupt doesn't mean that you should throw away the entire industry altogether. You should actually try to go into it and improve it. The big thing that annoys me about Occupy Wall

Street is that, yes, everybody knows there's a problem with the huge economic disparity between people, especially in New York City, but sitting in a park and yelling about it is not going to do anything. If you actually want to stop yourself and other people from being cheated out of money, it's important for people to be educated. You need to have a capacity or a willingness to learn about stuff, and you have to actually take the initiative to learn. I don't like it when people just sit on their butt and don't do anything about it, or just complain about it, versus actually going out and doing something about it. You're never going to overturn something unless you actually know what's going on. You can't just throw stones at it."

Her argument made a lot of sense.

It was my final day at NYU. I told Camille goodbye and then went to Chinatown to see Jonathan one last time. At Jonathan's apartment, I met his roommate Robert. Jonathan and Robert found each other as roommates through Craigslist. Robert was a 24-year-old college graduate who would soon be moving back to Canada for medical school. He wore thick-rimmed glasses and had messy hair. Jonathan and Robert were both wearing old-looking knitted sweaters. The three of us went on a walk through Chinatown and got talking about students who study finance.

"They're going to start working their 80+ hours a week not for happiness," Robert said, "but to be in a position of power. That's what I think."

"That's what everyone thinks," said Jonathan.

"So you think their only goal is power?" I asked.

"I do," said Robert. "Yeah, their goal is power."

"Do you think that's automatically bad, though?" I asked. "Is it possible to seek power and hope to use it for good?" I was thinking of Camille.

"I'm not sure they seek power for good though," said Robert. "Like, look at what people do for fun. My idea of a good time is getting together with friendly people for relatively cheap and doing interesting things. Compared to them having really expensive fun for the sake of having expensive fun."

"If their goal is power," I asked, "what is yours?"

Robert thought for a while. "I think my main motivation is to be important."

"I'd probably agree with that," said Jonathan.

I was impressed by their honesty. "But isn't importance the same thing as power?" I asked.

"It's similar," said Robert. "I guess the difference is that I hope I would use power in a way that isn't entirely selfish."

"Decadence is an interesting subject," said Jonathan. "You see a lot of it here, and the contrasts. Like how someone can be rich and drunk, walking down the street, and see a homeless dude who doesn't have any food. It makes you realize how differently people live."

"Yeah," said Robert. "I don't think the business students have any idea of how other people live, and that's one of the things you're supposed to learn in college. They're kept in the dark."

In some ways, I agreed with Robert: that week I had met a few finance students who did seem out of touch with the way other people lived. But I also disagreed, because I'd met Camille and Tim, and neither of them fit the stereotype that Robert was referring to. Similarly, I agreed with Camille when she said that the way to fix corrupt financial systems was not by protesting, but by educating yourself and actually doing something. However, I had met Jonathan, and he didn't fit Camille's stereotype of an Occupy Wall Street protestor who was just sitting in a park complaining. I felt that he was studying history and journalism precisely as his method of educating himself so that he could actually do something.

Mostly I found it strange that Camille and Jonathan had grown up together, had gone to the same high school, and were now going to the same university, but in less than two years they had had their worldviews shaped and solidified so much that they could hardly understand each other. In many ways, they were the two perfect people to get in a room together to have a productive conversation about money, financial systems, and income inequality, but when and where would that conversation ever take place? The dream of a college education is that students with diverse worldviews all come together to learn in the same place and along the way learn how to see the world in many different ways. But in a school with an unusual campus environment, it might be difficult for two students in different programs to find a place where such an exchange of ideas could happen.

13

RHODE ISLAND SCHOOL OF DESIGN

I would still become extremely nervous before meeting every new host. My habit was to park on the edge of campus and wait until nighttime to contact my host and tell them that I had arrived. I didn't know anything about Mary until I knocked on her door. I called her around 9pm, and she greeted me outside her house. It was an old yellow wooden house with insides that had been converted into dorm rooms for students.

"So I hear you're making a movie," Mary said. She was short with frizzy blonde hair pulled into a bun, and she looked at me through clear thick-rimmed glasses. She wore a fuzzy yellow wool jacket with big buttons. Her voice was quiet, and she spoke and moved slowly, like an old librarian.

The fact that she thought I was making a movie meant that there was a huge misunderstanding. The friend who put me in touch with Mary must have told her the wrong thing. Not only did I need a place to stay, I also wanted to follow Mary everywhere she went for a full week so I could write about her life. I tried to match Mary's librarian voice and whispered back to her like we were between book shelves.

"Well, no. I'm writing a book, actually," I said.

"That's nice," she said. "What is your book about?"

"College culture and student life. What did you think I was coming here for?"

"I heard you needed a place to stay for a few days while you were filming a movie."

"Oh, yeah, no, no, not quite," I said. "Actually I was hoping to write about you and your college experience, so like, I would follow you around and go to your classes and stuff."

"Oh, ok. Well that would be fine. I don't have a roommate, so there is an empty bed you can sleep on, but you should know it has some weird stains. Shall we go inside?"

Mary didn't hesitate at all. She was immediately ok with the drastic change of plans.

The inside of her house looked like a co-op, although Mary told me that nobody ever used the common areas. It was lonely there, she said. The stairs up to her room were old wooden planks that creaked as we climbed them.

"I'm getting over shingles," said Mary. "It's an old lady illness. I'm on a lot of medication."

Perhaps that explained why she was so calm.

All the dorm rooms and apartments I saw at RISD were decorated to the point of sensory overload. Mary had pieces of cloth, drawings, old dresses, bandanas, and small picture frames hung up all over her walls. Her furniture was antique-looking and matched the style of the house. She had no overhead lights, just warm lamps that glowed in the corners of the room, creating pools of light that illuminated the colorful porcelain objects, paint brushes, sketch books, and stacks of artwork on her dressers. The only untouched surface of her room was her former roommate's bed. Mary wasn't lying—the mattress did have some weird stains on it.

"My roommate moved out randomly for a roommate transfer," Mary said. "I admit it might be because of all my things."

"I like it here," I said as I looked around.

"Thanks," said Mary. "I'm kind of an old soul."

"How do you like RISD?"

"I sort of like it. But sometimes I'm frustrated by it, because I know it's so good that I can't leave."

Mary sat on her bed and I sat on her roommate's.

"I almost didn't go to school here," she continued. "I didn't want to go to college at all unless I got into RISD. And somehow I did, so now I'm here, and I feel like I can't leave. It's very, very expensive here. My grandparents have to help me pay for it. So I feel a little trapped, like I can't leave even if I sometimes want to."

"What makes you want to leave sometimes?"

"I don't know," she said. "You're expected to be very good at your art here. And you make a lot of it. So it's easy to feel afraid of not doing well, or of not doing as well as other people."

"What sort of art do you make?"

"I want to be a children's book writer and illustrator. So I'm in Illustration."

The artwork hanging around Mary's room was her own original art. She had a style that was whimsical and fanciful. In her drawings were things like fairies, magical forests, and kids riding on the backs of monsters. She was dressed like and had the demeanor of a grand-mother, but her artwork showed that she saw the world more like a child. Since I had arrived so late, it was already time for us to sleep.

"I usually listen to music while I sleep," Mary said. "Will that be ok?"

The room was quiet and still except for the soft music coming through Mary's laptop speakers. She played the album *Pink Moon* by Nick Drake. The only other sound was that of the occasional car passing like wind. The windows were cracked, and Mary's white lace curtains swayed gently in the breeze. A street light shone through the window, turning the curtains orange.

Mary and I were both still awake by the time the album ended.

"He was a sad soul," she said.

In the morning, Mary dressed herself twice. First she wore a black flowery dress, then she switched to a striped shirt with corduroy pants and red shoes. We grabbed coffee before class from a student-run coffee shop. Mary's first class was about archaeology, and we sat up front.

"He basically just shows old pictures of himself bare-chested, surrounded by women in South America, from his old trips and archaeological digs," Mary told me.

Mary's closest friend at RISD took a seat next to Mary. Her name was Zoey. She wore a black dress with white polka dots, and she wore bright red lipstick. During class, Zoey drew pictures on yellow scratch pads and handed them to Mary and me. One she drew for me was of an androgynous creature with hairy legs, a top hat, hooves for feet, holding a rose. Next to it was a note that said, "Welcome to RISD." I stared at the drawing for a long while, but I couldn't figure out what it was supposed to mean. I looked at Zoey with a raised eyebrow, and she smiled back warmly.

After class we passed by a student outside with a sword and shield practicing his fighting technique. He fought against an imaginary opponent with complete concentration. Mary and Zoey told me that he was also a nude model. Apparently he could be seen practicing at that spot on campus at all hours of the day, so the students were entirely used to him. Zoey left us, and I continued the day with Mary.

"RISD doesn't really have a college experience," Mary told me as we walked. "There are a lot of weekends where I don't go out, even if I want to, and I spend a lot of time getting ready for my adult life. I mean, it's here if you want it. But whatever the typical college experience is, I don't think I'm having it."

"I don't think there is such thing as the typical experience," I said.

"That makes me feel a little better. When I was touring other art schools, I got the feeling that art students were almost a homogenized type of person. But I didn't feel that at RISD. There was some variety to the people here, which I liked."

We went inside the Illustration building. Mary needed to look for one of her paintings that she had left behind after class. We looked in her classroom, but the painting was not there, so we went to the head office of the Illustration school. A woman sat behind her desk.

"How can I help you?" the woman asked.

"I've lost one of my paintings," said Mary. "This is the second time it's happened."

"What does this one look like?"

"It's this giant fluffy green man creature that looks like a fairytale yeti," Mary said.

"Ok, well you need to check everywhere for it. But if you can't find it, that means it was probably stolen. We have continuing education classes in this building at nighttime, and if you leave any art here that is halfway good, it has a high chance of getting stolen."

Mary sighed.

"If this has happened to you before, why would you leave another painting behind?" the woman asked.

"I guess I like to think that people are good people," Mary said.

"Nope," the woman said. "You'll learn that they're not. And it's even more true out in the real world. This is just preparing you for that."

Mary had a job in the campus mailroom. When she was not busy filing mail, she would work on her art. The piece she worked on that day was a watercolor painting of a woman and daughter making a banana pie. She usually starts a painting on Sunday if it's due the following Friday, because she works so slowly. She has to spend more time on each piece than her classmates because she has a small, meticulous style.

We went back to Mary's room where we would remain from 3pm until we went to sleep that night. She worked slowly and steadily on the same piece of art, the woman and daughter making the pie. During this time, she apologized repeatedly for not having anything interesting going on in her life. I didn't mind, and I liked being able to relax. The first day at a new school was usually stressful for me, but this made it easy.

"Freshman year at RISD you're in studio for eight hours a day," Mary said. "Just painting all day. They're trying to weed out the people who aren't serious. And there was this sort of competition of who spent the most time painting. So lots of people didn't sleep and would be like, 'Oh man, I only got two hours last night,' but I couldn't do that, so I just had to spend much more of my free time working on my projects instead of having a social life."

"Do you enjoy spending so much time painting?" I asked.

"It's ok," she said. "RISD can be really isolating. Like, if you weren't here right now, this is still what I'd be doing, but by myself. I guess it takes being alone to realize how much you like people. This house isn't very social or communal, as you can tell. And all my friends stay very busy. So I don't often see anyone in the evenings except for on the weekends. Sorry you got stuck with such an introvert."

Before bed time, Mary phoned her grandma and told her that she had accidentally taken too much of her shingles medication. She told her that it was hard to paint while high from the drugs. I took a shower in the communal bathrooms of the old house. When I returned, Mary was asleep on top of her bed wearing red flannel pajamas. The lights were off except for a string of Christmas lights. Her laptop was next to her playing *Pink Moon* again. I unplugged the lights and crawled into my sleeping bag.

In the morning, we went to Mary's still-life painting class. Fifteen other students were there, each setting up easels around a stage. On the stage was a random assortment of objects—an open umbrella, draped sheets, a chair, and stuffed animals. Before class started, a middle-aged man came onto the stage, unceremoniously took off all of his clothes, and sat down in the chair. The students then got to work reproducing the scene on their canvases. Since I hadn't been in an art class like this before, I was immature about his nudity and looked around the room for a minute with a little smirk on my face, but fortunately nobody noticed me.

The room stayed silent during class except for the rustling of paint brushes. About half of the class wore earbuds. Mary's easel was in the back center of the room. She straddled a tall stool like she was sitting on a motorcycle, and she leaned forward with one hand on the back of her neck and the other hand holding her brush. The teacher patrolled the room, stopping behind a student as they worked, watching them silently for a few minutes, then moving on to the next student. He had gray hair down to his shoulders and wore paint-splattered carpenter pants. If he did speak to a student, it was always practical and sensible. He would say something like, "Make this shape more defined," or, "Clean up this shadow," or ask, "Should these two lines really be parallel?"

RISD is modeled after an old-fashioned ideal of artist training where the young artist apprentices for many years before becoming a working artist. The goal of this class was to produce an accurate representation of the stage, the umbrella, the sheets, and the naked man. It was not about self-expression—it was about pure artistic skill.

After some time, Mary stopped painting. She was just sitting there. As the teacher walked around the room, he noticed that Mary was not painting, and he came to stand behind her. Mary's face contorted and her posture shifted as she reached for different brushes and mixed new paints, but still she didn't paint.

"How is it coming along?" the teacher asked eventually. His voice was gentle and understanding.

"I don't know," said Mary.

"Tell me about it," he said.

"I just hate my painting."

"Why?"

"It's not talking to me today."

"Why do you need it to talk to you? There is a lot of work you could do while you wait for it to talk to you. You could work on the perspective of the stage, or begin shading the umbrella."

"I just can't get anything down."

"Do you think maybe you're nervous because your friend is here watching you today?"

"No, that's not it."

"Why don't you go out for a little walk and come back in when you're ready?"

Mary left class to go outside and remained there until lunch. During lunch, Mary and the teacher sat together on a bench outside having what appeared to be a serious talk. Later, when studio began again, Mary had started her painting over on a black canvas and was painting the naked man above a floating rainbow instead of on stage with the other objects. I gathered that Mary was given permission to do an alternative assignment because of her difficulty with the original one. (Mary had also missed one day's work on the assignment because of her shingles, so she was behind the other students.) The whole incident seemed very sensitive.

Studio ended early that day because the teacher decided to take the class on a trip to the RISD art museum. We walked from painting to painting as he discussed the history and techniques used by the masters. He had the students look up close at brush strokes, he spoke of how paint used to be made, and in general he discussed art as a learned, technical skill, not as something mysterious or available only to the gifted. The class paid close attention to him and seemed to have sincere curiosity in what they were learning.

When class was over, I didn't ask Mary about what had happened to her. I figured that she would talk about it later if she wanted to.

That evening, Mary, Zoey, and I went to a presentation by a RISD graduate who was back on campus for an art show. (Students here pronounce RISD as *rizdy*, so "a RISD graduate" is correct grammar.) She had graduated two years prior and was now a freelance illustrator. Her art had been featured on magazine covers and in books. Her presentation focused on the practicalities of freelancing as an artist. She shared lessons about the technical challenges she faces in her screen printing process and about the logistical concerns she encounters when communicating with magazine editors who need her work on a fast deadline. While she spoke, she flipped through a slideshow of her work, and if she occasionally commented on its creative elements, it was casual and indifferent, such as, "I wanted to show something big in a small city." Everyone in the audience seemed impressed by the quality of her work, and the presentation seemed encouraging for future illustrators.

However, near the end of the presentation there was some discouraging news. The presenter told us that when she graduated RISD and moved from Rhode Island to a cheap apartment in New

York City, she tried for a year to make enough money to support herself, but eventually she couldn't sustain, so she had to move back in with her parents. Now she did her screen printing in the bathroom at her parents' house, and she was saving up money before a second try to leave home. This news came after having just showed us a large portfolio of commercial work. In theory, she had been very successful after graduation, but that level of success was still not enough to make a living wage in New York City. Mary and Zoey looked at each other with worried eyes: in a few short years, they too would face that challenge.

Afterward we walked to Zoey's apartment so Mary and Zoey could study. Zoey's roommate, Brooke, came out of her room wearing only a bed sheet wrapped around her. She studied sculpting and showed me with great enthusiasm some brass objects she had made. She had hair that was braided in a spiral and pulled up straight over her head. Zoey was making tea in a kettle, and David Bowie played from a record player. Hanging from the ceiling were dozens of fake flowers and butterflies. On the walls were floral quilts stretched out like wallpaper. The only light was a metal clamp-light shining onto the kitchen counter. Musky-smelling incense burned on the table and turned the air gray. Once Zoey's tea brewed, we all sat around the table drinking it. Zoey was holding a big loaf of bread.

"Before I went to college, my dream was to eat a huge piece of bread like this," Zoey said. "My mom would always catch me gnawing at baguettes like a beaver. And now I can do it. Freshmen are so excited because their parents aren't around. You can party every night because you don't have parents telling you not to. And if you have a boyfriend or girlfriend, you just live at their place because nobody's telling you not to do that either. But then sophomore year you realize you're paying so much, so you get serious."

"People party every night here freshman year, even with eight hours of studio every day?" I asked.

"Some of them," Zoey said. "Well, they try to, but not many of them make it work. RISD is a very old-fashioned version of an art school where you're supposed to work all the time. At our initiation, our president was like, 'Art is going to change the world. Art is just as important as business.'" She switched into a silly voice while speaking as the president and then resumed her real voice. "There were these big puffy chairs we sat in. But that's part of why I wanted to come here, because they took art so seriously."

Mary had not said much since we had been to Zoey's apartment, but she chimed in here and said, "Today I had a huge fit over whether I should even be here." That must have been what was going through her head during studio.

Brooke and Zoey nodded.

"I get those too," said Brooke.

"Me too," said Zoey.

After we finished the tea, Zoey grabbed a banjo and sang us one of her original songs.

"I like that one," Mary said.

"It's about my ex-boyfriend," Zoey said. "I felt like I finally got him out of my system when I wrote that song. I could feel him in my hands, like he was creating the song in me."

Mary, Zoey, and Brooke were unusual to me in a lot of ways, and yet I felt especially relaxed around them. In a way, at RISD it felt as if a person could do no wrong. Nothing was off limits socially, stylistically, or conversationally. For example, after seeing so many odd haircuts around campus, I started to suspect that there was no such thing as a bad haircut at RISD—anything that you did to your hair was just your unique method of self-expression. It was the exact opposite of the feeling at NYU of not having a pea coat. Here you couldn't dress incorrectly if you tried.

Mary had a test the following morning, and then she spent the rest of the afternoon working on her painting. That night we went to Zoey's again for dinner. The girls were going to make an experimental dinner out of the random foods they had in their refrigerators. The meal ended up being noodles, mushrooms, and some other vegetables, made into a big pot of soup. We were also joined that night by their friend Mason, who was studying digital image manipulation. His primary artistic tool was Photoshop, and he would start with an ordinary photo and turn it into visual art. Before dinner, Brooke rolled one small joint, and we passed it around. Neutral Milk Hotel played on the record player. Before smoking, the girls had used the word "beautiful" frequently, but after smoking they were using the word almost every sentence. Everything was beautiful now— the soup, the mushrooms, the kombucha Brooke was drinking, Mary's coffee. Zoey eventually said, "I think you guys are beautiful."

"I took a year off before coming here," said Brooke. "I think that really helped. It really informed me of what my goals were once I got here."

"I wish I took a year off," said Zoey.

"Me too," said Mary.

"In a way I'm doing college for my parents," said Brooke, "which is weird because they're doing it for me. It's kind of amazing that they're giving me this gift, so I don't want to take it for granted."

"It's weird going here," said Zoey. "Before you actually arrive, RISD is just a name. Even with a scholarship, my parents still had to take out loans, and I still don't know how to support myself. I'll have this cushion for a few more years, but after I'm out, I have no idea if I'll ever make money. That's a scary thought."

Brooke and Mary nodded their heads.

"I must say," said Brooke "I rip on school a lot, but I'm having the most amazing time here just making shit. We have such great facilities. It's like everything is at your fingertips."

The girls asked me if RISD was similar to other colleges. I told them that so far it was very different.

"See, we don't get any outside perspective here," said Brooke. "At art school you get put with all these people who are similar to you, so you forget how other people see it. It's almost incestual."

We smoked another joint and then watched vintage Disney cartoons projected onto the ceiling. The girls called each one beautiful. Then they put on another record, The Kinks, and we danced together as the record played from start to finish. When 'Waterloo Sunset' came on, I felt pure bliss. It was one of the nicest evenings of my whole trip. When it was late, Mary and I walked back to her dorm. She had been participating throughout the night, but I realized that she hadn't spoken much. It was mostly Zoey and Brooke doing all the talking.

"I get stuck being an observer sometimes, and it can be a curse," Mary told me on our walk. "I have to think, 'Oh, I haven't talked in a while, I should probably say something.' You seem like that too, how you ask a question and then sit back. You're almost like a traveling ghost, like you aren't a real person. Do you know what I mean?"

I felt touched that Mary had been paying attention to me and thinking about how I might have been feeling. "I think I know what you mean," I said.

"What's intoxicating about college is that you get a new face," Mary said. "I don't know if you care about any of this at all, but I used to have bad depression. I don't know if that's interesting at all for your book or if you want to hear about any of this. You probably don't."

"I'd like to hear, but don't feel pressured to tell me anything."

"Well, I had bad depression, and let's just say it got serious. And I had dealt with it during high school, and college presented an opportunity for people to not see me that way. But it also presented a challenge. When you're constantly being critiqued, it can lead to a very strange sort of anxiety. The point is, my life you're walking into, the only way I can describe it is that my knees are under water. I've been walking a lot on my own, and I have a very good friendship with Zoey, but my other friend is away overseas. Ultimately my point is that art school can be taxing because you're constantly being personally rated."

It was silent for a moment.

"I'm sure this is all stupid," said Mary.

"No, no," I said. "Not at all."

"Let's say tomorrow, what I turn in, if it gets slammed, it's like I'm being personally judged and valued. If my piece gets slammed, that's something I'm going to have to learn to grow with, and I've already had to go through a year of it. If I didn't choose to be more open with my intuition and creativity and speak freely, then I would probably be so consumed with my sadness that it would... not end well. And that's why I chose art. And this sounds so dramatic, but it almost saved my life."

In the morning, a group of students sat together on "RISD Beach," a grassy hillside in the middle of campus. The group included everyone from the previous night, plus a few new people. One of the new guys had drawn all over his jeans, and he wore yellow-lensed sun glasses with a bandana around his neck. It was not an unusual outfit to see around campus.

Mary and Zoey were in the same illustration class, and that day was "crit," short for critique or criticism, where students critique each other's work. At the beginning of class, each student tacked his or her project to the wall, which already had thousands of tiny holes from many previous days of crit. Then crit began, and the class went around the room discussing each piece of artwork, spending about ten minutes on each. Mary's piece was the watercolor of a mother and daughter making the banana pie. One girl in the class was particularly vocal in her criticism of both Mary's and Zoey's art.

The girl said to Mary, in a somewhat pretentious tone, "I also sort of wonder about the usage of the dots as the same background for each panel. It sort of links them together and sort of creates a weird flattening for me. I think maybe some subtle differentiations could help it."

While the girl shared her feedback, Mary and Zoey sat close to each other. Mary's arm rested loosely over the back of Zoey's chair, comforting her, and Zoey leaned slightly into Mary's arm. Knowing that Mary and Zoey were both so sensitive, it was simultaneously heartwarming and heartbreaking to observe them listening to the negative feedback together.

After the criticisms, the class split up to begin work on a new project. I took a seat at a random table, and one of the girls sitting there took the opportunity to tell me how she was feeling about RISD.

"I'm a little fed up with RISD because of the idea that we make good art when we're overworked," she said. "And this is how RISD is supposed to stay on this pedestal because of how hard the students work, and it's like a badge of honor when you graduate because you did it. Students don't get to eat or sleep, they're supposed to be martyrs for their art. But you don't make good art when you're over-worked! We need rest too. I haven't just sat around to shoot the shit with friends in forever except maybe over a meal. And the work you do, when it's so much, isn't even good enough to go in your portfolio, so something just needs to go. I want to be a teacher, and I'm going to teach in a really different way from how things are taught here. I didn't party once freshman year. I got all A's, but it was at a price. This year I'm getting all B's, but I'm happy. I used to cry at night freshman year when I'd spend 11 hours on one drawing and it still wasn't good. I just need to take a break. Sometimes you have to take a break to remember why you're here."

After class, Mary had work to do by herself, so I went on a walk with Zoey. She wanted to take me to a graveyard. She pushed her bike alongside her, sometimes stopping to pick a flower and put it in her hair. Everything was beautiful to her, even and especially the grave-yard. The trees in Providence were in full bloom with white petals that scattered across the streets. The sun sat low in the sky. Zoey wore primary colors—a navy polka dot jacket, yellow thick-rimmed glasses, and red lipstick. I liked the way Mary and Zoey saw the world, always noticing beauty and appreciating what was around them. By spending time in their presence, I had started to pick up on a whole new dimension of experience. Since so many of their conver-sations were based on pointing out things that were beautiful, I felt like I had to look around for things to call beautiful if I wanted to contribute. When I searched for things to comment on, I realized that pretty much everything was beautiful in its own way, or at least deserved to be looked at and contemplated. You might say, "I really like the cracks in this sidewalk," or, "I can't believe how tall these trees are," or, "That old woman was really lovely." Eventually I felt constant wonder at my surroundings. On the walk with Zoey, we were little kids exploring an environment that was constantly novel and infinitely pleasurable. Zoey might point at a bush and ask, "Can you believe how green this is?" and my sincere reaction would be,

"Oh my God—bushes are incredible. How does this exist?" Also, nothing was ever ugly. Mary and Zoey were art students, but not art critics. Neither acted like they were the arbiters of good taste and judgment. Someone who studied architecture, for example, might feel qualified to point out when a building is ugly. This would have been a faux pas for Mary and Zoey, since everything to them was on the spectrum of beauty. An ugly building might even be extra beautiful, precisely because it was so ugly.

The next morning was a Saturday. Mary, Zoey, and I took a long stroll through Providence. Mary and Zoey wore long yellow and orange dresses, respectively, and picked matching flowers to put in their hair. It was sunny and windy. On the walk, we stopped to look at flowers, to pet dogs, and to sit on benches. We went to a coffee shop, a vintage clothing shop, a yard sale, and a lunch cafe. This was the best I had felt in a long time—not just on this trip, but in years. At RISD, I felt like I did not need to perform. I could sit comfortably with no feeling that I had to act a certain way in order to be impressive or to fit in. I also adored Mary and Zoey and appreciated every moment I spent with them.

On the walk back toward campus, Mary noticed that Zoey was crying. Zoey had been a few steps ahead of us and hadn't spoken for a few minutes. Since Zoey was typically the main person speaking, that was unusual. When she sniffled, Mary asked, "Zoey?" so Zoey turned around, and that's when Mary and I noticed that Zoey's eyes were full of tears and her cheeks were bright red.

"Zoey! What's wrong?" asked Mary.

Zoey's shoulders drooped, and she stopped walking. She sucked in a slow, deep breath, then said, "I saw him earlier. I can't not think about it. I don't understand why he was so cold." She was talking about her ex-boyfriend, the one who she had gotten out of her system when she wrote the song on the banjo.

"He's a jerk. You can't worry about him," said Mary.

Zoey had passed him earlier in the day, and when she did, he pretended he didn't know her. The whole morning he had been on her mind.

"My body knows him so well," Zoey said. "I just want the pain to pass, to get over him. But then I see him."

"Zoey, I'm so sorry," said Mary as she gave Zoey a long hug.

After the hug, Zoey wiped her eyes with the backs of her hands, sniffled, then smiled.

It was my final night at RISD. That evening we met at Zoey's to get ready for an on-campus concert followed by a party.

The concert was in the basement of a building off the main street of campus. A guy played his guitar and sang while a small group of students stood in a crowd near him. There were about 15 people in the room, and more were filing in. The room was full of smoke, but you could only see the smoke when somebody flicked their lighter. We leaned against the back wall. It was Mary, Zoey, Mason, myself, and a few of their friends I had not met. When the next band, an upbeat rock group, came on, the crowd began to dance. There were more students now, and we nearly filled the room. Mary, who wasn't dancing, leaned over to Zoey.

"I'm going to go!" Mary yelled.

"You are?" asked Zoey.

"I'm more of a dinner party person!" said Mary.

Zoey, who had been dancing, shifted her focus into consoling Mary. After a moment, Mary looked at me and told me again that she was going to leave and that I should stay. In theory, I should have offered to leave with Mary, since she was my host, but it was my last night at RISD, and I wanted to stay out. I would say bye to Mary in the morning.

Mary left so that she could go to sleep, and the concert continued. Our group danced until we heard someone yelling.

"Get out!" someone yelled from behind. "Everybody! Out!"

I turned back after the third or fourth yell. Somebody was shining flashlights into the tiny basement. It was the police. The music cut off and the lights turned on. The shift in tone was so abrupt that it was awkward to look at anyone's face for a few moments. We filed out the door and each received a blast of flashlight to the face as we passed the law enforcement officer. This was our discipline. The after-party was supposed to be starting soon, so the night was still young, and the students from the concert huddled together outside.

Our group took a long walk along the streets to the party. It was Zoey, Mason, some other girl, and myself. The party was at a skinny, tall house in a residential neighborhood, and faint music could be heard through the front door.

"Are you ready?" Zoey asked me when we were outside, suggesting that I was in for something intense.

"I'm ready," I said.

"I don't think you're ready!" she said.

Up the narrow wooden stairs was a dance floor lit by a bare green bulb, and there was a DJ station in the corner of the room. Not much was happening. A few students stood in clusters and talked to each other over the loud hip-hop music. Nobody was dancing yet. There were so few people at the party that everybody turned to look at us when we walked in. There was a keg across the room in the kitchen, and most of the students were over by the keg.

I turned to Zoey, laughing. "This is what you were preparing me for?" I joked.

By RISD standards, this was as big as parties get. Our group went to the middle of the dance floor and began dancing. After we got the dancing started, most of the other students joined in. More students arrived, and within a few songs, the room was hot and everyone was sweaty from aggressive dance moves. I remember thinking that of all the dancing at all the schools I had seen, the dancing at RISD seemed the most comfortable, relaxed, and fun. I mention this because of an essay written by a Brown student called, "The Anatomy of a RISD Party," where he came to the opposite conclusion.

Brown University's campus is directly next to RISD's campus. Students from Brown and RISD will see each other around town, but apparently there is not as much socializing between them as you might imagine. A couple years before I visited RISD, a student from Brown decided to write an essay where he would write about what happens at a RISD party. Clearly, the two of us went to separate parties—they took place years apart, in a different place, with different students—but I like to imagine that we were observing the same party and coming to separate conclusions.

I don't have permission to quote the article at length, but I recommend that you look it up and read it. The writer basically takes a massive shit on RISD students. He wrote that there were no sincere dance moves on the dance floor, that the room contained a "choked energy," that the students were trying to "live as art," and that they were all self-conscious and unable to express sincere feelings.

I didn't read his essay until I left RISD, but that week I had heard about it from the RISD students. They had all read the essay and seemed upset by what it said. I wondered how the Brown student came to his conclusions. How can you ever really know what is going on inside somebody else's mind? If two people are doing the same dance move, how can you tell if one person is sincere and the other is insincere? If you feel that there is a choked energy in a room, how can you tell if everyone is feeling it or if it is only you? How can you tell if somebody is trying to live as art? And how can you tell if somebody's expression of feeling is honest or dishonest?

If you read the article, you can tell that the writer intended to criticize the RISD students from the outset. It was mean-spirited. He believed ahead of time that art school students would be pretentious and insincere, so that's exactly what he saw. The article pissed me off for a lot of reasons, but mostly it pissed me off because I personally found RISD students to be some of the sweetest and most sincere people I'd ever met.

Anyway, our dancing—which for me was some of the most authentic and fun dancing I had ever done—continued for hours. Unfortunately, after some time I started to have one of the most pathetic ailments that exists—a stomach ache. It was one of the worst stomach aches I'd ever experienced, and it made it hard for me to even stand up. Zoey offered to walk me back and said I could sleep at her place.

"I just feel bad for Mary," said Zoey as we walked. "She gets so overwhelmed. I think she just needs more people who understand her. It makes me sad."

I was keeled over in pain as we walked, holding my stomach. I barely managed a conversation. "I think it's hard to be alone," I said.

"I can't spend any time alone," she said. "I almost wish I were more of an introvert. I don't know what to do when I'm alone. It's scary to me."

Zoey made me a pallet on her floor with lots of pillows and blankets. My stomach ache was still brutally painful, but when I lay down, the sharp pain eased a bit. Her room was lit by one warm lamp. She put on a Bing Crosby record and turned the volume low. The violins were warm and crackly.

"Do you feel better?" she asked with a soft lullaby voice, sitting up above me.

"I do. Thank you."

"Can I ask you something?"

I was on my back looking up at her. I nodded 'yes.'

"Do you ever get jealous of your friends in college?" she asked.

I told her the truth. "Yeah."

"Why?"

"It's just so fun."

"It's not all fun."

"Not even for you?"

She shook her head 'no.'

I didn't say anything. Zoey was looking down at me in a caring, thoughtful way. Mary had been alone for hours, probably asleep the whole time.

"Anyway, thanks for taking care of me," I said. "I feel pathetic, like a 3rd grader in the nurse's office."

"I always liked that feeling," said Zoey.

"Yeah, I guess I did too."

"Do you need anything else?"

"No, I'm good right here."

14

TUFTS UNIVERSITY

For Nora, life is an absurdist tragedy that oscillates between boredom and depression. The only sustainable mindset that someone could adopt in such a world, she showed me, is one of disaffection. I joined Nora for one week of her disaffected life as a student among students at Tufts University. The week I stayed was a typical week for Nora, full of humdrum and monotony, except for two very unusual days—the first and last—which were full of excitement. Those two days book-ended my stay with chaotic entertainment that gave us both something to reflect on and to look forward to during the long, boring middle stretch of the week.

Nora was a different form of introvert than Mary from RISD. Mary had friends but preferred to be alone; Nora preferred company but had no friends. She lived in a shared house on campus in her own room and mostly kept to herself. However, she recently had started to become acquainted with some students who lived at a co-op up the street called the Highland House. The co-op received funds from the university to cook vegan food a couple nights a week for Tufts students. Students could go by and eat for free if they wanted, although it was unclear to me whether anyone ever took them up on the offer. It was the students at Highland House who hosted both of the chaotic events that brightened our week and made the rest of our time manageable.

I met with Nora moments before she would be leaving for the Highland House to attend their celebration of Passover. The co-op had no religious connection to the day of Passover, but the holiday served as a great excuse to have a feast. We walked from Nora's dorm to the Highland House and went inside. Some students were setting up a long dining table in the room next to the foyer, and other students could be seen coming and going from the kitchen in the back of the house. Nora and I stood together in the entryway. At first I deferred to Nora to lead the way, assuming that she had some friends there or knew where to go, but instead she only crossed her arms and looked around with a weak, nervous smile.

"You should talk to people," Nora said.

"Ok," I told her. "Do you know anybody here?"

"Not really," she said.

Standing next to Nora made me feel just as shy and uncomfortable as her. Instead of making small talk with anybody, we moved over to the dining table, took seats, and waited. Food was now being delivered and more students were coming downstairs for the feast. The event had been open to anybody from Tufts, but other than Nora and me, the only attendees were the students who already lived in the house. As more of the Highland House occupants joined us at the table, I became more and more confused as I tried to figure out what the event was supposed to be. Most of the students wore costumes of some sort, although there was no unified theme. One girl was dressed as Tinker Bell, another as a cat. Some of the girls had faces covered in glitter. The only students with costumes that had any relevance to Passover and/or Easter were a skinny, long-haired guy dressed as Jesus Christ, who wore only a white loin cloth and a crown of thorns, and a girl dressed as a sexy Easter bunny—she wore only a white bra, white skirt, and bunny ears. The dining table was mostly full when those two entered, so everybody was watching them. Before Jesus and sexy Easter Bunny took their seats, they made out with each other dramatically while everybody applauded and cheered. I was becoming rapidly desensitized to all of the strangeness.

One student was actually Jewish, so he explained to everybody what we were eating. The main food was matzah ball soup and matzah bread. Then he stood up on a chair and read some ceremonial chants. He was wearing a brown wool robe. His ceremonial chants had a call-and-response segment, and the students at the table echoed out their responses loudly and without bashfulness. Nora and I were still shy though, and we did not yell very loud. Her lips were frozen in an unchanging, nervous half-smile as she looked around. There were big jugs of wine on the table, and Nora poured herself another glass. Halfway through the meal, the students passed around a small stuffed-animal squirrel out of which you could smoke weed. The bowl came out of its chest and the pipe came out of its ass.

Afterward the students went outside to play some games for the occasion. First we stood in a big circle and tossed around a ball of yarn, each person holding onto a piece of the string. When you caught the yarn, you were supposed to say something for which you were thankful. Once everybody had a piece of the yarn, our task was to untangle the knots in the middle. This took quite a while. Next we went back inside for an Easter egg hunt. Nora and I took a break during this activity to drink more wine so we could loosen up.

"How do you know everybody here?" I asked her.

"I used to sleep with a guy who lived here," she said. "But he dropped out of school. And now his old friends are the only people I know."

That was the most she had spoken so far. Nora was tall and thin with black hair and straight bangs. She was very pretty. In social settings, she kept a slight smile on her face, but otherwise she wore a bit of a scowl. She laughed nervously any time she spoke. If you saw her walking down the street, you might think she was in a bad mood and didn't want to talk to anyone. In reality, she would love you to talk to her and become her friend. She didn't speak often, and when she did have something to say, she would speak in short, pithy statements. Her voice was so quiet that I often had to ask her to repeat herself three or four times. It took me a while to realize she was funny because her humor was so dry. For example, when I asked her what Tufts was like, she told me, "Tufts feels like high school, I just have even fewer friends here." Nora's primary friends were her internet friends. She was relatively popular as a poet among some online groups. It was easy to see that Nora was funny after I wrote down her words and reread them, but in person, her humor was often too subtle to elicit a laugh. Real life doesn't do Nora justice.

It was dusk. The Easter egg hunt had just ended. Nora and I stepped out onto the porch of the Highland House so she could smoke a cigarette (nearly everyone at Highland House smoked, and Nora had recently decided that she should also start smoking). On the porch, there was a guy named Anthony. I introduced myself and told him about the book. Usually people went about their normal business after hearing that I was there to document their lives, but occasionally a person would become eager to show me something especially entertaining. Anthony told me that they sometimes have big wrestling matches at the Highland House, and he wanted to show that to me, so he went inside to round up other students in order to start some wrestling right then. The group of us went to a large bedroom on the second floor.

In the bedroom, everybody sat leaning against the walls, passed around joints and pipes and jugs of wine, then we waited for the wrestling. Anthony set the mood by blasting the soundtrack from *The Lord of the Rings*. Then he stood up in the middle of the room with his hands in the air. He spun slowly like he was a wrestling referee in a big arena.

"I say ye, are there any challengers?" he screamed.

The guy dressed as Jesus Christ leapt to his feet to fight.

"Three rounds, ten second pin-downs," said Anthony.

Students cheered. "GO!" someone yelled. Anthony locked arms with Jesus then threw him to the floor and jumped on him. Jesus squirmed out from underneath, grabbed Anthony's torso, and spun him to the ground. For how skinny Jesus was, he was a pretty good fighter. Next Anthony wrapped his legs around Jesus's waist and threw him back underneath him, smashing Jesus's shoulder into the floor. Then Anthony pinned Jesus's arms behind his head, this time using his whole bodyweight to keep Jesus on the ground. Jesus fought to break free but didn't have the strength. A third guy started to count down.

"Three, two, one... WINNER!"

Round one was over—Anthony had won. Jesus won round two, then Anthony won the third and final round, which meant that he won the match. Match after match went on in the same fashion.

In the South where I spent the first ten weeks of this trip, there were profound gender differences between men and women. A man looked like a man and behaved like a man; a woman looked like a woman and behaved like a woman. In this co-op, however, gender played much less of a role. A man might have long braided hair, and a woman might have short hair and tattoos. And everybody wrestled. The room was full of both guys and girls, and many of the fights were co-ed. At one point, Jesus fought the girl in the sexy bunny costume, and they would make out with each other between each round, much to the crowd's approval.

"You're up next," Anthony said, pointing at me.

I wanted to resist, but the group pressure was too strong. They wanted me to fight one of the girls, and I agreed. Regrettably, I was overly scared of losing, so I was a bit too aggressive while fighting. When the round started, I immediately tackled the girl, and when our bodies hit the floor, there was a huge bang and the audience gasped. But the girl was fine, and after the fight was over she was all smiles. Afterward we all tried to encourage Nora to wrestle, but she refused in a way that assured us we had no chance of convincing her. No group pressure would have been strong enough. I rejoined her, and we stood together watching the next fight.

"A few weeks ago I was in this room, and I saw a girl's vagina," she told me plainly.

"How?" I asked.

"I saw an orgy, and I saw a girl's vagina at the orgy."

I was intrigued. "How did that start?"

"I was in the room hanging out with this guy, and people started coming in really drunk and on drugs, and eventually someone said, 'Let's have an orgy!' and I was like, 'That's a really funny joke,' but it wasn't a joke. I didn't partake. Somebody took my shirt off, but that's about it."

"Interesting," I said.

After we all had our fill of wrestling, everybody was clearing out. Anthony asked if I wanted to join him in his room for "a smoke and chat." I agreed—how could I say no? Nora headed back to the front porch for another cigarette and left me alone with Anthony. In Anthony's room, he rolled the two largest joints I'd ever seen, then we climbed through his window onto a fire escape. Tufts is located in a suburban area outside of downtown Boston, and we could see the Boston skyline in the distance. Our shoes were still off from the wrestling, and the cold metal of the fire escape stung our feet. Anthony handed me one of the joints and held his lighter out. We stood shoulder to shoulder as we looked out across the city.

"You must have some crazy stories," Anthony said.

I told him a few stories, selecting all the stories that were the most sensational and ridiculous.

After I had talked for a while, he said, "Oh my God, so our generation is just totally fucked?"

I laughed. That hadn't been the point of the stories, but taken in all at once, it made sense that he would feel that way.

"Well, I haven't made it around the whole country yet," I said.

"But still, based on what you've seen so far, would you say we're fucked?"

"You mean humanity?"

"Yeah. Are today's college students going to ruin everything?"

I didn't feel qualified to make any broad statements about college students, much less about the future of humanity. "I have no idea," I said. "I couldn't say."

Anthony appeared dissatisfied. "I bet the world ends in our life-time," he said. "We have the power to blow ourselves up, and I have a feeling there are enough people who want to do it. I think technology's going to be what ends us. I just don't see how we could survive another century after looking at the last one."

I nodded.

He continued, "And then you have environmental disaster, global warming, population growth. Have you met anyone who gives a shit about this stuff?"

I thought over each student I had visited. I wondered—who among them seemed personally concerned with those issues? Nobody in particular came to mind. Perhaps Jonathan from NYU. I said, "I've met some people who worry about those things, but I haven't met many people who are specifically devoting themselves to that stuff."

"Fuck. So absolutely nobody gives a shit."

I laughed again. It had not been my goal to send that message, but Anthony seemed determined to hear bad news.

"I've heard we're basically the most selfish generation to ever exist," he said. "And right now is the most important time for us not to be selfish." He shook his head and gave me a dejected look. "It doesn't mean anything if people want to care about something but still don't do anything."

"That's true," I said. "But our generation doesn't run things yet, so it's hard to say what we'll do. People are still in school, learning."

"Yeah, but what are they learning?"

"You're right, I don't know."

He took a drag of his joint. "Civilization is falling apart and we're all just watching it happen."

I wasn't sure what to tell him or how to cheer him up. I don't think he wanted to be cheered up—some people just like to believe that the world is about to end. Maybe he was right, I'm not sure.

After our "smoke and chat," we went inside and were greeted by Nora and a guy I hadn't seen yet. He had mischievous, foxlike eyes and was there to buy weed from Anthony. He had been smoking cigarettes with Nora on the porch before they came to the room. Nora introduced us. His name was Theo.

"You should invite him on Friday," Nora said to him, talking about me.

Theo glanced back and forth like there was some kind of conspiracy.

"What's Friday?" I asked.

Theo put his palms together and tapped his finger pads in waves like a movie villain. "Well..." he said. "It's a wine party, and it's also an ecstasy party." He paused for dramatic effect. "And it's also... an orgy. Are you in?"

Nora and I went back to her house, which was a house like the one at RISD—an old house that was remodeled and converted into dorm-style bedrooms with communal showers. On the second floor of the house there was an unoccupied bedroom where I would be sleeping. Since we were both drunk and tired, we went to bed right away. I lay awake for a long while, pondering both the end of the world and the orgy that Friday.

The following morning was the start of Nora's regular week. Over breakfast, Nora told me about her ex-boyfriend Santiago. He was sort of an alcoholic, but then went to Japan and lived with Buddhists and came back with a new sense of spirituality. That is when Nora met him. They were sleeping together while he was still officially dating another girl long distance, because he was worried the other girl would hurt herself if he broke up with her. Nora refused to continue the situation on those terms, so he agreed to break up with the other girl. He was in his final year at Tufts but didn't think he was doing much of value there, so he dropped out and had been traveling around ever since. Other than that, Nora doesn't know where he is or what he has been doing. He used to live upstairs at the Highland House, and he was the person who first brought Nora there. During their relationship, Santiago had been her only real-life companion. She relayed all this information to me with a slight smile and a hint of tragic humor.

After breakfast, we went to Nora's classes for the day. One was on Chinese culture and the other was called Literature of Chaos. In her

Literature of Chaos class, there was a girl named Aliyah who Nora was obsessed with. Nora had never talked to her, but she thought she was gorgeous and smart and fascinating, so Nora wanted to find out a way to become her friend. Both classes that day dealt with the theme of disaffected youth. That night, Nora and I watched a Chinese movie, which was homework for the class on Chinese culture. Since the theme of the Chinese culture class was "disaffected youth," so too was the theme of the movie. It was hard to sit through—an hour into the film there was a three-minute shot of the protagonist repeatedly trying and failing to kick-start a motorcycle. We figured that it was a metaphor for the meaninglessness of life. The rest of the movie contained long shots of young people smoking cigarettes and staring out windows, presumably while pondering the meaninglessness of life. Nora was terribly bored throughout the movie. After it was over, we stepped onto the porch so Nora could smoke a cigarette of her own.

"Damn, you look disaffected," I joked.

"It's because I am disaffected," she said.

"Why's that?"

"I don't know," she said. "I feel a lot more down to just do whatever now. After a year here, it's just too boring if you don't."

"Are they really having an orgy Friday?" I asked.

"It's the Highland House, so probably."

"Are you going to participate?"

"I don't know. Are you?"

"I don't know either. How do you know Theo?"

Nora told me that Theo had been friends with Santiago. Theo was going to be the host of the orgy that Friday night, although apparently he didn't have plans to participate in it himself. His goal, according to Nora, was to feed everybody MDMA and wine, then sit in the corner of the room to watch the ensuing orgy. He planned to wear big headphones and listen to classical music while marveling at his creation.

Perhaps I was more of a prude than I had realized, but I didn't feel cut out for group sex. The idea seemed fraught with danger. What if I was impotent? What if I was premature? What if everyone else had STDs? I could only think of the risks.

That evening when I tried to enter the room I was staying in, the door was locked. I had locked myself out. My belongings were still in the room, so in order to get inside, Nora and I had to call campus security. When the security guard came and unlocked the door for me, he told me that I was not allowed to be inside the room and that I had broken campus policy. He said that Nora would have to be written up because she was the one who let me into the room. The security guard explained this to Nora with a slightly condescending, patronizing tone. Nora handled herself with unflinching disaffection. To combat his patronizing tone, she gave him a continuous look of belittling contempt. It was like a teenager rolling her eyes at her dad, except it was far more refined and effective. Her performance gave the interaction an absurdist quality, as if we were trapped in some infinite bureaucratic web, and our captor was an incompetent moron. He told me that I was "in violation of commandeering unoccupied living space," and that Nora would be written up for "assisting in the commandeering of unoccupied living space." Nora laughed when she heard him say this. The security guard stayed talking to us for an incredible length of time, talking in circles about how it's against policy to have guests stay in unoccupied rooms. The whole time it seemed as if he were waiting for us to say, "We're sorry, we understand," but we never did. We stood there looking so unamused that when he left, he seemed to feel a little bit guilty about the ordeal. Afterward Nora smoked a cigarette, took an extremely long shower, and went to sleep. That night I slept on her floor in my sleeping bag.

On the way to Nora's Mandarin class in the morning, she said, "I don't want to do anything anymore." I asked her to elaborate, but she had nothing more to say—it had been her version of a one-liner. "I don't want to do anything either," I said.

After class, we went to a see a guest speaker from China who was speaking about Chinese business. We attended so that Nora could receive extra-credit points. The man had flown from China just to give this speech, but there were only six students in the audience. It was horrible and embarrassing for everybody—in a giant auditorium that could seat at least 500 people, there were only six people in the audience, and we were spread far apart and seated far from the stage. The man spoke from the stage in Mandarin while a woman translated for him, and it was a strange, almost comedic form of translation, because he would speak for a few minutes, and then she would summarize his words into one quick sentence. For example, after he had been talking for a few minutes, she translated everything he said as, "It requires lots of focus to get ahead." The speech lasted quite a long time—so long, in fact, that even the translator was having trouble staying awake. Her eyelids would go heavy like a dog's in its final moments before slumber until the Chinese man would finish a thought, and then she'd jolt awake to give a quick translation to the crowd that didn't care anyway, then she'd almost nod off again. I could sense Nora's boredom. Throughout the speech, Nora picked fuzz off her black corduroy pants and did not appear to listen at all. I watched her long slender fingers up close as she picked off tiny pieces of fuzz from all over her pants. I watched her carry out her useless task, each of us in a trance-like state, as the Mandarin droned on unintelligibly through the auditorium sound system. Dear God, I thought, did he really come all the way from China for this? Even with the reward of extra-credit, only six students had showed up to hear him speak. What an embarrassment. What humiliation. And his speech was so long—what was he even talking about? The boredom made my chest tighten, which caused me real physical pain. Despite all my struggles, I managed to hear something particular that the translator said. Again she was summarizing a few minutes' worth of speech into only one sentence. She said, "Sometimes in life, the clearest view is from the outside." Since I hadn't been paying attention before that line, it stood alone without context. Even though it was a bit of a cliché, I tried to imagine that the line contained rich significance. "Sometimes in life, the clearest view is from the outside." I swirled the idea around in my head. I wondered if, perhaps, this applied to me. I'd always thought that the fact that I didn't go to college was a detriment to my credibility as somebody writing about college life, but now I wondered if I had a clearer view because I was an outsider. As the speech continued, I looked up at the speaker and tried to understand what he was going through. Absolutely nobody was listening. His presentation was a disaster. And yet he still seemed to care. He had not sulked, had not walked off the stage, had not once shown a look of resignation. This provided me a vague sense of comfort, and I began to admire him. I imagined his life growing up. My imaginary montage of his adolescence contained long shots of him in China as he stared out windows, smoked cigarettes, and tried to kick-start motorcycles. In these images, he was not disaffected but instead was filled with courageous resolve. I felt my spirits lift.

As we left, I asked Nora what makes her so disaffected.

"Disaffection is the hallmark of postmodernism," she said. "Some people think postmodernism is a phase we'll pass through and people will be sincere again, but I think that's just wishful thinking."

We ate a large dinner, Nora smoked a few cigarettes, and then we went to sleep. In the morning, Nora took another very long shower; the water ran for a solid 30 minutes. Afterward we left to go to her part-time job at the school library. Nora's job was in the mail room of the library.

"You get to see how fun my job is," she said sarcastically.

For Nora's job, she would take a stack of newspapers and put stickers on them indicating where in the library they were supposed to be located. Then she would put various books in boxes and label the boxes. After that, her task was to load a cart full of books and place them on the shelves of the library.

"This is a good day," Nora said. "Usually the cart has more books in it, so it's heavier and I don't like it. I used to hate this job because it was so boring, but now I like it because it's so boring. It's like a break."

"A break from what?" I asked.

"From other more boring things."

I laughed.

"Sometimes we get new shipments of books," she said. "That part is kind of fun. Lots of the books have very boring titles and you get to wonder, 'Why does this book exist?'"

After work, we ate lunch in the cafeteria. I noticed that the sidewalks outside were wet.

"It's raining," I said.

Nora looked outside and said, "It rained a lot last year."

That night, Nora talked with her internet friends in a group video chat. Nobody spoke out loud; they instead typed into the chatroom. Some were poets, some comedians, some wrote novels. They were all kind of like Nora in that their typical evening involved socializing online.

"I wish all those people were in my room right now for real," said Nora. "I had girl friends in high school. But here I don't have any girl friends. I just don't really like the girls at Tufts. But I really like these girls on the internet, and I'm like, 'I wish you were here so I could have a female best friend at Tufts.'"

"You could ask Aliyah to be your friend," I said. Aliyah was the girl from Nora's Literature of Chaos class.

"I wish," said Nora. "I really want to."

Nora had a lot of similarities with Mary from RISD. They were both quiet and shy, they both had jobs in the school mailroom, and they both liked to fall asleep while listening to sad music. Nora's bedtime music of choice was the band Bright Eyes. That night as Nora listened to Bright Eyes, I took the opportunity to ask her a barrage of personal questions, which led to a conversation about existentialism, disaffection, and love.

"Existentialism to me seems like the ultimate philosophy," Nora said, "but it gets a bad rep, because like, a lot of teenagers will discover existentialism and use it as an excuse to say it's ok to be resigned and depressed. But it's never good to follow a philosophy or a theory exactly, because it's just pure abstract thought. You can be informed by it, but like, you shouldn't subscribe to it. It's good to take from it what you will. I think the bottom line of existentialism is the belief that you are what you do, so it's no use to sit around and have lofty ideas but not act, because really you're making literally no difference in the world if you're doing that, no matter how pure your intentions are. I think in the end, it's essentially uplifting. If you believe in something, then do something about it."

"Do you think young people, college students, are mainly disaffected, or are they trying to do something to help the world?" I asked.

"I feel like at Tufts, it's nice to see a lot of people that seem to genuinely care about what they're studying. A lot of International Relations kids are really into political justice. They want to make the world a better place, and they really believe in that, so that's kind of inspiring, I guess. When I think about that stuff, I feel much more cynical than those people. Or there are people who are studying biology because they want to be doctors, not to make money, but to help people or to do research in science. But this is a small school, I don't think it's representative of America's youth culture."

"If you are disaffected, how do you get out of feeling that way?"

"This is going to sound really cheap, but it seems like everyone, a really common solution, is finding love. It's like, a cop-out almost, I feel. Maybe that's what it comes down to, it sounds really stupid, but yeah. Once you find your love, you're not disaffected anymore, it feels like life has a purpose again. I feel like all of society believes that the ultimate thing you can attain in life is your soul mate. Maybe that's just human psychology. I don't know if that's a construct or if it's biological, but that's like, the ultimate thing, to find the person who makes you happy. But that's not a good existential answer at all, it's like a cop-out."

"I see."

"But then the whole matter of earnestness vs. irony comes in, because if you tend to favor irony, then you really can't aspire to things like making the world a better place. You think, I'm going to die, and then we're all going to die, so whatever I do to try to make a difference, it's not really going to have any effect; I'm not going to live to see the world become a really great place or anything like that. So, finding love, would be like a personal way out, because it directly affects yourself. It's a tangible thing for yourself. But it's not going to make the world a better place."

"Love is the way out of disaffection?"

"Yeah. Because if you can actually care about another person, then you're not disaffected anymore."

"Then you're affected."

"Right. But that seems really depressing to me. It feels like a cop-out."

I had talked to Nora for so long that she fell asleep in the middle of our conversation. Bright Eyes was still playing. I paused the music, closed her laptop, and fell asleep shortly after.

Nora had another part-time job at the campus art gallery. She called herself a "gallerina"—a portmanteau of gallery and ballerina —someone who stands around and answers questions at an art gallery. Nora was using the term with some irony, since the term "gallerina" typically has a negative connotation.

"I just get paid to stand there and answer questions," she told me, "but most people don't have any, so it's incredibly boring, and if they do have any questions, I usually can't answer them."

"Do you ever go up and ask people, 'Do you have any questions?'"

"No. Most people have a bit of anxiety. They feel shy about talking to the person standing there. They don't want to make small talk about whatever. I mean, I feel that way."

Nora wants to become a museum or art gallery curator someday. She's not sure exactly how she'll go about it, because she doesn't like the way commercial galleries operate. At commercial art galleries, the only goal is to sell art, so if somebody is there just to look, they will be actively ignored. Nora's favorite class at Tufts was on the economics of art.

Nora's shift in the gallery was over. The rain had stopped, and now the sun was shining and the birds were singing. Nora had the idea to bring a blanket outside so we could sit on a big hill near the library. She said that the hillside was a popular spot for students to gather, but she had never sat there before. When we reached the hill and spread out our blanket, Nora appeared to have a genuine smile on her face.

"This is nicer than I thought it would be," she said. "I guess I could sit out here by myself... when I'm alone again. I'm thinking about the future."

We sat reading for a while then eventually put our books down and lay on our backs. It had become a lovely day.

"I wonder if it was like this every day, if I'd still like it, or if I'd just become disaffected," Nora said.

The hillside was full of other students sitting on blankets in big groups. Nora looked around at them.

"Last year I passed up some opportunities to make friends with some normals. I thought I'd have a million chances at making friends, but I didn't. I should have tried harder freshman year to make friends, because those friends stick together. Now nobody wants new friends."

"What do you mean by 'normals'?"

"Some people are more unusual and interesting and weirder. Other people are normals. I always wonder what normals are thinking about. Some people are just really happy-go-lucky. They don't get stuck in their own head."

"Am I a normal?" I asked.

"I'd say you're a normal."

"No way, you're the normal!"

"You should want to be a normal," she said, "trust me."

Down the hill there was a girl sitting by herself. Nora was watching her and, I think, building confidence: if that girl could sit pleasantly alone, then so could Nora. But a little while later, a guy walked over and sat down next to the girl.

Nora asked, "If I come here alone, will that happen to me?"

"I think he already knew her," I said.

"Everyone knows everyone except for me."

The week was over, and it was the night of the Highland House orgy. Although the week was objectively boring, like Nora told me it would be, Nora's company had made it amusing and fun for me. After we ate dinner, we bought ourselves beer and wine to bring along with us to the Highland House. We still didn't know if we would take the MDMA or participate in the orgy. Nora seemed to share my mindset, which was ambivalence. I mostly just wanted to be there to witness whatever happened.

Nora and I walked up the street to the Highland House and sat inside drinking our beer. We were early—nobody was there yet. Eventually Theo arrived, walking in with a cute girl. He had the same mischievous look as always, like he was plotting something.

"You guys want to come upstairs while I clean up?" he asked Nora and me.

We followed him into his bedroom, which is still the messiest room I have ever seen. There were bongs and pipes and gas masks and old cigarettes and bottles and plates and wrappers lying all around the room. The bed was covered with laundry, and strangely, inflatable innertubes. He picked up huge piles of junk and threw them into a trash bag. Then he vacuumed the room. Nora and I sat squeezed in the corner as he vacuumed and bobbed his head with nervous energy.

"Are you having it here?" Nora asked Theo. I assumed that she was referring to the orgy.

"I'm going to start it here and then move it to the other rooms," said Theo. "We're getting close to 20 people tonight. I'm not letting anybody go to sleep until 8am. It's going to be wonderful."

Nobody would use the word 'orgy.' In fact, I never heard the word all night. We sat nervously in Theo's room for about an hour as more students arrived and joined us.

When two new guys arrived, Theo asked them, "Do you guys want to play dress-up?"

The guys weren't sure what to say.

"I have some soft shirts and some fishnets and some nipple tassels," Theo said.

I had no idea if playing dress-up was an MDMA thing, an orgy thing, or if that was just some bizarre part of Theo's plan. The two guys politely declined. Nora and I glanced at each other and took big swigs of wine. Eventually everyone took a cigarette break, and we rounded up more students while outside, then we headed back up to Theo's room where everybody was getting ready to take the MDMA.

The students sat circled around a coffee table in the middle of the room. It was a big group now, about 20 people. Nora and I returned to our familiar corner with our bottles of wine. Theo handed out little baggies of white powder to the students who were gathered around the coffee table, and they paid him on the spot. It was $30 for each dose of MDMA. Nora and I didn't take any MDMA, but at that point in the night, we had had so much wine to drink that we were probably the most intoxicated people in the room.

"I'm thinking about my life right now," Nora said to me, "and I'm like, 'I'm sitting in the corner with wine.'"

The students rolled up dollar bills into straws to snort the powder. Theo had turned on loud soul music. The students dumped their baggies of MDMA onto the table and pushed the powder into lines. A majority of the students appeared new to the process of using MDMA, and they glanced around while waiting for other people to go first. Once the leaders—Theo and a few others—had snorted their MDMA, the rest of the students joined in. At some point, Theo loudly announced, "Welcome to doing drugs in college."

After they had taken the MDMA, the students dispersed into small groups around the house. My goal for the next couple of hours was to roam from group to group while trying to witness the beginning of the orgy. I was curious about a number of things: How do orgies begin—formally or informally? What was the etiquette of entering and exiting an orgy? Would the mood be lighthearted or serious?

A variety of activities were taking place around Highland House during this time. In one room, a small group of students was dancing in a circle while passing around vodka and energy shots. To be chugging liquor and energy shots on top of snorting MDMA meant that these students had grand ambitions for the night. Aliyah, the girl from Nora's Literature of Chaos class, was one of the students in this room. I joined them for a few minutes and then moved on, still looking for the orgy.

In another room, one girl had removed her shirt, bra, and pants and was sprawled across the floor as other students used crayons to draw on her body. I joined in on this too. One girl kept saying, "You're in Nirvana, this is the happiest moment of your life," and the half-naked girl kept exclaiming how great it felt to have people drawing on her. Eventually they switched to drawing on people's faces, and during this time I was coerced into letting them draw all over my face with crayons and glitter.

"There are some people who are on this earth to learn a different thing than you are," one girl said. "And my current path or whatever, in this lifetime, might be different from yours, or yours, or yours. Like, we're all here to learn a different thing, and they have different experiences in their past lives than the experiences that I've had. Maybe they're more karmically advanced, or more towards reaching Nirvana than I am, or maybe I'm more toward reaching Nirvana than other people. So when you meet people who are so much more in tune than you, or so much more in touch, maybe they're just on a different path."

"I feel like people at the Highland House always make me feel like that," said another girl. "Everyone's just so much more in tune with themselves."

"Exactly!" said the first girl. "So I was always so down on myself last semester, thinking that other people are just so in it, and so down with themselves, and just on a different plane than I am. And now I'm like, 'That's ok! This is what I'm doing right now, and this is what they're doing right now.'"

Downstairs in the room where we ate the Passover feast at the start of the week, there was a strobe light flashing and loud dance music was playing. A group of girls was here dancing, and two of the girls were topless. Their nakedness didn't feel erotic, however, it felt more like the nakedness you would find at a nudist colony. At most of the schools I had been to so far, nakedness would automatically have been somehow related to sex, but at Highland House it seemed to be more an expression of freedom than of sexuality. Nora and I joined this group to dance for a little while, and then I continued my search for the orgy.

In another room, a group of students was passing around a pipe and sharing stories. Theo was in this room.

"Do you guys remember when Oliver asked me to give him a blowjob?" one girl said. "We were sitting on the balcony stoned. I said, 'Ok, but only if Theo puts three fingers inside me.'"

"And then I said, 'No, only one,'" said Theo.

"And I said, 'Two.' And you said—"

"—'deal.'"

They burst out laughing. It had been a fond memory.

It was nearly 4am, and there was still no orgy. Feeling drunk and tired, I went to the bedroom where the students were bodypainting and lay down on the bed to go to sleep. What happened next may have been the closest thing to an orgy that happened all night, but I should warn you: the story is incredibly disappointing.

As I was lying on the bed, two girls walked over and lay down on either side of me with their heads resting on my chest. This was a welcome experience; I wasn't particularly attracted to either of them, but I was enjoying what was happening. I put my arms around them and began caressing their backs. They had both clearly taken the MDMA, because they started whispering in my ears, "Oh my god, this feels so good. This feels so good." The cuddling started to become more intense—the girls had wrapped their legs around me and were rubbing my chest and reaching their hands under my shirt. Eventually I felt one of them start to slowly unbutton and unzip my jeans. I opened my eyes and looked down toward my crotch to see who was doing it. I was surprised—the person unzipping my jeans was a fourth person who had just joined us, and he was a dude. If I had been a more daring person or a more interesting writer, I would have gone along with this and taken it wherever it went. I half-wished that I was one of those cool, laid-back, bisexual guys who would have been cool with this, but I simply wasn't. Instead of letting him unzip my pants, I politely took his arm and moved it away from my penis. He understood my signal and moved his hand away, but only for a little while. A minute later he went for my zipper a second time. I moved his hand away again. But he was persistent—he kept trying a third time, a fourth time, and a fifth time.

Here's the disappointing ending: at some point while this was happening, I either blacked out from having had too much to drink, or I fell asleep. I have no idea how things ended. I woke up in the morning, sleeping on the floor, fully clothed, with nobody else in the room. I never saw those students again.

(I've told a few friends this story, and they've all asked, "Are you sure they didn't have sex with you while you were asleep or blacked out?" I feel almost certain that they didn't. I'm not sure what could have possibly happened. If I could go back in time, at the very least I would try to remain conscious or awake so I could know how things ended.)

"Wait, so was there ever an orgy?" I asked Nora in the morning over breakfast.

"I don't think so," she said.

The Highland House party had been a let-down. Theo was never able to get the orgy started. However, Nora had some good news from the night.

"Remember Aliyah, from Lit class?" she asked me.

"Of course," I said. This was the girl that Nora was obsessed with.

"Yeah, I just think she's really pretty and I want to be her friend. Well, last night we were on the porch, and she took a picture of me with her phone, and I was like, 'Yes! I've made it into her phone!' Do you think I should friend request her?"

"I think you're safe to at this point."

"I don't know," she said. "I used to have a crush on this really attractive TA. I talked to him a few times in the library, and then I friend requested him. Now we never talk. I screwed it up. I don't know how to do these things. I hope I don't screw it up with Aliyah."

"I think a friend request is pretty innocent."

Nora took out her phone and sent the friend request.

"I don't wear my anxiety on my face," she said, "but if only they knew. Maybe they'd feel sorry for me and be my friend."

It was my last day writing about Tufts. Nora and I were walking together on campus.

"If you're so disaffected, are you into guys who are disaffected?" I asked Nora.

"I don't know. I was like, really obsessed with Santiago, and he was only sort of disaffected but not really. Even though I only knew him for like two months before he left and I never saw him again, I told him I loved him. It was over email."

"Did he reciprocate?"

"Well, he told me he was like, exploding with feelings, but he wanted to wait until he saw me again before he told me anything. Then he visited me again, but he never said it back."

"I'm sorry," I said. "But wait, then why do you like Bright Eyes so much?"

"What do you mean?" she asked.

"Why do people who are disaffected like music that's so emotional?"

"Because we're not actually disaffected," Nora said, "we're actually really, really affected."

By complete coincidence, Aliyah, who Nora had just friend requested, was walking past us on the other side of the street. As we passed her, Nora waved, and Aliyah waved back.

"Oh my god, she's so pretty," Nora said softly.

"I think you two are friends now," I said.

We walked in silence for another minute.

"Wait, I just got really sad," said Nora, "because I realized Aliyah is about to graduate."

"She's a senior?" I asked.

"Yeah, she's a senior, so she's about to be gone. It's all for nothing. It's like a metaphor for life: good things can happen to you and then you die."

15

HARVARD UNIVERSITY

Henry

My original host at Harvard, Henry, was a little bit embarrassed to have me following him around. He told me I shouldn't tell anyone that I didn't go to college, that I should instead say I'm a high school senior who wants to go to Harvard. We tried this lie out a few times, but each time Henry would become too uncomfortable and end up telling the other person the truth, which of course would always make me look like a dick, because I had just been lying to their face. Since Henry didn't have a place for me to sleep, I spent the week commuting from Tufts as I still slept in Nora's dorm. Nora and I had become close friends by that point.

One night, Henry and his friend Josh were studying in one of the dining halls. Henry and Josh were having a smart-sounding conversation in front of me that didn't actually make much sense. I'm pretty sure they thought I had no idea what they were talking about. Their conversation had a formal and sophisticated tone, as if they knew that what they were saying was highly intelligent.

"What are you writing about?" Henry asked Josh.

"Hegemony," said Josh.

"Who are you going to mention?"

"I think I'm going to mention Hume."

"Ah yes, Hume was an empiricist."

"Yes, he was."

Then Henry looked at me and said, "If you have any questions about Theory, Josh is the guy to ask."

Josh didn't respond with any humility. Instead he looked at me confidently, pursed his lip, and nodded, as if to say, "Yes, I can answer all of your questions." Two years at Harvard and he was already an expert on social theory.

Maybe I'm still too stupid to understand their conversation, but here's what I think happened. Hume did write about hegemony—he wrote about the balance of power theory of international relations. And he was an empiricist. But Hume's writings about international relations, where he wrote about hegemony, have almost nothing to do with his epistemological writings, where he wrote about empiricism. So I'm pretty sure that when Henry said, "Ah yes, Hume was an empiricist," it was a non sequitur spoken exclusively for the purpose of sounding smart in front of the guy who only had a high school education. But again, maybe these guys were actually geniuses, and I'm still too stupid to understand what they were saying.

With that said, I now think it's badass that at Harvard you can be respected for being an expert on social theory. The truth is that I did not actually know all that much about what they were saying. If I could go back in time, I would now be excited to meet a guy like Josh, a supposed expert on social theory, and I'd likely have many questions to ask him.

Henry ended up being the only person at Harvard who thought it was embarrassing that I didn't go to college; the rest of his friends were apparently fine with it. Accordingly, I ended up not writing much about Henry. Instead I split my time between a number of his friends and some other people I met.

. . .

Ivey

Ivey and I sat across from each other eating lunch at a Mediterranean cafe. She was one of Henry's friends. I had explained to her what I was doing, and she had invited me to lunch. She wore a sleeveless turtleneck sweater and had to eat quickly because she had a meeting afterward.

"I had incredible ambitions to get into Harvard for a very long time," she told me. "And it worked."

"How so?" I asked.

"My application basically said, 'I'm the shit, and you're going to want me on your alumni list.' I'm very type-A in that way. People make fun of me because I have this 25-year life plan and everything."

"What's the plan?" I asked.

"Well, I don't want to go into all of it. But it starts with doing the 2+2 plan, then going into consulting."

Ivey explained that the 2+2 plan lets college seniors apply to grad school, and if they get in, they're able to work at a real job for two years before beginning grad school. It's meant to encourage students to come back to Harvard to get their MBA instead of getting too used to making lots of money in their jobs. Ivey said that it's also so women don't start families before getting their MBA.

"Why do you want to do consulting?" I asked.

"Because I didn't want to do I-banking," she said.

I found her answer revealing. I meant my question, "Why do you want to do consulting?" to ask, "What is it about consulting that excites you enough to dedicate your life to it?" But Ivey hadn't chosen consulting because the work itself excited her, she had chosen it as a binary choice between consulting and investment banking.

"I'm confused, so those were the only options?" I asked.

"Well, like 50% of Harvard grads get recruited into those two careers."

"What's the appeal of consulting and I-banking for the students?"

"Well, I think it's twofold. First, it's incredibly high pay right out of school, so part of it is monetary. But second, I think it has to do with people wanting to beat out the competition. Getting those jobs at a really good firm is really hard. So you work incredibly hard to be number one so you can get into Harvard, and then if you were to get one of those top jobs, you are number one of the number one."

I nodded.

"In 5th grade, I got straight A's one time," she said, "and my dad said, 'If you keep making straight A's, you could really go to Harvard,' and I sort of latched onto that idea, I guess, and I kept making straight A's."

"And now you're here."

Ivey sighed. "I used to have this huge confidence that I would make a big difference in the world, but I don't really have that anymore."

"How'd you lose it?"

She looked up from her food and rested her head on her hand, fingers stretched out over her chin and across her face. "I call it the I Can No Longer Be President Syndrome," she said. "Every kid grows up with their parents telling them they can be anything they want, but then you grow up and realize you can't do that. Like, there will always be poverty and AIDS. You come to reevaluate what impact means. You don't have to be Mother Theresa to make an impact."

We finished eating and went outside. I asked if I could come along to her meeting.

"Sure," she said, "but you'll need your walking shoes to keep up with me."

Alexandria

On the weekend I visited Harvard, it was "Pre-Frosh Weekend," which meant that high school seniors who were accepted to Harvard would come from their hometowns to visit. The high school seniors would stay with Harvard freshmen and sophomores for the weekend to see what it was like to live as a student. Alexandria was one such high school senior. She was also the little sister of my host's friend. As such, she would be spending some time with us over the weekend.

A few days before Alexandria arrived, Henry and Wyatt—my host and his friend—told me that she had never had alcohol. Their plan was to change that, and it had become a bit of a conspiracy among everybody who knew Wyatt that they were going to get his little sister drunk for the first time. At first, Alexandria didn't know that this was everybody's goal, but she figured it out soon enough. I sat with Alexandria, her brother Wyatt, and Henry, in the courtyard of one of the dorms (here called "houses") named Lowell.

"These two are the first of six siblings," Henry told me, referring to Wyatt and Alexandria. "And they're both at Harvard. So basically they're the next Kennedy family."

"I could run for office once I make my billion," Wyatt joked.

"Do you skip class from high school when you come to Pre-Frosh weekend?" I asked Alexandria.

"I did," she said. "This is the first time I've been to campus."

"Do you like it so far?"

Alexandria appeared to have more weighing on her mind, but she only said, "It's very pretty."

We were on our way to a weekly event known as 'Tea Time.' Freshmen students are divided equally between eight houses, all of which have their own dining halls, sitting rooms, and courtyards. Each house has an adult figurehead called the House Chair. For Henry's house, Lowell, the House Chairs were two elderly women. They live in a house attached to the back of Lowell, and regularly host 'Tea Time' for students.

As we left the courtyard and headed to Tea Time, the casual atmosphere of student life faded away, and we were transported into an old-fashioned, formal setting where everyone was on their best behavior. As we entered the house, we formed a single-file line and shook hands with a row of older women wearing formal, boxy dresses and pearl jewelry. The floors were made of thin strips of polished wood, the furniture was antique and shiny, and the walls were adorned with old, original artwork in thick brass frames. There were caterers who served us pastries and tea on fragile china. When somebody finished a plate of dessert, he or she could set it down onto an end table, and one of the caterers would pick it up. On the back wall of a main room was a giant portrait of the Dalai Lama sitting in the same room we were in, seated next to one of the elderly women whose hand we just shook.

After filling up our plates with pastries and making some polite small talk, we stepped out into the backyard area where we could speak louder and act like kids again.

"I'm gonna get you drunk," Henry told Alexandria.

"Oh, I don't know," said Alexandria.

"I think you're going to cave. This is college, this is just what happens."

Alexandria's brother Wyatt only smiled, neither helping Henry nor defending his sister.

"Well, I don't drink," said Alexandria.

Alexandria was tall and had freshly cut hair that stopped at her shoulders. She walked and spoke gracefully and had a hint of maturity or wisdom about her.

"We'll see about that," said Henry. "Look, you can either take the path of your brother or you can start drinking now."

"What is the path of my brother?" she asked.

"He came here and said he didn't drink, just like you," said Henry. "Four months later, he was on his knees vomiting into my toilet."

"It's true," said Wyatt.

"That's quite a lovely image," said Alexandria.

"Look, alcohol is the epitome of the college experience," said Henry.

Henry was right.

Alexandria said, "I'm sure it is."

Back inside Tea Time, Alexandria and I were standing next to each other.

"Why'd you choose Harvard?" I asked her.

"Well, I wanted to go to Yale or The University of Chicago my whole life, but when I found out I was accepted to Harvard, I had to go."

"Why is that?" I asked, though I already knew the answer.

"Well, I don't know," she said, "I guess it kind of feels like you have to."

"That makes sense," I said. "By the way, I don't want to contribute to trying to make you drink, but if you do happen to drink this week-end, I want to be there to write about it."

"Fortunately I'm not very easily peer pressured," she said. "My aunt is an alcoholic, and I don't want that." Alexandria looked out a window toward Henry and Wyatt. "But it is college, so I don't know. We'll see, I guess. But I hope not."

The pressuring of Alexandria persisted for hours. The pressure was coming from everyone who Alexandria was introduced to.

For example, a girl named Fiona walked up to our group and said, "Oh my god, Wyatt, is this your sister?"

Alexandria said, "It's nice to meet you."

"I'm so excited you're here! I've heard all about you."

Alexandria glanced at Wyatt, then said, "Oh, that's nice, I hope."

"Are you looking forward to the weekend?" Fiona asked.

"Yes, I am," said Alexandria.

"We're going to paaartayyy!"

Henry cut in and said, "Alexandria doesn't drink."

"Wait, you don't believe in drinking?" Fiona asked Alexandria. Fiona already knew that Alexandria didn't drink, but she was pretending to be surprised. She gave Alexandria a huge look of sudden disapproval.

"It's not that I don't believe in it," Alexandria said, "I just don't drink."

"Oh, I understand, really, you can trust me," said Fiona. Her disapproving look turned into a big smile. "I didn't drink in high school either. But you will soon! Starting tomorrow night. You can start with just a little." Fiona and Henry high-fived from across the table. "I've been waiting for this moment a long time," Fiona said.

Alexandria managed a polite smile before letting out a sigh. She continued to tolerate the pestering but was becoming more removed from the conversation. Beneath her polite demeanor she appeared to be thinking deeply.

Fiona, Olivia, and Sarah

I told Fiona, the girl who was pestering Alexandria about drinking, that I wanted to hear about social life at Harvard, so later that night she invited me to her dorm room to have wine and cheese with her roommates. This led to a fascinating and depressing conversation about Final Clubs and the unequal power between men and women at Harvard. Final Clubs are single-sex social organizations similar to fraternities and sororities, but they tend to be even more exclusive and elite.

"So you want to hear about social life, yeah?" Fiona asked me. "Where do I start?"

"Start out with freshman fall and how awkward everyone is," said Olivia.

Fiona: "Yeah, so freshman year is really awkward. I think the difference is that there are a lot of kids who haven't partied at high school, but here, there are even more who never did."

Olivia: "I love cheese, this is so college."

Me: "Wine and cheese is college?"

Olivia: "Well, wine and cheese isn't college, but wine and cheese like this is college."

Fiona: "So sophomore year people start joining Final Clubs. Girls join just to hang out with other girls, versus the guys. The guys just want to rage."

Olivia: "They want to pound girls. It's disgusting."

Fiona: "Yeah, so the thing about guys is that they have mixers with Harvard girls, obviously, but they also have mixers with girls at schools who don't go here, like Northeastern, Wellesley, BU, BC, Suffolk, Boston Conservatory School, just like any school you can think of, and they just like, slay chicks on the reg, which makes Final Clubs awesome if you're friends with them, because you can just go hang out on the weekends or something, but it also makes them a place where the dynamic is just so, just like, so skewed."

Olivia: "Yeah, it's so sexist. And it's so hard to not play into it. Because that's the only thing."

Fiona: "It's the only social outlet. And I'm not saying I don't hang out there, because I do."

Olivia: "I do too."

Fiona: "But I'm just saying like, if you wanted to date a guy, I don't know how you'd do it."

Olivia: "No, especially when they first get in. Guys are just... d-bags. I don't know how to phrase it in a nice way. Like, you can quickly see a boy change when you realize—like, they don't have a social life all freshman year. All of sophomore fall they're busy sucking up to older boys so the older boys like them and think they're suitable for their club, and then they can finally do what they do and have an actual going out life sophomore spring, and by that time they've become douchebags."

Fiona: "I feel like sophomore year is the worst time for a boy."

Olivia: "Yeah, it is. I don't know, they're just like, 'Oh my gosh, there are so many girls who are coming to clubs, and there are so many girls I can hook up with,' and it's true, but they just don't need to suck up to girls, or be curious, or like, open doors for girls, because girls are just flinging themselves at them."

Fiona: "Yeah, they don't need to like, date you. If you're looking for that at Harvard, I feel like that's pretty hard to find."

Olivia: "It is. People say that if you want to 'find a boyfriend' you have to find him freshman year, or as a junior."

Fiona: "Hold on to him."

Olivia: "Yeah, hold on to him."

Fiona: "Hold on to him, and then if he goes club, make sure he doesn't go astray. Or just find a boy who isn't in a club. But a lot of girls won't date a boy who isn't in a club because he doesn't have that social status."

Olivia: "Well, it's not even social status, it's just awkward when you're going to a Final Club when all that goes on is people get drunk and grind. Your boyfriend is going to be like, 'Why are you going?' and you're like, 'Well, I just want to hang out with people, and what else am I going to do?' and it's just awkward."

Fiona: "Yeah, so it gets awkward. So let's say there's a party to get in. The members of the club get a +3. So there was a Grey Goose party last week, and to get in you have to be friends with one of the boys in the club. So you just see the same people circulating at every club because it's the members' friends."

Me: "Hm, and so, the guys who are in Final Clubs, is it that they're attractive because they're cool guys who are attractive anyway, or is it because they're in a Final Club?"

Olivia: "I'd say it's because they're in a Final Club."

Fiona: "But that doesn't mean there aren't cool, hot boys who aren't in a club, but it's like, that's where you're going to find the pack of them."

Olivia: "Yeah, like if you want to increase your odds."

Fiona: "But if you're going to a Final Club, you're not going to find a boy who's going to date you."

Olivia: "No."

Fiona: "You're going there to hook up. Or you're going there to hang out with your friends who aren't anything more. It's one or the other extreme."

Olivia: "Yeah, for sure. The social scene is just weird here."

Fiona: "Yeah, it's tough, because as a sophomore girl, I'm still in that stage where it's fun to go out and rage at night, and I don't know, I'm not ready to just have casual, I don't know, random things in dorm rooms. And Boston is so strict with fake IDs, so unless you have a ridiculously good one, you can't go out to bars where people who are 21 go, and that's when they can finally get out of this bubble."

Me: "Is there an answer? A way it could end?"

Fiona: "No, because there's always someone to feed into it. Even if it's not Harvard people, it'll be people from other schools. The sad thing, well not the sad thing—this is going to sound douchey—but every girl wants a Harvard boy, and some girls will do anything to get one. They even have a twitter group called Harvard Hoocheys where girls tweet about like, 'Oh my god, I saw this Harvard boy.' It's husband hunting."

Olivia: "And when they say Harvard boy, they don't mean just like a random Harvard boy, they mean a Final Club bro type that every girl wants to get with, and every girl does, but he's not a boy who dates you."

Me: "They dream of taking a guy who hooks up with a ton of girls but decides to stay with you."

Olivia: "Yeah, I think that's it for every girl, like the bad boy that turns good boy, who turns good boy for you and only you."

Fiona: "But that doesn't happen, because they have like 20 hot biddies, like throwing themselves at them. Why would they?"

Olivia: "And people go, 'Oh, it gets better post-college,' and it does, like maybe in NYC because there are so many other people, but at the same time there's just a bunch of fashion girls and New York biddies, and so I think being a boy in a Final Club, it's the entitlement and prestige, and what you can do with that, it's pretty tremendous, it's kind of insane."

Me: "So why did you say sophomore spring was so bad? It's sophomore spring for you right now, right?"

Fiona: "When the guys go through Punch their sophomore fall, they aren't allowed to do anything, so they're suppressed. Well, I don't want to say suppressed, but basically they haven't been able to go out."

Olivia: "But it's also one of those things where they see older guys do it and they all want to be 'legends.' I feel like the word 'legend' is overused at Harvard. Every boy wants to be a legend here."

Fiona: "But I feel like by junior year to senior year they all mellow out, you know? Sophomore spring is the time you want to stay away. Junior fall is bad too, because it's the other side of Punch. It's like, junior spring is where it all goes, but it just goes downhill."

Olivia: "It's just all so annoying. It's hard to not, as a girl, let this whole social scene kind of change, like—not change you—but just change how you view relationships with guys."

Fiona: "Or change how you view relationships with other girls. With guys, it's like you have to go in there knowing that you shouldn't expect anything the next day, even if you had the most amazing time studying or going on a date, or maybe having a little kiss on the dance floor. You should not expect anything the next day. Even if you do get a text, you should be like, 'Oh, it doesn't mean anything.' You have to guard yourself, because it's all their plan of attack. I've heard that guys have a list in the club, being like, 'Oh, this is who I've hooked up with,' and stuff."

Olivia: "I've heard guys in some of the clubs have a list. It's like the easiest girls at Harvard. When you walk in the door, you get attacked. It's like, 'Oh, I've hooked up with her, I've hooked up with her.'"

Fiona: "It's like a game with them."

Me: "What do the girls here think of the girls from the other schools who go to the guys' Final Clubs?"

Olivia: "I don't think any of us like them."

Fiona: "We hate on them, but like, we're in this environment where we should all actually be like, sticking together, and be like, 'You guys suck,' and like, 'You boys need to change your perception of girls,' but at the same time, we view them as not the only reason, but a big factor in the reason, of why boys are so cocky. Because they're throwing themselves at them every night."

Olivia: "Like let's say you meet a boy and you really like him and you have class with him. Let's say you want to date him, so you don't hook up with him that night. Well if you don't, some other girl will. And the other girl is probably a girl who doesn't go here."

Fiona: "Exactly."

Olivia: "Because think about it, Harvard girls don't actually put out all that much. I mean some girls do, but not most."

Fiona: "There's the exception, but the thing is, if you think you're..."

Olivia: "...the only girl they're talking to..."

Fiona: "...and if you think, 'Oh, I'm going to show him,' and storm out of the club, he's just going to make out with some other girl and not even think twice about it. That's the problem. You're not showing him anything, because he can just get another one."

The third roommate, Sarah, walked in. She said she had to stop her homework because she could hear our conversation and she wanted to join. After a few minutes, the conversation led back to boys in Final Clubs.

Fiona: "Another thing that pisses me off is that boys don't need to court girls. Because they know that if they take you to an event, you're going to bang afterwards anyway. Guys are able to get with any girl they want without taking them on a proper date."

Olivia: "Well, they can do that with almost any girl."

Fiona: "Yeah, that's what I mean, and so they do."

Olivia: "This is going to sound really dorky, but that's why I'm still sort of talking with my guy from freshman year."

Sarah: "Wait, really? That's literally my exact situation."

Olivia: "He's not cute, he's not in a Final Club, but he's got like a really good future at the number one hedge fund."

Sarah: "He's not cute, like he's ugly?"

Olivia: "I mean, he's like, a redhead."

Sarah: "Hey, not all redheads are ugly. Johnny was so sweet to me all sophomore fall and took me to all his date events, and I had so much fun with him, but then he disappeared off the face of the planet. But then I hooked up with him this weekend, and now I'm like, 'Oh, you're back in my life now,' and he's been like texting me."

Olivia: "I'm going to give you some legit advice. Just maybe be like, his flirty friend, and then catch him in New York. Because he doesn't look like he could do Models and Bottles."

Sarah: "What?"

Olivia: "Models and Bottles is like, the next phase of Harvard douchebag. You guys don't know this?"

Sarah: "I'm really worried, I'm really worried."

Fiona: "You should be worried, it's not good."

Olivia: "So when boys in clubs go into finance..."

Sarah: "No, no, no, no, no, I already know where this is going!"

Olivia: "So they go into finance... work in investment banking..."

Fiona: "They're all in New York..."

Olivia: "They're all in New York. And they get bottles, and instead of BU girls and Northeastern girls, it's fashions girls in New York."

Fiona: "Who are hot as fuck."

Olivia: "Who are hot as fuck. And that's two more years."

Fiona: "Probably doing coke."

Olivia: "Right. So you catch them, if you want to marry them, my theory, is buy-side."

Sarah: "What is buy-side?"

Olivia: "Buy-side is when they get out of finance and they hit private equity and venture capital."

Sarah laughed out loud.

Olivia: "No, I'm serious. You know who told me this? My guy friend Connor told me this last year."

Me: "What is the bottles part of Models and Bottles?"

Olivia: "Bottle service. They buy the girls classy shit."

Me: "Why do you go for these guys? If this is their life, what is the real appeal?"

Olivia: "Ok, here is the appeal—"

Sarah: "—it's all the good-looking ones."

Olivia: "Yeah, mostly."

Sarah: "There are some cute ones who aren't in Final Clubs, but they're much harder to find. Because where are they? WHERE ARE THEY? I want them, and I don't know where to find them."

The answer they gave me—that the real appeal of a guy in a Final Club was his looks—didn't seem entirely true. I'm sure the guys are handsome, but more important than that, they are the handsome sons of the wealthiest and most powerful people on Earth, and as Final Club members at Harvard, are themselves on track to become the wealthiest and most powerful men of the future. I'm sure that has something to do with it also.

At some point during the night, Sarah said that she wouldn't be willing to date a guy who was shorter than 6'2". I was surprised to hear this. I'm not 6'2", but I was still significantly taller than Sarah—

tall enough that my chin could comfortably rest on the top of her head—so I stood up next to her and said, "Really? You wouldn't date a guy who was my height?" She looked up at me, thought for a second, then said, "Well, are you 6'2"? This cracked me up. In the middle-class suburbs where I'm from, a guy's height is only important relative to the height of the girl he's dating—he just needs to be a little bit taller than her. But here, Sarah was comparing a man's height relative to the height of other men. The 6'2" requirement also seemed to be more like a linguistic requirement than a real judgment of a man's size. It would be like if I saw some amazing breasts, but I was not willing to touch them until I knew that they were at least a C-cup.

Something bizarre happened next. Fiona and Olivia were leaving to go to a party, so I said I was going to leave to go back to Tufts. Once I said I was leaving, Fiona insisted that I stay behind with Sarah and sleep in their dorm. Every excuse I tried to make—I needed to shower, to change clothes, to charge my phone—she had an answer for. Her insistence began to take on an almost aggressive quality after I had refused so many times. The only reason I could imagine that she wanted me to stay so badly was that she wanted me to hook up with Sarah. This was Sarah who had just spent the entire night explaining all the ways that I didn't meet her high standards. As Fiona was insisting that I stay, Sarah sat on her bed with a subtle look of resignation that seemed to say that she knew what Fiona was doing, and she wasn't entirely opposed to at least making out with me or something, but she was going to be a little bit ashamed about it afterward. It was as if Fiona and Sarah had recently had a conversation about how Sarah needed a random hookup with someone for a confidence boost, and they both knew that I was her chance. There was also a sense that I would be ready and willing—honored, even—for the opportunity. I didn't like the way this felt.

(I have to state the obvious here, which is that my intuition could have been completely wrong. Perhaps Fiona was just being an aggressively good host, and perhaps Sarah's resigned look was her wondering what she should eat for a late-night snack.)

Fiona and Olivia left to go to the party once I agreed to stay there a little longer with Sarah so my phone could charge. Once we were alone, Sarah asked me if I had done any writing about students involved with the Occupy Wall Street movement. I told her about Jonathan at NYU. Sarah told me that her family was a part of the richest 1% of families in America.

"I think most people don't understand the 1%," she said. "Because within the 1%, there's a HUGE range of wealth. Most people don't know how expensive it is to live in Manhattan. Like, once you get an apartment, a car, you pay for private school, you pay for groceries and the rest of your basic living expenses, you're already spending maybe $500,000 a year. If you're in the lower part of the 1%, that can still be a hard number to reach. And that's just barely getting by. What people don't realize is the difference between one million and ten million, or 100 million and a billion. My dad works all the time. He's always working just to support us. People think it's all yachts and that sort of thing. Well, that might be true with the super-rich, but the sort-of-rich aren't doing that. My dad has to put almost all of his time into just paying college bills and mortgage and those things. It's not like he's lazy. We had nannies growing up because he had to work so much. When people call him lazy or say he's a bad person for trying to make money, that's when they've crossed the line."

Sarah was telling me something that I didn't comprehend until years later. When I originally quoted Sarah's monologue, I assumed that all readers would have the same reaction as me: "Wow, Sarah is extremely spoiled. Her family makes over $500,000 a year and she is still complaining about not having enough money." But I think Sarah was telling me something much more subtle.

There is a tendency for protesters to begin with a complaint about a legitimate problem and then, because of the processes of group psychology, to slowly devolve into a religious, Manichean worldview of light and dark, good and evil, and then to label the people perceived as the culprits of that legitimate problem as the sole source of evil in the world. The Occupy Wall Street protests began with a legitimate complaint about the injustices of extreme wealth inequality and corrupt financial systems and then devolved into a Manichean worldview where the 99% was the embodiment of good-ness and the 1% was the embodiment of evil. Unfortunately, evil doesn't work that way; society is an ecology, and evil has no source— no beginning and no end.

Sarah seemed to be telling me that her dad, as he accumulated his money, had simultaneously accumulated responsibilities, so that although he had become rich, he had in some ways become a slave to his money, and he was now stuck living a life of obligation and responsibility instead of a life of freedom and joy. While he did have a huge income, he also had huge bills—a house in Manhattan, chil-dren in college, etc.—and he now had to work all the time in order to pay those bills. He did not have an easy life. And who knows how Sarah's dad made his money? Perhaps he was a doctor, a surgeon, a healer of some sort, doing much needed work for society as a way to take care of others in support of his family. Maybe he was a great man and a loving, attentive father. Meanwhile a very popular social move-ment was marching around calling her dad evil. Sarah seemed to be telling me, "My father is not evil, he is a good man."

But I was not even listening to what Sarah was trying to tell me. Instead I just thought she was a spoiled rich girl, complaining about nothing.

I left shortly after that, as politely as possible. Sitting on the train headed back to Tufts, I felt sick with despair. I'd had a fascinating evening listening to the girls talk about their dating lives, but I found the conversation incredibly depressing. At the beginning, I felt terrible for the girls because of how skewed the power dynamics were at Final Clubs. But then I realized that I was not in a Final Club, and I was crushed with envy at the thought of how good those guys have it. Theoretically I was not even tall enough, even if I were in a Final Club. I didn't go to Harvard either, and I didn't even go to college! I was the lowest of the low in this big power game, or at least that's how it felt at the time. So that was depressing. And then I was depressed further when I realized that people living at the very top of society could still be horribly dissatisfied with their lives. You can be accepted to Harvard—which is often considered the pinnacle of success for a young person—but still feel inferior relative to your peers at Harvard. Or you can come from one of the richest families in the country and still feel poor relative to families that are even more rich than you. It was awful to think about. When I arrived back at Tufts, Nora was still awake, and I told her all about what I had just heard.

Aisleen

The Harvard students who I had spent time with so far had all been from the same group of friends. In order to observe a different side of Harvard, I split up from them and instead tagged along with a couple of students who were studying social theory and feminism. The first student who I spent time with, Aisleen, was a feminist activist on campus, and I was curious to hear what she thought about Final Clubs. While taking a walk around campus, she explained:

"Final Clubs are different from fraternities, because the whole concept is that you don't rush for it, you get 'punched,' so what happens is that they door-drop for the sophomore men who they think should get into their Final Club, so it's sort of like a rush process, except only the people who are invited are allowed to attend their events, and then they narrow you down. So obviously they first pick people who are within circles that are full of traditional privilege. So you have legacy students, you have rich students, you have athletes, you have all those groups. And they're mostly white. Basically, Final Clubs are extremely misogynistic, because you have groups of extremely privileged men in environments where they have lots of connections to lots of really powerful alumni who are able to give them job offers or hook them up with other connections. And they're misogynistic because Final Clubs control most of the social spaces at Harvard, because Harvard doesn't have many social spaces. That's kind of an issue, because night life here, you get all of these girls flocking, getting bussed in. You have women at Harvard going to Final Clubs and blatantly being objectified by men. The traditional way is that women scrounge for alcohol, men scrounge for sex—it's that exchange. I mean, that's extremely heteronormative and that's not how it always works, but in Final Clubs, that's the thing that usually happens. So you get a lot of freshman girls going into Final Clubs, not really knowing what's going on. Apparently, most of the sexual assaults on campus happen at Final Clubs. So my roommate that you met, she's actually in a sorority and visits Final Clubs. And that's sort of a problem for me. But it's just so entrenched that it's just what happens. It's a very small percentage of the actual community that are in Final Clubs, but a lot of people participate in the structures, because Harvard doesn't have spaces for people to go out at night. In Final Clubs, you have to be on a list to get into parties, so you'll have like one dude, and maybe 50 or 60 girls. So you'll have 20 or 30 Final Club bros that won't let any other guys in, because they want access to all these women who want alcohol. You know? So things like that are interesting power plays that reflect larger power plays that they have access to. It's interesting shit."

"I never thought of it as small power plays reflecting larger power plays," I said.

"That's all it is at Harvard," she said. "Think about who has access to power in different collegiate systems. Especially at Harvard, there is tons and tons of access to amazing opportunities. But there are specific people who have access to specific opportunities. Think within the financial sector. A lot of the people here that go into finance are actual terrible bro-y Final Club dudes. Or a lot of the people who go into really influential political positions, I can't look at them, because I know that some of them are those people that I've seen at these Final Clubs. It makes you have this dark cast over everything you see, when you see a Harvard degree. It's sort of scary."

I agreed with most of what Aisleen had to say—she was right that these men were taking advantage of extreme levels of power. However, I disagreed in one important way. Aisleen's idea was that the men in Final Clubs want sex, and the women attending Final

Clubs want alcohol. That can't possibly be true. Highly educated college women aren't getting bussed in from all across Boston and lining up outside these Final Club parties just so they can get drunk. If these underage women were so desperate for alcohol, they'd make friends with 21-year-old women and get their booze that way. Aisleen's worldview discounted the fact that these women actually want the men. I had met three of these women the previous night, and that's what they told me they wanted—not the alcohol but the men. In my understanding of the situation, the women attending Final Clubs are equally responsible for the unfair power dynamic, because it is the women's desire for the men that gives the men their power. If the women weren't attracted to the men and didn't line up outside their door, the men wouldn't have any power over them. But the women are attracted to the men—extremely attracted.

Aisleen did live by her word, however. She never attended Final Club parties, and her boyfriend—who I met briefly—gave off vibes of gentleness and compassion and thoughtfulness. It's possible that Aisleen's tastes in men were so enlightened and progressive that she could no longer understand the tastes of women who were not so far along.

Before I split up with Aisleen, she brought me to a library, and I sat next to her as she delicately flipped through an original copy of *Our Bodies, Ourselves*. I didn't know much about the book at the time, but I later learned that it was a very important book in the history of women's health. A lot of men on the internet think that feminism is all about hating and shaming men—and maybe sometimes it is—but every time I hear those criticisms, I am reminded of Aisleen delicately turning those pages.

Jacob

Jacob was friends with Aisleen. I met him during one of Aisleen's meetings, and when she had to leave, Jacob and I got talking about my book. Somehow he struck me as particularly wise, and I ended up talking to him as if he were my therapist. I spoke to him at length about my primary anxiety, which was that I had no idea how to view the world. For all of my life, I believed that I had a strong set of values. However, while traveling to different colleges, I realized that my values were weak. Each week while living with a different student, I would adapt to their way of seeing the world, and I would end up valuing whatever they valued. If I didn't have my own set of values that I brought with me wherever I went, that meant I was just a product of my environment, and I had no self. I told Jacob that I was ashamed of a lot of the things I had done so far. Every school I visited, I was just dying to fit in. Based on who I was visiting, I changed not just how I behaved, but even my deep beliefs about life. I'd always thought of myself as a nonconformist—I had gone against the crowd by skipping out on college, for example—but now it was like I was so desperate to fit in again, to be liked again, that I would try to conform completely and totally everywhere I went. The best example of this was my opinion of myself switching from South Carolina to Charlton. The girls at South Carolina shamed me for my behavior, so I felt ashamed, and then the guys at Charlton were proud of me for the same behavior, so I felt proud. But how was I supposed to feel about my own behavior independent from social feedback? How was I supposed to know how to act when I didn't experience the rewards and punishments of the group? How was I supposed to know how to live? I looked to Jacob, a college sopho-more, for answers.

"I mean, there's an internal logic to every single group you're looking at, or every little subculture," he said. "I did some reading for this class, and it was about how—it sounds so simple—but that the way people behave, and the way people's values and morals are, it's based on the fucking context! Which sounds so insane, but it is! Here at Harvard, I'm in so many progressive communities, and a lot of radical communities, but I go back home, and my friends are like fuckin' white dudes from Maine who don't understand anything about that stuff. But what am I supposed to do? I'm not gonna be like,

'Guys, we have to stop everything we're doing.' And frankly, I'll behave in ways that, probably, frankly, aren't good."

"What you just said is very profound in its simplicity—that morality is contextual," I said. "Because that's exactly what I'm experiencing while writing this book."

"It doesn't mean that if you put anyone in any situation, they're going to necessarily fit the situation," he said. "But it does mean that sometimes people act very good or very bad in one situation, and from that you can't necessarily infer that they'll act good or bad in another situation. But that's the key thing you have to do in ethnography. To the greatest extent possible, you leave your preconceptions and beliefs at the door, and understand that the value system you're seeing makes sense internally. Being in a Final Club makes sense. It totally makes sense. But when you step back, it doesn't."

"Right."

"I feel like a dick bringing in ideas that I've learned from class, but like, Weber—he's one of the three founders of social studies or sociology—and this is exactly what we're talking about, but he calls them Spheres of Rationality. Basically, every institution of any kind, or any kind of cultural thing, makes sense internally, and you have smaller and smaller spheres, and when you're within each sphere things make sense internally within that sphere. And then, if you're outside of a given sphere, nothing makes sense. Like, if you're within the U.S., certain things make sense. If you're white, certain things make sense. If you're a fuckin' Harvard student, certain things make sense. But if you look at it from a different perspective, none of it makes sense."

"That's exactly what I'm talking about," I said. "And it's tough, because, where is the right sphere to be? It feels like there's no answer."

"Exactly. I don't think there is an answer. But still, you just discovered what this fuckin' dude wrote about. That's incredible."

Not only did Jacob help to soothe my anxiety, he also showed me that what he learned in class could directly apply to what I was experiencing in my life. I was deeply grateful for the conversation.

(And if this chapter seems critical of Harvard overall, I want to emphasize here that perhaps the most wise, thoughtful, and intelligent student I met on this trip was also a Harvard student. Our conversation lasted about two hours, and I wish I could share all of it.)

All Together

At the end of the week it was Henry's birthday, so all of his friends took him out to a nice restaurant. Inside, about 20 students filled a long table and were eating dinner and drinking margaritas. Among them were Ivey, Sarah, Fiona, Alexandria, Wyatt, and a few more familiar faces. I was the last person to arrive, because I had been with Jacob and Aisleen that day. Henry was sitting at the head of the table, and I sat in an empty seat near him.

"Did you guys get Alexandria drunk yet?" I asked.

"No! We need to do that!" said Fiona. She screamed down the table. "ALEXANDRIA! Do you want a margarita?"

Alexandria yelled back. "No, thank you!"

"We're gonna order some more for the table! You can pour yourself some!"

Alexandria didn't reply.

As soon as the students started to drink their margaritas, they became more and more unruly. We were the loudest table in the restaurant, and the restaurant's other patrons were giving us unfriendly stares. If one of the students wanted food, he or she would yell out at the waitress as soon as she was through with another table. Alexandria observed all of this going on around her, and she appeared completely dejected. She was hardly able to maintain her polite smile anymore.

"Alexandria! Drink! You have to drink!" Henry yelled.

"No, no, no, thank you!" Alexandria said.

"Make Alexandria drink!" someone else yelled.

"I really don't want any!" said Alexandria. "But thank you!"

"It's Henry's birthday! You have to drink!"

Sarah had ordered a gin and tonic for herself, but she thought there wasn't enough gin in it. She called the waitress over.

"What do you need?" the waitress asked.

"Can I get a *gin* and tonic?" Sarah asked with a rude tone and squinted eyes that signaled contempt for the waitress.

I was amazed when I heard this. Usually when someone asks a waitress to make them a new drink, it's full of apology: "I'm so sorry, but I don't really taste gin in this drink, is there any way you could possibly, maybe add some more?" Sarah was also using a fake ID to drink underage, so she really had a lot of nerve to be so rude. I was able to empathize with Sarah when she defended her father against the Occupy Wall Street protests, but it's much harder to empathize with someone who is needlessly rude to a waitress.

As the waitress kept returning to our table trying to take orders and keep everybody's drinks filled, she started to become flustered. We were too loud for the waitress to communicate with us. Fiona, Sarah, and some other girls, after drinking a couple margaritas each, started to sing loudly. They belted out in falsetto while bouncing in their seats. Alexandria was watching from down the table and looked even more dejected than before. Then, sometime in the middle of all this, our waitress began to cry. Tears rolled down her cheeks, and she tried to wipe them off with her shirt sleeve, but, unable to gain composure, she walked away in the middle of taking someone's order. We never saw her again, and instead two new waitresses took over in her place.

By the time the bill came, half of the 20 students had already left. The ten of us who were still there had to split the cost ourselves. We assembled enough money to pay for the bill, but we still needed to leave a tip. When nobody wanted to pay any more, we hurried out of the restaurant without tipping.

We walked to the subway to head back to campus. At a back entrance to the subway, one student swiped his ticket, and the rest of us ran through underneath the metal arm without paying. The other people in the subway—who had presumably each paid in full—eyed us with apparent disdain. Some musicians were playing in the subway with open guitar cases asking for tips. The Harvard students danced to the music while they waited for the train but did not tip the musicians either.

We boarded the train and took seats. For some reason there was a delay with the train, and it didn't start moving right away.

"Oh my god," said Sarah. "We should just take a cab."

"No, we can't do that," said Ivey. She looked at me. "He'll say we're snobs."

Henry and I went back to his dorm, where there were a few new Pre-Frosh high schoolers hanging out with Henry's roommates. The roommates were trading a bottle of vodka back and forth taking shots. Some electronic dance music was playing from computer speakers. The high schoolers were a guy and a girl. The girl sat next to me on a couch with her hands sandwiched between her legs and a look of worry that reminded me of Alexandria. She had the same look of fear masked with politeness and the same freshly cut hair.

"Is Harvard like you expected?" I asked her.

"I tried not to expect much," she said. "I didn't know anything about college. But this? This is... I don't know. It's... campus is really pretty. It's really picturesque."

It was the same answer Alexandria had given at the start of the week.

"That's all? Campus is pretty?" I asked.

"Well, it's my first time here," she said.

"What about everything else?"

"I don't know."

"Has everyone been trying to get you to drink?"

"I had half a shot today," she said.

"Had you ever had alcohol before that?"

"No."

The high schoolers were supposed to go to a big foam party that night without their Harvard hosts. I was heading the same direction as them, so we walked together. Once we were in private, away from the current Harvard students, the high schoolers spoke openly to me. They had been quietly panicking all weekend.

"I had no idea drinking was so big here," the girl said. "I thought it was Harvard so everybody was more into studying."

"Yeah, is it always like this?" the guy asked.

Everybody likes to give good-sounding advice to people younger than themselves. I was no exception.

"You know," I said. "You don't really have to drink at college. Most people are in their rooms right now not drinking. You only see the people drinking because they're the ones who are loud and visible. A lot of people cave to social pressure when they come to college, but not all of them. It's still possible to stay true to your ideals and the reason why you came to college in the first place. Now is the most important time for you to do that."

"That makes me feel better," the girl said. "It reminds me of an article I read in The Crimson that said people come to Harvard trying to change the world but end up majoring in Econ and working in finance."

The guy seemed surprised to hear that news. He asked, "How could that happen?"

———

Throughout this book, I haven't been sharing many updates about what has happened to the students since I left. I'll make an exception, and that is the story of Alexandria. After her visit to Harvard for Pre-Frosh weekend, she changed her mind and decided that she no longer wanted to attend Harvard. She took a year off before college to study abroad, and then she accepted her offer to The University of Chicago, the school she had wanted to attend for her whole life. As of the last time I spoke to her, she still didn't drink alcohol.

———

I feel compelled to share one more story about Harvard. When I was a few years into writing this book, I had a dream that my mom secretly took my high school transcript and applied to Harvard on my behalf. I was accepted. When I heard that I was accepted, I felt the most profound, euphoric feeling of validation imaginable, almost as if the dream had allowed me to experience the neurological maximum of happiness associated with validation, acceptance, and prestige. When I awoke alone in my bed, I was extremely disappointed to realize that it was just a dream.

16

MIDDLEBURY COLLEGE

Middlebury is a small school in Vermont with about 2,400 students. In spring and summer, the land around campus looks like those idyllic green rolling pastures pictured on milk cartons. Campus is so beautiful this time of year that going to class feels like a leisure activity. Like Furman University, the students here say that their school feels like a country club, and they accordingly call it "Club Midd." Meal times were a highlight of each day. The cafeterias offer a buffet of healthy food, much of it sourced from an organic farm on campus. Students pay for their food as part of their tuition, so they are able to come and go from the cafeteria without paying. My host, Dominic, was the unofficial leader of a large group of male friends who would gather each day to eat together. Over lunch or dinner they would catch up on their personal lives, trade stories, and joke around.

Dominic was a model student. He was intelligent and spoke often in class, had a warm smile and commanding voice, and was involved in many activities and groups around campus. Middlebury tries to be very environmentally friendly, and Dominic went to great lengths to embody those values. He didn't eat beef for environmental reasons, he was a stickler about recycling, and he would always take the stairs instead of the elevator to save electricity. If one of his friends took the elevator, he would tease him and call him "lazy." (That teasing actually worked here; it was embarrassing for students to be caught wasting resources.) When Dominic spoke, his eyes were big and sympathetic like he was adoring some new puppy.

The night before I arrived, Dominic had run into an ex-girlfriend who he hadn't spoken to for many months, and they ended up talking for a while. Dominic was telling his large group of friends the story over dinner.

"It was weird to be talking at first, but we were both surprisingly mature about the whole thing," Dominic said, "and I was thinking maybe we could become friends again, because I still think she's a really cool girl. We parted ways last night on good terms, so this morning I decided to text her. And I was like, 'Hey, so I have this plan. I'm tired of us being awkward around each other, and I know you are too, so for the next two weeks, every time we pass each other, we should give each other a high five. We won't even talk, just a high five to slowly get rid of all the tension that built up from not talking.'"

Everyone was smiling. "So did she respond?" someone asked.

"It's horrible," Dominic said. "After I wrote that super long text, all she writes back is, 'Nah, I'll pass.'"

Dominic gave us a look with his big, sympathetic eyes as we all laughed. The guys told Dominic that they thought his plan was pretty creative. Two of them patted Dominic on the back, and soon Dominic was able to laugh it off with us.

But Dominic wasn't too upset over it, because he had a new love interest who he had just started to date. He told me about her the following morning over breakfast.

"She's one of Middlebury's leading voices of feminism," said Dominic.

"How so?" I asked.

"Well, she's been talking a lot about this event called 'It Happens Here' about rape and sexual assault. The event was extremely successful. There were over 500 students there to listen to the speakers. The whole theme of it was that sexual assault even happens at Middlebury."

"What do you mean by 'even happens' at Middlebury?"

"Well, a lot of people think nothing bad can go on here because Middlebury's just this perfect sort of community. So the event was saying that's not necessarily true. Anyway, it's been really interesting with her. Like when we hook up, she's incredibly good at being vocal on her end."

"What does she say?"

"Well, for example, when we first hooked up, she was like, 'Can I take your pants off?' and I was like, 'Hell yeah!'"

I was amazed to hear that. "Dude, that's awesome," I said. "'Can I take your pants off?' Incredible."

(Today it is fairly common for a woman to ask a man's consent before removing his clothes, but five years ago it was revolutionary.)

"I know," Dominic said. "She really lives by what she says. I think all girls should have that equal responsibility. If guys need to ask for consent whenever they make moves on girls, girls should be expected to do the same, even if it's just a courtesy thing. Because of course I'm going to say yes."

"That would solve a lot of problems," I said.

"Yeah, it solves so much when both people are vocal about their intentions and know where the other person is coming from. You're hooking up, and you can be sure she's enjoying it. And not just that, you know that she wanted it beforehand and didn't have any doubts."

"Brilliant," I said.

"And it's also nice if a girl is taking at least a bit of action. Instead of me taking my own pants off and just hoping she's gonna be cool with it. I think it's the right way to do things."

"How did you two meet?"

"We were in this club, in a meeting. I didn't know her yet, but she spoke up and said she didn't support race-based affirmative action and thought it should be more socioeconomic. I didn't completely agree with her, but I liked the way she shared her thoughts. That's when I fell for her."

"Very romantic."

I met Vivian, Dominic's new romantic interest, that day. She was short and pretty.

"College has this glow," she said over lunch. "When you're young or when you go on college visits, there's a glow around it. Once you're inside though, it feels more like a grind. You don't see the glow from the inside."

The next day, Dominic bought Vivian chocolates and left them on her dresser with a note that said "D." She texted him when she found it and said, "I don't know if you are D, but whoever he is, he certainly knows the fastest way to a girl's heart is through her stomach."

Dominic replied, "This D sounds very mysterious and romantic."

That evening, Dominic went to Vivian's place for some alone time, and I hung out with Dominic's roommates. His roommates were Ian, Michael, and Tyler.

"So is there a shared interest or something that connects your friends group?" I asked. Dominic had at least ten close friends who were always together.

"A lot of our friends don't have much of a scent trail like a lot of people here," said Ian. By 'scent trail,' he meant that they didn't have a stereotype.

"What are those people like?" I asked. "The ones with scent trails."

"Well, there's a big mountaineering club," said Ian. "Those people are kind of obsessed with outdoors and have their own social structure. Then there are the Febs, people who arrived here in February, it's like this late arrival program. For some reason there's a generally negative attitude toward Febs, so all the Febs stick together."

They decided that instead of continuing to explain the stereotypes to me, they would just show me a music video called "Midd Kid" that covered all of it. Some Middlebury graduate had made a parody music video of what students are like at Middlebury. The stereotype is basically that people at Middlebury are flannel-wearing, Nalgene-bottle-carrying, granola-eating, mountaineering types. It made some sense—Ian, for instance, wore flannel, had a scruffy beard, had massive forearms from rock climbing, and always carried a Nalgene bottle. At some point he told me, "I get real restless staying here during the week, so on weekends I have to find an adventure of some kind. I get this urge to just go far away outside and sleep on the soggy ground."

Dominic and his friends were all sophomores. Ian and Tyler were roommates freshman year, and Dominic and Michael were too. By sophomore year, all four of them lived together in a suite. Ian and Tyler told me that the first few nights of school freshman year, they didn't really talk to each other.

"I didn't know how I would relate to this guy from England and Beijing," said Ian. "But after a few days of not talking, we were sitting next to each other, and he farted. We both chuckled, and after that we were all good."

Later that night, while Dominic was still with Vivian, a group of guys and girls came over to their suite to play beer pong. Between games I got talking to one of Dominic's friends, Max.

"Where's Dominic tonight?" Max asked.

"I think he's staying over at Vivian's," I said. "Do you know her?"

"Oh yeah, I know her," he said with the particular tone of someone who has more to say.

"What do you mean?" I asked.

"Honestly man, Vivian is really hot, but she's kind of lame. She just sucks."

"How so?"

"Don't tell Dominic this, but that girl is crazy. Actually, you can tell Dominic I said that. I already tried to warn him before. He didn't want to listen."

"Really? I met her and she seemed pretty cool."

"Sure, she's cool. But she's also crazy. I dated her for like one week freshman year."

"How is she crazy?"

"I couldn't even begin to explain it. But I think Dominic really likes her. Maybe she's changed, but I doubt it."

That night there was a girl visiting Middlebury from Washington University. She was drunk, and she was flirting with a lot of Dominic's friends. She also had a boyfriend back at Washington University. The guys all discreetly spread the news that she was in a relationship, and the subtext of this news was, "Therefore, don't hit on her." For the remainder of the night, all the guys treated her as if she were off limits, and nothing more happened with her. This was refreshing for me to witness. At LIU Post, I had taken a group vote about the ethics of sleeping with someone who had a boyfriend, and the group said it was ethical. If I had taken the same group vote here, they would have said it was unethical.

All week I slept on a giant beanbag in their kitchen. When I woke up the following morning, Dominic was back from Vivian's and was sleeping in his own bed. After breakfast, Dominic's group of friends met up to play basketball. Afterward we sat around on the court.

"I got my penis touched last night," said one of the guys. "Broke a two-month cold streak."

"Good job," someone said.

"Congrats," said another.

"The thing I love about Middlebury," said Dominic after a minute, "is that we learn how to work really hard. And we do. But we have like two days a week where we chill really, really hard. We have a really high quality of life. We play sports and hang out and drink and smoke and hook up. Even though it's artificially constructed—the whole 'college on a hill' thing."

"I don't think it's artificial," said Michael. "Maybe it's an environment that's been created, but I think there's something real. It's the people. The people are here."

"Yeah, you're right," said Dominic. "I honestly feel like Middlebury has 1,800 people with my exact value system."

"Some time in my life, I want to just move to Vermont and live this exact sort of life again for two more years," said Michael.

"It's not the same though," said Dominic. "It's not just Vermont that's good, it's the people, like you said."

Someone changed the subject and asked, "Dominic, what were you doing last night?"

"I was hanging out with Vivian," said Dominic.

"Did you fuck?"

"No. I saw her boobies though."

"Not bad."

"It's weird, though. She wanted to have a talk."

"A talk already? You've been hooking up for like a week."

"Yeah, I don't know what to think, because she told me that she wants to be non-exclusive."

"Nice."

"Yeah, it should be good, right?" Dominic said. "It seems like that's supposed to be my dream. But is it?"

"Non-exclusive," I said. "So you're together, but you can still see other people?"

"Right," said Dominic.

"That sounds ideal to me," someone said.

"And I always thought that would be ideal, too," said Dominic. "But something is weird about it. I can hook up with Vivian and other girls if I want, which should be awesome. But I feel like it's weird that she's the one who's so adamant about it."

"As long as you're hooking up with her as much as you want, you're good to go, right?" someone asked.

"I think so," said Dominic. "I think so."

That afternoon, Dominic, his roommates, and I went on a long walk. Middlebury is so beautiful that it is common for students to go on long hikes or walks between classes. We brought one small joint to share between the five of us. Our hike took us across rolling pastures and through dark woods. The day was so lovely that we kept extending the walk farther and farther. Eventually we sat in a gazebo overlooking Middlebury's solar farm, which provides much of the power for campus. The school's long-term goal is to become self-sufficient.

"I grew up in a house in the woods," said Ian. "But when I was ten or so, we moved to the suburbs, and then I started spending all my time inside. I played a lot of video games and stuff. But then I went camping with my dad, and he was about 50 at the time, and he told me I had to do adventurous things while I was young, because I'll never be in as good of shape. So I started to love the outdoors, and now I can't get enough."

"It's almost a necessary part of resetting," said Dominic. "When you're camping, your only motivation is to exist. You aren't worried about your job or relationships or trying to impress people. It's invigorating."

On our walk back, Dominic said, "Let me ask you guys this—what about sleeping over at a girl's place? Vivian told me last night I couldn't stay over, but it was already 4am. That's almost morning."

"Weird," I said.

"She had me over, we hung out and talked about how we wouldn't be exclusive, and then at 4am she asked me to leave."

"You hooked up, right?" Michael asked.

"Yeah."

"How far?"

"Handjob," said Dominic.

"Hm, that's an interesting question then. Do you sleep over after a handjob?"

"It depends on the handjob," Ian said with a smirk.

"Yeah," said Michael. "There's a huge range of handjobs. But the gist is you thought you should stay over, and she kicked you out?"

"I guess so," said Dominic. "I'm just not used to that, I wasn't sure what to think."

We didn't know either. We talked it over but couldn't make sense of it.

Dominic's friends made for a great support system. Any time a conflict arose with Vivian, Dominic had a large group of guys to consult for feedback. Throughout the week, as complications escalated—the non-exclusivity, the kicking Dominic out at 4am, and some other small things—all of Dominic's friends would put their heads together to try to make sense of it and to offer advice and encouragement. Ian told me that when Dominic was anxious, everybody else would become anxious too. Dominic had somehow become the moral center of the group, and it was in everybody's interest to make sure that he was doing well.

Near the end of the week, something would happen between Dominic and Vivian that would lead to the strangest conflict he and his friends had yet encountered.

It happened on the night of Middlebury's biggest party of the year. Somewhere on the edge of campus is a group of modified trailers that students live in known as The Mods. Once a year, the students who live there throw a collective party called Modopolooza. It's a big dance party where electronic dance music is played and most of the student body is present. Before we left for Modopolooza, Dominic's friends all came over and we played some drinking games in the dorm room. I asked Dominic about how he got himself involved in so many different organizations on campus.

"I started kind of being on my own early, so that's probably why I take initiative here. It's interesting how for so long you think your family is going to love you unconditionally, but you realize that's not really the truth. It's really just chance who you're born with. My parents are both alcoholics, and they're paying for me to be here, but they're not really where my support is. Like we were talking about yesterday, the support group, mine isn't my parents. I get all my support here at Middlebury."

"Does their alcoholism play a part in your life, you think?"

"Well, of course I still drink and stuff. I don't think a firm pro-alcohol or anti-alcohol stance is a very good way to be. But I'm conscious of it. I like to always put that last drink down, to always drink a little less than others to show myself I'm in control."

Their pregame was more ambitious than usual. Since the guys were preparing for the biggest party of the year, there was a lot of beer to consume. Once all the beer was gone, Dominic and his friends took off on a path through the woods to Modopolooza. Everyone was hammered. They climbed trees, screamed, and fought each other along the way. We passed by some large houses in the woods where the guys would all be living the following year. These houses were like the cabins that a family would pay good money to rent for a week's vacation. I imagined that living there would make Middlebury feel even more like a resort.

The party was outside in front of the trailer homes. When we arrived, a huge group of tightly packed students was dancing together. In the middle of the students, there were two large speakers on raised platforms. Aggressive trance music was playing, and it had everybody either grinding or, if alone, air-thrusting. The students who weren't dancing were inside the trailer homes drinking beer and liquor. Most of Dominic's friends disappeared into the sea of students as soon as we walked up, so I spent the next few hours walking in circles around the party, occasionally wandering inside to grab a new drink. (I prefer partner dancing—like swing or salsa—to grinding; there are rules for me to follow, the sexuality is more sublimated, and after enough lessons I might even look elegant while doing it.)

While I was walking around inside the trailer, I passed two guys who were trading long chugs from a bottle of vodka. I joined them and tried to show off by chugging the vodka for a long time, then I immediately blacked out and fell asleep on the couch. The party's hosts had to wake me up once the party was over and everybody was gone, and they had to call Dominic from my phone so he could come pick me up. This actually wasn't embarrassing—the next day on campus, lots of students would come up and pat me on the back while saying things like, "Hey dude, I heard you passed out at Modopolooza! Awesome!" Middlebury was small enough that my emails looking for a host had reached a large number of students, and a lot of people knew that I was the visiting writer. The students seemed proud that their party had made me pass out.

While I was inside asleep on the couch, Dominic and Vivian were outside dancing together in the middle of the students. This is when the strange event occurred. I didn't witness it happen myself—Dominic had to tell me about it later. He told me the story late that night, then again the following morning, and then he told the story to all of his roommates. We spent the following two days trying to understand it, but after two days of discussion, we still came to no conclusion. Here's what happened:

Dominic and Vivian were dancing together at Modopolooza. Both of them had been drinking. As the party became more intense, they decided to step up onto the platform that was holding one of the speakers in the middle of the students. So now they were elevated above the crowd, grinding, and highly visible to everybody else. For a few minutes, everything seemed fine. But eventually Vivian leaned back and told Dominic, "Quit being so nice. Be mean to me."

"Basically, we were dancing," Dominic told me, "and she kept insisting that I, like, objectify her, and like, feel her up."

"She used those words, 'Objectify me'?" I asked.

"She kept insisting that I act like an asshole. The words she kept using were, 'Be an asshole for ten minutes. Just be an asshole!' And whatever I was doing just didn't feel like enough."

Dominic's response to Vivian's request was to grind with her more aggressively. He would rub his hands all over her body and grind into her harder and harder. And yet, whatever he was doing didn't seem to satisfy Vivian. Then, as he was rubbing his hands across her thigh, something happened.

"So at one point, I was feeling her up," Dominic said, "and my hand caught on her skirt and lifted it up, and she flashed people. I wasn't even aware of this in the moment, but she was infuriated. And fair enough. If someone did that to me, I would be super pissed."

Dominic accidentally lifted up Vivian's skirt, exposing her ass to the students below. He said she was wearing underwear, so she wasn't completely exposed. Nevertheless, as soon as it happened, Vivian jumped down off the platform and took off running away. Dominic ran after her out of concern.

"Where are you going?" Dominic yelled.

Vivian didn't respond, she just kept running, so Dominic kept following her. When Dominic was about to catch up to her, she turned around, made a big X symbol with her forearms, and screamed, "Stay back!"

Dominic quit running and put his hands up in surrender. "Whoa, what happened?" he asked.

"I said, 'Stay back!'" she repeated.

Vivian turned and kept running, presumably toward her dorm, and didn't speak with Dominic again until the following morning.

In the morning, Dominic and Vivian texted a little bit, and that's when she told him about her skirt being lifted up. After Dominic explained that he didn't mean to lift her skirt, Vivian still maintained that his behavior had been inappropriate. They made plans to meet up and talk about it later that day.

In the meantime, Dominic and his roommates spent the morning trying to make sense of what had happened. We were a bunch of 19- and 20-year-olds deliberating over Vivian's possible motivation like members of a jury deliberating over the details of a crime. One person would make a long speech while pacing around the room, then the next person would go. Our main question was, why did Vivian, a vocal feminist, want Dominic to be an asshole to her? And what exactly was Dominic supposed to do in that situation to satisfy her request?

"My ex was somewhat feminist," said Michael. "When we were in a relationship, we were on equal terms. But when we were in the bed, we were not on equal terms. Like, she was not a feminist in bed. You know what I mean?"

"How did she change?" I asked.

"She wanted to be dominated. And I feel like that's a thing, like, this happens. People who are feminists on the outside—I'm all for that—but I feel like there are times when they want to be dominated. There's just this thing, where in bed, for some of them, it changes. So my theory with Vivian all along was that that's the case with her. She gives very strong hints of that, and gives many glimpses of that. And if you go one step too far, you get what happened with Dominic. You said she lives very intentionally. So this is a case where something that she feels sexually doesn't jive with the way she thinks theoretically, rationally, intelligently. And she hasn't come to terms with that yet. And I don't know if she will. She may want to suppress it."

"I think the other explanation is that she's self aware," Dominic said. "I'm not defending her, and shit's bizarre, and there's totally the possibility that it doesn't work out between us. But the other explanation for her behavior is that she wants to tap into the primal satisfaction of those things—partially for the fact that you want what you can't have, kind of like how being a criminal is so exciting to people, because you're breaking some rule or whatever. She wants that rush without actually undermining her self-respect. So the idea is that you get someone close who you can trust, and then you do those things, instead of the other way around. So her self-empowerment is the defining charactcristic in the dynamic between her pleasure-seeking self and her empowered self."

"You are the human form of her internal struggles," Ian said. "You're the battleground."

We couldn't agree, and our discussion came to no good conclusion. I was curious to hear what Aisleen from Harvard, who, like Vivian, also identified as a feminist, would say about the story. I texted her and gave her a super vague outline of what had happened. Aisleen wrote back and disagreed with Vivian's approach. Aisleen believed that even sex was political. Her theory was that if a woman wanted a man to be an asshole or be dominant toward her during sex, or if a man wanted to do that to a woman, that they were roleplaying existing power structures within a patriarchal society. Aisleen believed that people should maintain an equal balance of power, even during sex. I found their differing perspectives interesting. A lot of people who disagree with feminism don't understand that there is a huge range of thought and a great diversity of perspective within feminism.

A few hours later, Dominic left to go talk things over with Vivian. They spent a few hours together, and then I met up with Dominic over lunch so he could give me the new details. I would be leaving for Dartmouth later that afternoon, so this was our final conversation.

"I think I've managed to salvage it," Dominic told me. "She was mad, and she's no longer that mad. We sort of talked through what happened, and we realized that stuff went awry, but she believed me that it wasn't intentional or whatever. So we talked about the context and sort of realized that, ok, there was probably some communication that should have gone on before she asked me to be an asshole, so I'd have some idea of what that meant. Now that she's explained it to me, basically she wanted to feel wanted. Which is totally fair enough."

"Interesting," I said.

"And we got talking about other things, and she explicitly said, 'I want our relationship to be centered on the fact that I think you're hot, and you think I'm hot, and not on the fact that we are kindred spirits. That's not the side of things I want to explore.' So I was like, 'So are you down for a Tuesday afternoon booty call?' and she was like, 'Yes, exactly.' And there's clearly a big learning curve in acting like that towards someone, because that's never how I've acted toward someone. And she keeps saying how 'sweet boys' don't understand this stuff. She keeps describing me as a 'sweet boy.'"

"She's saying you're sweet, meaning you don't understand it?"

"Yeah," Dominic said. "She kept insisting last night that I was being too sweet and too nice. And so now I realize what I should have done—and I came to this conclusion myself—I should have been like, 'Pause, I'm not comfortable with what you're asking me to do right now.' So in some twisted way, I realize that I fucked up, in not doing that."

"Calling you a sweet boy is a pretty condescending way of saying that you're respectful," I said.

"It's weird, but at the same time, partially out of the fact that I still have a crush on her, and partially out of the fact that I've never had that kind of relationship with someone, and partially out of the fact that sex is fun, I'm gonna try to do this whole, you know, physically based relationship with her. The question is, is it a net good? Maybe it ends badly, but if it's good for a while, then I think it's a net good."

"The only way it would be a net bad, I think, is if you change—like if you eventually modify yourself to fit this weird mold that only pleases her, and it pleases nobody else."

"And I think I'm ok," Dominic said, "like I think I can toe that line pretty well. I'm very confident that I'll be ok."

There was a strange, almost sad irony to Dominic's situation. In some sense, Dominic had a quality to him that would make him the ideal boyfriend for a large number of women. And yet, he was now dating someone who wanted to rid him of that exact quality. But at the same time, lots of women want a man who's full of sexual desire, who's assertive about what he wants, and who is capable of being a bit of an asshole at times. So another way of looking at it might be that Dominic was lucky to be with a woman who was willing to so patiently teach him how to be sexy. Whatever was happening, I agreed with Dominic—I was very confident that he'd be ok, mostly because he had so much support from his friends.

We finished our lunch while talking about other things. Then on the walk back to Dominic's dorm, he brought up Vivian again.

"The thing about it, like, if we were having sex, and she were to be like, 'I want you to just dominate me and not care about me at all,' I'd respond to that being like, 'Ok, maybe I can do that.' But you know, I might not be that comfortable with the idea of doing that to someone. Especially not someone that I kinda have a crush on. Oh well, that'll be a bridge to cross, when it comes."

17

DARTMOUTH COLLEGE

Dartmouth was a two-hour drive from Middlebury, but even so, I allowed myself a three-day break before beginning my time there. I watched every movie playing at a local theater and spent the rest of my time hunched over a 24-hour diner, where I listened to old waitresses sincerely use expressions like, "Look what the cat dragged in," and "Where you been hidin'?" Each night I drove to a Walmart near the diner, bought a few cans of beer, lay down in the back of my car, and stared wistfully into the bright lights of the parking lot as they shone through the moonroof onto my sad face.

Everyone had been telling me that I had to visit Dartmouth because of a popular Rolling Stone article about the school's apparent "vomit culture." A disgruntled Dartmouth student had leaked stories to a journalist about one fraternity's hazing rituals, which apparently included lots of required vomiting. The article's most sensational anecdote was that fraternity members were forced during pledgeship to drink until they vomited into a kiddie pool, and then they'd have to swim in the kiddie pool that they just vomited into. (The phrase "kiddie pools full of vomit" had swept the nation.) This sounded interesting for me to write about, but unfortunately, all the negative attention Dartmouth was receiving had made the students there wary of journalists, and I was having a difficult time finding someone to host me.

After months of no responses from Dartmouth students, good fortune connected me at the last possible moment with the perfect person to write about. It was Dominic's roommate's cousin, and I was connected to him only one day before I arrived at Dartmouth. He was a 6'3" legacy on the rugby team, he was popular and good-looking, and he was a member of one of Dartmouth's top fraternities. If anyone could acquaint me with Dartmouth's "vomit culture," it would be him. The trouble was that he wanted to meet me first before agreeing to be the subject of the Dartmouth chapter—a reasonable request.

Todd and I met in the street while he was on his way to a sorority event. He was wearing a green Dartmouth sweatshirt with the hood pulled over his head, leaving his face in shadow and making our conversation feel like it was top-secret. It was night already, and I had to muster up all the energy I had in order to speak, due to my three days of silence leading up to the interaction.

He wasted no time. He asked, "So how can I know you're not making us look bad? People are pretty pissed around here about that article."

"Well, my book isn't supposed to be an exposé like the article was," I said. "I just write down everything that happens, so whatever it is that you show me, that's the story I will tell."

"But what about you?" he asked. "What's your perspective that you're bringing to this?" Todd's assertiveness was refreshing.

"I don't really have any affiliation," I said. "I just want to tell a good story. If I have any bias at all regarding the Rolling Stone thing, it's probably that I want to show that it's not true, in order to show the other side of Dartmouth. There'd be no point in me being here if I just said, "Yeah, it really is like that.'"

"Alright, maybe this will be good then. Right now the whole country's opinion of Dartmouth is based on one bad apple who took out his own personal inadequacies on everybody else."

"So I can stay?" I asked.

"Yeah, you can stay."

We turned onto a street with rows of sorority houses. Many of the girls we passed waved at Todd or otherwise pivoted their heads to look at him. When we stepped into the sorority house, a dance performance was in progress, and students filled the room sitting cross-legged on the floor or standing against the walls. Eight girls were dancing to choreographed songs. The dancing was artful, expressive, and intimate. At the end of each dance, the students clapped politely. Todd went his own way and would belt out "YEAH GIRL!" each time with a mighty voice, after which all the heads would turn, and the girls would give him looks of curiosity and/or admiration. After the dancing ended, girls with shaky hands and soft voices recited original poetry. A recurring theme in many of the poems was the idea of romance without alcohol. A very pretty and nervous girl's poem repeated the phrase, "Kiss me sober." For a Greek event, the students were quite racially diverse, at least compared to the South. The event also seemed inclusive to students who I wasn't accustomed to seeing in Greek houses—for example, some somewhat scrawny guys with artsy haircuts and thick-rimmed glasses. Todd yelled out "YEAH GIRL!" after the poems too. By the end of the event, my impression was that what I had witnessed was the polar opposite of "vomit culture." Afterward, Todd and I headed to his fraternity house.

"You should have seen it earlier," he joked. "We were all swimming around in kiddie pools full of vomit."

I chuckled. "That was one of the most wholesome things I've seen on the whole trip."

"Yeah, but this kind of thing never happens," he said sarcastically. "We usually just make people swim in urine."

Outside, more girls yelled out to Todd or hugged him or just stared at him. He gave massive hugs, sometimes lifting the girls off their feet. I pretended like all the attention he received was normal, as if it would be the same for me if he were the one visiting my home.

Inside the fraternity house, Todd led me through a maze of basements into a beer-soaked room where students were playing what was apparently the original beer pong. It's kind of like normal beer pong, except you use paddles. The guys who weren't playing beer pong stood around the table sipping beers.

Todd gave one of his friends a hard fist bump then swung an arm over his shoulder and patted his chest.

"No biddy tonight?" his friend asked.

"Nope, no biddies tonight," said Todd.

"Ah, too bad."

Todd didn't live at the fraternity house, so we headed to his dorm after a little while. Todd's apartment-style dorm that he shared with three roommates had a TV and game console set up that remained turned on for 24 hours a day, exclusively dedicated to Tetris. (It seems ridiculous for me to mention their video game habits, but trust me, Tetris was a central part of Todd's life.) One of Todd's roommates had the high score for the game on their console. His record score was so incredibly high that it was still unbroken after months of constant play by the other three roommates. Todd considered it unbeatable at this point, but he still spent almost all of his free time trying in vain to beat it. Nearly every conversation I had with Todd that week took place while he was playing Tetris. As he played on my first night at Dartmouth, he asked me why I didn't go to college.

I gave him my typical answer.

"I understand your logic," Todd said after my explanation. "It's admirable, really. But to me, college is just too fun. I don't care what else you say. It's just too fun."

It was the best argument for college I had ever heard. "You're right," I told him. "That's the one flaw in my whole philosophy."

"See, at college you just show up and learn whatever you want," he continued. "You show up and study hard at your classes. Dartmouth encourages you to take random interesting things that you like. And then you just have a shit ton of fun the rest of the time. People say it's the best time of your life, and it probably is, as far as I can tell."

The Dartmouth student who had been the whistleblower about fraternity hazing was an ever-present topic of conversation that week.

Todd was not in the same fraternity as the whistleblower, but Todd's fraternity had a pledgeship process that was just as challenging, so he had a lot to say about it.

"It really pisses me off that people are thinking of Dartmouth in a negative way," Todd said. "It's really frustrating that reporters have so much control. People just kind of believe what they hear. My fraternity's pledgeship is known for being one of the hardest. It's hard, but for me it's hard in a way that's understandable. We are one of the closest brotherhoods on campus because of it."

Todd went on to describe a number of the hazing rituals he underwent during his pledge term. He told me the details off-the-record, so I won't describe them here, but I will say that, to me, they were just as bad as swimming in kiddie pools full of vomit—although there were no bodily fluids involved. Todd's fraternity had one night of especially intense hazing. Now that Todd was an active member of his fraternity, he wanted to get rid of this night for future pledges.

"Why be mean to these kids that are going to eventually be some of your best friends?" Todd said. "Why would I want to perpetuate this terrible cycle? So after that night, I was like, I'm going to change this. Whenever it comes up, I'm going to be like, 'Hey, I think we should get rid of that night, I think it was pointless.' And I was planning to do that, you know? And then this fucking kid comes out with this article that makes us all look like douchebags, and he goes about it in the most pussy way possible. This kid is the fucking douchebag. And it just infuriated me, and really pissed me off, that people are now seeing Dartmouth with this view, when the kids here are some of the most genuine, nice kids I've met in my whole life."

Regarding the so-called "vomit culture," Todd said that it was partially true, but it wasn't the full story. His fraternity, for instance, had one member who didn't drink alcohol. During hazing, that member would have to pour beer over his head instead of drink it. He also said that the older guys in the fraternity told the pledges on the first night of hazing that if they were ever concerned or didn't want to do something, that they should come talk to them. Todd never felt any concern that he would be kicked out if he spoke up.

"Brothers take care of brothers when they're drunk" Todd said. "They'll make sure they're not crazy drunk. And the puking thing? It does have a functional purpose. If you're really drunk and you need to puke and get it all out of you, you do it."

"Makes sense," I said.

"Maybe after having gone through pledge term, I've been brainwashed," Todd said. "But like, I enjoyed pledge term, and sure, there were things I didn't enjoy, but as a whole, it was entertaining and it was a challenge. It's pretty cool. It's kind of fun in a way to be quote-unquote 'fratty' and be kinda gross. It's like playing in the mud, you just have no regard for anything. It's your time to just let loose. Part of that's kinda fun, just throwing up on the ground, and you keep drinking, and just being messy and gross, and you're just kinda drunk and you're with your friends, and it's like 'What the fuck?' It's a good way to blow off steam. The whole point of hazing is that you have to go through things together that are tough as a group, so in that way you all come closer. Challenges bring people together."

One of Todd's roommates had joined us. "It's the most fun you never want to have again," he added.

During this conversation, I started to realize that Todd thought I would somehow be the savior for Dartmouth's reputation. This led to an odd pattern in our interactions throughout the week. As Todd began to trust me, he would reveal worse things about Dartmouth, which would in turn make it harder for me to save their reputation and still tell an honest story. I had told Todd that I wanted to show that the Rolling Stone article wasn't true, but so far, all evidence seemed to show that it was completely true. Everything in the article —the forced vomiting, swimming in vomit, swimming in urine—all of that was true; the only surprise was that most of the guys here apparently enjoyed it.

One more thing about Todd: Todd was prescribed a really high dose of ADHD medication. If the average dose that somebody would take as a study aid is one pill, Todd took between five and ten pills each day. Todd's roommates told me this information one day while he was gone, and then Todd told it to me himself later in the week.

Todd would sometimes crush up a pill or two and snort them before a party, which allowed him to drink until blacking out and to skip an entire night of sleep. This led to the most intense partying I witnessed at any college.

In the morning, we went to Todd's classes, followed by a meeting, and then Todd went without me to rugby practice. In the evening, he had a cappella practice. To my dismay, Todd also had a wonderful singing voice. In the suburbs where I'm from, a child gets to choose between being either smart, athletic, or talented; you can only pick one—maybe two if you're especially gifted. But Todd had somehow chosen all three, which seemed to violate a law of nature.

One night while on the way to Todd's fraternity house, we stopped by the campus art building so Todd could show me the galleries. At the entrance to one of the galleries, there was a cute girl in a red dress standing by the guest book. She was the "gallerina" here like Nora from Tufts. Todd was good at almost everything, which included being smooth with women, so it was enlightening to watch him operate.

"Are we supposed to sign in?" Todd asked her.

"You don't have to," she said, smiling.

"Ok, just checking," he said.

There was a subtle shift in Todd's demeanor after their exchange. We were the only two visitors in the gallery, so I could sense that everything he said to me from then on was meant to be overheard by the girl standing near the door. I played along, hoping not to screw it up.

"What do you see in this one?" Todd asked me, pointing to an abstract painting.

"Hm," I said. "Mountains."

"Nice, I gotcha, I gotcha. You see these clouds too?" he pointed. "Right there?"

"Nice call," I said.

"Do you ever paint?" he asked.

"A little bit. I do mostly abstracts."

"I'm into landscapes myself," he said. "Lakes and snowy mountains, clouds, that sort of thing."

I felt pretty certain we were both lying. Admittedly, I was less concerned with impressing the girl than with not disappointing Todd. We made our way slowly around the room while bullshitting about each painting until we had circled back to the entrance.

"The art's pretty good here," Todd said to the girl.

"Yes, it is," she said. She had a slight accent.

"Are you an artist?" he asked.

She blushed. "No, not really."

"That's too bad," said Todd. "You look like an artist."

She blushed more.

"What's your name?" he asked.

"Noelle," she said.

"Do you work here a lot?"

"Sometimes," she said.

"Ok, see you later Noelle."

We walked out and closed the glass doors behind us.

"I think she was down for a three-way," Todd joked.

I said, "Definitely."

That night, Todd's fraternity was hosting something called "Tails," a weekly mixer with a sorority. "Tails" is short for cocktails, which is what everyone drinks, as well as short for the phrase "get some tail," which is what the guys aim to do with the girls.

Before the girls arrived, Todd said, "Don't let me stay out past 10, ok? Please. I gotta study. No matter what I tell you, don't let me stay out."

I agreed.

Pretty soon there was a group of about 20 girls in the middle of the main room at the fraternity house. This was Tails. A cocktail bar stretched from wall to wall lined with liquor bottles, and the girls were having their drinks made by some of the guys in the fraternity who were acting as bartenders. Some music was playing from speakers in the corner. This was a strange night, however, because the guys in the fraternity were barely talking to the girls.

"I'm showing you a bad Tails," Todd told me. "These girls aren't that hot and they aren't that cool. We have to be nice and have a Tails with all the sororities, so sometimes we get the bad ones."

I was witnessing something that I had never seen before. The sorority girls here were huddled together in the middle of the room, waiting for the guys to talk to them. Only about eight guys had even bothered to show up for this Tails, and those guys were standing on the edges of the room talking to each other instead of the girls. Meanwhile, the girls were terribly nervous. They were looking around the room, smiling at the guys so they'd hopefully come and talk to them, but the guys were mostly giving them no attention. The girls mistook me for a member of the fraternity, so if I made eye contact with one of the girls, she'd smile weakly, look down at her feet, then slowly look back up at me a second later with her ego at risk to see if I was still looking. I've said it before, but I'll say it again—I've never had girls be as attracted to me as when they mistook me for a member of a fraternity. I wondered, how many kiddie pools full of vomit is this worth? For most guys, probably quite a few.

Todd and I went into the basement to play beer pong while we waited for more girls to arrive. He managed to remain the loudest person in every room we entered. We played beer pong on the same team, and any time we'd score he would yell something then affectionately slap me across the chest.

After beer pong, we went upstairs to see which new girls were there. As a complete coincidence, Noelle from the art gallery had showed up. Todd and I walked over to her. Todd smiled at her and said, "Noelle," with an intense gaze. She seemed flattered just to hear her name come from his lips. We talked to her for a few minutes then stepped away to pour ourselves new drinks.

"She wants some," Todd said to me.

"Yeah, she does," I said. "We should invite her to come with us." Later that night we were headed to a big party at another fraternity.

"Do you want to do it?" Todd asked.

I didn't want to screw it up. "Ah, I'll let you do it." I said.

He didn't hesitate. He walked up to Noelle and said, "Hey, we're gonna go smoke, wanna join?"

She smiled and said, "Ok."

It was too easy for him. We left Todd's fraternity with Noelle, her friends, and a few other guys to sneak onto a dorm rooftop and smoke a few joints. The campus security guards kept driving in laps around the building, so we had to duck down out of sight. The pot made Todd even more charismatic by mellowing him out a bit and revealing some gentleness. I, on the other hand, became extremely paranoid and even less charismatic. ("What the hell am I doing on this rooftop with these strangers?" I kept wondering. "What insane sequence of decisions has led me to being here in New Hampshire on this rooftop with these people?")

Eventually we climbed down and headed toward the big fraternity party. I checked the time and remembered what Todd had told me earlier about not letting him stay out. Our group was walking in the dark across a grassy field. I walked up to Todd.

"Todd," I said. My voice was all soft and weak now from the paranoia. "Todd, hey, just a reminder. You told me earlier not to let you stay out past 10. It's midnight now."

"Yeah, man, I know, I know. I'm not gonna stay long. I'm not gonna stay long."

"Ok, well, you told me that you'd argue with me, and that I shouldn't let you."

"I know. I know I said that. Trust me, I'm already mad at myself. But I gotta. I just gotta."

"Ok, that's cool," I said.

After this, Todd's excitement doubled as if he had just outsmarted a babysitter and was now allowed to stay up late. He came to a stop, leaned way back, then let out a long howl at the moon, and then he ran up to Noelle and grabbed her from behind while she was walking and lifted her off the ground in a giant bear hug. She cackled with laughter and screamed "Todd!" When he set her back down, he rested his hands on her shoulders and left them there for a moment while she stood frozen, then he let go and moved immediately to the other side of the group to start talking to one of the guys as if his thing with Noelle had never happened. I played a little movie in my mind of what would have happened if I had tried that same move. It was horrible and devastating, and I had no sense of humor about it.

Down the hill a white wooden house was blasting music that shot deep throbs of bass across the lawn. It was so loud that you could feel it in your feet. Groups of students like ours flocked toward the noise from all directions. Campus security guards stood at the edge of the property with their toes on the grass. Two members of the fraternity stood on the porch letting the newcomers inside.

"PRETEND I CARE!" one yelled. "PRETEND TO SHOW ME YOUR ID! S.N.S. IS WATCHING FROM THE STREET! PRETEND TO SHOW ME YOUR ID! PRETEND I CARE!"

We filed past him, played along by flashing our IDs, which he didn't look at, and joined the party. Dartmouth fraternities are the opposite of Harvard Final Clubs—they are completely inclusive. At Dartmouth, any student is allowed into fraternity parties, and they can have as many free beers as they want.

As I passed through the doorway, the music punched me in the face and woke me right up. Everything was glowing and moving about in rapid motion. The students all wore white, which glowed purple under black-lights, and the room was speckled with bright spinning dots of neon green. (I think it was a black-light party, which meant you were supposed to wear white; I was the only person not dressed appropriately.) The entire house was a dance floor, and it was packed with a few hundred students, all of them dancing. The music was loud enough that I couldn't hear my own voice, which meant that conversation was absolutely off limits—all you could do was dance. The students had mashed themselves together and were throwing their fists in the air as one ecstatic, selfless whole. Until I witnessed this party, I had always thought that nobody really liked this kind of atmosphere, as if its raging intensity had surpassed any individual's desire for fun. But nope—these students were loving it; they were going nuts. Even the guys who didn't have girls with them shame-lessly stood in little clusters, bobble-heading with reckless abandon as beads of sweat poured down their foreheads and sprayed violently from their hair. It was as if Dartmouth had invented partying and every other school was a cheap imitation.

And Todd was right at home. I was still standing a step inside the entryway, stupefied, when I saw that Todd had managed to push himself to the center of the party and was dancing with fury, already sandwiched between two hot blonde girls. It was impressive.

I had no idea how to behave or interact in this environment. The group I arrived with had dispersed, so I was alone and paranoid at the craziest party I had ever seen. Where was the "kiss me sober" girl? I ended up walking in laps around the house so I wouldn't look too out of place. There were more students in a downstairs basement, and some of the girls were dancing on tables in their bras, and some of the guys had their shirts off too. At Tufts when there were girls dancing topless, it didn't feel sexualized. Here at Dartmouth, the girls in their bras felt very sexy.

At some point in the night, I stood next to Noelle from the art gallery for about ten minutes. We stood shoulder-to-shoulder, watching Todd from the second floor as he danced on the first floor. It was quiet enough upstairs that we could talk, and Noelle used the opportunity to ask me about Todd. "How do you know Todd? Oh, you're writing about Todd? How cool. What is he like?" Nothing ended up happening between Todd and Noelle while I was there, but I was certain that Todd could eventually make something happen with her if he wanted. That night I saw Noelle on a few occasions wander onto the dance floor to try to dance near him, but she never got his attention.

(About an hour after this happened, Noelle actually made a move on me. She walked up to me, put her hand under my shirt, and started breathing heavily into my ear. I was way too paranoid to think about women, and I had too much pride to be someone's second choice, so I stood there without reacting until she eventually walked away. Do I regret it? Absolutely.)

Todd's dance style was absurd. He would grind with a girl with one—or sometimes both—fists in the air, and he'd keep his eyes closed. It was full-body, fully immersed dancing. He wasn't just sort of dancing, he was completely dancing. Fortunately, Todd's closed eyes gave me the luxury of being able to be a loser at this party without humiliating myself in front of my host. For the next couple hours, I continued walking in laps around the party while waiting for Todd to get tired.

Todd never got tired, but at some point I saw him step outside onto the porch, so I tracked him down. It was 3am and the party was still raging.

"Hey, man," I said to Todd, "I was heading out, but I realized I don't have a key to your place."

He looked like he'd just been on a rollercoaster. "Crazy, huh? Oh my god. You do well in there? Hah! Woo!"

"Yeah, it's awesome in there," I said. "I'm just too wiped to keep going."

He gave me the card to unlock his door. "Gotcha man, yeah man, I hear you," he said. "Well, I'm gonna stay. I know I said I'd leave, but I just can't leave. It's too fun."

I said, "I know what you mean."

When I woke up, Todd was next to me playing Tetris. He had already been to his sunrise rugby practice, eaten breakfast, and spent some time studying. He never went to sleep the previous night.

"Aren't you tired?" I asked.

"I'm absolutely exhausted," he said.

"You don't seem it."

"Yeah, so the thing is, I told you about my ADHD. I'm prescribed a pretty crazy amount of medication. I'm trying to drop down, really. I don't like how it makes me feel. But I just take the pills throughout the day to keep my energy going."

"And that works?" I asked.

"Sort of, yeah," he said. "It feels like two layers. Up top, it feels like I'm full of energy. But down below, if I think about it, I can tell I'm completely exhausted, and it's almost like I'm half asleep."

"I see."

"And at parties, me and my friends will like, snort the pills sometimes, so that we can keep going. It's sort of dangerous, because you can't feel how drunk you are. So you just keep drinking until you pass out."

"Ah, so that's how you party so hard."

"I don't actually recommend it. But once you've started doing it, it's just too awesome. It feels incredible. You can just go absolutely wild, and it feels perfect. Like, last night. That probably wasn't the most academic thing, you know? But I feel like that experience and the cumulative effect of all those experiences will be worthwhile."

"That's a good outlook," I laughed.

Todd spent the day studying at the library, so I split up from him and spent some time with his roommate.

"They talk about this thing called the Dartmouth X," his roommate told me. "Guys are one line of the X, and girls are the other. Guys' status tends to track upwards, whereas girls' status tends to track downwards. So as a freshman guy, you're kind of at the bottom of the social hierarchy. And senior girls are sort of at the bottom of the social hierarchy. They're kind of the least desirable, because they're used up, or used goods or whatever. So senior guys tend to pair up with freshmen girls."

(For a contrasting perspective on women's age and desirability, consider this quote from Benjamin Franklin: "In all your amours you should prefer old women to young ones ... for they have greater knowledge of the world.")

Todd's roommate went on to tell me that practically any guy from a good Dartmouth fraternity has a job on Wall Street waiting for him when he graduates. Apparently the fraternity alumni networks are very well-connected, and they try to give jobs to fellow fraternity members. If it's truly as easy as he says, that might be yet another reason to swim in the kiddie pools full of vomit. At some point it just becomes a worthwhile investment.

On the subject of the whistleblower—the guy who leaked the information to Rolling Stone—Todd's roommate also used the phrase, "personal inadequacies" to describe his motives. The general consensus among Todd and his friends was that the whistleblower was simply inadequate—just plain weak—and that's why he told the secrets to Rolling Stone. My guess is that in addition to being angry at the guy for worsening Dartmouth's reputation, they were also mad at him for breaking the rules of honor culture. In honor culture, you don't report your problems to a higher authority, you handle them yourself. The whistleblower, by reporting his fraternity's hazing rituals to the media, broke that ancient code.

There did seem to be a "vomit culture" at Dartmouth, as mentioned in the article, though I never witnessed anyone vomit. The guys I spoke to seemed to think that vomiting was a natural, expected consequence of heavy drinking. Since there was apparently so much vomiting during pledge term, the guys who had finished pledge term were accustomed to vomiting, and for them it was no big deal. So many guys had this attitude that it was starting to rub off on me: after only five days at Dartmouth, I was starting to think that vomiting was a little bit cool. (I kind of wanted to throw up and have Todd see me do it.)

It was my last night at Dartmouth, and we had another big party to attend. Todd must have recognized that I didn't fit in very well at the party the previous night, because he was determined to get me extremely stoned for my last night, thinking that the weed would work as a social lubricant. Unfortunately, weed does the opposite for me.

Todd stuck a giant bong to my mouth and lit the bowl for me. We were at his fraternity house in an upstairs bedroom.

"Suck suck suck suck suck," he said.

I did.

"Hold it in hold it in hold it in."

I did.

"Ok, good," he said. "Now another."

We repeated this process a few times. I knew this was a terrible idea, but I was powerless against Todd's peer pressure. When they taught us as kids not to do drugs, the hypothetical people offering you drugs were always scary, creepy people in trench coats, but in real life, the people who offer you drugs are usually the really cool people who you're desperate to impress. (Note: After Todd read an early draft of this chapter, he apologized for this and said that he was just trying to "smoke a brother out." And he's right, it was definitely my fault that I didn't assert myself.)

Todd was already drunk and high when I met up with him a few minutes earlier. I wasn't sure if he had recently snorted his pills, but I assumed so, because he was acting manic.

"Follow me," he said.

I followed Todd across the house. While walking, I started to feel terribly unsettled from the weed I had just smoked. Todd had an intense, nervous energy, and I didn't know what he was planning. He led me to one of the fraternity basements, then into a dark room. The air had the musty scent of beer and urine.

I couldn't see much of the room because of the darkness. Once we were in the corner of the room, Todd unzipped his pants and pissed onto the shadowy floor in front of him. I gathered that it was some sort of fraternity ritual to piss on the floor of that room.

"This is a secret room," Todd said. "Never look at the floor. Don't even shine your phone on it. You don't want to know."

"Alright," I said, laughing.

When he was through, we stepped back into the hallway. Then Todd put his hands on my shoulders and bent down so we were eye level. He asked, "Are you ready?"

"For what?" I asked.

"I'm going to get you laid," he said. "We're going to a dance party. Are you sufficiently drunk and high?"

"I'm only high," I said. "I just got here."

"What? You should have said something. Let me get you a beer." He grabbed a beer from their large industrial refrigerator, cracked it open, and handed it to me. "Chug it," he said.

The weed we smoked was way too strong. Already I was even more stoned and paranoid than the previous night, and we'd only smoked five minutes earlier. When I put the beer can up to my lips, it was not a can of beer, it was pure drugs—just a can of drugs. My lips and tongue almost froze to the can because it was so cold, and it felt like I might swallow my tongue. Also, my face was numb and felt like it was expanding. The room was spinning too. Even in this state, I was aware that it was noble of Todd to want to get me laid, but I really didn't want to get laid. Nothing sounded more awful at that moment than interacting with strangers and trying to have sex with them.

"Did you put something in the weed?" I asked. "I feel fucking weird."

He threw his head back with laughter and ignored the question. "Let's go see some fucking people, man! I love people! Ah! Are you fucking ready?"

"I'm ready," I lied.

"I said, are you fucking ready?" he repeated like a coach giving a pump-up speech.

"I'm fuckin' ready!" I said. (How pathetic—I can't believe I participated in that interaction.)

My tongue was now three times larger than before, and I was sure I would eventually choke on it. Once I finished the beer, I felt the need to burp, but no burp came. The burp sensation grew and grew with no release. My need to burp was so strong that it was stinging my chest, and I found it hard to speak. I could feel my heartbeat in my chest, my fingers, and my brain. I was on the brink of a panic attack.

"We're going to a dance party and we're getting laid," Todd said again. "Let's fucking do this!"

I followed Todd outside across campus. Nighttime had a gritty haze to it; the darkest blackness of my vision was a milky gray. Todd was now yelling.

"People go with me great! Mmmm, people! WAHOO! YOU FUCKING READY!?"

Then he shifted into actual gibberish.

"Wamdiddlydoo! Blehblehbleheeeemmo!"

My face was numb, and I worried that the numbness was permanent. What if I still had a numb face when I was 60? I still hadn't burped and needed to more than ever.

"Dude, I can't feel my face!" I said.

Todd said, "I know, right?"

We went into a house on campus—maybe another fraternity, I wasn't sure—and went down the stairs into the basement. This party was similar to the party the previous night, except instead of darkness and strobe lights, the overhead lights were turned on so the basement was bright and clear, leaving no blanket of darkness for me to hide in. The room was packed wall-to-wall with students dancing the Dartmouth way. Todd pushed his way to the middle of the dance floor like he had done before, but unfortunately this time he remained aware of me and made sure that I followed him into the mass of dancing students.

One of Todd's friends, another tall, muscular dude, was near him in the middle of the dance floor and gave Todd a big high five. Then Todd looked around at the girls in his vicinity. He stared at a seemingly random girl for a second, then pulled her by the hand toward him, spun her around, and started grinding with her. She went along with this happily. Todd went into his normal dance mode, except instead of closing his eyes, he kept them open, watching me.

My task now was to do the same thing as Todd: grab a girl and start grinding with her. But this task seemed enormous or impossible. I still did not like grinding—I prefer to hump in private—but I had no choice. There were two girls dancing near me, but I felt that I couldn't possibly grab them like Todd had just done. Other people's personal space felt like a sacred barrier. How horribly violating to touch another person! My God, they can actually feel it if you touch them!

I tried to get myself to start dancing, but I couldn't do that either. I was standing there motionless, like some sort of psychopath, just staring in awe at everyone around me. But I had to do something because Todd was still watching me, so I did the only thing I could think of. I took a step closer to Todd and raised my hand to give him a big high five like I had just seen his friend do. Huge mistake—what was I thinking? It was one of the dumbest things I'd ever done, but my hand was already in the air, so I had to leave it there. There was already a big grin on Todd's face, but underneath it I could sense him thinking, "What the fuck?" Still, in a truly generous gesture, he went through with it and gave me the high five. (To receive a high five out of pity is a truly terrible thing. When a high five is given out of pity, especially in public, it means that the superior individual is sacrificing some of his or her accumulated value for the sake of the lesser person; I was literally sucking away Todd's coolness, as if coolness itself were a magical resource that begins with God then trickles down through society, and I was reaching up way too high, trying to take more than my fair share. Todd seemed to know all of this instinctively.)

But the coolness I had stolen from Todd was still not enough to get me dancing. I went back to standing motionless and staring. C'mon, dance, I told myself. Move your body. But I couldn't move. How much time had gone by? Had I been standing there for a couple of seconds or had it been more like ten minutes? Shit, I had to do something, quick.

You're not going to believe what I chose to do. After some time had passed since the first high five, I took another step closer to Todd and raised my hand up in the air to try to give him a second high five. Shit. Goddamnit. Oh, fuck, dude—what was I thinking? The first high five was one of the dumbest things I'd ever done; the second high five was the dumbest.

I managed to save myself a little bit. As my hand was in the air and Todd was looking at it, cringing, I switched the high five gesture to a "give me just one moment" gesture with my index finger raised. After that, I promptly turned around and walked up the stairs and out of the basement.

At the top of the stairs, I saw a small room with nobody in it, so I walked in there. There was a couch in the room, so in order to seem busy, I pretended to search for some imaginary lost object underneath the cushions. The only thing I had really lost was my dignity. For almost 20 minutes, I scratched my chin and pursed my lips while saying out loud, "Where the hell is it? Where could it be?" This was the party-going equivalent of eating lunch in a bathroom stall. After

18 straight weeks of living with college students, you'd think I could do better than this.

Eventually a student walked into the same room. He was huge and muscular with a young-looking, round face.

"Are you looking for the bathroom?" I asked.

"Oh, no," he said. He held his phone in his hand. "Just checking something."

"Cool, me too," I said.

We stood looking at our phones for a moment until we both accidentally glanced up at each other at the same time.

He coughed, then asked, "You liking the party?"

"To be honest, I'm kind of tripping out right now," I said. "I'm trying to hide. I feel fucking pathetic."

He laughed. "Don't worry, I feel uncomfortable too. I'm new here."

We were like two kids eating lunch in separate bathroom stalls who, after months of familiarity, begin sharing food.

He told me his story. He was a football player who had just transferred to Dartmouth during his sophomore year. He hadn't planned to join a fraternity when he transferred, but now that he had been at Dartmouth for a little while, he felt he had no other choice but to join one. It wasn't because he thought it would be fun to join, it was because he thought he would be an outcast if he didn't. This is the other side of the vomit debate. Imagine that a student arrives at Dartmouth expecting a certain social life, only to find that he must swim through vomit and urine to get it, and he's an outcast if he doesn't. He's not technically forced to jump into the kiddie pool, but since social pressure is higher than he anticipated, he realizes he didn't have the full information when he chose this school and not another one, and now he feels deceived. Is he a "bad apple" or the victim of "personal inadequacies" if he finds a way to voice his dissatisfaction?

Then I told him my story. Eventually he asked me which school was my favorite.

"I had a really good time last week at Middlebury," I said.

"What'd you like about it?"

"I couldn't really say. I just felt good while I was there."

"It's the students, right? Because what else is college without the students?"

I thought for a moment: the students, yes, the students.

I don't think he meant to be profound, but I took it that way. I thought it was so profound that my whole pathetic journey that had brought me into that room had been worth it.

Eventually I thanked him for the chat. We exchanged names and shook hands with much respect.

"Well," he said, "I guess I'm gonna go back in."

He smiled and disappeared down the stairs.

I left the party soon after and enjoyed a long, restful sleep. Todd was a machine—he stayed awake all night again, apparently hooked up with two girls separately (though I think he included making out in his definition of 'hooking up'), and then went to rugby practice in the morning. He was already playing Tetris when I woke up.

Todd had blacked out that night, as well as the night before. I asked him if he remembered arriving at the party, and he said he didn't. I wasn't sure if he was telling the truth, or if he was letting me save face over the high five fiasco. I admitted to him that I didn't usually smoke weed and that I'd been terribly paranoid at both parties. He said he didn't notice anything strange, but again, I think he was just being polite.

The night before, Todd told me, all the girls left the party at around 2am, so the guys threw on some classic '90s music and "just bro'd out, hard" until 5am. Todd was explaining to me how incredibly fun it had been when the conversation came to a sudden halt. He was still playing Tetris and right now was having an incredible round. As he kept playing, the roommate who was the current record-holder happened into the room, so he sat down to watch. As Todd got closer to the high score, the roommate watched more nervously, since he hoped to maintain his record. When Todd was moments away from beating the record, he started yelling, "OH! OH! OH!" Then he did it —he beat the high score—but we all stayed calm. It wasn't time to celebrate yet, since Todd was still alive. In Tetris, the score increases exponentially, so as Todd kept playing, his score kept doubling, tripling, quadrupling, and in the end, he absolutely shattered what had been thought of as the roommate's unbeatable record. When Todd's round finally ended, he ceremoniously set down the controller, then raised his arms into the celebratory v-shape pose of a gymnast. He showed all his teeth in a gigantic grin, his chest rising and falling with euphoria.

His roommate hung his head. "Motherfucker," he said. "You and your performance-enhancing drugs."

Still grinning at the ceiling, Todd shook his head like a dog shaking water from its coat and let his tongue hang out and flop all around. Then he let out a rich, hearty laugh that lasted an absurd length of time. What he was experiencing was the state of utter joy. For most of us this feeling is rare, but for Todd it appeared to be a daily experience. His roommate remained unamused.

This was all very funny to me, but it was somehow a little more than just funny. I sat there on the ground, looking back and forth between the two roommates, unsure whether to laugh or to sigh.

18

UNIVERSITY OF CHICAGO

The University of Chicago was an unusual week. My host asked me if she could tell me things "off the record," and I said, "Sure." That was a mistake. Throughout the week, virtually everything she said that was interesting would be followed with her saying, "Wait—that was off the record." I decided to honor her request. Accordingly, I have no story to tell you. Instead, I'm going to tell you a few amusing things that happened or that I noticed, then I'll share a short conversation I had with some Economics majors who were chain-smoking on a balcony, and then I'll end with some advice for high schoolers.

The students at U Chicago were very smart; however, one thing missing from their intelligence was the knowledge of how smart other people were, especially people who didn't go to U Chicago.

For example, U Chicago students assumed that everybody was working their way through reading the Great Books. A rather cute girl asked me, "Have you read *Ulysses* yet?"—which implied that all people have either read the notoriously difficult 700-page book or were planning to read it eventually. I don't remember if I even knew who James Joyce was at the time, so a better question for me might have been, "Have you heard of the book *Ulysses* by James Joyce?" in which case my answer might have been, "No." But instead, since she was rather cute, and she was asking if I'd read it *yet*, I said, "No, not yet," and then tried to change the subject.

Another example was in their use of big words. U Chicago students were either assuming I had a large vocabulary, in which case they were wrong, or they were assuming I had a small vocabulary, in which case they were mean. They would ask me a question with a big word in it, and they'd position the big word in such a way that I had to know its meaning in order to reply. They'd ask things like, "Would you say it was perfunctory?" and then look at me expecting an answer. I didn't have the confidence to say, "I don't know what that means," so I'd say, "Uhhh... yeah, I mean, somewhat... but not entirely," and then try to change the subject.

One more thing about word choice: U Chicago students would often list big words that were almost synonyms, but not quite, in order to describe something. One word wasn't enough—it seemed like they needed to create a collage of words to paint around their precise, intended meaning. I sat through a screening of the 1951 film *The River*, and as the credits rolled, two guys in front of me started discussing the film. One of them said, "It was didactic... almost, moralistic." Perhaps this style of speech is what helped everyone have such a big vocabulary. If someone listed three large words, you only had to know one out of three in order to know what they were saying, and as a consequence you'd learn the meaning of the other two.

One day I sat in on a Sigmund Freud reading club. These students were reading Freud as an extracurricular, pleasure activity. There was a kind of rivalry between these students, who were interested in the mind, and other students, who were interested in the brain, and it was clear that these students were losing. One guy angrily said, "Those fMRI people just don't *understand* the unconscious!" as if the scientific pursuit of understanding human nature was actually the pursuit of understanding his own nature, and he felt misunderstood. At the time, I thought these students were a bit ridiculous, but a few years later, I developed a minor interest in psychoanalysis, and I found myself wishing that I could join a similar club back home.

One student shared with me a big secret about himself, one that nobody else at U Chicago knew. The secret was that he had gone to a public high school, as opposed to a private high school. All of his friends thought that he went to a private high school, and he wanted to keep it that way. It had never occurred to me that going to a public high school could be shameful (I went to a public high school), but for some students here, it apparently was.

Students all around the country kind of dislike Harvard, but students here especially seemed to dislike Harvard. Rarely on this trip did I make myself the center of attention, but on certain occasions a group of students would gather around and ask me about which school was the best, worst, most interesting, etc. For a brief ten-minute window this week, I had a large group of U Chicago students completely enraptured by my every word. What was I saying? I was telling the story about how the Harvard students made their waitress cry and then didn't leave a tip. This story about Harvard students being rude to a waitress made the U Chicago students so happy and amused that I can safely say that those ten minutes were the most entertaining I have ever been.

(The actual truth about Harvard students is that while yes, those 19- and 20-year-olds were somewhat immature, they were also being rapidly socialized through things like Tea Time, their very well-run meetings, and lots of formal events, such that by the time a Harvard student turns 22, he or she is probably more mature and sophisticated than I will be in my whole life. I, of course, left this part out when I was sharing the story with my audience at U Chicago.)

On my last night, I switched from my official host and spent some time with an unrelated group of students. It was about ten students chain-smoking cigarettes on a balcony.

Me: "College, would you say so far, is the best time of your lives?"
    Eloine: "No, I'm going to U Chicago. I want to cry every day."
    Daniel: "It's just something to prove."
    Eloine: "Yeah, you gotta prove yourself to everyone."
    Daniel: "It's just fear."

Me: "Fear? Where does the fear come from?"

Daniel: "It's just the knowledge that there's always someone way ass smarter than you. Not just a little bit but like, a hundred times better than you in every way."

Mason: "In every way Math and Econ related."

Daniel: "I don't know. I wonder how much of the U Chicago stereotype is self-fulfilling, where we like hate ourselves because we hear other people hating themselves."

Mason: "It's definitely a self-fulfilling prophecy. It's like the culture of this school. I don't even know if it's like, an actual deep self-hatred of oneself. Maybe it's just a symptom of sociality."

Daniel: "Informed entirely by like, being with your peers. Because last year, I didn't feel this at all. And then this year, I started taking harder classes and I was like, 'Oh so it is real! There it is!'"

Me: "But do you enjoy the classes, or is the work really just miserable?"

Daniel: "Oh, I love it. I love math. It's incredibly rewarding. The proof clicks and you're like 'Oh shit!'"

Mason: "Especially on the proofs that are four pages long."

Daniel: "Right!? Oh God! I did my first three-page proof, and I was like 'Ahhhhhh!'"

Mason: "It's very nice."

Daniel: "Another thing people hate on is when people say, 'We go here,' or say that it's hard because we go here. I'm sure it's fucking hard at many other schools, but like, we should appreciate the hardship rather than that we're at this specific school at this specific time."

Mason: "There's an artificial exceptionalism brought on by the insecurities of a lot of people. It's like 'I'm going to a top five school instead of Harvard.'"

Daniel: "Right, right. Also, fuck them for not letting me in."

Me: "Did you guys apply to Harvard?"

Daniel: "I mean, I did. But whatever. The point is, I've come to like, hate the idea of networking, and the realization that this major —like when I first came here I thought I might go the Goldman

Sachs route and just sell my soul to Wall Street and call it a day and take the big check and be like, 'Oh, that'll be fun,' but now I realize that like, fuck, if I had to hang out with those people all day, it'd be like..."

Me: "What do you prefer? What are you doing instead of that?"

Daniel: "Academia."

Mason: "We both want to go to grad school for Econ."

Daniel: "The department here for Econ, if you want to go to grad school, they want you to go to Harvard, Yale, MIT, or Stanford."

Mason: "I feel like I'd be lucky if I got into fucking UT for grad school."

Daniel: "I'd go to NYU. I think that'd be fun."

Mason: "That's a much better school than UT though."

Daniel: "So the deal is that NYU is top 12. But this kid Vladimir, he's like, so... the pre-Meds here are big fucking dicks."

Mason: "Big fucking dicks with small fucking dicks."

Daniel: "All they think about is getting into medical school. That's it, right? This is Vladimir for Econ grad school. He's not that smart of a person, I'm just gonna say it. And part of my motivation of getting in is to prove to him that he's not that smart."

Mason: "Maybe not him but that type. He's the ideal type."

Daniel: "I mean, he is the platonic form. Yeah, that kid's a fucking douchebag. But the thing is like, this path that I have chosen, is not free from the thing I'm escaping. It's just statistically less probable to encounter the thing I'm escaping."

Me: "What's the thing you're escaping?"

Daniel: "Just like, the people who say, 'Oh, I want to be published in this journal, or work at this firm,' right? It's not about, 'I want to do cool research. I want to improve human knowledge. I want to do something that's fulfilling and interesting to me.' It's about, 'I want to be published in Econometrica and I want a hot wife.' Those are his goals. Verbatim."

Mason: "I just want to be published. And have some acknowledgement. No matter how small it is."

Daniel: "You do? I'm not saying it's bad to want to be published. But if that's like, the only thing, then what?"

Mason: "I feel like it's almost the aesthetic of academia. It's like, 'Oh, you're doing something that's not just for making money.'"

Daniel: "Right. That there's some other, perhaps more noble idea that we're pursuing. I feel like if you have to sum up U Chicago, then 'a bunch of fucking nerds' could be the chapter. Then just move on."

Mason: "U Chicago is a bunch of fucking nerds."

Me: "Everyone's been reading 10-20 pages per chapter, and then this one is just that one sentence."

Mason: "What's funny is that within this pool of nerds there's a plurality of more nerds trying not to be nerds. That's the sad thing."

———

The older I get, the more I am impressed with The University of Chicago and its students. It is my opinion that every college should have an intellectual social climate, and it is my experience that most colleges do not. But why not? I discussed this briefly in the Furman chapter, but allow me to elaborate. An intellectual social climate is a social climate where students regularly discuss outside of class what they are learning inside of class, and they do it for fun.

Students in intellectual social climates are more excited about what they are learning, they are more motivated to study hard, and they have much more fun and enjoyment in their academic lives. Students who graduate from schools with intellectual social climates are on average far smarter than students who don't. I would guess that these students are more likely to become lifelong learners, more likely to contribute useful gifts to society, and are more likely to enjoy their professional careers than their counterparts. Intellectual social climates are a good thing, and all college students should have the opportunity to be a part of one. (It took me visiting U Chicago, and to a lesser extent, Harvard, to finally admit to myself, "Holy shit, I am not very smart! I better go home and study absolutely everything!" What began as a vain desire to not appear stupid in front of my peers transitioned into a sincere desire to learn for its own sake, and I thank the U Chicago students for this inspiration.)

But most of the schools I visited did not have intellectual social climates. Why might this be? I have narrowed it down to one main reason: most college students today are going to college too early.

It is my belief that most people need to gain a great deal of general knowledge and life experience before they can unlock their deep curiosities and passions. Before a person can figure out what subject they want to devote their lives to, they need to somehow develop an intuitive understanding of how all the various subjects fit together. They need to figure out how the world works before they can figure out what role they want to play within that world. When a young person goes straight from high school into college and chooses a major that is mostly job training, they foreclose on their identities and skip a necessary stage in their development—the stage of exploring the world and searching for an identity.

The reason most colleges do not have intellectual social climates is not that the students there are not as smart as the ones at U Chicago. The reason is that too many college students have never experienced learning as fun and exciting, so they don't even realize that it's possible to enjoy their classes. High school is all about getting a high GPA, not about enjoying or thinking deeply about the material. Students who enjoy their classes will feel motivated to discuss with their friends what they are learning. If students don't enjoy their classes, these discussions will never take place.

Take me for example. If I had gone to college straight after high school, I would have absolutely hated my classes. But today I think there is nothing more enjoyable than a good college lecture. The best college lectures are more entertaining than television, more exciting than sports, and more profound than drug use. When you step outside after a good lecture, the trees should look a little different.

And yet I have met, and continue to meet, so many college students who do not care at all about their classes. They treat their college classes the same way they treated their high school classes— which is to say that they view them as a necessary evil. They go through the motions of their college education because they feel that is their only choice.

My favorite poem is, "The People, Yes," by Carl Sandburg. This book's title is an homage to that poem. One part of the poem is called, "A Father Sees a Son Nearing Manhood," although the advice applies to daughters as well. In the poem, Sandburg says a young person should have "lazy days seeking his deeper motives," and that he should "seek deep for where he is a born natural" so that he may understand "free imaginations bringing changes into a world resenting change."

If a young person ever wants to become a free imagination bringing changes into a world resenting change, she will need to have lazy days seeking her deeper motives. She will need to seek deep for where she is a born natural. She will need time to explore and to think with no outside pressure. But when in a young person's life is this supposed to happen?

College today is too expensive to be a time of exploration. If a student spends two years studying math but then decides she would prefer to study psychology, this change in majors might be extremely expensive. It is expensive because it might require additional years at college in order to complete all the necessary credits. Because changing majors would be so expensive, the math student will not even consider switching majors. As she encounters material from psychology that interests her, her mind will cut itself off from enjoyment because she is already so invested in math. She will not daydream about a career as a psychologist because the costs of switching are too high. Her mind closes down and stops exploring.

To avoid this fate, her strategy instead should be to do her exploring prior to attending college.

Filmmaker Werner Herzog recommends that aspiring movie directors do two things: read a lot of books, and travel 5000km by foot. According to Herzog, doing these two activities will allow the young director to experience "the depth and intensity of existence." I think that's what all young people—not just directors—really want to do: to experience the depth and intensity of existence. Herzog's prescription is basically two things: study and travel. My guess is that once someone experiences this depth and intensity of existence, they will become insatiably curious about almost everything. Only then should they choose what they want to do with their life. And only then should they go to college.

I am not a person who should give anyone life advice, but allow me to give advice about the one thing I know most about—the question of whether a young person should go to college straight out of high school. (Although don't forget what Hunter S. Thompson said about giving advice: "What is truth to one may be disaster to another.")

If you have no idea what you want to do with your life yet, do not feel like you absolutely have to go to college straight out of high school. It is a really bad life decision to invest $100,000 in professional training for a field you don't even enjoy, because now you're $100,000 in debt and the only way to pay it off is by doing the thing you don't like. I have far too many brilliant friends who are in this situation right now, and I have seen that it is a very bad situation to be in. If you have absolutely no idea what you would like to do with your life, why would you invest heavily into education for a specific career?

Your goal when you are young should be to discover your life's task. This is not something you can easily discover by flipping through a course catalogue when you're 17. You actually have to go searching for your life's task. It could take a decade. But once you find it, your entire life becomes imbued with meaning and significance. Now you know what you're trying to do. You have a goal and a purpose. You will be excited to wake up in the morning, and you will enjoy your work. No setback or obstacle will get in your way.

I'm sure there are some college programs that actually expand minds, that allow students to explore, and that help students discover their purpose in life, but I almost never saw this happening. Instead what I observed was that most students were being initiated into a specific and singular worldview, they were being taught job skills that made them useful in one and only one sector of the job market, and they were having their minds closed down to the possibility of ever pursuing something else. College, for most of the people I wrote about in this book, represented a great narrowing of possibilities.

What could you do instead? Another option is to travel around, work odd jobs, and give yourself a broad general education through personal study. Sleep in your car if you need to keep your costs low. Read lots of books, or take long walks while listening to lectures. Study a little of everything. The adults of society will try to recruit you to their own worldviews, but you must resist this. Read books from all political and social perspectives, and keep an open mind. If you grew up in one political or social or religious climate, read works from the people who disagree with you, and try to understand their perspectives. It is physically painful to read books written from a worldview other than your own, and physically pleasant to read books written from your own worldview. You must chase this pain and avoid this pleasure. If you are able to put a label on your beliefs, and if you feel solidarity with other people who label their beliefs in the same way, then you are probably viewing the world from only one perspective. Your goal should be to view the world from as many perspectives as possible.

Follow your curiosity wherever it takes you. If you follow your curiosity, you don't need any self-discipline, because the curiosity will be pulling you from ahead. Do not worry about "following your passion," because most people don't start off passionate about anything. Instead, follow your curiosity, and have some faith that it will lead you somewhere good. Do this until you feel called into a specific profession, until you feel so completely obsessed with a specific field that you want to devote your life to it, and then go to college. Some people call this a gap year, but it may take two or three or five years. What's the rush? This is your life, your one life.

If more college students went to college not because they felt forced to, but because they wanted to pursue a vocation, a calling, then maybe more students would be excited to go to class, and then maybe more students would want to discuss outside of class what they are learning inside of class, and then maybe there could be an intellectual social climate at every school.

19

TEXAS A&M UNIVERSITY

An individual raised in the home of his parents has experienced nothing of the world outside the context of his own childhood, and so he cannot yet know what there is, what he may do, or who he may become. He leaves his parents for the first time not grown up but entirely fresh, completely unformed. The previous 18 years have widened his potentials, but none have been decided. Right now he is nothing. He exists entirely as energy, an incredible force of action, a raging, screaming possibility. What he seeks he cannot see or know. His desire is for a sensation of wholeness, of maturity, of arrival, and so far, the desire is without content: arrival of what? maturity how? what is it that a whole human is supposed to become? This is the time of adolescence, when a young person asks himself, "Who am I?" In the course of his life, this may be the most important question, because the quest for identity is also a quest to belong. When a young person asks, "Who am I?" he is also asking, "How will I fit into society?" He can only answer these questions properly after a period of free exploration, when he has surveyed humanity broadly and considered how each role works together. For the individual to self-define and obtain a sense of identity, he must find some placement within society that feels perfectly suited for him. This is necessary for society at large as well, because each new generation must question the actions of the generation preceding it. (Only in a perfect world would it be acceptable for the youth to become unquestioning copies of their parents.) As society progresses or regresses, grows or shrinks, moves in one direction or another, conduct within that society must adapt. It is the special power of youth to observe the world for what it is; that is, if society is a vector in motion, a newborn will perceive this constant change as stillness. With these perceptive powers, then, each new generation must question its elders, accepting the good and rejecting the bad in accordance with the changes the world has undergone since the elders were themselves adolescents. With this in mind, the wandering, uncertain adolescent who seeks meaning and purpose functions as society's method of redefinition. The collective articulation of a new generation is composed of the self-definitions of its individuals, and so the seeking, searching, exploring nature of young people is the same force that directs the future of humanity. The young person's soul, that centered place of the personality, whether it is of mind or matter, of neurobiological or of mystical origins, craves this exploration.

Gabe wanted to go to any college other than Texas A&M. His mom, dad, sister, and brother had all gone to A&M, and it was expected that Gabe would go as well. For Gabe, A&M represented his succumbing to familial expectations. It meant that he would not go off into the world and invent himself, but instead that he would become exactly what his parents had always wanted him to become. As a high schooler, Gabe applied to a number of long-shot dream colleges in hopes that he could go to school far from home—somewhere where he could escape the culture of his youth, meet students from different backgrounds, and form a new identity for himself. He also applied to Texas A&M as a backup and because his parents wanted him to. When the college letters rolled in, he was rejected by all of his dream schools. The only college that accepted him was Texas A&M.

Gabe was now nearing the end of his sophomore year at Texas A&M, and I was visiting him for one week before I returned to Austin for the summer. When I arrived, we took seats in his apartment, and he began telling me about his life.

At freshman orientation, incoming A&M students are told about the Two Percenters. Two Percenters are the 2% of A&M students who don't show school spirit and aren't eager to participate in school traditions. Gabe identified as a Two Percenter, and he claimed that Two Percenters comprised 30% of the student body. The majority of the students—the diehard Aggies—tended to be Christian, politically conservative, and obsessed with their school.

As Gabe was telling me about A&M, he received a text from Mikayla, a girl who he hadn't spoken to for a couple months. She was inviting him to come with her to an event the following night called Breakaway. Breakaway is a church service that takes place on campus. It is held in either the football stadium or in an auditorium, and it has a weekly attendance of 9,000 students, making it the largest Christian gathering on a secular campus in the nation.

"Who's Mikayla?" I asked.

"She's just some girl," Gabe said. "She used to like me until I dropped the bomb that God's not for me. That's what it's like here— dropping a bomb. Now she just invites me to Breakaway every now and then to see if she can still convert me."

"What are you going to say?"

"Oh, I always make some excuse."

"Do you want to go? I'd be down."

"No way. I couldn't do it."

"Dude, we should go."

"I really don't want to, but I've always been curious. I'm worried there's gonna be a lot of this thing." Gabe imitated the worship style seen in certain Christian churches—eyes closed, one hand in the air, swaying forward and back.

"Is that what it's like?" I asked.

"Yeah, I'm pretty sure it's that kind of Christian."

We spent a while debating whether or not to go. Gabe didn't want to go because anything church-related made him uncomfortable, and also because he didn't want to lead Mikayla on. If he accepted her invitation, he thought, he would be signaling to her that he might be a romantic prospect. I suggested that he tell Mikayla I was his friend visiting from out of town, and that I was the one who wanted to go. This would take the pressure off the romantic aspect of the night, and it would also allow Gabe to hide the fact that he might have any personal interest in Breakaway. Gabe was convinced. He texted Mikayla and told her that we were interested.

"This might actually be good," Gabe said. "This semester my mom told me, 'Gabe, please go to church for me three times.' And my sister has already asked me to go with her."

Gabe stopped going to church with his family sometime during high school. His mom thought it was because their church was too boring, and she figured that Gabe would start going again in college. Now that Gabe was in college, he still had no interest.

"Why did you stop going?" I asked.

"Well, fuck. I don't have the answers, and I'm not going to. I'm indifferent, but I thought about it. I took a long time to think about it and decided I didn't know the answers. It's a lot better to just tell people I don't care."

Gabe was drinking a beer and eating a plate of baby carrots. The television was on, and a local jewelry ad was playing. It said, "She loves the Aggies. You love the way she makes you feel."

"I'd say it's like 98% Christian here," Gabe continued. "The atheists are all the goths or lesbians. Or like, the fat kid with the Pokemon shirt and the mustache. And it really is a huge deal to tell somebody you aren't Christian. They just expect it. And if they find out you're not, they're like, 'Oh, it's one of them.'"

Mikayla texted back. She was excited to take us to Breakaway. She was even willing to pick us up and drive us there herself. Gabe let out a big grin and shook his head, then he stood and walked to the bottom of the stairs.

"Logan!" he yelled. "Logan! C'mere!"

Gabe's roommate Logan came to the top of the stairs.

"What is it?" Logan asked, sounding vaguely annoyed like he had been interrupted from something important.

"We're going to Breakaway with Mikayla tomorrow," Gabe told him.

"Oh god, I gotta hear this," Logan said while hurrying down the stairs.

If Gabe was unenthusiastic about his social life, he was even less enthusiastic about his academic life.

"It's not like what you see in movies," Gabe told me, referring to college classes as we walked through campus the following morning. "Like, in movies you see this witty professor who teaches you things and shows you new ways to see the world, and you meet new people who are all different but who you bond with. But in real life, you get here and you might have one good class, and the rest of the professors are like, 'We're gonna hammer out this material. I know you don't want to take this class.' And the four kids you're working with aren't interested either. It's pretty much high school, but with even less interaction."

Gabe had a natural passion for the subject of criminology, and he had considered studying this field and trying to make a career of it, but after some consideration he had decided to pursue the safer route of studying business. This was also the route his parents most approved of. The result was that he was utterly bored by all of his classes. These classes had hundreds of students, and the professors were typically reading off of PowerPoints. As soon as the professor switched to a new slide, students would quickly type up all the words on the slide, then immediately return to browsing the internet as the professor spoke. Nobody was listening. (There was one exception, which was Gabe's class on management. This class was great. The professor was an old guy who sat and told educational anecdotes for the duration of class, unaided by PowerPoints. The students didn't like the class, though, because it was hard for them to figure out what they would be tested over.)

"Didn't that fucking suck?" Gabe asked after an economics class. "When I was little, my idea of college was something so studious, without PowerPoints and that shit and just awesome professors with an hour of lecture about something really intellectual. It's amazing to think what I used to think college was like ten years ago. I always saw those Northeastern schools with perfect campuses and autumn trees and all that."

While walking around campus, Gabe told me about various Aggie traditions and then made sure to show me that he didn't follow them. In the middle of a long sidewalk called Military Walk, there is a large Aggie seal that students are not supposed to walk across. According to tradition, if a student walks across the seal, he will not graduate.

"Do you walk around it?" I asked.

"I always walk through it," Gabe said.

Gabe did as he said. We walked right through the middle of the seal as the rest of the students on the sidewalk changed their routes to avoid it. (Gabe did go on to graduate.)

When we returned to Gabe's apartment at the end of the school day, his roommate Logan had some news for us: he also wanted to go to Breakaway that night. Logan wasn't particularly religious either, and he had never been to Breakaway, but since Gabe and I were going, he wanted to go too. Logan had an ulterior motive for attending beyond sheer curiosity. He had an ex-girlfriend who had started attending Breakaway regularly after she got into a new relationship. When Logan dated her, he knew she was a Christian, but he didn't know how serious her beliefs were. Now that he knew she was a regular attendee of Breakaway, he realized that he never knew her as well as he thought. His desire to attend Breakaway seemed to be a desire to learn about the girl he had been so close to, and to see who she had become after they broke up.

Mikayla was small with a soft voice, and as she looked over the steering wheel, she seemed to glow with pride at the idea that she was transporting three newcomers to Breakaway. She and Gabe had an immediate rapport, a flirty closeness and familiarity, especially considering they hadn't spoken for two months. If Mikayla and Gabe stopped their courtship for religious reasons, it seemed to be a lost opportunity. Over the car speakers, Christian music was playing, upbeat and modern with sentimental lyrics.

"You have to admit, it's pretty cool that something like this happens on our campus," Mikayla said. "Breakaway has a bigger turnout than men's basketball games."

That week Breakaway was held in a large auditorium, and since the auditorium couldn't seat all 9,000 attendees, service had to be broken up into two smaller services. Traffic was bumper to bumper all around the building, and huge groups of students were walking inside from all directions. We parked and followed the crowd.

The auditorium was packed. It was a real challenge to find four seats next to each other, but after about 15 minutes of searching, we finally found four adjacent seats in the front row. I sat on the outside of our group next to Mikayla, and we made small talk while we waited for the service to begin. Mikayla was a business major like Gabe, and she grew up in Houston.

A band walked out and played a few songs to begin the service. They were dressed in hip, casual clothes and played rock music. The lyrics were projected on large screens above them with no punctuation and trendy lowercase i's. The 5,000 students in the auditorium sang along to the music, and when I glanced behind me, I noticed that many of them did in fact have one hand in the air with their eyes closed while swaying back and forth. Mikayla was singing; Gabe, Logan, and I were not.

After the songs, the preacher Ben came onto the stage and said, "Howdy!" The students echoed, "Howdy!" Ben is apparently highly regarded by the students and is the main reason most people show up each week. He was young, handsome, and a bit muscular, wearing a tight black hoodie and nice jeans. He made a few administrative remarks about an upcoming retreat and then quickly went into a long prayer. We closed our eyes and bowed our heads. The prayer didn't have the tone of a recitation; Ben appeared to be speaking straight from his heart, spontaneously and passionately moved to say each word. "God, we love you and want so much to praise you tonight. Please fill our hearts with your love, God." The prayer went on like this for quite some time, and about halfway through, the band's guitarist began to accompany the prayer with some dreamy, reverby guitar notes, making the ordinary prayer sound much more profound and badass, and as the prayer neared its end, more of the band members joined in and began to grow louder with perfect timing, such that a split second after Ben uttered his final, "Amen," the band exploded with a huge crash of drums and a blast of bass that vibrated in my chest as they swelled into a huge wall of sound reminiscent of the climax of an Arcade Fire song, so that when I finally raised my head and opened my eyes to look up at the stage, I couldn't tell if I was physically disoriented or in communion with God or both. When I turned around, all 5,000 students were singing along—"We cannot dare to imagine all the love of God"—and now there were twice as many hands swaying in the air as before.

The sermon that night was about the meaning of the phrase "hallowed be Thy name" from the Lord's Prayer. The actual content of the sermon was not particularly notable—in fact, I still don't think I know what "hallowed be Thy name" means—but the delivery of that content was astonishing. Ben had prophetic charisma, and his message seemed divinely inspired. He would speak at a rapid pace for a few minutes as if he couldn't get the words out fast enough, then suddenly slow down into incredibly slow speech, all the while making dramatic gestures with his body.

He put his hands in the air. "God, may you be glorified." His fists clenched. "Exalted." He put his hands over his heart. "Loved." He crouched down, as if hunched over with passion. "In all that we do."

At one point, he said, "Because the feeling of awe is contagious," then repeated himself three times with different emphasis each time, similar to how Chris Rock tells a joke. "Awe is contagious. Awe is contagious. Awe is contagious." And even though I knew what he was doing, the third time he repeated it, I got goose bumps.

We never told Mikayla that I was there to write a book. During the sermon, I took notes in a notebook, and this seemed to inspire Mikayla to take notes as well (perhaps there was even a slight spirit of competition). Mikayla's legs were crossed, and she'd play with her pen as she took notes on the little comments that stuck out to her.

This is exactly how my mom would take notes during church when I was growing up, and I felt a fleeting impulse to give Mikayla a hug.

At the end of the sermon, Ben asked the audience to repeat the phrase, "Hallowed be Thy name," with passion in our voices to represent all the meaning that exists in the phrase. I said the words along with the other 5,000 students. Once we said the words, Ben let the room drop to silence. Slowly the guitarist built another dreamy soundscape as the band joined in. Ben said, "Thanks," then walked off the stage just as the band swelled into another epic musical climax with all of the band members harmonizing. The students were still seated, but slowly they stood to join in with the music. The standing up followed the same logic as a spontaneous standing ovation; you didn't stand up at the same time as everyone else—you were supposed to stand up as you felt individually compelled to stand. I timed my standing to be one moment after Mikayla's, which was perfect timing. Gabe and Logan both felt they missed their window of opportunity to stand, and they remained seated for the whole song (we joked for the rest of the night about how perfect my timing was). Gabe and Logan had debated ahead of time about whether or not Mikayla was going to put her hands in the air during the singing portions of Breakaway. So far, her hands had remained by her sides, but now that Breakaway was nearing its end, she seemed unable to resist. While singing she put not just one, but both hands in the air. Gabe, Logan, and I remained stoic.

After the song was over, the lights slowly came back on, and it was now time to leave. The students began filing out the same way they had filed in, except now there seemed to be a slightly different tone in the room. Before Breakaway, everyone seemed to be in separate groups. You were a stranger to everyone in the room except the friends you had arrived with. But after Breakaway, there was a vague sense that everybody in the room was a part of the same thing, that you could no longer think of someone in that room as a complete stranger. I didn't ask Gabe how he felt when the lights came on at the end of Breakaway, but I liked to imagine that he also felt some vague warmth, some slight sense of renewed connection to his peers. He didn't agree with them necessarily, he might not have even liked them, but he was one of them, and that meant something.

"Was it like you expected?" Mikayla asked us in the car on the way home.

"It was pretty good," said Gabe.

"I liked it," I said.

"Yeah, he's really funny," said Mikayla. "And it's not so serious. I know you were worried about crazy people, but most people aren't like that."

Mikayla dropped us off, and we walked back into the apartment. The third roommate, Ryan, was in the common room. He was a Christian, but of a more old-fashioned denomination, so he had never been to Breakaway and had no interest in going.

"How was it?" Ryan asked.

"You're talking to a new follower of Christ," Logan joked. "We're all converts."

"The first five minutes, I felt super awkward," Gabe said. "The awkwardness flooded over me, but then it was ok."

For the next hour, we replayed our experiences at Breakaway. During Breakaway, we had to remain quiet observers; now we were bursting with energy, excited to share our thoughts and feelings. We agreed that it was more intense than the church services we were used to, and that the worship style of hands-in-the-air singing was a little bit uncomfortable to witness. However, we also thought that Ben was highly entertaining, the prayers were badass, and that overall Breakaway was not as bad as we expected.

"I have to admit, he was better than most 60-year-old preachers," Gabe said. "Although there are still some things he believes fully that I just don't, so I can't really get into some of the stuff. But I'd still give him a solid B or B+."

The conversation shifted into a discussion of the religious songs we had grown up with as kids. I don't know exactly how it started, but someone would remember a song and say, "Oh! Remember this one?" and then start singing. We all knew the same songs, and we would all join in to sing each song together. We were mostly making fun of the music, but occasionally there were strange moments when our initial mockery would subside and we were left standing together, singing the songs with complete sincerity. This singing seemed to inspire a sense of nostalgia in each of us, a nostalgia for the comfort of a child's religion when God was an all-powerful, all-loving man in the sky, guiding our lives and keeping us safe, and somehow this childhood's comfort was baked into the melodies—at least in our minds—so that although we were cringing, we were simultaneously feeling a warm, communal contentment that lasted the rest of the night.

"This is one of those things where if my mom asks me in a few weeks if I have been to church with my sister," Gabe said, "I can say, 'No, but I did go to Breakaway,' and when she asks how it was, I'm going to say, 'Oh, it was pretty good,' and she'll ask if I'm gonna go again, and I'll say, 'We'll see,' and that'll be enough to let her think it's all ok."

PART III

20

BRIGHAM-YOUNG UNIVERSITY

School was out for summertime. I spent the three months of summer living alone again in my Texas apartment. Looking back on these three months, I was very depressed, but I didn't realize it at the time. Before I had traveled to colleges around the country, I had convinced myself that I wasn't missing out on much fun. Now I was painfully aware of all that I was missing. More than just fun, though, I felt that I'd missed the opportunity to begin my life. College gives a person a sense of direction and purpose. It shows you what life is and then teaches you how to begin. I was still only 20 years old, but psychologically I felt like I'd reached the end of the road, like I was old and finished before ever getting started.

That summer I took an intellectual interest in suicide, and I read Emile Durkheim's classic work on the subject. I was not personally suicidal, but I recognized that I might be experiencing some of the sociological drivers of suicide that Durkheim had discovered. Durkheim found four sociological types of suicide, which he called egoistic, altruistic, anomic, and fatalistic. The ones that I thought applied to me were egoistic and anomic suicide.

From the Wikipedia article: *"Egoistic suicide reflects a prolonged sense of not belonging, of not being integrated in a community. It results from the [suicidal person's] sense that s/he has no tether. This absence can give rise to meaninglessness, apathy, melancholy, and depression. Durkheim calls such detachment "excessive individuation". Those individuals who were not sufficiently bound to social groups (and therefore well-defined values, traditions, norms, and goals) were left with little social support or guidance, and were therefore more likely to commit suicide."*

"Anomic suicide reflects an individual's moral confusion and lack of social direction, which is related to dramatic social and economic upheaval. It is the product of moral deregulation and a lack of definition of legitimate aspirations through a restraining social ethic, which could impose meaning and order on the individual conscience."

To outsiders it might have looked like I was in the middle of an incredibly fun trip, but that wasn't exactly true. Friends and family would ask me to tell them about all the fun times I'd had, as if I were returning from a long and happy vacation. Surely there had been fun, and I had a lot of good stories to tell them, but there was a lot that I couldn't tell them, a lot that I didn't know how to tell.

It seems bizarre to complain in any way about my life, which was still mostly good. My material needs were met, and I had friends and family who loved me. Nevertheless, that summer I was followed by a pervasive sense of dread that I could not escape. Perhaps everybody else already feels this way, but for me it was new.

Everyone I'd met so far on this trip seemed to have a clear worldview, a clear map of reality. Each person had a different worldview, but each worldview seemed self-contained and complete. They knew their place in life, and they knew the way forward. If you studied finance, you saw the world as the flow of money. If you studied evolutionary biology, you saw the world as survival and reproduction. If you studied history, you saw the world as the rise and fall of civilization. By comparison, I felt that I'd ruined my map of reality. Every week I'd spent with college students had confused me a little more, and now I didn't know where I was. The only thing I knew to do with my life was to keep visiting colleges, and I was going to keep doing it until I felt like I was complete.

It was also starting to feel embarrassing to be on a college campus and not be a student. Why was I so desperate to hang out with college students? I didn't even go to college. I did not belong; I was not welcome. Everyone must have been able to see right through me. My entire project was beginning to feel pathetic and full of desperation. I was beginning to fear that I was the laughing stock of my community, that people would cringe when they thought of how far I was taking my ill-fated, pathetic project. I dreaded the idea of visiting another college, but I felt that I needed to see a few colleges out West to give the book some geographic balance. I had gone East, now I needed to go West.

It was with this psychological backdrop that I met the Mormons.

My host at BYU was an old acquaintance from middle school who had moved out to Utah after 8th grade. I didn't know she was a Mormon when we were acquaintances in middle school, but I remembered that she always had sleepy, half-opened eyes because she went to 6am church service every day before school. When she responded to my Facebook post and said that I could stay with her at BYU, it all made sense.

Nicole invited me to meet her at a Mormon camp retreat. The retreat was an hour away from BYU in the mountains west of Provo. I was always nervous to meet each week's new host, but this week I was especially nervous. Part of this was because I had been alone all summer and my social skills had regressed, so I felt shy and uncomfortable, but mostly I was nervous because I didn't know anything about Mormons. I was scared of offending someone, breaking a rule, or doing something humiliating.

When I arrived at the campsite, I saw a couple hundred students gathered together under a big pavilion, brightly lit within the darkness of the surrounding woods. After parking, I stood outside the edge of the pavilion, looking for Nicole in the light. The environment felt more like a family reunion than a college retreat. It was noisy, and the students were separated into groups playing little games, all of them energetic and joyful. When Nicole saw me, she walked over from her group.

"Wow, you made it!" she said. "I didn't think you would actually make it all the way out here!"

She brought me over to her group, and I sat down in the circle next to her. When I arrived, the students had been broken into groups of ten to play icebreaker games. Everybody was here on account of being in the same "ward," which is a division of Mormons grouped together within the Latter-Day Saints church based on where each person lives. This was a "singles' ward," meaning that everybody was unmarried. Since a new school semester had begun only a few weeks before I arrived, the students were still getting to know the other students in their new singles' ward, and this was the first retreat.

I didn't talk much with Nicole but instead jumped right into the icebreaker games with everybody else. The game they were playing when I arrived involved saying specific facts about yourself based on the colors of Skittles you picked from a bowl. If you drew a yellow Skittle, for example, that meant, "Say one fact about your family." For this fact, the students in my circle all shared the number of siblings they had. One girl had six siblings, another had nine, one guy had seven. They all had giant families. When I drew a yellow Skittle and said I had only one sibling, they all gave me sympathetic looks as if I had just shared some bad news. "That means you two must be extremely close!" one student told me, as if to cheer me up.

Over my shoulder, the rest of the students played the same icebreaker game, and as I looked around, I noticed an abundance of smiles. The interactions seemed profoundly wholesome, and I knew I wasn't just imagining it. There was a gentle friendliness on each face that made me feel much older than everyone, perhaps because I was associating wholesomeness with childishness. In the world I knew, a person becomes more cynical as she ages, so nobody over about 13 years old would ever play these icebreaker games unless she were forced to. But these students were loving the games, and everybody took a genuine interest.

The other thing I noticed was that the guys didn't seem to be judging me. I was accustomed to walking into a fraternity house, for example, and receiving judgmental stares until my host convinced everybody that I was cool, safe, and welcomed. At BYU, the guys seemed to welcome me immediately and without caution. Their eyes were warm and inviting from the first moment. I followed their lead, and after about an hour, I felt a little less cynical and a little more wholesome.

One of the games we played involved Student A covering his or her head in shaving cream while Student B tried to throw Cheetos into the shaving cream. Another involved sucking Skittles through a straw. Another was a big race to see who could be the first to remove all the tissues, one by one, from a tissue box. (Nobody made a joke about masturbation, because Mormons aren't supposed to masturbate.) For the last game, my team pushed me to the front to be our representative against the other teams. I tried to decline, because I typically hate games like this, but my team insisted, and I eventually agreed. The competition was to fetch gummy bears from a big bowl of pudding using only your face. I walked to the front of the pavilion and lined up with the other contestants at a long table. Someone shouted, "GO!"

I slammed my face into the pudding to fetch the gummy bears. The students were screaming and cheering. Ice-cold pudding covered every inch of my face. Eventually somebody won, so we stopped, and when it was over, I wasn't embarrassed but instead felt strangely exhilarated. My fellow contestants and I were given paper towels to wipe off our faces, and as we stood to the side cleaning up, I had a big smile on my face, a real one.

"That was crazy!" I said. "That pudding was so cold!"

"I know!" said one of the guys. "It's all up my nose! Gross!"

We all gave each other high fives, and nobody seemed to remember or care who had won the race. When I returned to my team, they gave me high fives too and said things like, "Man, you did awesome!" I won't lie, this felt great even though I'd heard them say the same things to everybody else.

When I started talking to the students on my team and mentioning why I was there, the first question I usually got was about whether or not BYU was different from other schools. I had only been there for two hours, but already I could tell that BYU was unlike any school I had visited. The students were amazed to hear this. They thought that BYU was just like any other college.

After the games, we had an hour of free activity time. Some people tossed footballs. Lots of students sat around chatting. Some of them played board games ("Mormons love board games"). During this time, I noticed a guy and girl engaged in some aggressive, elementary-school-style flirting. They were standing alone, facing each other.

"What?" he said with a slight smile.

"What?" she said back.

He got louder. "What!?"

She did too. "What!?"

He raised his arms to his sides, pretending to be angry, and cocked his head to the side. "WHAT!?"

She did the same as she choked back laughter. "WHAT!?"

They took steps toward each other as their pretend altercation escalated, getting up close in the other's space as they cocked their heads in mirrored, opposite directions and raised their arms. As the flirting reached its crescendo, they burst out in laughter, put their arms down, then chuckled off the remaining tension while looking into each other's eyes. It was cute, as well as a little bit cringeworthy. Nobody else had been watching them—everyone was busy engaging in other silly activities. There was goofy dancing, games of chase, and loud jokes. Lots of smiles. It was the sort of environment where, if I had arrived with a friend, I could have sustained a cynical attitude, but since I was there alone, I had no choice but to go along with it.

Up next was a "fireside," which meant a religious lesson. We lined up chairs in church-pew-style rows and took our seats. One of the students prayed to begin the fireside, and I peeked during the prayer to see if I was praying correctly. Mormons pray like the average Christian, except they cross their arms instead of clasping their hands. After the prayer, a woman who was no longer a student came to deliver the lesson, speaking into a microphone.

"Hey everybody!" she began. "So we've all come out to this campout for a number of things: for friendship, for fellowship, but most importantly, for relationships."

I raised a brow.

She continued. "So before we get started, I want all of you to switch seats so you're sitting boy-girl-boy-girl. Ready? Go!"

I knew this was a single's *ward*, but I didn't realize the campout would be the Mormon version of single's *night*.

I was on the outside of a row sitting next to Nicole, who was sitting next to her boyfriend; technically, I was already in a boy-girl-boy sequence. This meant I didn't need to stand up to look for a girl to sit by, a task I thought was potentially disastrous. But in front of us was a row of only girls who now had to stand up to look for boys. One of them stood up, saw the empty chair next to me, then came and took a seat. This put her on the outside of our row and made me her sole adjacent boy.

"My name's Kayli," she whispered.

Immediately I felt a strange pressure. She was looking at me all sweet-like, and while I tried my best to be kind to her in response, I had to repress my urge to tell her that if there's a Mormon heaven, I almost certainly won't be joining her there. I whispered back, "Hi Kayli, I'm Drew."

The woman up front gave a talk about three different girls she knew. One of them was an 18-year-old just dying to get married. The next was a 21-year-old who got engaged but eventually broke it off. The final girl was a 24-year-old who had written off marriage to focus on her life but was surprised when she was wooed by a 21-year-old man, and now she's happily married. The twist was that all three girls were past versions of the speaker. The moral at the end was that a person needs to learn how to be happy, and only then will marriage happen, and any age that happens is ok. For some people, 18 years is old enough, and for others, "even as old as 31" is ok. At some point when she was talking about physical attraction, she said a line that received universal laughter, which was, "Oh c'mon guys, don't tell me you've never looked at a girl and thought, 'Oh yeah, she could be my eternal companion!'"

(Mormons call their husbands and wives their "eternal companions." Apparently Mormon men don't think, "I'd sure like to take her to bed!" but instead, "I'd sure like to take her to heaven!")

During the fireside, Kayli arranged then rearranged her hands on her knee, uncrossed then recrossed her legs, and even looked over toward me once or twice. I was terrified, not only because of my responsibility to Kayli by virtue of our proximity, but also because of what was happening all around us. One row ahead of us, a guy had reached over to hold his adjacent girl's hand (she accepted), then he kept looking at her sentimentally at specific, uncomfortable moments —for example, when the speaker said, "Sometimes it hurts not to know love, no matter how young we are, so you singles really need to help each other through this time," and at that moment he gave his girl a smile while nodding slightly and squinting his eyes as if to say to her, "Hm, that sounds kind of nice, doesn't it?" As I watched them, my cringe meter was all the way up. This fireside was so uncomfortable for me that I felt real physical pain in my chest, a tightness of my heart, and I felt I needed to recoil and shield my face, but since the circumstances prevented me from doing so, I had to just sit there with a mortified grin.

Did that guy and girl in front of us really just meet each other? Were they really already holding hands and trading sentimental glances? Were Kayli's occasional glances at me her attempts to initiate similar little moments? I was too afraid to find out, so I ignored her completely. I couldn't decide if I was supposed to hold her hand or not. It seemed completely insane to hold her hand, but it somehow felt like I was supposed to. (Even if I had wanted to, my hands were too sweaty from nervousness.)

I also felt lousy because I started thinking that, even if I did talk to Kayli, I would only be a bad influence for her. She was innocent, and I was bad in some fundamental, unchangeable way. So as Kayli sat next to me, in addition to feeling strange for obvious reasons, I also felt a little guilty, like she was good and I was bad, and I could only harm her. People don't really work that way, but that's how it felt, and I sat there unable to move, thinking, "If only she knew... if only she knew..."

After the fireside, a student with a guitar came to the front of the pavilion and played some songs as everybody sang along. The first song was something from *The Little Mermaid* ("Mormons love Disney"). The next song, "I Want To Grow Old With You," he introduced by saying, "This one's good for flirtatious guys." The last song he played was, "The Middle," by Jimmy Eat World. At first, I thought this was a strange song selection, but then I heard all 200 Mormons sing along, and I understood at once why they liked it. (Check out the lyrics—it's very wholesome.)

After the music performance, we prayed again, then the students rose to mingle amongst each other. I told Kayli it was nice to meet her before she slipped away.

"I'm so sorry," Nicole said. "That was so weird. I didn't know it would be like that. That was even weird for me. I'm sorry."

I laughed. "No, it wasn't too bad. I just didn't know if I was supposed to make a move on that girl."

"Why? Did you want to?" Nicole asked, excited.

"No! I just didn't know what was going on," I said, laughing.

"Ok, well don't worry, I don't think that will happen again. That's not what it's usually like here."

It was an overnight campout. There were a few guys' cabins and a few girls' cabins, and everyone started splitting up to claim their beds in their respective cabins. I went to my car to grab a sleeping bag but ended up sitting there alone for 30 minutes to take a breather and collect my thoughts. When I eventually went to one of the guys' cabins to find a bed, I accidentally walked in on a rather risqué co-ed game that was taking place out of view of the adults who were facilitating the campout. One of the students was explaining the rules.

"Ok, one guy tries to kiss whoever is *it*," he said, "while the other person who is *it* tries to kiss their face."

When I stepped into the cabin, the 15 or so students playing the game turned my direction and stared at me, so I froze for a second and then slowly turned around and walked out. I had a conversation about the game a few days later with Nicole's boyfriend and his roommates. The students I walked in on were considered the bad kids, they told me. The game is called Kissing Rugby. It involves one person trying to make it from point A to point B without being kissed by the other person of the opposite gender. Occasionally the game escalates into tackling, pinning, and hugging-type maneuvers. Accordingly, the game is considered inappropriate by most students.

One of the guys in the conversation who hadn't heard about Kissing Rugby before said, "Whoa, that's basically lip rape!"

Because he said 'rape' someone asked him, "Why all the bad words?"

The first guy said, "Bad words? You mean because the other day I said 'sex'?"

"Yes!"

"I don't know, but that game is sketchy. I don't really want to tackle girls. Just too sketchy."

Someone else said, "Yes, sketchy for a Mormon boy."

The first guy said, "All I'm saying is it takes a certain sort of girl to play it."

The night of the campout was bitterly cold. Nobody brought warm enough clothes. Under the pavilion, we drank hot chocolate and played board games while other students were in the cabins. Nicole and her boyfriend Isaiah were rumored to be off in the woods making out. The board game I played was a roleplaying card game where you shoot people and take their possessions. Somehow everybody played this game humanely and with mercy. Winning wasn't important. In fact, everyone was going so easy on each other that it took a very long time for the game to end. When someone was in the position to defeat an opponent, frequently they wouldn't do it; they'd just pass on that turn so nobody would lose and the game could keep going forever.

Later that night, I met back up with Nicole, Isaiah, and Isaiah's roommates. They were standing in the dark, away from the pavilion, looking at the sky. We were far enough outside the city that it was dark enough to see the center of the Milky Way jutting across the sky. We stood close together, shivering, looking up.

"Do you know about our missions?" a guy named Eli asked me. He had a gentle voice and spoke to me like an old friend.

"No, not really," I said.

"Well, pretty much all Mormon guys go on missions from age 19 to 21. We get assigned somewhere, and our only job is to teach about God. But it's pretty difficult. We work from 9am to 10pm seven days a week for two years straight. And we can only email our family once a week, and we can only call them on Christmas and Mother's Day. We don't watch movies or anything like that. We're just outside in the area we're assigned to all day, every day."

"What kind of places do you go to?" I asked.

"All over the world," he said.

"They all change so much when they're gone," Nicole added.

"How so?" I asked.

"They just grow up. Most of the boys are immature before they leave, and afterward they're just different."

Almost all the guys at BYU have been on their two-year missions before starting college, which means your average guy is two years older than the girls in his graduating class. Nicole's boyfriend and his friends had already been on their missions. They were all 22 or 23, while Nicole was only 20, but they were in the same class. In the starlight, the guys retold stories of crazy times on their missions like encounters with gun runners and drug users, getting chased by wild dogs, and, funniest of all to me, the many times they had to do an excessive number of chores for people who ended up not actually interested in Mormonism (the typical agreement is that a Mormon missionary offers to do "service" for a person with the understanding that the recipient will allow them to discuss Mormonism afterward; this means that missionaries often spend all day mowing yards, cleaning homes, and moving furniture, only to be brushed off in the end and asked to leave before they give the Latter-Day Saint sales pitch).

It occurred to me that Mormon missions are a nicely designed modern rite of passage. The children are raised with a huge emphasis on family, but during their missions they are separated from family for two years as they learn to be independent. It's true that sometimes college itself separates a student from her family and serves as a rite of passage, but it doesn't always work that way. A surprising number of college parents keep up with their child's life so completely that they know about their child's day-to-day workload and can ask questions like, "Have you finished your Calculus assignment yet?" The Mormon prohibition against regular emails and phone calls was an interesting solution to this problem.

One of the guys told a story that made me feel a little bit sad. He was the youngest of three brothers, and both of his older brothers had become "inactive" Mormons, which was a more pleasant way to say that they didn't believe in Mormonism anymore. The youngest brother—the guy who was telling me the story—was the only brother so far who had gone on his mission. The other two brothers openly state that they will never do a mission. The father of the three boys quotes the Bible and says, "First is last and last is first." The implication is that his boys will follow a Biblical path and go on their missions in reverse order, youngest to oldest. The father and the youngest brother are still holding out hope, waiting for the other two brothers to go on their missions. As he concluded his story for me, he smiled and said, "So whenever my oldest brother goes on his mission, it'll all be complete. First is last and last is first." I wondered whether the brothers were truly "inactive" or if they were completely gone, and I wondered how long the family would hold out hope. For the person with true religious belief, death isn't real; you and your loved ones, as long as you remain believers, will live together in Heaven. The real death is if your loved ones lose their faith, because it means you will be eternally separated. Heaven isn't so great if the people you love aren't there too.

"It's so cold!" said Nicole.

"We should all huddle together," said Isaiah.

Everyone agreed, so they formed a tight circle with their arms wrapped around each other.

"Aren't you going to join, Drew?" Nicole asked.

"Yeah, c'mon in!" said Eli.

"Yeah, yeah, ok," I said, before taking sheepish steps toward them.

They opened up a hole in the circle, and I filled it in. At first the group hug was too wholesome, too sentimental, and I felt that same tightness in my chest from earlier, but after I took a deep breath, I was able to relax a little and enjoy it.

Nicole asked, "Isn't it warmer in here?"

In the morning, we ate French toast and sausage, then headed back to BYU. I joined Isaiah and his roommates to watch the BYU football game on TV. It was like watching football at any other college, except there was no beer.

"Hey, what do you think of Nicole's roommate?" Isaiah asked Eli.

"I don't really know her," Eli said.

"Yeah, but do you think she's attractive?"

"I don't know if she's attractive, because I don't know her personality."

"Oh, c'mon. You can think a girl's attractive before you know her personality."

"Not me. I have to know about her personality first."

The football game carried on. A few quarters passed. Then, without warning, a Victoria's Secret commercial came on the TV. It was a very sexy lingerie ad.

"Hide your faces!" someone yelled.

There were six guys present. Partially for humor and partially in earnest, the guys shielded their faces from the TV. At the time, I found it a bit pathetic—did they think they weren't allowed to look? But months later, it occurred to me, "Oh my God! They were trying not to masturbate!" Mormons aren't allowed to have any sexual contact before marriage, and they're also not allowed to masturbate or look at arousing images. It's quite possible that seeing a surprise lingerie ad on TV is the sexiest thing that's ever happened to a 22-year-old Mormon. If that's true, then the Victoria's Secret commercial probably sent a lightning bolt of arousal through these guys, and they had to shield their eyes so they wouldn't be tempted to masturbate. (I

met a Mormon later at Stanford, and when I asked him if he mastur-
bates—not that this was a common question that I asked people—he
said, "Sometimes, but then I feel really bad about it"; he had gone his
entire two-year mission without masturbating, but ever since, the
longest he could last was about 60 days.) Today when I see these
commercials, I always shake my head and think, "Poor Mormons."

The next day was Sunday, the Sabbath. On Sunday everybody
went to church at the temple, but this particular Sunday was a special
one where you had to be an official Mormon to attend. Accordingly, I
had to miss out. Outside, huge flocks of girls in colorful dresses
marched toward the temple. Slightly smaller groups of sharply
dressed guys also made their way to the temple. The smallest groups
were the many students attending temple as couples. Going to
church together is a common activity during a relationship, as well as
for a first or second date.

After church, I joined Nicole at her apartment with two of her five
roommates, Erin and Juliette. On the wall was a large poster of the
famous WWII V-J Day sailor kiss. Tucked behind the thermostat was
a small picture of Jesus Christ. There was a television that they had
agreed would be given to the first of the roommates to be married. As
we made small talk, Juliette told me she was a "BYU baby," which
meant that she was born while her parents were still students at BYU.
She said to me, "Tell me more about yourself," so many times that I
had soon told her everything I felt I could share. Erin played a few
songs on her guitar, all of them about love or marriage.

"Why do you call your husband or wife your eternal companion?"
I asked.

"Well, we believe that when you get married to someone in the
temple, when you go to heaven, you and your family and their family
and everyone is there. So you stay together with your family forever."

"So getting married is a huge deal," I said.

"Definitely. You'll see at BYU that we spend a lot of time talking
about marriage and families. I don't know what it's like at other
schools, but that's really important here."

Isaiah and Eli came over to Nicole's after they changed out of their church clothes. They each took turns on the guitar and sang songs. Mormons grow up singing in their church choirs, so nobody is bashful about singing, and they all have nice voices. Almost everybody I met could at least play the guitar and maybe also the piano. We all sat listening as people passed around the guitar and took turns singing.

"I love Sundays!" said Nicole.

"What do you like about Sundays?" I asked.

"Because nothing else matters!" she said. "We have church, and then we just get to relax. We don't do any work or any chores on Sundays. Some people think it's ok to shop for food or watch some TV, but most people don't do those things either."

"And that's to 'honor the Sabbath'?" I asked.

"Yep! And people think Mormons aren't Christians," said Nicole. "I mean, look, we have a picture of Christ on the wall."

"What exactly is the difference?" I asked.

"Well, we're Christians," she said. "It's just that most Christians only believe in the first two testaments of the Bible. But we have one more, the Book of Mormon."

"Old Testament, New Testament, and the Book of Mormon."

"Exactly."

When I was little and learned about the concept of the Sabbath day, my reaction was, "Really? You don't get to do anything?" and I imagined a horrible day full of nothing but lying on the couch; now that I was a little older and rethought the concept, my reaction was, "Really? You get to do nothing?" and I imagined a wonderful day full of nothing but lying on the couch. As great as that may sound, Sundays at BYU are even better. It's a day of rest not just for you, but for all of your friends. Since nobody is busy, everybody wants to hang out. And then you get together and do nothing, together. It's guilt-free, God-sanctioned leisure time. In Provo, Utah, nobody is productive on Sunday, so you don't fear falling behind the way you might if you were surrounded by working people. An individual in the secular realm acting like a Mormon on a Sunday would be a "lazy piece of shit," whereas a Mormon on a Sunday gets to behave identically and be a "leisurely child of God." On Sunday, the students didn't use phones or laptops or TVs, which meant that they spoke to and listened to each other with full attention. Everyone participated and everyone was present. (I was the only person slightly disengaged, since I was still taking notes in my phone.)

Next, we all went to feed ducks. We left Nicole's apartment with a few loaves of bread and walked to an on-campus pond. Again I anticipated that this would be boring and wholesome, but it turned out great. We tossed hunks of bread into the water then watched dozens of ducks fight for the scraps. The pond was busy with toddlers running around and young parents pushing babies in strollers ("Mormons love babies"). Nicole was sitting with Isaiah holding hands. Juliette was with Eli. I was standing by myself. Across the pond, I saw Erin talking to a small boy, maybe three or four years old. She waved and smiled to a woman who was probably his mom, then she crouched down and handed him a piece of bread. He tossed the bread into the water then watched without reaction as the ducks swam over. Erin, still crouched next to him, put her hand on his shoulder, pointed her other hand at the ducks, then gasped with wide eyes in that uniquely maternal way that magically makes small children amused. After seeing Erin, the boy who had previously seemed apathetic about the ducks now looked delighted. He smiled and clapped, then wanted to throw more bread, so Erin supplied him.

After seeing Erin with the little boy, a warm, innocent feeling came over me that reminded me of how boys feel about girls in elementary school, before they are attracted to them, per se, and they instead feel a kind of pre-sexual adoration, a kind of happy, magical curiosity. Erin was definitely pretty, which was causing some of the feeling, but there was also some other quality there that I was noticing. The average person is beaten down by feelings of anxiety, meaninglessness, and cynicism, but these Mormons didn't appear touched by those feelings. They were giving off the impression that they had never experienced pain or sorrow, that life was always getting better, and that it would never end. This quality made the girls at BYU especially alluring to me, and I spent the week fantasizing about converting to Mormonism, marrying one of the girls, and making a giant Mormon family with nine or ten kids.

When we all returned to Nicole's apartment, we went back to sitting around on couches, fully engaged with each other. Eli continued to sing and play love songs on the guitar. What happened next was unusual to me. One of Nicole's other roommates, Jane, came into the room and joined us. Isaiah was sitting on the edge of one couch with room next to him. Nicole was on the floor leaned over the coffee table eating a bowl of cereal. When Jane chose her seat, she went next to Isaiah and lay down with her head on his lap. (Isaiah was Nicole's boyfriend, remember.) Isaiah didn't flinch or treat it as unusual at all; instead, he rubbed her head and ran his fingers through her hair. Nobody reacted at first. Everything was the same, except now, Nicole wasn't looking over at me; she must have been aware that I would find it odd. As time went on, Nicole's head dipped farther and farther into her big bowl of cereal, and her cheeks became a little red. Then there was some loaded eye contact between Nicole and Erin, after which the tension spread around the room— except to Jane, I think—and then, a moment later, Isaiah said to Jane, "Ok, I'm gonna go cuddle with Nicole now." Jane sat up innocently, then Isaiah joined Nicole on the floor to rub her shoulders as she finished her cereal.

A little later, Isaiah and Eli left because Nicole and Erin were about to have their "home lesson," which meant that two guys would come over to give them a religious lesson. The men teach the women because in Mormon religion, men have 'priesthood,' which is a kind of divine authority. Women don't ever attain priesthood. In most ways, men and women at BYU existed as equals—as far as I could tell —but this was one glaring exception.

Since the school semester had just started, it was the first home lesson of the year, and Nicole and Erin hadn't yet met their teachers. The two guys arrived wearing gray suits. When they came in, we all sat down in the living room area. One of the guys said he was studying business and hoped to one day become the president of the United States.

"So do you have boyfriends?" he asked. This was part of their get-to-know-you small talk.

"I do," said Nicole. "His name is Isaiah."

"Have you talked about marriage yet?"

"Uhhhh, no!"

"Alright, alright," he chuckled. "How about you Erin? Do you have a boyfriend?"

"Nope," she smiled. "But I'm fine."

"Are you sure?" he asked. "I know some pretty great guys who are also single. I could set you up if you'd like."

"No, no. I'm fine. Really, it's no big deal. Really."

Both of the guys had girlfriends, so asking about the girls' relationships wasn't because they were interested themselves. At BYU there is a constant, collective effort to put single people into relationships. Everyone was constantly playing matchmaker.

"Ok, ok," said Nicole. "Let's start the lesson."

The guys pulled out a copy of Ensign magazine. They retold a story from the magazine about a guy on an airplane who brought with him a Book of Mormon. The woman seated next to him happened to bring up Mormonism in their conversation, and since he had a copy of the book, he was fully prepared to tell her about the church. The lesson was to always be prepared. The guys had a mildly condescending attitude during the lesson, and the girls had an attitude of subtle contempt—kind of a "let's get this over with" attitude. I think the girls realized that these two guys had no justification to be lecturing to them, even if the church said so.

At the end of the lesson, the two guys took turns praying for the girls. They prayed for Nicole and Erin to have strength during the week, then they assigned the girls to either pray for a missionary experience or to pray for the opportunity to help someone. The girls said they would, and the guys said goodbye.

Before I left for the night, Nicole played one last song on the guitar. It was the oldie called "Last Kiss." I knew the song well, but it took on a new context to hear a Mormon sing it. "He's gone to Heaven so I gotta be good, so I can see my baby when I leave this world."

Since I wasn't allowed to sleep at Nicole's apartment, at night I stayed with a student named Bobby. Bobby lived in an apartment complex, and the first night I stayed with him there were dozens of students sitting by the pool with their feet in the water. He had recently met a few girls who wanted to hear some of his original songs, and those same girls were out by the pool, so Bobby grabbed his guitar and we joined the girls. Bobby played finger-style guitar and sang in a smooth, high-tenor voice. After the first song, one of the girls, Miranda, said, "Marry me, *me gusta*. Oh, it sounds like Heaven." (Bobby and Miranda would start dating each other two weeks later.) The girls could sing and play guitar also, so they all traded songs and harmonized with each other. The singing was rather intimate—two of them would sing together while making eye contact for an entire song. And these girls weren't singing cheesy wholesome songs, they were singing cool folk songs. This went on for nearly two hours. As a listener it was extremely enjoyable, one of the most peaceful and pleasant times of the whole trip.

After singing songs, we headed to one of the girls' apartments. There was a curfew at BYU, but it wasn't too strict—guys couldn't be at a girl's apartment after midnight. BYU students aren't allowed to live at apartment complexes that don't enforce BYU rules, so all the apartment complexes near campus enforce the rules, otherwise they'd have no tenants. When we were inside, one of the girls mentioned her "Marriage and Family" class.

"Today, we were talking about if we thought certain things were ok. Just a discussion where there wasn't a right answer. It was like, can you watch TV on Sundays? Can you kiss on a first date? Can you get married as a freshman?"

"What did people say to those?" I asked.

"People said different things. Some people thought it was ok to watch TV on Sundays if it's every now and then and with your family, but most still choose not to do it. Some girls thought it was ok to kiss on a first date if the situation was right."

Another girl asked her, "Would you?"

"No," she said. "You don't have to kiss all the frogs to find the prince."

This was a funny inversion of the familiar expression, which, as I'd learned it, was, "You have to kiss a lot of frogs to find the prince."

"How about getting married as a freshman?" I asked.

"It's possible," she said, "but I don't think it would be a good idea."

"How strong is the focus on marriage here?" I asked. "Are you thinking about marriage on a first date?"

She laughed. "It's probably in the back of your mind, but it's not as serious as it sounds. Although one of my teaching assistants starts every class by asking if any girls are recently engaged."

"So people must be getting engaged all the time here," I said. "What if you're someone who never gets asked on dates?" This was a rude question for me to ask, I realized later, since it could have referred to any number of girls in the room.

"Well, then you wait," she said. A moment later she added, "And you probably feel sad."

On my first day at BYU, I had overheard Nicole on the phone with her parents discussing a friend at BYU who had overwhelming, crippling depression that left her bedridden for days at a time. Nothing so far had helped her, not even a blessing from a priest. Nicole also mentioned that a few more of her friends had mild depression. For some reason, I didn't write this down in my notes at the time; it's as if I wanted to ignore it.

With so many outwardly happy BYU students, it was hard to imagine that some were depressed. Of course, depression may be mostly biological, in which case Mormons would have the same rates of depression as anywhere else. But if depression is somewhat environmental, then I wondered what might be causing depression at BYU. One possibility is that the prescribed path through life is too narrow and too strongly enforced for some people. At BYU, everyone was assumed to have identical goals: worship God, fall in love, get married, be fruitful and multiply. But what if you were receiving no attention from the opposite sex and your prescribed purpose seemed unattainable? What if you were gay? What if you didn't believe in the literal truth of Mormonism? Mormonism is full of rules to guide its followers' behaviors, so if an individual's identity falls outside the bounds of those rules, then her life might take on a difficult, labored quality, as opposed to the happy, care-free quality exhibited by those whose identities fit in easily with the rules.

I met one student at BYU who told me that he had become an atheist. Nobody else knew except his brother. Although he was an atheist, he continued to attend class at BYU, go to Temple, and live as a Mormon. This is not entirely unusual. There are groups of people who live as Mormons, but they don't have sincere religious belief. They call themselves Cultural Mormons, and they communicate with each other anonymously online. Most Cultural Mormons were raised as Mormons, lost their faith, but still prefer the lifestyle of Mormonism. Others were never Mormons, but they liked the lifestyle, so they converted to Mormonism without ever truly believing in it.

"Are you allowed to touch a girl's breasts?" I asked Bobby. It was after midnight, so we were back at his apartment without the girls.

"Nope. It's the law of chastity. It kinda sucks. We can kiss though. Kissing is awesome."

In the morning, I went with Nicole to her Marriage Prep class. Although it's a required class, it's still a favorite for students. At the beginning of class, one student went to the front of the room and played a Mormon hymn on the piano while the class sang along. The professor had otherworldly charisma. He wore a shiny suit and had a bright face that kept your attention. During class he referenced a Mormon document called the Proclamation to the World. The Proclamation to the World claims that the family is the central unit of society and the most important part of life. When the family is not the central unit of society, civilization will crash. "Pick a civilization and watch it die," the professor said.

Next, he said that women are destined to be primarily mothers and little else. I was worried that the lecture was about to take a sexist turn until he made the complementary statement that men are destined to be primarily fathers and little else. The idea was that the social duty of both men and women was to be good parents first and foremost. In this regard, there was no gender difference.

"Heavenly Father takes it very seriously how his daughters and how all his children are treated," the professor said. "In much of society, daughters have not been treated as well as sons, and that has very serious consequences." He continued, "If you're not prepared to be stay-at-home parents here on Earth because you spend all your time at your job, then you won't be prepared to be stay-at-home parents for all of eternity when that's your only job."

His conviction made his words very intense. When he said "eternity" and meant it, I felt vertigo.

On politics, he said, "We take no stance in parties and never back candidates, but we will always support God's proclamation to us." The Mormon church never officially endorsed Mitt Romney, for example, even though we can safely assume that most of its members did.

The lecture switched into its main focus, which that day was education. "What did the gospel say about education?" he asked rhetorically. "To get all of it." Then he quoted the current president of the Church of Latter-Day Saints, President Hinckley, who said, "You are moving into the most competitive age the world has ever known. All around you is competition. You need all the education you can get. Sacrifice a car. Sacrifice anything that is needed to be sacrificed to qualify yourselves to do the work of the world. That world will in large measure pay you what it thinks you are worth, and your worth will increase as you gain education and proficiency in your chosen field."

The professor continued in his own words. "I fear too many of you see education as career development. Sure, it's good to get more money to feed your family. But education has a supreme importance aside from money. The more education you get, the lower the divorce rate." He showed some charts that showed the correlation between education and low divorce rates. (It was true only until the PhD level, i.e., people with PhD's divorce more than those with master's degrees.) He said, "Education is profoundly important to families. Teach your child to understand truth and they will not part from it."

One of the students raised his hand and said, "If you only get a high school diploma, you set yourself up to not stimulate your mind." The professor agreed with him. (As someone with only a high school diploma, this idea bothers me, but maybe I can sort of sympathize with people who think it.)

The professor continued with why college graduates do better in marriage: "Literally just jumping through hoops and enduring college to the end is great for building character, which helps marriage."

Marriage was still more important than education, however: "But don't work so hard on your education just to make so much money that you don't have time for your family."

"Lord bless you," he said, "and have a beautiful day." And that was Marriage Prep.

After class, I sat with Nicole and Erin on campus and ate ice cream. They asked me to explain my perfect, ideal girl.

I thought it was a funny question, so I said, "I'm just trying to find someone who's nice to me."

They didn't catch the joke and both said, "Awww."

Another girl came and joined us. She told Nicole and Erin that she had just set up their mutual friends on a date, and that sparks flew, and now the two of them were in a relationship. It wasn't a strange thing to hear—students were getting into new relationships every day.

Since students here weren't making drunk decisions or having sex, stories like this never had bad endings. The gossip at BYU was never juicy or inappropriate. If you heard someone say, "Oh my gosh, guess what happened to Brad and Carol!" the story wasn't going to be that Brad just gave Carol gonorrhea, it was going to be that while Brad and Carol were eating burritos, Brad told Carol he liked her, then they held hands, and now they're a couple.

(Actually, some students are having sex at BYU. While writing this book I met a Mormon woman who would in fact have sex while attending BYU. The sociology of the BYU sex scene is fascinating. At BYU, the costs of getting caught having premarital sex are huge: you are kicked out of school and your credits do not transfer. So you better not get caught. The most likely way that you would get caught is that the person who you had sex with will confess his or her sexual activity to a priest. Therefore, if you want to have sex at BYU, not only do you have to find someone who wants to have sex with you, you also have to look for someone who is guaranteed to never feel any remorse about it.)

On Mondays, Mormons across the world have "family home evening," which they call FHE. It means that families stay together, keep the TV turned off, eat dinner, and probably play board games. At BYU, since the students are away from their families, FHE takes place at the home of empty-nest parents who live in the area. The hosts open their homes for the members of specific singles' wards in the area.

It was Monday now, and about 30 students from Nicole's ward were gathered outside the apartments and were separating into cars to caravan to FHE. Again, since it was the start of a new semester, they hadn't yet been to their new FHE house and met the leaders. Once we arrived, we filed in and were greeted by two smiling adults in their 50s or 60s. It was a medium-sized suburban home, nicely decorated, with warm cozy lighting. The seating in their family room had been supplemented by a few dozen fold-out chairs, and we all took seats. The students began with a hymn, which sounded like a professional choir singing. Then one of the students stood up front to present his "spiritual thought," a prepared teaching from the Bible. He was small with straight-cut bangs, a digital wrist watch (not the trendy kind), and wire-rimmed glasses—all things that might have subtracted from his authority in another setting—but here he seemed prestigious and respected on account of his piety and religious knowledge. His lesson was about seeking perfection in God's eyes, how you can never reach it, but how you have to keep striving for it. Afterward he led a prayer that lasted a long while. With my eyes closed so long, I started to feel the same warm, communal feeling that I remembered from A&M. (Prayers can be nice, even if you don't believe that anything supernatural is taking place.) After the prayer, we started to play more icebreaker games. In the middle of the room, there was a big bowl of apples picked from an apple tree in the front yard, and each student ate two or three. Meanwhile, the homeowners prepared home-made apple pie and ice cream for us to eat. Even though the adults hadn't met the students until that night, everybody acted like they were a close-knit family.

The evening wore on, and what happened naturally was that the guys and girls separated into one-on-one conversations. All the conversations had a sweet, slightly romantic vibe to them. If two people were talking, they'd look right into each other's eyes and give their full attention for the duration of the conversation.

After some time, Juliette noticed that I was sitting alone, so she came to sit across from me.

"Isn't this home nice?" she asked. "It feels so nice being inside of a *home*, you know?" She gave the word 'home' a special emphasis, squinting her eyes and leaning forward a little each time she said it. "I like our apartment, but this is really a *home*. You can feel the difference in a *home*."

Juliette was tapping into my deepest need—the need for home and belonging. I felt as if she were repeating the word 'home' to taunt me, tantalizing me with dreams of domestic bliss, sexual fidelity, and lots of children—the Mormon status quo. I stared into her eyes in a sort of trance, again thinking, "If only she knew... if only she knew..."

At the end of the night, once we had filled up on apples, pie, and ice cream, the husband addressed the group with some closing thoughts. "It was great to have you all. If any of you want to come over at any time, please do. If you ever have a bad day at school, please come talk to us."

"Truly," the wife added.

Mormon culture even had an answer for the so-called empty-nest syndrome. These parents had completed their productive, child-rearing years, so now, instead of becoming burdensome old people, they were growing into respected elders who could share their wisdom with younger generations. The students formed a line and hugged the adults on their way outside. We loaded into cars and caravanned back to campus.

It was nighttime now, so I went back to Bobby's apartment to sleep. Before bed we did something insane. I'll try to be brief about it, because it is completely random and not very much related to college social life, but it was possibly the most fun I've ever had—sober, drunk, or otherwise.

Bobby had recently purchased a full-body chicken costume for no reason in particular, so we decided it would be fun to run around Provo while he wore it. In order for me be disguised as well, we bought a cat mask from a grocery store. Out in the streets, Bobby would tap a student on the shoulder and then run away, encouraging them to chase us. Right before I left for this leg of the trip, I bought a banjo, and I could play one small song on it. I brought the banjo along with us, and I'd play a musical soundtrack whenever we were chased. It felt like the chase scenes from the movie *Raising Arizona* with the banjo and the yodeling. The combination of the chicken costume and the strumming of the banjo was endlessly entertaining. I was surprised that the students really would chase after us. Almost everybody thought our antics were hilarious, and they would immediately join in on the fun. We worked up the confidence to try knocking on random apartment doors, then run away when someone answered. The students would chase us even in that situation. Eventually we would knock on apartment doors, then run *inside* their apartments, getting them to chase us around their apartment, and then outside. These were complete strangers but fellow Mormons. Nobody was frightened; they just laughed and tried to rip off our masks. The next day Bobby and I were so sore from running all night that we both walked with limps. Two weeks after I left BYU, Bobby texted me an incredible photo. Somebody had placed around campus multiple fliers that said, "WANTED: Chicken Man and Cat Boy," with very accurate drawings of us in our costumes and with phone numbers to call. I was so flabbergasted while sitting alone in my car that I had to step outside just to laugh loud enough.

That night after we took showers and were about to sleep, Bobby and I started talking about Mormon missions. He told me that before a guy goes on his mission, he is called a "Preemy," short for pre-missionary. I asked if girls ever go out with Preemies.

"Definitely not," Bobby said. "You pretty much get stiff-armed by girls. I don't like it. Girls don't take them seriously at all. A lot of girls want to get married, so they won't date a Preemy, since he's going to eventually leave on his mission. The girls date older guys."

"Do the girls ask about the guy's mission and try to figure out if he's a Preemy?"

"Yeah, in the first 30 seconds. A girl will ask where you went on your mission, and if you say you haven't gone yet, she's gone. She'll just walk away basically."

"Do you think that makes guys go on missions? Is that lack of respect what pushes some guys to do it?"

"I can honestly say that some guys go on missions just so they can say they've done their mission to girls. But if you do it that way, it's truly hell on Earth. That's not why you should go on a mission."

The next day, I ate lunch with Nicole at a place that makes their own ice cream and serves burgers.

"Since there's so much focus on marriage here, do you think there's an issue for someone who's not even being asked on dates?" I asked.

"Oh yeah. Oh yeah. I think that's a big issue," Nicole said. "We talk about boys a lot. It is an issue. I have a roommate who's never been asked out on a date. And her idea of self-worth is kind of low, but I think at the same time, we preach so much about your worth versus your worthiness. I don't know if you've heard this term yet in the classes here, but we try to have an eternal perspective on things."

"Right."

"We try to see things as God would see them," she continued, "so we can be more like Him. So that does change the way we deal with trials and hard things in life. They're not necessarily a blessing, but they're there to help us grow. So that changes our perspective a bit, but I still think girls not going on dates is big. I would assume at other colleges people don't date quite as much, is that true?"

"Not at all," I said. "Do you know what goes on at other colleges? Do you want me to tell you?"

"Tell me."

"A lot of the time, people meet each other and have sex right away. If they keep having sex, then they might talk about getting into a relationship, but maybe not. People call it 'hooking up.'"

"Wow. When we say 'hookup' here, we mean to go on a date. That's literally what we mean. That just would not bring satisfaction to me. It really wouldn't. Like, he doesn't even want to be with me because he likes me, but just because we had sex and he thinks I'm cute. I'd have a really big problem with that. That's so sad. I don't think that brings as much satisfaction out of getting to know someone."

Bobby and I spent every remaining night of the week at Miranda's apartment playing music. He would become giddy with excitement before heading over to her place, one time even exclaiming, "I love girls!" as we walked out the door. I spent my days going to class with Nicole and hanging out with her oddly alluring roommates. Throughout the week, I witnessed students do small acts of service for others. Doing acts of service had become a lifestyle for the students who had completed their missions. Isaiah, for example, saw a parked car with a badly bent fender, so he left a note under the windshield wiper that read, "It looks like you might need some service," along with his phone number. (By the way, he meant service as in 'an act of service,' not 'mechanic service.')

That week was my 21st birthday, but since I was surrounded by Mormons, I didn't have any alcohol (I did not have a drink all week). Despite its strangeness, BYU was the happiest week I spent among college students. When I was finished with all my traveling for this book, and I had to begin the long, difficult process of piecing my life back together, it was the Mormons who would prove most inspirational for me. As soon as I returned home from this trip, I gave up alcohol, and I didn't have a single drop for a year while I worked on the rough draft of this book. I also gave up sex outside of relationships, and I quit trying to compulsively sleep with everyone I met. I even tried to give up masturbating, and I made it 100 days in a row without. Today as I finish writing this book, I'm back to all my old vices, but I think I indulge them in a slightly healthier way, thanks to the Mormons.

It was the morning of my last day at BYU. The previous night, one of Bobby's roommates took a girl on a date to a trampoline place—some sort of giant room full of trampolines—and then they went to a sandwich shop. When he was dropping her off at her apartment, she asked, "Wanna come in for some water?"

As he told me about the water line, I burst into fist-pounding laughter.

"The best is when they ask you to come in for milk," he said.

"You're kidding," I said, wiping tears from my eyes, "Girls really ask you to come inside for milk at the end of a date?" (To be clear, my laughter was friendly, not insulting.)

"Yep," he said.

All the guys smiled and nodded, indicating that they had heard the same lines.

I don't know why I was tempted at the end of the week to see what everyone thought of casual sex—but I was, and I couldn't help myself —so I explained it to them and then asked what they thought. (I really did have to explain it—at first they couldn't even comprehend casual sex conceptually.)

"You mean they like, make out?" one roommate asked me.

"No," I said. "They go all the way."

"Wow," he said. Then after some thought, he added, "I think if you don't have a sense of purpose, then you resort to more base desires."

Another roommate who was from Mexico and had converted to Mormonism later in life joined the conversation. "I used to drink a lot down in Mexico and try to get girls," he said. "You can get those same feelings without it."

"Do you like it here more than Mexico?" I asked.

"Oh yeah," he said. "There weren't many blonde girls in Mexico. When I came here, I was like, 'Oh man, this is the Promised Land.'"

I told the guys goodbye, then I went by Nicole's to say goodbye. The girls insisted I share one more meal before I left. Erin prayed before we ate, like we'd been doing all week. She prayed for my safety and for me to have a happy trip out to California. This was nice to hear. After eating, Nicole gave me two parting gifts. The first was a handful of granola bars, chewing gum, and water. The next gift was a copy of the Book of Mormon. I was honored, even though the Book of Mormon is handed out in Provo like strip club flyers in Vegas. Nicole told me I didn't need to read it or even look at it, but she thought maybe I would want to learn more. I told her I would definitely read it. (I'm so sorry, Nicole, I still haven't read it.) Then I said my good-byes, gave everybody hugs, and stepped outside into the sun feeling elated, ready to continue west.

Down the street, a car had run off the road, and one of its tires was jammed into a ditch. A few students were gathered around the car figuring out what to do. Since I had seen people doing acts of service all week, it seemed natural for me to join the group of students and offer my help. The driver of the car wasn't a Mormon, just a girl passing through Provo. Eventually one of the guys left to find a car jack. While we were waiting for him to return, a dozen or so more students who were walking down the sidewalk stopped to offer their help as well. At this point, we only needed a car jack—additional bodies weren't going to help us—but the growing number of students gathered around did serve as moral support. Once the guy returned with the car jack, he was able to lift the wheel out of the hole. However, the car still needed to be reversed out of the ditch. It would require an aggressive, jerky movement that might damage the car. The girl was too afraid to do it herself, so I offered my service. She gave me her keys, I took the driver's seat, turned the car on, and floored it backwards out of the ditch. All the students cheered from the sidewalk. I had done very little, but I felt like a goddamn hero.

After the girl thanked us and drove away, the BYU students stayed gathered around to share in the afterglow of victory.

"I feel like this is something that would only happen at BYU," one guy said to his friend.

"I don't know," his friend said. "I think people are nice everywhere."

They went back and forth in disagreement for a while. As I listened to them, I felt like I could have chimed in to settle the debate, but I didn't want to ruin their fun.

21

UNIVERSITY OF CALIFORNIA BERKELEY

For most of the students in this book, I was only able to see a one-week snapshot of their lives. UC Berkeley was different—I had the pleasure of meeting my host on three separate occasions. Some people have relatively stable identities; if you see them every few years, they will be more or less the same person each time. Others have ever-changing identities; each time you see them, they have different interests, a different worldview, and a different plan for the future. Vishal was one such person.

When psychologist Erik Erikson was studying the process of identity formation, he found that many geniuses share the trait of having extended adolescences. If adolescence is characterized by the search for identity, then an especially gifted person may have trouble with adolescence. They recognize that they may have the potential to do great things in the world, but they struggle to find a social role that allows them to put their potential to full use. A normal person may figure out his social role by his late teens or early 20s, but the especially gifted person may continually redefine himself, trying on different social roles, until he is in his late 20s or early 30s. If you study his biography, you find an extended adolescence full of twists and turns and a life story dictated by a bizarre inner logic, knowable only to himself.

I first met Vishal before I had thought of writing this book. I was 18 years old on a solo road trip and passing through San Francisco when a mutual friend told me I should visit Vishal, a freshman engineering student who lived in an all-male dorm at UC Berkeley. The plan was just to grab coffee with him, but I ended up sleeping on his floor for almost two weeks. From my first interaction with Vishal, it was clear that he had been going through some profound life changes. He was a new convert to a certain political philosophy, and he was fiery and passionate about it. He spoke about the evils of corporations and the monetary system, the injustice of wealth inequality, and the need for intentional communities and a redistribution of power. I kept asking Vishal if there was a name for his philosophy, but he didn't like to give it a name. His activist friends, however, were quick to tell me the name of their movement: radical anarchism.

A college freshman is significantly older than a high school senior. To me, Vishal was a wise teacher, and I was his naive pupil. During my two weeks with him, he taught me a number of things. His lessons consisted of how to steal cafeteria buffet food in plastic containers, how to dumpster dive, and how to eat food communally. Eating as a group off a single plate of food teaches you how to share finite resources; at first, the instinct is to overeat, but quickly you learn that you can't enjoy what you're eating until you're sure that everyone else has enough. Learning this lesson about food made me more sympathetic to what Vishal was trying to teach me about politics.

Vishal's life outside of school consisted mostly of attending protests or planning for protests. The first protest we attended was a 20-day hunger strike against the Arizona law that allowed police to racially profile anyone who looked like they might be an illegal immigrant. We didn't join the hunger strike, but we sat in solidarity with the strikers for an afternoon. During that afternoon, a group of protestors—Vishal and I included—marched around chanting, "20 day hunger strike!" At one point, Vishal even gave a crowd-pleasing speech into a megaphone. The event gave me the satisfied feeling of being a part of something. It felt like important things were happening here.

On another day, a large group of students gathered outside the UC Berkeley president's house to protest the privatization of the university. This protest was accompanied by a long row of riot police prepared to arrest protestors for any illegal activities. While the protestors were lined up parallel to the riot police, I overheard a student have the following conversation with one of the police officers.

"How are you doing?" she asked.

"Doing alright, ma'am," he said with a smile.

"I want you to know you live a sad life," she said, "and that you're a failure to your family."

The police officer chuckled. "I'm sorry you think that," he said. Some other officers laughed too.

Then she said, "Fuck you, pig!" and moved to a different place in the crowd.

Her comment seemed rude and unnecessary. If earlier I had been on the side of the protestors, now I didn't know whose side I was on. If earlier I had felt compelled to chant along with the protestors, now I felt more compelled to stand to the side and simply watch. As we left the protest, Vishal told me not to tell our mutual friend that he had gotten involved in the anarchy scene. He didn't want his friends back home to find out, and he especially didn't want his parents to find out.

My final disillusionment with these anarchists came when Vishal and his friends asked me to drive them to court. None of them had cars, so about six of them piled into the back of my mom's minivan to drive from Berkeley to Oakland, where they had been arrested. Before I arrived in Berkeley, nearly 300 protestors had run onto a freeway and stopped traffic, again protesting the privatization of the university. The only people arrested were Vishal and a few of his friends, and now I was driving them to their court date. When I was parking, they assured me that I wouldn't get a parking ticket if I parked right in front of the courthouse, but a few hours later as we were leaving, I had in fact received an expensive parking ticket. The anarchists complained about the injustice of my parking ticket the whole way back to campus but never offered to help me pay for it.

In some ways, the anarchy movement was a social club just like any other. One of Vishal's roommates had also joined the anarchy movement once he came to Berkeley, but Vishal questioned his motives. When I asked why he thought his roommate was involved with anarchy, Vishal said, "For the friends."

An anarchist must have a fundamentally optimistic, Rousseauian view of human nature: "Man is born free, and everywhere he is in chains." Although anarchists focus on abuses of power and the corruption of authority, they also have to believe that humans are capable of governing themselves without authority figures. Individuals are good; it's power that leads to corruption. Beneath all the protesting and anger, there's a strand of utopianism: if only we could tear down our existing systems and rebuild them without unjust hierarchies of power and ownership, then life on earth could be equitable, peaceful, and happy. And that was Vishal as a college freshman —idealistic, passionate, and hopeful to rebuild a better world.

By the time I visited Vishal to write about him for this book, it was three years later, and he had recently graduated. He was unemployed—happily, he said—and living in Oakland. He had dropped out of the political scene and was now putting his energies toward life as a graffiti artist. He warned me that if I were to follow him around for the week, I would have to engage in some minor illegal activities —mostly trespassing. In the three intervening years, Vishal had changed his appearance dramatically. As a freshman, he was clean-shaven and dressed like someone out of a Gap catalogue. Now he had a long beard, disheveled hair, and wore mostly loose, black clothing, which gave him a tough look. He had the same wise, all-knowing vibe, but his optimism had shifted into a world-weary cynicism.

"Oakland was a booming town in the '50s," he said. "Lots of industry was here. Then in the '70s, all the industry left. What's left behind is run down and in ruins. I want to expose how decrepit the city is and how much it's falling apart, and how there's this culture of beautiful graffiti art that people don't even notice, because it's on these buildings people have stopped caring about. It's almost like this secret haven."

We took a drive to see some of the graffiti in the area. Vishal could tell me what graffiti was old and what was new, and he could often identify which artist had done each piece.

"Berkeley made me realize how corporatized schools are," Vishal said. "I got in trouble with some of the stuff I was involved with, and there were a lot of stresses in dealing with the charges and still trying to graduate. So I got out after three years instead of four. Looking back, during school the urge to do graffiti was kind of like a trance. And I realized after I graduated that I'd built up this passion, so now all I really needed to do was follow through with it."

Vishal had a girlfriend, Bailey, who lived with him. She had the unusual job of being a dominatrix. (I've somehow met two dominatrixes in my life, and oddly enough, they were two of the sweetest people I've ever met.) She worked at a legal dominatrix place where the women would act out scenes with paying customers, but no sex was involved. She would often come home from work ecstatic about how good of a performance she had given that day. One day she was asked to roleplay being a cop who interrogates a male customer for stealing jewels. "You should have seen me, babe," she said to Vishal. "I was so good. You would have been proud."

Bailey was extremely supportive of Vishal's life as a graffiti artist. She viewed him as a sort of hero who was beautifying the world and giving back to all the people who didn't have the ability to create graffiti art themselves. She looked at Vishal adoringly and always seemed excited to be in his presence. Vishal never let Bailey do graffiti with him, saying it was too dangerous, so she would stay home and wait up for him. On nights when we'd do graffiti, she would walk us to the door and say, "Alright soldiers, kick some ass!" Then when we'd return home—often at 3am or 4am—she'd be awake and eager to hear how everything went.

Vishal was unemployed, but he wasn't looking for a job either. He had done some freelance web design work since he graduated, but when I was visiting him he ignored two phone calls from a man who wanted to hire him for more work. At the same time, Vishal was applying for food stamps. We spent three mornings that week at the Self-Sufficiency Center waiting in line for Vishal to complete the next phase of his paperwork. The process seemed to be intentionally frustrating. One day we waited for three hours to talk to one of the social workers. When it was our turn to talk to them, all they did was give us a phone number to call. When Vishal went home and called the phone number, it went straight to a voicemail box that was full, so he couldn't leave a message. We had to wait another three hours the following day to receive a new number to call. That phone call allowed us to schedule another appointment at the Self-Sufficiency Center, and so on.

Vishal was a smart guy, so the irony of this situation—that Vishal was turning down paid work while applying for food stamps—could not have been lost on him. I suspect he did it on purpose: the urge that compelled him to do graffiti was also compelling him to apply for food stamps the same week a writer was there to document his life. It was a rebellion, a statement. Vishal could have hidden the fact that he was turning down paid work, and he could have chosen to apply for food stamps on any other week. What was he trying to express, then? Perhaps it was his disaffection with society. He had given up trying to help or change society, and now he was resigned to get by as easily as possible.

During the day, Vishal spent his time looking for new spots to graffiti, and after he had picked a spot, he would do sketches of his graffiti in a notebook. He also spent a lot of his free time playing Grand Theft Auto, and he was reading the Marquis de Sade. Camille Paglia wrote that "all roads from Rousseau lead to Sade," and this seemed to be Vishal's exact journey. As a freshman, Vishal's worldview assumed the inherent goodness in human nature. At 22 he seemed to be dwelling on the bad—the violence, cruelty, and sadism.

"Do you want to do any drugs while you're here?" Vishal asked me. "I could probably get anything we might want from one of my old co-op friends. Mushrooms, acid, but also pretty much anything you can think of."

"What's a bad mushroom trip like?" I asked.

"Well, speaking for myself, one time I got into a thought loop where I couldn't stop thinking about how once all of humanity is gone, the universe will be no different without us. The thought of the meaninglessness of all life and existence became so intense that it was almost palpable."

"Hm," I said, "I think I'll have to pass on that."

Vishal did unfortunately bring me to one party while I was visiting him. My joyous week of sobriety at BYU didn't inspire me to change my life in any way, and I was already back to drinking heavily. Each night I would drink a bottle of wine and feel that everything was right with the world. In the morning I'd feel the opposite, and that bad feeling would persist until the following night when I'd begin drinking again. Each morning I'd promise myself that I wouldn't drink that night, but as night would approach, I'd decide to drink again for just one more night. At the beginning of this trip, it was my hosts encouraging me to get more drunk than I usually did; now I was the one encouraging my hosts to get more drunk than they usually did. (I was on a budget, by the way; these were $2 bottles of wine.)

I'd been drinking at least a bottle of wine to myself every night with Vishal and Bailey, and then on the night of the party, I drank a bottle before we left, then brought another bottle along with me. The party was a house party full of recently graduated students from Oberlin College who had moved to Oakland after graduation. The partygoers were mostly straight women and guys who seemed gay, and everyone was wearing thick-rimmed glasses except for Vishal and me. For snacks, the host had baked kale chips.

The only good thing about me becoming embarrassingly drunk is that there's usually a one-hour window of time along the way where I'm abnormally charismatic. Fortunately for me, this one-hour window coincided with my arrival at the party, so I was operating at peak charisma when I made all of my first impressions. There also didn't seem to be any male competition at this party. I was the only guy giving off any sexual vibes, and I counted at least three girls who were sending sexual vibes back my way.

After I had consumed my second bottle of wine, I quickly became a sloppy drunk and a walking embarrassment. After that, I still thought I needed more to drink, so I would repeatedly fill my empty bottle of wine with beer from the keg and drink that too. I wasn't even trying to write about Vishal—I was completely in my own world at this point.

One of the girls who had flirted with me a bit—I can't explain why, but I led her into the bathroom for the purpose of looking in the mirror at a hat she was wearing. Within a few seconds, we were making out. After a moment, she pulled her head away.

"I'm really bad at monogamy," she said.

It took me a moment to process what she was trying to tell me. When I realized what she meant, I was extremely disappointed. I was so tired of girls with boyfriends.

"You have a boyfriend?" I asked.

"Unfortunately I do," she said seductively, as if it were going to turn me on.

"Do you want to fuck in the shower?" I asked. I wish I never asked this, but I did.

"This shower?"

"Yeah, right here, right now."

She seemed shocked, but then she said, "Ok."

I had hoped that she would say 'no'—that although she's bad at monogamy, she still has to do it because she promised somebody who she cares about that she would.

"Sorry, we can't," I said. "You have a boyfriend."

When you stare into the eyes of so many people cheating on their significant others without apparent remorse, it becomes very difficult to imagine that your own future significant other would behave differently under identical circumstances. As a life-long romantic, I found this hard to stomach.

I left the bathroom before I could see her reaction. Then I walked immediately over to one of the other girls who I thought I had a shot with and kissed her on the mouth. It was the party's host who had baked the kale chips.

"Wait," she said. "Were you just hooking up with that girl in the bathroom?"

"No," I said.

"Promise?"

"Yes."

"Ok, follow me."

I followed her to her bedroom, where we started making out on her bed. After our clothes were off, I tried to finger her, but my fingers wouldn't go in.

"Ow, dude! Be gentle!" she said.

"What? Sorry."

"Ouch, dude! I said be gentle!"

"Sorry, I'm hammered."

"I can tell."

She sighed with frustration, then pushed me over onto my back and gave me a quick hand job, which was generous of her, then she put her clothes back on. By the time we left her bedroom, the party was over and everybody was gone, including Vishal. We went back into her room and sat down on her bed.

"Can I stay over?" I asked.

"No, you have to go," she said.

I was in desperate need of affection. "Can I just stay?" I asked again.

"No, I have to wake up early. You have to go."

"We can go to sleep right now. I won't take up too much room. Please?"

"No, you have to go. I'm sorry. I'll call you a cab. Where does the guy you're staying with live?"

"Wait. Please can I just stay?"

"No, you really can't."

"Ok."

What was I even doing at this point? My happiest moment with a girl on this trip was still when I kissed Autumn on the cheek, back in Oklahoma, so many months ago.

I gave her Vishal's address and then sat on the edge of her bed with my head hung low. She left the room and came back with a glass of water for me to drink. As we waited for the cab to arrive, she gently scratched my back with her fingernails. Perhaps she was doing it out of pity, but I appreciated the gesture and thought of it fondly over the next couple weeks. When the cab arrived, she gave me a $10 bill, which I accepted for some reason, to pay for the ride. It was nice of her to pay for the cab, but she was also paying money for me to leave, which hurt.

When I arrived back at Vishal's house, he wasn't answering his phone, and all the doors were locked. I was still very drunk, and I went around knocking on the windows, waking up Vishal and all of his roommates in the middle of the night. I don't even remember doing this—Vishal had to tell me about it later.

I woke up the following morning feeling the same as usual; the feeling of complete disappointment with myself had become the commonplace flavor of my existence, and that morning was nothing new. I knew I wasn't going to sort myself out before the end of this trip, that I was headed toward some sort of emotional collapse, and that I had no control over what was happening. I was in desperate need of a therapist, a priest, and a psychiatric evaluation, but instead all I had was three more weeks of hanging out with college students.

Doing graffiti was a simple process. When it was around 2am, Vishal and I would dress in all black and then drive to the spot that Vishal had scoped out. We'd park about a half mile away and then sneak to our intended destination. One night, Vishal brought me underneath a highway that he called the MacArthur maze. According to Vishal, the Oakland highway system was poorly designed using inefficient, complicated, and flawed construction methods. The city, instead of redesigning the highway, just kept adding more and more highways to the same area to the point where it had become a ridiculous tangled web of concrete. Beneath the tangled web of concrete was land that could have been put to good use, but instead there were fences there to keep people and animals out. Over time, the land had become inhospitable to everything but weeds, which grew out of a bed of trash that had floated down from the cars passing by on the highway overhead. It was a failure of urban design, the sort of sight that reveals in one quick glance the worst of what careless human activity can do to destroy an environment.

"I don't want to get looked at or get any attention," Vishal said. "The whole graffiti culture is about anonymity, so you never know who a person is outside of it. I just want to create something new in all the blight."

We jumped some fences to get underneath the MacArthur maze. Vishal found a large blank pillar that suited him, and then he spent the next hour writing the word "SIN" in huge, 3-D letters with his cans of spray paint.

"At first, it seemed like there was a threat," Vishal said, talking about being outside at nighttime, "but eventually I began to feel the peace of it. In a lot of ways, I feel I'm indebted to graffiti for making me come alive."

When we were done for the night, we'd go home and stay up with Bailey. Bailey hadn't gone to college, but she planned to eventually.

"I just know that when I go to college," she said, "that's more of a marriage than anything else I'll face in my life—more of a serious commitment, a lifelong commitment, that will stay with me and affect the rest of my future. It's not a decision I want to make when I'm 18. That's not a decision I see any 18-year-old making. I mean, Vishal sure as fuck made that decision and rocked it, but me at 18? Holy hell. Even me at 20 is like, blue hair dye and trying to do my thing. It's just, when I go to college, and have to pay for every penny of that, I want to be married to my cause, and go at it with as much devotion and passion as Vishal had when he faced all his classes. But I just—I'm not there yet."

Before I left Berkeley, I asked Vishal why he fell out of the anarchy movement.

"I dropped out of the political scene because of lack of motivation," he said. "It's hard to reflect on. Was I just following the typical Berkeley radical student path? I felt like I was a revolutionary, but maybe I was just a bougie middle-class activist."

Vishal's life as a graffiti artist didn't have the same sense of community as his life as a political activist. To remedy this, Vishal hoped that sometime in the future he would find a partner to do graffiti with him.

"If I keep doing this for maybe two more years, and I don't meet anyone," Vishal said, "I might have some second thoughts. Because I don't want to be doing this alone forever."

A couple years later, I ran into Vishal at a Christmas party in my hometown of Austin, Texas. Vishal appeared to have gone through another surprising shift in identity. Now he was living in Manhattan, he was employed at a steady job for a corporation, and he was working in his free time on creating the next big smartphone app. He was clean-shaven, and his cynicism had shifted back into an excited optimism. He had broken up with Bailey and had a new girlfriend. He didn't seem disaffected anymore; instead, he seemed hopeful about the future after having learned to pursue a mostly conventional life. And what was he wearing? I could hardly believe it. It was the last thing I'd have expected Vishal to wear, but I should have known better. He was wearing what the students at NYU had taught me was a Manhattan rite-of-passage. Yes, he was wearing a pea coat. It seemed that not even Vishal could resist.

22

UNIVERSITY OF SOUTHERN CALIFORNIA

USC was a bad week. I was running out of energy as a writer, as a traveler, and as a person. At the start of this trip, I would open my map of the United States and feel complete joy as I imagined all the miles of unexplored terrain before me. Now I saw those miles as a burden. Additionally, the thought of having to meet another group of students filled me with dread. There was the small talk, the smiling, the enthusiastic telling of stories. I had no will to keep going. I felt like a traveling salesman, far from home, who had been fired from his job but who still knocked on doors from force of habit. What I wanted most of all was to go to my parents' house and take a long nap in my childhood bed.

USC has one of the top film schools in the world. Located in Los Angeles, it is thought of as the school that sends its students directly into the Hollywood system. Aspiring filmmakers compete for acceptance into USC, and then, once accepted, continue to compete to come out of school as one of the most promising young filmmakers.

When I arrived at USC, it was another week where I hadn't spoken aloud or communicated with anyone for many days. It took me a while to find a host there, so I'd been driving around California, sleeping in parking lots, and cleaning myself in bathroom sinks.

Every night before bed, I'd drink at least one bottle of wine in the back of my car. While drunk, I would gaze up at the stars and fall in love with life and my place in it. I still kept telling myself that I needed to quit drinking alone at night, but I didn't stop. This nightly ritual lasted until the end of the trip.

I didn't know anything about my host, other than that he was a senior in film school. I was worried he'd be a cool, hard-partying extrovert—kind of like a 22-year-old Michael Bay—and that I'd have to use a lot of energy to keep up with him, but I was relieved when Kent answered the door. He was wearing a t-shirt with a giant picture of The Dude on it, a tribal print sweater, and thick-rimmed tortoise-shell glasses. He had a Beatles haircut, scraggly sideburns, and a soft voice. I could relax—thank the Lord.

Kent was getting ready to rehearse a scene with two actors for his class on directing actors. They were performing a scene from *Juno* and rehearsing in his apartment foyer. It was the scene where Michael Cera says, "You broke my heart. I should be royally ticked off at you. I should be really cheesed off." During the rehearsal, Kent kept a hilariously serious demeanor. He'd walk around as the actors performed, sometimes watching them from across the room and other times watching from just a foot away. As this was going on, other USC students kept leaving the apartment, presumably all headed to the same party. The girls were wearing skimpy neon outfits, and the guys were wearing fake mustaches and sombreros. Kent joked, "They're all waiting for us so they can get the party started."

After the rehearsal, Kent and I went up to his room, drank some wine, and listened to a Simon and Garfunkel record.

"College is an experience to get you in touch with who you are," Kent said. "It's almost cathartic. And I'm just a different person than who I was brought up as. The standards are different. Going away from home wasn't hard, but going back is different. It's kind of like a re-entry."

In the morning, Kent was headed to the eighth and final shooting day for the thesis film he was working on. He was one of two production designers on the short film, and his role would count as his undergraduate thesis project. Each thesis film had one producer, one director, one writer, one assistant director, two cinematographers, two production designers, and two sound mixers, all of whom were receiving thesis credit for the film. Apparently the film professors assigned the students their roles based on the aptitudes they had shown in their previous years as film students. This system would have annoyed me endlessly if I had been a film student. To me, it goes without saying that most of the students wished they were the director, or at least that's what I would have wanted. With this in mind, you might pay roughly $35,000 a year, plus living expenses, for four years, not to be the director, but for the opportunity to be one of two boom operators on another 22-year-old director's short film, which would be the most important project of your undergraduate education.

Back in high school, we used to have representatives from different universities come talk to us about their schools. We were allowed to skip class any time we wanted to attend one of these talks, so I went to as many as I could. I specifically remember the representative from USC talking to us about their famous film school and making us feel as if getting into USC would automatically make you the next Steven Spielberg. Of course, it's the representative's job to sell us on their school, so I understand why they wanted us to believe that. What I can't understand, however, is why these sales pitches were supported by our parents, teachers, and administrators. I remember the NYU representative telling us that at NYU, students are so accustomed to seeing actors "like Will Smith" filming movies on campus, that they don't even react and keep walking normally so they can be extras in the backgrounds of the shots. It's disappointing that stories like this are told to easily influenced middle-class 15-year-olds from the suburbs, even if the stories have a grain of truth. It's important for young people to have dreams and ambitions, but it's an injustice when the dreams sold to young people are grandiose or delusional—and in the case of USC and NYU, unfathomably expensive.

The students were shooting a scene in an apartment hallway. The script supervisor told me, "It's a confrontation scene between the neighbor and the protagonist. The neighbor has been stealing the protagonist's possessions, but then they start having sex, and it gets even weirder after that."

The shoot went smoothly for the ten-hour day (except for a few students thinking they were food-poisoned during lunch). There was a bittersweet tone throughout the shoot, since it was their last shooting day. For the students, working on the thesis film was a lot of fun, and there was a pleasant camaraderie that had developed over the previous months. Since it was the last day, it would be the end of all that.

"That's a wrap!" the assistant director yelled.

The students high-fived and gave each other hugs. After an hour of wrapping cables, waiting for lights to cool, and packing equipment into cars, the crew gathered outside.

"I love you guys so much," said the director. "Thank you so much. It's been so fun, I'm gonna cry!"

The crew clapped again and more hugs were given. The hugs were long embraces of ten seconds each between every member of the film. It seemed nice.

Kent and I went back to his apartment for another night to sit and drink wine.

"What's your favorite part of filmmaking?" I asked.

"I like all the collaboration on set," Kent said. "You're on so much of a personal level. You have to interact and communicate. At an office, you just take a small piece of work and go back to the cubicle. I think the creative collaboration is the main joy of filmmaking."

"Do you get a lot of that at USC?"

"Yeah, for sure. Although I'm not sure how different of an education I'm getting at USC compared to a less expensive college."

"How so?"

"I feel poor as shit going here. My family doesn't have a lot of money. It was really tough for me to even go here this semester, because we were a few thousand dollars short."

"Do you feel it's been worthwhile though?"

"I hope so. I guess I won't know for a few years. But if having the degree helps me do what I want, then it will have been worth the cost."

In the morning, I went with Kent to his film production class, the class that facilitates the production of the thesis films. The day's agenda was to watch the footage shot over the weekend by the four groups and give critiques. The classroom was in a screening room with a large projector screen up front and movie theater seating. Each group's director stood at the front of the room and spoke briefly about the weekend's shoot, then the footage began, each group having around 20 minutes of footage to show.

The student critiques were gentle, heavy with hamburger method to reframe negative remarks into positive ones. For example, "That scene was really great. I noticed the actor's hair wasn't wet after he stepped out of the shower, so I'm sure you'll have lots of fun working with that footage when you edit."

The professors were less kind, although their remarks were still generally positive and still full of hamburger method. The harshest comment of the screening was, "I question the reality of what I just saw."

For Kent's film, the professors all questioned the use of the bright red boots as a wardrobe piece, a decision that Kent had made. I walked through campus with Kent and a fellow crew member after class.

"I still feel it," said Kent.

"Me too," she said.

"Feel what?" I asked.

"Margaritas," said Kent.

"Hah! You guys got drunk for class?" I asked. It was still morning.

They didn't respond. They both seemed depressed.

"I don't see what isn't believable about red boots," Kent said. "This is a movie. They were bright red because they symbolized her sexuality. Of course they called attention to themselves."

"Yeah," she said, "the red boots were a central part of her character."

I never learned if they drank before class because they just liked drinking, or if they did it to cope with the feedback from the professors.

Kent's film crew met to have lunch at a place on campus called Traddies. When the crew was back together, Kent and his crew members seemed to cheer up. The camaraderie from set was back, and even though shooting was over, they would still be working together through post production.

During this lunch, I sat to the side and made no effort to talk to anyone. For most of this trip, I was sincerely curious to learn about other people, to ask them questions and try to understand their social worlds. But at this point, I didn't care anymore. My project had carried on far too long, and I was becoming miserable. To lose one's curiosity is a terrible thing. There is a crew photo from the last day of their shoot. In the photo you can see the smiling crew all grouped together, and then down a hallway you can see me sitting entirely alone.

Whatever my opinion was about the value of film school, it didn't matter. The students here appeared to be having a warm, loving time, doing what they wanted, surrounded by close friends. Maybe none of them cared who was the director. They just wanted to make movies, and that's what they were doing. Perhaps many or most of them would in fact be sent directly into Hollywood, where they would get to keep these positive feelings going for the rest of their lives.

23

STANFORD UNIVERSITY

In the 2012 Fiesta Bowl, one last-second field goal kick determined the outcome of the game between #4 Stanford and #3 Oklahoma State. The kick was missed, and Stanford lost the game. After the missed kick, television cameras zoomed in on the anguished face of the kicker—a 19-year-old student named Jordan Williamson—and broadcasted his emotions to millions of curious onlookers around the country. It happened in an instant: Jordan could have been the school's hero, but instead he became the school's disappointment. He could have been admired by sports fans around the country, but instead he was ridiculed.

It was a year later, the next football season, and Jordan was still Stanford's field goal kicker. I met up with Jordan and his teammate Adam after one of their practices. When we met, Jordan tried to give me a cool handshake, but I went in for a normal one. Then Adam tried to give me a normal handshake, but I went in for a cool one. Goddamnit—22 colleges for practice and I still couldn't shake hands.

(Note: Jordan gave me permission to use his real name in this book.)

I wasn't going to bring up the Fiesta Bowl with Jordan unless he did first. I didn't want to be another person asking him about the missed kick, even if it was presumably one of the central stories of his life.

Jordan and Adam were about to head grocery shopping, so I got into the back seat of Jordan's truck. In the parking lot of his dorm, a few other football players were walking past, and Jordan told me their names and positions.

"Most of the guys on the team are pretty cool," Jordan said. "There are a few dicks, but everyone is pretty nice."

"How are they dicks?" I asked.

"Well, there are always gonna be those guys who hate kickers, but Stanford doesn't have too many of those."

At the grocery store, Jordan and Adam filled their shopping carts to the brim. It was interesting—college athletes, no matter how good or famous, are still just students. Watching them shop was strangely hilarious.

"Shit, man, I think I'm gonna get some provolone," said Jordan.

"Not cheddar?" asked Adam.

"Nah, I don't really like cheddar."

"Suit yourself, man."

We loaded the groceries into the truck and headed back to campus. That's when Jordan brought it up.

"Did you see the Fiesta Bowl or hear about it?" he asked me.

"What? Oh yeah, I saw it," I said.

"If we go out Friday night, you might hear some interesting stuff around campus, like people talking shit about me."

"Really?"

"Yeah, like most people here were really supportive and all that, but sometimes those same people talk shit when I'm not around. Like last week, I was walking past a party and saw this girl who's usually really nice to me, and she didn't notice me near her. And she was saying like, 'Man, our kicker sucks, he totally lost the game,' and stuff like that. Then when I went up to her later, she acted super nice to my face. So there are people like that. And then sometimes drunk people will see me from like, a balcony, and yell, 'Wide right!' or say I suck. But most people are supportive."

"Who was the girl?" asked Adam.

"That girl Hayley," said Jordan. "You'd recognize her. I got pissed, and I usually don't lose my temper. But the girl I was with calmed me down and was like, 'No, Jordan, the reason people respect you is because of how you handled it, so you can't throw that all away now.'"

"Was that girl one of the first times that happened, or does that happen often?" I asked.

"I've been in places where people don't know who I am. I went to Jack in the Box with a buddy of mine, and it was pretty late. This group of guys walked in, one of them was talking about the Colts, and we started talking to them, and my buddy made a joke like, 'They better not draft the kicker,' talking about me, and the guys got the joke, but one of them wasn't paying close attention and was like, 'Yeah dude, the Stanford kicker, he fucked up! He missed that kick and lost the game for us!' and they were like, 'Dude, stop, stop,' and he's like 'What?' and they're like, 'That's him!' and he just froze, so I said, 'Yeah, he fucking sucks, right?' and put my fist out to give him a fist bump, and he put his head down and scooted to the back of the group and didn't say anything the rest of the time. So things like that happen."

"That's rough," I said.

"But what I found is that those people are the ones that don't really get the sport," Jordan continued. "People who understand kicking understand that things happen and there are a lot of variables—it's not always just the kicker. You have to have guys blocking for you, you have to have a good snap, a good hold, and what I haven't told a lot of people is that I didn't get the best holds during that game."

"That makes sense."

"The kicker is literally the biggest scapegoat in all of sports. Nobody gives a shit that we fumbled on the one-yard line and gave up the ball earlier in the game."

Jordan and Adam split up so they could carry their groceries to their separate dorms. Everybody at Stanford lives on campus, and the athletes don't live in segregated athlete-only dorms. This meant that football players might live next door to chemistry majors. Stanford places a high priority on mixing the athletes with the non-athletes, going as far as requiring that athletes room with non-athletes during their freshman year.

Jordan brought me down the hallway and introduced me to a group of guys from the football team. The dorm room reminded me of the Charlton baseball team's dorm rooms, because all the furniture was pointed toward a television where the guys were playing a football video game. This is what they did on most school nights.

It was well past midnight when Jordan and I headed back down the hall to his room. He had a twin mattress on the floor at the foot of his bed for me to sleep on. Jordan flipped the lights off and we got into our beds. Jordan began to tell me the story of his previous football season.

"I was 11/12 on field goals for the season, which is phenomenal, but then I tore my groin, and I was out for four or five games. When I came back, I kind of wasn't the same. I kept missing. Then we went to the Fiesta Bowl, and I could kick, but not everything was back to the normal. And so I missed a couple kicks, obviously we lost the game. There was a lot of publicity for it. But at the beginning of the season, I started getting cocky and arrogant because I was doing so well. I felt like I couldn't be touched. I started to become a douche, and I could tell, but there was nothing I could do to get myself to stop."

"Really, in your head you knew you were being a douche, but you couldn't get yourself to stop?"

"Yeah, kind of. Kind of. And when I got hurt, it kind of went down a little bit. But when I came back and took over my position, even though I hadn't kicked in four weeks and the guy who replaced me was 4/5, which is good, they still just stuck me right back. So my arrogance came back. But after the Fiesta Bowl, all of that just went away. I started looking at everything totally different. You know, I was like— I was pretty depressed for probably two months. I couldn't sleep for two weeks. I'd always tear up."

"You couldn't sleep?"

"No. I couldn't sleep, because my head kept thinking about the game. It was awful. It made me realize, as much as I didn't want that to happen, if I had made that kick, who knows how arrogant and cocky and a total douche I would have been. I wouldn't have been the guy I wanted to be if I had made that kick. But because I missed— yeah it cost the team the game and the Fiesta Bowl—but I think it was probably best for me in terms of my personal growth and going through the tough experience."

"Yeah, I never thought about that," I said, "but it's true that the opposite would have happened."

"Yeah, so for me it was a really humbling experience. I used to see kickers miss field goals that would ultimately lose the game and be like, 'How'd they do that?' but once you go through it, it's like, 'Holy shit, how was I so ignorant?' I was a kicker, and I didn't see how they could do that. But now I've done the same thing, and I've learned a lot from it."

"Did you ever tell yourself that it's just a game?"

"I definitely did. I realized how ignorant and caught up in sports some people get just based on that experience. So, I didn't have any death threats, but I've had friends at other schools who missed game-winning kicks who got death threats. But I definitely had ignorant people who said, 'Oh, you suck,' blah, blah."

Jordan sat up and explained where on the football you're supposed to kick and how a misplaced hold by the kick-holder could affect the kick.

"So if you're hitting this spot, you're hitting the far edge," he said. "You're not getting any contact, any meat. All the ball can do is spin off to the left. Literally, both the kicks I missed were leaned that way and gave me laces. But nobody could see that, and they thought I just fucked up. But I think it happened for a reason. And I think it's better for me that it did happen."

"Yeah, I can see that," I said.

I don't think Jordan was intending to place blame on anyone else. Instead, I think he was trying to say that there are more variables in a field goal kick than just the kicker. In a free-throw in basketball, the only variable is the person shooting the ball; if a player misses a game-winning free-throw, it is entirely that player's fault. But in a field goal kick, there are 22 players on the field who can influence the result. You have the guy snapping the ball, the guy holding the ball, the defensive line trying to block the kick, the offensive line trying to block the defense, etc. The kicker's swinging leg is the most important variable, but it's not the only variable. If something goes wrong during the snap or the hold, there is nothing a kicker can do. With this in mind, the kicker should not receive all of the praise if he makes a kick, and he should not receive all of the blame if he misses.

"This past week, I had one of my best games ever," Jordan said. "I made a 48-yard field goal at the end of the first half that put us up 10-3. They tied it up 10-10. I hit a 27-yard field goal to put us up 13-10. In the first half, when they were up 3-0, they sent us out for a field goal. I hit the ball clean, but our line let someone through, and they blocked it, and of course you can't make it. I had some dumbass post on my Facebook, "Ha! Nice fuckin' miss! Thanks for the win!" Some random Notre Dame guy. He tagged his friend in it. His friend was like, 'Haha, what a legend!' These guys were just talking shit, and I had pretty much the best game of my career, because I hit the longest field goal I'd hit at Stanford. What I realized was that if you're a kicker, if you do your job and make your kicks, that's what you're supposed to do. You're not glorified for it, that's your job. But if you miss, everyone just shits on you. But there's no kicker who's ever been 100%. So many of these fans are just so ignorant and don't understand the position that it's just stupid. It's actually made me not like my position as much, in a way. I feel like I can never satisfy everybody."

"That would be difficult," I said.

"It is. Alright, you about ready to get some rest?"

Jordan left around 8am to eat breakfast at the football team's mandatory breakfast. Afterward, he returned and napped for 30 minutes before waking up again for his developmental psychology class. He sat next to me on his futon and put his head in his palms.

"Aw man, I really don't want to go," he said, as if he were asking me, "Can we not go?"

I didn't say anything, trying not to sway his decision. I actually did want to go to class to see what classes were like at Stanford.

"Alright, well, you ready?" he asked a minute later.

During class, the professor had the students do an in-class assignment, which was 5% of their grade. It was about attachment theory, and he showed clips of children and their mothers with different levels of attachment. Jordan had no idea what was going on between the babies and their mothers. This was the second time I'd sat through this lecture on the trip, so I was able to give him the answers.

"You saved me," said Jordan as we left. "There's no way I would have gone to class if you weren't here. I would have made a zero on the participation grade."

"How often do you go to class?" I asked.

"Maybe 30% of the time."

"That's not much."

"Yeah, football makes it really hard to go to class. You're practicing all day, and it just completely sucks all the energy to do something else."

We walked around campus before we ate lunch. The Stanford campus is one of the largest in the country, so most students ride bikes everywhere. While walking, we saw some of the Stanford band playing the Stanford fight song from a balcony near the center of campus.

"Our band is awesome," said Jordan. "They dress up real crazy, not like any other band. They're banned from some airlines, because one time they all got on one side of the plane and then ran to the other side to try to flip the plane."

[Note: I think this is just a myth.]

Since Stanford was playing Cal—Stanford's biggest rival—the next day, campus was decorated with all sorts of pro-Stanford and anti-Cal signs. A fountain was filled with red water that week, and some of the buildings hung massive flags from their rooftops that said things like "Beat Cal."

"The girls aren't very good here," said Jordan. "The hot ones are either stuck up or not interested in athletes."

"Why not athletes?" I asked.

"I don't know. One time I went on a date with a girl, and she didn't know I played football. I told her I played while we were on the date, and she said she wouldn't have showed up if she knew I played football."

"That's dumb."

"We did end up doing stuff later though, so that was ok."

"Do people text and call you after games?" I asked.

"Yeah, I usually get 35-40 texts after every game."

"Do you write back to everyone?"

"I try to, but sometimes it's hard to get to everyone."

"What about after the Fiesta Bowl?"

"I got about 100 texts. 200 emails. 600 friend requests on Facebook. My name was trending on Twitter."

"What do you even do at that point?"

"I don't know. I didn't want to talk to anyone."

Throughout the week, Jordan told me a number of stories from football games. Usually fans from the other teams taunt him, yelling things like "You suck!" or "Wide right!" or "Remember the Fiesta Bowl!" Jordan tries to ignore them, tune them out, and forget about what happened, but he does hear them, and it does make him angry.

It was the night before the game. Jordan and the rest of the team were going to drive an hour away to Berkeley to stay overnight in hotels, so I stayed behind at Stanford by myself. Before Jordan left, he received a text from his grandma that said, "Sweet dreams. Enjoy beating Cal. I'll be watching."

Another Stanford tradition during the week they play Cal is that the theatre program puts on a play about the rivalry. The play is just "shitting on Cal," according to Jordan. I bought a ticket and went to see the play since Jordan was gone with the team that night.

The auditorium was nearly full of students, even though the play had been running all week. I took an empty seat near the back row, hoping to remain by myself, but the seats around me all filled up with students. The house lights dimmed.

Somebody came onto the stage and starting yelling something—I don't remember what—and this led to all of the Stanford students launching to their feet and yelling back in a coordinated, memorized cheer. I was sitting among them, and the natural thing would have been for me to launch to my feet as well, but I didn't have the strength or the will to stand up, so I remained seated. The students engulfed me as they screamed and screamed. I should have expected that something like this would happen, but it caught me completely by surprise. All at once I felt a tightness in my chest, a splitting headache, and a dizzying anxiety that made me feel like I was about to lose my mind.

The feeling of being an outsider, of not belonging, was becoming unbearable. It felt physically painful to be so isolated. The situation I found myself in was the purest manifestation of me not belonging—a giant mob of students, all belonging to the same group, standing and screaming a coordinated cheer, as I sat silently in the middle of them. If I had been a professional writer sent on assignment to cover this event, I would have at least had an official reason to be there. But I had chosen to be here by my own volition with no authority or guidance, no one to report back to, nobody who even knew where I was. Whatever situation I had put myself in, I was utterly responsible for it. I could have chosen to go to college, and I could have been one of 20 million screaming college students somewhere in America. But I had nothing to scream about, no group to be a part of. I had no alma mater—no nourishing mother. It occurred to me all at once: I chose this freely, and I made the wrong choice.

I felt so completely and totally alone that I couldn't bear to stay seated. I'd known loneliness before, but never loneliness so intense that I felt I had to escape. I stood up and shuffled past the students in my row, then walked to the back of the room to lean against the wall for a minute.

A small student walked up to me with some official lanyard around his neck. "You need to take your seat," he said in a squeaky voice.

"I know," I said. My head was still buzzing with anxiety and I desperately wanted this guy to leave me alone.

"Take your seat!" he said.

"Ok," I said, not moving.

"In or out!" he commanded.

My hatred for this guy was so pure that it almost manifested as physical violence, but I was able to resist. Instead I gave him the meanest look I could give, then I turned and walked out of the auditorium.

That night I stayed alone in Jordan's dorm room drinking my familiar bottle of wine. That night, however, the wine didn't lift my mood but instead sunk me deeper into depression and self-pity. I had been visiting colleges for far too long.

I woke up the next day feeling a bit better. Jordan got me tickets to the Cal game and connected me with two of his non-athlete friends, a 23-year-old Mormon named Reid, and a 21-year-old engineer named Jeff, who previously skipped a semester at Stanford to create a successful iPad accessory. These guys were great company and made my sour mood manageable. Reid was not a typical Mormon—he looked like a Ralph Lauren model, he cursed frequently, and he admitted to being so horny that he sometimes breaks the law of chastity to fool around with girls.

We drove an hour to the game at Cal, took a close parking spot at a Mormon temple, then headed to the stadium.

Fans of Stanford and Cal swarmed to the stadium from all directions. Stanford is a private school, and Cal is a public school, so Reid started chanting, "Go endowment! Go private education!" as we walked in. While chanting, he walked up to an elderly couple wearing Stanford colors and gave them high fives.

"How much do you guys care about the outcome of these games?" I asked.

"I don't go to many games," said Reid, "but I do get seriously angry when we lose. It takes me at least an hour to cool down after a loss."

"Me too," said Jeff. "It's weird. It's like your clan has been defeated and you're watching them lose."

We bought hot dogs then took seats about 40 rows up in the Stanford student section behind the goal posts as the teams warmed up. Jordan warmed up separate from the rest of the team, first standing off by himself, and then when the team cleared off the field, he stepped out for a few practice kicks.

A Stanford student walked past us with a shirt that said "F<#* Cal" on the front and "Because it's so easy to get in" on the back. In a nearby row, a six-month-old child wore a Stanford onesie.

Jordan kicked off to begin the game. In the first quarter, Stanford fumbled the ball, and the Stanford students were abruptly quieted. At the same moment, the Cal students erupted with cheers. Even though I had written about Cal Berkeley just two weeks earlier, I felt sincere anger, bordering on hatred, for their student section across the stadium.

Stanford had the ball back and progressed down the field. On first downs, the Stanford students did a chant, something that ended with "Fuh-fuh-fuh-first down!" Stanford got the ball within field goal range and set up for a field goal.

"We're just setting it up for Jordan Williamson to miss it," said the Stanford student next to me. I did not expect to hear that coming from a Stanford fan.

Jordan came off the sidelines and lined up, pointing his arm toward the goal and taking a few calculated steps away from the placeholder. The ball was snapped, Jordan's leg swung, and he missed the kick.

"See what I mean?" the student said after the miss.

I looked over at Reid and Jeff, halfway hoping that they would start an altercation to defend Jordan, but they didn't. (For the record, Jordan was having a very good season, and I happened to witness his worst game.)

Because we were at the Cal stadium, every advertisement from the announcer was directed toward Cal fans: "Cal fans! Keep your money at the bank that loves the Bears as much as you do!" "Cal fans! Put a jar of Ro-Tel in your favorite dish at your next Cal party to go bold with flavor!"

Later in the game, Stanford was again in a field-goal-range fourth down situation. It was Jordan's next field goal, a 34-yard kick.

"You fucking suck, Williamson!" said the same guy from before. "Watch, he's gonna miss it."

Jordan lined up as before, took his same steps, and missed again.

"Wide fucking right, of course! Why do we keep putting that guy out? He fucking sucks!"

Another guy a few rows behind us yelled out, "You suck!"

Nobody else yelled anything in Jordan's defense or in support of him.

Sports bring out the best in some people and the worst in others. I played basketball growing up, and while I was not a great athlete, I was a good teammate. If someone on my team missed a shot, I'd say, "Good shot! Keep shooting!" If you criticize a teammate for their mistakes, or even show a slight look of disapproval or disappointment, they are going to lose confidence and play even worse than before. The proper attitude you should have toward someone on your own team is one of encouragement, of what the therapist Carl Rogers called unconditional positive regard—and this is not just because it's the nice thing to do, it's because it's actually the best strategy if you want to win games. With this in mind, I couldn't comprehend how Stanford students were yelling out "You suck!" to their own player. Jordan may have missed a few kicks, but he was still the best field goal kicker at Stanford. Who else was going to do the team's kicking?

Stanford ended up winning the game, but Jordan remained 0/2 for the day, so we left with mixed emotions.

We met up with Jordan later in the day. He was surprisingly composed after his poor performance. He explained that on his first kick that day, the ball sailed directly over one of the goal posts, which is good in the NFL but not in the NCAA. One of the refs put his arms up, but the other didn't. The first kick messed with his mind, then he just outright missed the second kick. He said he's glad they won, but it was still frustrating for him. "You can never win," he said.

Jordan asked us if any of the Stanford students made any negative remarks about him during the game. Reid lied and said that he didn't hear anything, so I followed along and told Jordan the same thing.

There was something tragic about the situation. Jordan was sensitive and we didn't want to hurt him. He seemed truly nice and didn't seem to have any resentment toward anybody for treating him so badly. I couldn't imagine how Jordan must have felt walking around his own college campus as his peers yelled "You suck!" and "Wide right!" to him from balconies. One more variable in a field goal kick is the kicker's psychology, which is influenced by all of his social relationships. Surely if his peers are yelling "You suck!" to him throughout his school week, that will lower his confidence and make him a worse kicker on game day.

Everyone's heard that football is essentially symbolic warfare, and that football is so exciting to watch for fans because it taps into a kind of tribal warfare spirit. But you would hope that students at a university as prestigious as Stanford would be smart enough to recognize the differences between football and actual warfare. The costs of losing a real war are death to you and your loved ones, economic ruin, destruction of cultural artifacts, and collapse of civilization. The costs of losing a football game are a few hours of disappointment and perhaps a few additional cases of erectile dysfunction across the student body on the night of the loss. And yet, athletes are susceptible to receiving more praise or blame than military generals. Jordan, by missing the game-winning kick at the Fiesta Bowl, underwent a massive public shaming that was heaped on him not just by the other team's fans, but by his own fans, the people who were supposed to be rooting for him and supporting him—and the shaming didn't end on the night of the Fiesta Bowl, it was apparently still going over a year later. When Jordan puts on his football uniform, he is acting as a representative of Stanford, and it makes sense that his fans would scream at him or cheer for him in accordance with their own emotions during the game. But when Jordan was not in uniform, he was just a 19-year-old student, a nice and gentle guy, trying to have a pleasant college experience like everybody else. You would hope that the Stanford student body would have found some way to say to

Jordan, "We're not mad, we still love you, we know you did your best," but I don't think they ever did.

Later in the night, Jordan and I went to dinner with a linebacker from the team. A few crowds of girls walked by and congratulated the linebacker on the win, but they didn't speak to Jordan or even look at him. After dinner, we stopped to buy beer. We bought a lot of it.

"It's not a sipping kind of night," said the linebacker.

"I just wanna get fucked up," said Jordan.

We brought our alcohol back to one of the dorms where some of the football players were sitting around and drinking. It was 10pm. Even though Stanford had beat their rival, the atmosphere was not celebratory—it was the same as all the other times I'd been in there. After a few beers, I got the courage to start asking interview questions to the team.

"What's it like playing football?" I asked loudly as a general question to everyone in the room. Sometimes stupid questions get great responses.

"Repetitive," said one player.

"How so?" I asked.

"It's just repetitive and dead. There's so much pointless energy put toward it. It's all we do. You've probably noticed, we don't have time to do anything else. It's all we do."

"So you don't enjoy it?" I asked.

"No," he said. "Not anymore."

"I have respect for anyone who can put in all the time and energy and still enjoy it," said Adam. "But for me, all the meetings and all the tape we watch, it's meaningless. They don't mean anything."

"Me too," said Jordan.

Nobody provided any other viewpoints. They all agreed: football was their day job, not a source of pleasure.

The players said that they only get one or two weeks a year to go back home. They have practice all through Thanksgiving break, and if they have a bowl game, they play during Christmas break too. During summer break, they only have one week off from practicing. Some of them even said they hope they don't win any more games, so they don't have to play a bowl game. At that point in the night, their post-game victory celebration was somber. Even though they had won against their rival, the football players all seemed depressed. And their depression was rubbing off on me. I kept drinking.

The plan for the night was to pregame with the football team in the dorms, then move to some other dorms where there was a party, and then go to a fraternity house for a dance party.

Jordan and Adam both had rough nights. Adam drank heavily and stayed at the dance party until almost all of the girls were gone. The ones remaining, he said, were the ones who were looking to have sex with one of the football players. Adam chose one of these girls, went to her dorm, and had "dangerous, unprotected sex" with her. In the morning, he apparently recognized that she was "really thick," so he told her he wasn't interested in anything else with her. Since they had unprotected sex, he then drove her to buy a morning-after pill and made sure to watch her swallow it. He had no sense of humor about the night when he told us the story.

Jordan was in a tough predicament that night. Stanford beat their rival, so it was supposed to be a crazy night of celebration, but Jordan missed both of his kicks that day, so he wasn't supposed to let his peers see him celebrating too much. In some sense, he was supposed to act happy, but not too happy. As the pregame at the dorm was ending and the football players were about to head out into the broader social world of partying Stanford students, Jordan styled his hair and put on a flashy wristwatch and large, dark sunglasses, even though it was nighttime. This gave him the vibe of being ready to party, while also serving as a sort of mask. During the night, nothing dramatic or unusual happened with Jordan, but he drank enough that he lay in bed the following day until 2pm. After he woke up, he spent an hour on the phone with his kicking coach while still lying in bed. Jordan's voice was groggy and defeated, and the conversation sounded more like a therapy session than a conversation about sports. At one point Jordan said—presumably talking about the Fiesta Bowl—"Yes, of course I still think about it. I think about it every fucking day."

That night was also the last night of my trip. Because it was the end of my story, I must have had a subconscious desire for there to be a cathartic ending. This manifested in me drinking a ridiculous amount of alcohol, led to me humiliating myself, and ended with me feeling the worst despair of my life.

During the night, I drank right to the threshold of alcohol poisoning, and I accordingly blacked out for most of it. Oddly enough, I was still instinctively taking notes, and I was later able to read these notes to piece together the source of my shame.

Early in the night, I tried to recite poetry to the football team. That week when Jordan was at football practice, I'd been reading in the library, and I found myself truly appreciating poetry for the first time. I was excited about it; the football team wasn't. (In my defense, I was trying to read them *All is Vanity Saith the Preacher* by Lord Byron, which is an excellent poem, and I still think they would have appreciated it, had they been willing to listen.)

After this, there was an hour or so where I was talkative, loud, and obnoxious. I was acting this way with no positive social feedback. Being obnoxiously drunk might be acceptable from time to time if you're around friends, but when you're a guest in somebody else's life, it's not ok. The ancient Greeks had a word called "xenia," which was the sacred code of hospitality between a host and a guest. In America we don't have such a strict code, but even so I felt myself to be in violation of something sacred, and yet I was too drunk to stop.

Then I became aggressive and belligerent. When we left the dorms to head to one of the parties, one of the linemen was carrying a long 2"x4" for some reason. I snatched it from his hands and sprinted away with it. He eventually chased me down while threatening to kick my ass, then pried it from my hands. I was less than half his size, so I was fortunate that he didn't go through with kicking my ass.

Jordan told me the next day that at some point during the night, somebody threw an empty liquor bottle at the exterior door of somebody's dorm room, causing the bottle to shatter everywhere. The large student who lived there came outside ready to beat up whoever threw it, and the football team had to collectively calm him down. I have no memory of this happening, but I would not be surprised if I was the one who threw it. In fact, I'm pretty sure it was me.

I didn't make it to the fraternity house for the dance party at the end of the night. Instead I took off jogging across campus by myself for at least 30 minutes. I know this because I have a 30-minute audio recording of myself breathing heavily as I jogged. I don't know why I did this. When I reached a distant part of campus, I must have gone around trying to open random doors, because I somehow wandered into somebody's dorm and into an empty bedroom, where I locked the door behind me and went to sleep in the student's bed. All night and for most of the morning, I could hear somebody banging on the door trying to get inside, but I ignored it. In the morning I was missing my phone, my wallet, Jordan's hat, my sunglasses, and one shoe. I felt no anger or humor at this fact. I was the most hungover I'd ever been, but the pain wasn't physical, it was psychological. The most disconcerting aspect of the hangover was the feeling that my flesh was inanimate, that my physical body was not attached to my mind.

Looking back, this is a somewhat funny story, but at the time, I felt deep, painful shame, a kind of despair about who I was and what I'd become. I believed I'd ruined my life by skipping college and trying to write this book. My decision felt irreversible, and I thought that the sadness and loneliness I was now feeling would never go away. In the grand scheme of human suffering, what I was experiencing was barely a blip on the radar; nevertheless, in the context of my own life, it was the worst I had ever felt, and I believed it would be permanent. By writing this book, I had hoped that I would go through a challenging and interesting experience and come out the other end better off, more grown up, and happier, but none of this happened. Instead I felt worse off in every conceivable way.

I unlocked the door and took timid steps outside, fearing that I might be justifiably beaten up. Two students—a guy and a girl—were sitting on some stairs by the front door. I didn't want to spook them, so I tried to speak, but my voice made no noise. I cleared my throat and tried again.

"Excuse me," I said.

They turned and watched me walk up to them, not speaking as they eyed me with cautious curiosity. As I stood before them, I felt like I might start crying at any second, but I managed to keep my face frozen and my voice calm.

"I don't know where I am or why I'm here," I said, "but could you tell me how to get back to Mirrielees dorms?"

They laughed. "You have a really long way to go."

"That's ok, I think I can make it."

"Do you not go here?"

"No."

"Where do you go?"

"I don't go anywhere."

STAY IN TOUCH

If you want to discuss this book with other readers, there is a subreddit called r/thestudentsyes.

I am going on another big solo road trip back to all the original colleges in order to promote this book. If you want to follow along, follow my Instagram @drewott1. That's Drew Ott and the number one.

If you want to contact me, email me at drew@thestudentsyes.com

If you want to hear about my future projects, subscribe to my mailing list at www.thestudentsyes.com. I am working on a book of essays, a feature film, and an album of piano folk songs.

ACKNOWLEDGMENTS

There are many people who I need to thank and acknowledge for helping me to complete this book.

Believe it or not, my biggest supporter for this project was Randy from Auburn. Randy texted me at least once a week for five straight years telling me to "hurry the fuck up" because he couldn't wait to "crush some chapters." Randy's enthusiasm kept me going when everyone else thought that I would never finish. Randy, you are a shithead, a disgrace to the human race, and a great friend. (By the way, five years later and Randy still has never spoken to Dream Girl again.)

There is a massive list of people who I can't thank, because it would give away the anonymity of my hosts. These are the countless people who helped me find hosts at the start of the project. You all know who you are. Thank you. (By the way, when I first had the idea for this book, it was extremely hard to find people who would let me write about them. Almost everyone said no. So I eventually said, "Fuck it," and left home when I only had two or three hosts lined up. Once my emails said, "I am traveling *right now* on a road trip, and I've already written about Texas, Baylor, and Oklahoma, and I'm looking for my next school," suddenly everyone wanted me to write about them. The lesson here is that if you have a crazy idea, nobody is going to believe in you until you've already gotten started.)

Thanks to the professors who let me sit in on their classes. I sat in on the classes of at least 50 different professors throughout this year, and I found the lectures extremely enjoyable. This year of traveling was the most educational year of my life not just because of what I was learning about student social life, but also because I sat in on so many random lectures. I began this project by rejecting higher education but along the way discovered that education is my highest joy and my deepest need. (If you're curious, I had a 100% success rate asking professors if I could sit in on their classes. Before class started, I'd walk up to the professor and say, "Hi, I'm writing about your student Nora. Is it ok if I sit in on your class?" They'd say, "Absolutely! Glad to have you!")

I had many early readers who gave invaluable feedback. These people were Ben Rehder, James Powell, Natalie Parma, Jayhee Min, Reid Beauchamp, Luis Caffesse, Katherine Brown, Bryan Ott, Mike Ott, Gwen Harmon, Jeff Jutras, Chris Donahue, David Walsh, Andrew Willard, Kelsey Willard, James Burns, Tamara Raimi-Zlatic, Morgan Catching, Stephen Mick, and Daryn Hughes.

Thanks to my friend Brian Morgan. At the very beginning of this project, I wrote Brian a check for $1,000—a huge amount of money to me—and told him that he could cash the check if I ever quit. After I wrote that check, I never even considered giving up because I so badly didn't want that bastard to take my cash.

The cover of this book was designed by my godmother Alison Cannon. Alison heard that I had been struggling for months to commission a satisfactory cover from freelancers on the internet, so she sent me the final cover you see right now and said, "I spent 30 minutes on this. What do you think?" I said, "Yeah, I'm gonna go with that." Thanks!

The book was proofread by Robert Macias. I thought he might find three or four errors, but instead he found... significantly more. Thanks Robert!

My parents have been a huge source of support, not just for this book but for everything in my life. After their initial shock when I told them that I wasn't going to college, they quickly went back to loving and supporting me as they had always done. I've met many young people who've told me that their lives are dictated by fear of parental disapproval or loss of parental love. I've never had this fear, and that has given me a great feeling of freedom and strength.

I'd like to thank you, dear reader, for reading all the way to the acknowledgments. This book was self-funded, self-published, self-marketed, self-everything. If you've found it enjoyable in any way, I need all the help I can get to spread the word. The best way you can help is to write a review and to tell your friends about the book. Thanks!

Finally, and most importantly, I owe a huge debt of gratitude to all the people who hosted me and who agreed to be the subject of a chapter. If you found this book entertaining at all, all credit goes to my hosts. One thing I didn't mention throughout the book was that I was always terrified to say goodbye to my host each week. I would typically stay with someone for seven days. Two or three days into my stay, I would start stressing about my departure. Would we hug? Shake hands? If I told them how much I enjoyed my stay, would they believe it? Could I possibly relay how meaningful the time was for me without it being awkward? Today I think about these people all the time. For each of my hosts, I was just one strange week in the middle of their college years. But for me, these people have been my entire life for the last five years. I have fond memories of everyone I met on this trip, even the people who I might have made look bad, and I am sure that I will be reliving these memories for the rest of my life. I am deeply grateful that I was able to meet so many people who showed me such a good time and who taught me so much.

FAQ

What was your favorite school?

My favorite school was Middlebury. The schools I found most interesting were BYU and Harvard. My favorite chapter is Spring Break. If I could choose to attend any college I wrote about, it would be The University of Chicago. And as a native of Austin, TX, I'll always love The University of Texas.

Are there any schools you wish you wrote about?

Yes, many. Most notably, a historically black school, a military school, and a school that does a Great Books reading program—for example, St. John's College.

How did you afford this?

The year I spent traveling to colleges was the least expensive year of my adult life. I spent well under $10,000 that year. By comparison, many of my hosts were spending over $50,000 a year on tuition alone. I wasn't paying for an apartment back home, I was still on my parents' health insurance, and I was sleeping on couches or in the back of my car. My only expenses were gas, food, and alcohol.

Did you write about any [insert race, gender, or sexual orientation here] students?

Yes. Many of my hosts or their roommates or friends were persons of color, but I didn't mention it unless it was critical to the story (usually it wasn't). One of my hosts was gay, but that didn't affect the story, so I didn't mention it. With that said, the diversity in the book was completely random, because I didn't really have any choice over who would host me. It was hard to find any hosts at all, and I had to accept whoever would agree to be in the book. Often I showed up to someone's door with no idea who they were or what they looked like. What I was looking for most of all was cognitive diversity—diversity of thoughts, values, and worldviews, and I think I did a pretty good job. I was not able to tell every type of story or include every type of person—because that would have been impossible—but I did my best and I'm proud of the result.

Why are you self publishing?

I hate being rejected. Part of the reason I didn't want to go to college is because I didn't want to apply to my dream colleges and have them reject me. Part of the reason I didn't want to traditionally publish is because I didn't want to write query letters to agents and publishers, only to have them reject me.

Also, I've heard that traditional publishers give authors really bad deals on their first books. Well, this book is going to be the most marketable thing I ever produce, so I want a good deal on it. Self publishing gives authors a higher percentage of profits.

One of the best reasons remaining to choose a traditional publisher is that it'll help you get laid. Women used to reject me because I didn't go to college; now they reject me because I'm self publishing. "Wow! You're writing a book? Who's your publisher?" "I'm self publishing." "Oh... well, good luck! Bye!"

But traditional publishers come with other benefits. Writing this book has caused irreparable damage to my mental health, and I still wonder what it would have been like to write this book with the collaboration and guidance of an experienced editor. I will never know.

Will you write a sequel? Will you write another book like this?

No. After writing this book, I have a newfound respect for privacy —both for other people and for myself.

This book is also somewhat narcissistic and self-indulgent. I think a person should only create a few self-indulgent works in their lifetime, rather than make a whole career out of it.

Did writing this book make you want to go to college?

Yes, but I'm old enough now that I no longer care about the social experience, the degree, the job training, the connections, or the prestige of being a college graduate. I highly doubt that I would ever try to go to college, but if I did, it would be entirely for the pleasure of learning. Since discovering the pleasure of learning, I often find myself thinking about how fun it would be to somehow be a college student forever.

51259219R00288

Made in the USA
Columbia, SC
15 February 2019